Identified with Texas

The Lives of Governor Elisha Marshall Pease and Lucadia Niles Pease

Elizabeth Whitlow

University of North Texas Press
Denton, Texas

10 9 8 7 6 5 4 3 2 1

Permissions:
University of North Texas Press
1155 Union Circle #311336
Denton, TX 76203-5017

The paper used in this book meets the minimum requirements of the American National Standard for Permanence of Paper for Printed Library Materials, z39.48.1984. Binding materials have been chosen for durability.

Library of Congress Cataloging-in-Publication Data

Whitlow, Elizabeth, 1944– author.
  Identified with Texas : the lives of Governor Elisha Marshall Pease and Lucadia Niles Pease / Elizabeth Whitlow.
     pages cm
  Includes bibliographical references and index.
  ISBN-13 978-1-57441-866-8 (cloth)
  ISBN-13 978-1-57441-877-4 (ebook)
  1. LCSH: Pease, E. M. (Elisha Marshall), 1812–1883. 2. Pease, Lucadia Christiana Niles, 1813–1905. 3. Pease family. 4. Governors—Texas—Biography. 5. Governors' spouses—Texas—Biography. 6. Texas—Politics and government—1846–1865. 7. Texas—Politics and government—1865–1950. 8. LCGFT: Biographies.

  F391.W625 2022
  976.4/050922 [B]–dc23
                        2021052489

The electronic edition of this book was made possible by the support of the Vick Family Foundation. Typeset by vPrompt eServices.

Contents

Preface

In 2006 when a prairie-style house built in 1917 on Parkway in the west Austin neighborhood of Enfield became subject to "demolition by neglect" by the owner, its status on the National Register of Historic Places could not save it. The Austin City Council could have done so by giving it a historic designation, but to take that action Council members needed details about the history of the house. For those details, I, as a native of the city and a Texas history researcher and writer, living nearly across the street from the house on Parkway where Enfield Road begins, turned to the Austin History Center of the Austin Public Library for information. The threatened house, built for Ethel Felder Webster, was among the first constructed by the Enfield Realty and Homebuilding Company. Its founders in 1914 were Julie Pease, daughter of Governor Elisha Marshall Pease and Lucadia Niles Pease; their grandson, R. Niles Graham; his sister and brother-in-law, Margaret and Paul Crusemann; and her cousin Murray Graham. The company gradually developed hundreds of acres of land owned by the Pease family into a high-quality neighborhood from Enfield Road at Parkway to the north and west, reaching Woodlawn (the Pease home), and beyond. The City Council did not give the Webster house protection, but it was purchased and then sensitively rehabilitated by several Austin residents.

The history of Enfield seemed to deserve an article in the *Southwestern Historical Quarterly*, but Randolph "Mike" Campbell, then-editor of the *Quarterly*, suggested instead that I undertake writing a biography of Governor Pease. I quickly concluded that the work should be a dual biography, because Lucadia Niles Pease's life was inseparable from her husband's. It was March 2015. Five intense years followed as I read thousands of letters and papers saved by the Pease family and housed in the Austin History Center of the Austin Public Library, as well as in the Governor's Papers in the collection of the Texas State Library and Archives Commission.

Why a biography of this governor has not been published until now is unknown. Born in Connecticut in 1812, Elisha Marshall Pease came to Texas in 1835, participated in events of the Texas Revolution, served in the first three state legislatures after Texas joined the Union in 1845, was elected governor in 1853 and re-elected in 1855, and returned to the governorship as an interim appointee from 1867 to 1869 during Reconstruction. His achievements in all these positions were substantial. He was also a highly successful and respected lawyer and a large landholder with properties in Travis and many other Texas counties. Pease owned slaves, but he did not take a strong proslavery position, and when secession came in 1861, he continued to support the Union. He and his family remained in Austin during the Civil War, and when it ended, he did his best to heal wounds and restore Texas to the United States. Perhaps Pease's northern birth, his lack of a military career, and his quiet unionism largely explain why a man who made so many extraordinary contributions to Texas has not received the major biography that he deserves.

Lucadia Niles Pease, also a Connecticut native (born in 1813), grew up there. She married Marshall Pease in 1850 and came to Texas as a newlywed. Lucadia did not become a public figure—after all, in nineteenth-century Texas career opportunities for women barely existed—but she was known as the Governor's "Lady." Moreover, her early independent travel, her stated position as a "woman's rights woman" in the 1850s, as well as her support of sending a daughter away to college in the 1870s to earn a degree, all serve as markers of her intelligence and the strength of her convictions. She had a very close, loving relationship with her husband that influenced every aspect of his long and productive public life. Soon after Marshall arrived in Texas, he became, in his own words, "identified with Texas." Lucadia joined him in that identity when she arrived, and a biography of Marshall must reflect how the two became as one and remained so until his death in 1883. Like Marshall, Lucadia is notably absent from the biographies of nineteenth-century Texans. A 1973 University of Texas at Austin doctoral dissertation by Roger A. Griffin focused on Elisha Marshall Pease's public and political work, but Lucadia was virtually ignored. Thus, *Identified with Texas* is properly presented as a dual biography.

The Peases left a voluminous documentary record of their lives, and I have made an effort to allow them, where possible, to tell their own story, in their own words. Writing this book has been work, but far more, it has been a joy to come to know these people, and it is a rare privilege to bring them, a remarkably loving, intelligent, principled, and compassionate couple, to print at last.

An interwoven connection to the Peases has been lifelong for me, although I did not recognize all the connections until work on this book began. I have researched and written it while living on Governor Pease's first land purchase in Austin in 1855, adjacent to Shoal Creek, on what became the eastern edge of the Pease homestead tract. It is near Woodlawn to the west, and the Governor's Mansion is to the east. My childhood home was in Tarrytown on Pease land. Attending Pease Elementary School, I first heard the Governor's name. Perhaps becoming the Pease's biographer was meant to be. Certainly, it has been a delight and an honor.

Acknowledgments

Marshall and Lucadia Niles Pease were both dedicated record keepers, and so were their families. The couple's letters to one another and others, plus letters to them, form the rich, honest, and immense primary source of information about their lives. Therefore, the first acknowledgment is to them and to all the others who saved records, and then to those in the archival holdings that faithfully preserve them. The largest collection is The Pease, Graham, and Niles Families Papers. It is a mega-collection of documents from six sources filling more than 250 boxes at the Austin History Center of the Austin Public Library. The majority of the Pease Papers were donated by the Pease's grandson, R. Niles Graham. It was a priceless gift. No one deserves more credit than Mike Miller, then-Managing Archivist, for his knowledge of this collection and its enhancement. Most every staff member of the Austin History Center cheerfully pulled every box I needed, some multiple times. The other major source of primary Pease documents is the Governor's Records collection held by the Texas State Library and Archives Commission. Tanya Wood and the dedicated staff serving the reading room of the Archives have been ever-helpful. Also, the equally capable reference librarians of this priceless agency have always found what I needed. The archival material of the Texas General Land Office, including military service records, were made available by Deputy Director of Archives and Records Mark W. Lambert and his knowledgeable staff, who also helped to locate information. The agency's holding of the first draft of the 1836 Texas Constitution, which I believe to be in Pease's handwriting, was an astonishing find there.

Other sources include the Westfield Athenaeum of Westfield, MA, for original records of the Westfield Academy, provided by Jan Gryszkiewicz; the Masonic collection in Waco for some early Pease letters, and the Brazoria County History Museum, Angleton, for the District Court Minutes documenting Pease's entry into the Texas Bar. Other assistance was provided by Catherine Best, Librarian of the Dolph Briscoe Center for American History at the University of Texas at Austin, for research on the rare Niles book and its map; as well as archivists in the National Archives regarding Senator Niles's role in Texas's admission to the Union. Jeffrey Bassett of the Bassett Family Association confirmed information about that family at Eltham Plantation, where Lucadia visited as a young woman.

Greatly appreciated financial support for the years of research and writing of this book has come from several grants: Laura and Jeff Sandefer, who live in the Pease's home, Woodlawn, and the Old Enfield Homeowners Association made grants that were matched by the Summerlee Foundation of Dallas, TX, with enthusiastic encouragement from John Crain, its former president, and Gary N. Smith, its current president. Jan DeVault's son, Bryan, also generously contributed to my work after his mother passed away. Special thanks are also extended to former Woodlawn neighbors Richard and Martha Coons who have also contributed to the writing fund and been graciously supportive.

The only extant published biographical source about Governor Pease except for minor references was the 1974 University of Texas doctoral dissertation of the late Roger A. Griffin. His widow, Wilma Griffin, encouraged me to write a larger work and made his notes available before they were donated to the Austin History Center. Additional topical information has been provided on a variety of subjects by several Austinites, including Bill Butler, an expert on historic brick and brickmaking in Austin, Mark Lambert on Pease's law practice, and Laura Sandefer on details of Woodlawn's construction. She has guided tours of the historic house and invited me to make presentations about the Peases in the gorgeous parlor of that home. The Docents of the Governor's Mansion thoughtfully provided a helpful private tour of that historic home.

Assistance with valuable writing advice and encouragement has come from Texas historians Paula Mitchell Marks and Andrew Torget. Two others offered enthusiastic support from the beginning of this project: one was my dear friend Jan DeVault, who read a preliminary draft, and the other is Carol Clare Chowdhry, a close friend since our undergraduate years whose knowledge of Texas history and publishing has been valuable.

Two more people deserve grateful acknowledgement: Frances J. Nesmith, an extraordinary teacher of American and Texas history at Stephen F. Austin High School in Austin and a TSHA Junior Historian chapter sponsor, and James M. Day, director of the State Archives, who employed me to work there part-time during my years at the University of Texas. By their knowledge and enthusiasm, they shaped my abiding interest in Texas history and in researching and writing it.

The person to whom I owe the most gratitude for making this book possible is Randolph B. (Mike) Campbell. In March 2015 while he was Editor of the Texas State Historical Association Press and Chief Historian of the organization, he asked me to write this biography. He became the developmental editor of this book, providing endless and valuable guidance. His only quality that equals his patience and wisdom is his kindness.

Elizabeth Whitlow
Austin, Texas
August 2021

Chapter 1

The Early Lives of Elisha Marshall Pease and Lucadia Niles Pease, 1812–1837

"I had a strong desire to try a new country."

E. M. Pease

Lorrain Thompson (L. T.) Pease and Sarah Marshall Pease welcomed their second child and first son on January 3, 1812, in Enfield, Hartford County, Connecticut. The boy was named Elisha Marshall for the first and last names of his maternal grandfather, and his family called him "Marshall" all his life. He signed his letters to them with that name or sometimes by his legal and public signature, "E. M. Pease." No surviving evidence indicates that he was ever called "Elisha" by anyone who knew him, although many made the assumption during his life (and later) that he was called by his first given name and should be addressed as "Elisha M. Pease." Those who did not address him as "Marshall" or "E. M. Pease" addressed him as "Governor Pease," once he held that office, and a few close associates sometimes wrote to "Friend Pease."[1]

Young Marshall came from a long line of ancestors who had settled in Massachusetts, and then Enfield, in the Connecticut River Valley even before Connecticut became a colony. Robert Pease (the first of the family

1

to settle in America) and his son, John, left Great Baddow, northeast of London, and arrived at the Massachusetts Bay colony in 1634. John and his son, John, were among the settlers of Enfield in 1679. A century later, Marshall's grandfather, John Chauncey Pease, fought in the Revolution at Bunker Hill and elsewhere. Marshall's father, Lorrain Thompson (L. T.) Pease, was a farmer, attorney, probate judge, and state legislator. He and Sarah had seven children—four girls and three boys. Marshall later wrote that all the children were born in Enfield, and except for the first one, in the same room of the "Old Kibbee house near the centre of the Town on the West side of the street." Marshall's parents apparently valued education because he remembered that the children were sent to school while very young and that one schoolmaster was a thorough disciplinarian. Also, the Pease family named one son for Jean-Jacques Rousseau, the eighteenth-century philosopher whose Enlightenment values helped inspire the French Revolution; a naming that probably alluded to their admiration of Rousseau's values, which included the education of children.[2]

Most of Marshall's education is not documented in surviving records, but he and his siblings probably attended one of the public district primary schools until he went to a coeducational boarding school in Westfield, Massachusetts, when he was fourteen. Marshall's student listing was "E. M. Pease," but he was credited as an actor in a play as "Marshall." One contemporary biographical source indicated that he attended this academy for two "terms," but the school charged by the quarter and made no reference to "terms" or semesters. Westfield Academy was a rare coeducational institution in its day: It admitted 96 "lads" and 110 "misses" in 1826. What academic courses the girls were taught with the boys was unspecified, but the school catalog notes that "young ladies are taught drawing, painting, and needlework by a preceptress, who is employed from June to December."[3] The relatively progressive educational environment of New England would also the shape the life of Marshall's cousin—and future wife—Lucadia.

A year-and-a-half after Marshall's birth, a child named Lucadia Christiana was born to Richard and Christiana Griswold Niles on June 25, 1813, in Poquonock, a section of the town of Windsor, about fourteen miles south of Enfield. She would be the second of four girls.[4] The Pease and Niles children were second cousins with "shared Marshall blood," as Lucadia later wrote; they had a great-grandmother, Naomy Marshall, in common.[5] The Marshall family first came to Connecticut in the early seventeenth century and were among the founders of Windsor, the colony's earliest English settlement. The Niles family also settled early in Connecticut.[6]

As a child, Lucadia was probably educated first in the public district schools in Poquonock. She and her sister, Juliet, attended the Hartford Female Academy in 1828, and Lucadia took notes on ancient history from lectures that year. Richard Niles likely felt gratified when he received a note saying that the teachers "are happy to inform the parents of Misses J. and L. Niles that their conduct during the past term has given them great satisfaction. Their improvement both in their studies and the others duties of a scholar has been worthy of recommendation. They have apparently been desirous to please their teachers and to perform everything required of them in the best manner." Lucadia's academic record was excellent: a note addressed to her father stated that her examinations in Rhetoric, Arithmetic, Geography, and Grammar "have been without mistake."[7]

A twelve-dollar receipt for tuition payment for Miss L. Niles was dated October 22, 1828, and signed by Catharine E. Beecher, a cofounder of the Hartford Female Academy in 1823. Beecher was an American pioneer of the idea that both girls and boys of every class should receive a full education, including physical education, and she went on to promote the idea that women should be teachers. From age sixteen, Beecher had reared her younger siblings, including three who shaped American social values: Harriet Beecher Stowe, abolitionist and author of *Uncle Tom's Cabin*; Henry Ward Beecher, clergyman and social rights activist, and Isabella Beecher Hooker, suffragette. Although Catharine thought that women should not vote and that women's influence was in the home, she believed that because their role of nurturing children and caring for the home was so important, men and women were equals. Even if Lucadia attended the Hartford Female Academy for only a year at the impressionable age of fifteen, she absorbed values that would affect her entire life.[8]

Lucadia continued her education at the Springfield Female Academy between 1829 and 1832, although it is unclear if she was in school for the whole period. Since she was there at age nineteen, it seems probable that she received at least some education that was equivalent to high school or perhaps college-level work. Lucadia's letter of July 14, 1829, written when the quarter was half over, described French as difficult, although she liked it. Painting was "a pleasing and polite accomplishment and yet I consider it as rather a secondary object and shall not arrive so near perfection in the art as you might expect." She wrote to her parents in June, 1832, that Mrs. Potter was a "very pleasant, agreeable woman" who treated her with "extreme kindness." Lucadia had "commenced Mental Philosophy by Geometry, Rhetorick [sic], Arithmetic, and Composition." J. L. Hawks, apparently one of her teachers, noted that she had "sustained the character of a good scholar, has almost universally recited good lessons, and has gained the affection of her affectionate teacher."[9]

While Lucadia's schooling lasted into early adulthood, Marshall had to leave home and school to go to work while he was still fourteen. He likely did not want to leave school at an early age. Even while quite young, he possessed a fondness for study and an excellent memory. His first job was as a clerk in a store owned in part by Richard Niles in Poquonock. Over a two-year period, Marshall developed accounting skills and work habits that well-served him in later life, and he must have seen Lucadia more than he had before, since her family lived there. He was, however, away from his own parents and siblings. Decades later when his oldest daughter, Carrie, wrote to him from school, he replied that he was sorry to hear of her homesickness and knew what the feeling was, "for you know that I left my home before I was as old as you are, and never was there afterwards except as a visitor."[10]

Beginning in 1829, Marshall served as a clerk in the Hartford post office where John M. Niles, brother of Richard Niles, had been appointed post-master by President Andrew Jackson. Over the next five years, Marshall did not have an interesting job, but he made numerous friends in town, and he called his time in Hartford among the happiest of his early years. One of his friends was Gideon Welles, who, along with John Niles, was a leader in Jacksonian politics in Connecticut. Welles, who was ten years older, began cultivating Marshall's interest in politics. The Pease family knew about politics firsthand, since Marshall's father, L. T. Pease, had been a probate judge as well as a legislator. Also, while living in Hartford, Marshall wrote a letter to "Cousin Lucady" and sent two books to her and to Juliet. This is the earliest surviving communication between Marshall and Lucadia.[11]

While Marshall was working in Hartford, his father apparently was not earning enough to support his large family comfortably. This economic unease had a driving effect on Marshall, who could not see a way to make a better living for himself in New England at the time. Thus, when E. M. Pease was twenty-one, he left a none-too-promising career as a clerk and struck out in search of a more economically secure life west of his ancestral home. He was not alone in the urge; he soon found many others, mostly young people, headed west. He wrote letters home recording what he saw and thought. He began by going across New York, where one of his first experiences was having his trunk stolen by an Indian. After seeing Niagara Falls, he went to Buffalo to join emigrants from the eastern states in numbers that he called "astonishing," all headed for Michigan and the northern parts of Indiana and Illinois.[12]

At Gainesville, Ohio, he attended a district court session and then wrote to his father, "This western country is the field for lawyers. Those who have a talent for speaking succeed. They are well paid and if economical can soon get rich." So, he ventured an idea: "I had the vanity to think that I could make a[s] good a one [lawyer] as any I heard then, and was almost tempted to read Law, but it seems like throwing away two of the best years of my life to qualify myself. What do you think of it?" L. T. Pease's response is unknown, but as a lawyer who had not made enough money, he might have advised against his son's reading law, unless he foresaw a better financial future in new territory.[13]

Upon arrival in Chicago, Marshall wrote that since his last letter, "I have passed through trials by land and water, I have been sick and home-sick and *shipwrecked*. I am now in ... good health and spirits." He was in such irrepressibly good and youthful spirits after a storm that he "took a bowl of milk for breakfast and in the course of the day felt quite smart." That day a boat took passengers to get their possessions from the sinking vessel on which they had arrived. Marshall rescued shirts and collars from his trunk, wrapped them in a coat, retrieved his boots and hat, and waited for the next ship. He lost everything else except his money, which was rolled in a handkerchief tied to his waist. The ship's cabin was very small, and the men had given it to four ladies. In his usual good humor, Marshall commented, "I slept on the softest plank I could find, no covering but the heavens above." He wrote reassuringly that he had not been afraid of drowning in the storm that wrecked the ship because he could have clung to a plank until he floated ashore.[14]

"Michigan holds out great inducement," Marshall wrote, as he began to gather information about land and its prices as well as business opportunities. He saw that the numerous immigrants made a good market for produce, and farmers who had come three or four years previously had cleared from $8,000 to $12,000 annually. He noted, however, that speculators had already bought up most of the good sites for villages. He suggested to his father a purchase of a quarter section, but in trying to think of the possibilities, he said, "I wish you were here with me that I might have the benefit of your experience." He warned his father that a person coming to settle had to submit to hardship for four or five years, but over time could not fail to improve their condition. He then described where land in Michigan was available, noting that two federal land offices would soon be open, and provided further information about speculation. "I would not think it safe to invest anything here at present," perhaps expecting the market to settle down and also because titles may not have all been clear. He ruled out the mercantile business, because "it is those only who have dealt in lands [who] have made much money." He also commented that he had not yet found any business he wanted to engage in. Marshall's letters displayed an intelligent and sophisticated grasp of the facts by a young person without previous experience in real estate.[15]

In late July, Marshall wrote about plans to meet his father in New Orleans to evaluate conditions there. He thought that if they did not move to Louisiana, buying an Illinois farm would be wise. "I shall be willing to settle down with you. You will find it something of a trial to leave Connecticut." He traveled farther south in Illinois, where he saw land along the Illinois River that appeared to be the richest in the world and the most easily cultivated, and thought about settling there; after all, corn was sixteen feet high. Over the summer, his view of the West evolved. Marshall wrote from St. Louis that during his trip he had seen beautiful land and fields, but he wisely realized that most were too far from transport. He told his father that he had looked at enough western country to form an opinion by then, "but I have not yet made up my mind to spend my days in it. I have no doubt that I could do better here than at the East, yet ... a residence near the Sea Board is [needed] for preferable society ... and the means of intelligence are more abundant. Still if you should conclude to emigrate [sic] I am willing to join you." He wrote from St. Charles, Missouri, in mid-August that he thought he "could stand the southern climate well for I am sure they never had warmer weather at New Orleans than I have experienced since I left Chicago." Although he provided no temperature readings, his comment would prove true: over the years he was known to suffer from cold weather and only infrequently complained about heat as others did.[16]

Father and son did not meet in New Orleans; rather, Marshall returned to Enfield, and subsequently the two went to New Orleans, where they heard about Mexican Texas and its Anglo-American settlers. They were impressed when they read Mary Austin Holley's book about the settlements of her cousin, Stephen F. Austin, and they heard talk about how rich the land was and how wealth could be acquired. Among those heading to Texas was Don Carlos Barrett, a noted lawyer from Erie, Pennsylvania, who planned to settle in Mina (present-day Bastrop). He invited Marshall to read law in his office. Marshall agreed, and his father went along to see the country. In January 1835, the schooner *San Felipe* carried Barrett, the Peases, and others to Velasco. There on the east side of the Brazos River at a drop-off point for increasing numbers of immigrants, twenty-three-year old E. M. Pease first set foot in Texas. He already had his first independent experience in evaluating business opportunities, including land evaluation; he had found that his disposition permitted him to deal well with physical discomfort and uncertainty; he was ready to explore the possibilities of practicing law; and he was driven to succeed financially.[17]

His first landing in Texas did not mark an auspicious beginning. Rough water prevented the *San Felipe* from crossing the Brazos River bar, and as

Pease went to the beach with the pilot in a small boat, they were drenched. The weather remained cold and rainy. He found Velasco, "by no means an inviting place" with "six or eight houses only and forty or fifty inhabitants." He stayed at a public house with poor accommodations on the opposite side of the Brazos at Quintana for about two weeks before the ship could enter the river. He was very homesick, and he wrote later that had there been an opportunity to return to New Orleans he might have left Texas forever.[18]

His time in Velasco was used to good advantage, however, because he met people who were or would become important, and he began to learn Spanish grammar and Texas history. He met merchant Thomas F. McKinney, who had just started a mercantile establishment at Quintana, "a man of indomitable energy and perseverance and considerable business talent" whose firm would contribute a great deal to the government and the army in the revolution that began later that year. He made the acquaintance of Colonel James W. Fannin, an ill-fated leader of the coming revolution. He met Patrick C. Jack, then practicing law in San Felipe; eventually they became close "brother lawyers" during the days of the Republic of Texas. He also met Michael B. Menard, a shrewd observer of men and a future founder of Galveston; Colonel Joseph Morgan, later of New Washington; and Dr. Branch T. Archer, a chief actor in all that immediately preceded the revolution and a member of the first Texas Congress. Pease called him "a man of singular purity of character." The new arrival noted that many of the people in Velasco were not living there; they were awaiting passage either to New Orleans or upriver into the interior of the Colony. Looking back on those days, he remembered that he had borrowed a Spanish grammar book from Barrett as soon as he arrived and began to devote all his leisure time to it, because all the laws were in Spanish, and only a few of them had been translated into English. Also, all land titles to the colonists were in Spanish as were most legal contracts between individuals. He noted that before the summer was over, he was "able to read and translate it very readily." He also learned some Texas history when he visited the site of the Battle of Velasco that had occurred in 1832.[19]

After two weeks, the *San Felipe* made its way thirty miles upriver to Brazoria. Pease was disappointed to see that the largest Anglo-American community in Texas was small and unimpressive. He counted two hotels, four one-story brick buildings used as stores or saloons, and thirty or forty homes for 200–250 people. All business was conducted on Main Street; a weekly newspaper was published, and the principal store was the forerunner of R. & D.G. Mills, for many years afterwards the largest mercantile house in Texas. On Pease's one day in Brazoria, he met John Austin Wharton, who would later make him his law partner. Wharton was about twenty-seven or twenty-eight years old and had an arm in a sling as the result of a wound received a few months earlier in a duel with Colonel William T. Austin. Pease left Brazoria hardly able to imagine that it would become his home for sixteen busy, profitable years.[20]

The Peases and Barrett continued to San Felipe, and then rode seventy miles overland to Mina. The elder Pease called that land "a succession of verdant groves and lawns ... of the most surpassing beauty and loveliness." He then returned home, with the thought that he might return later with his family and a stock of dry goods.[21]

At Mina, the younger Pease began to settle in, reading law in Barrett's office and serving as his clerk. On April 13, 1835, the lawyer and the clerk took the oath of allegiance to the Mexican government. Pease reflected no qualms at the time or later about renouncing his US citizenship. He may well have thought, as many other Americans did even before the Texas Revolution, that it was simply a matter of time before Texas joined the United States, and that becoming a citizen of Mexico was a mere and perhaps brief formality.[22]

His first exciting frontier adventure was a near-encounter in May with Indians who had murdered three men along the trail he planned to take. He wrote to his father in 1841, recalling that he had been riding horseback on a trip for Barrett, headed to San Felipe and thence to Columbia. When he could not find corn for his horse, he let the animal loose on the prairie, lost him, and could not buy another. He walked to San Felipe—about sixty miles in two days—bought a horse, and was headed back to Mina by the Wilbarger trail when someone saw fresh signs of Indians. He changed his route and took the La Bahia road, crossed the Colorado, and approached Mina on its east side. He arrived in Mina, however, with "billous [sic] fever," and was in bed for two weeks and remained ill intermittently for some time thereafter.[23]

Pease thus experienced some personal adventure upon arriving in Texas, but the province itself was on the cusp of far greater excitement—revolutionary excitement. The thousands of Anglo-Americans who had settled in Mexico since the mid-1820s had become increasingly dissatisfied with the Mexican government, and Stephen F. Austin, having traveled to Mexico City to present a request for separate statehood for Texas, wound up imprisoned there in early 1834. At the same time, President Antonio López de Santa Anna began to move toward making himself all-powerful in a completely centralized government of Mexico. In response, the Mina municipality established a Committee of Safety and Correspondence in May 1835. Pease's friend Barrett was elected to the committee, and Pease found himself in public life for the first time when he became its secretary. During the summer the situation escalated to violence with a skirmish at Anahuac between Anglo colonists led by William B. Travis and Mexican troops, but many Anglo-Americans, including Barrett and Pease, still wanted a peaceful settlement. On July 4, the Mina committee of safety called other councils to come together at San Felipe to discuss averting a war. Barrett and another representative planned to meet with General Martín Perfecto de Cos, but before that could happen, the Mexican general ordered Travis and other Texian leaders arrested. Dangerous conflict was brewing. A meeting of representatives from all the municipalities in Texas was called for mid-October. Mina residents had internal disagreement, because war party leader R. M. (Three-legged Willie) Williamson had arrived, disagreed with Barrett's conciliatory efforts, and questioned his patriotism. Pease defended Barrett, and in mid-September he advised Barrett, who was at San Felipe, to come home, lest the citizens be too harassed by Williamson and "soon be divided and distracted as any in Texas."[24]

Pease's position changed when Gonzales *alcalde* Andrew Ponton was ordered to surrender the community's little cannon, loaned to them by the government for protection against Indians. Ponton's call for volunteers to help defend Gonzales reached Mina on September 27, and as Pease wrote his father later, "I was among the first to volunteer." He described the battle, and apparently his only discomfort in the event was incurred from waking up stiff and in pain from the cold. The Battle of Gonzales did not last long, and the troops then met Austin, just released from prison. Austin still wanted to see a federalist Mexican regime established and believed that the focus should be on the struggle to preserve liberty, not a war for independence. However, he was elected commander of the army on October 11 and two days later ordered an advance to San Antonio. A few miles east of town, the Texian forces skirmished with enemy pickets, and the event concluded. Pease's army days seemed to have come to an end, because his bilious fever reoccurred and was made worse by exposure. He was granted a discharge and went home to Mina to recuperate.[25]

The work of the Consultation resumed at San Felipe on November 3. Barrett, the Mina representative, continued to side with Austin. The Consultation created a provisional government with Henry Smith as governor and Sam Houston as army commander; they also created a General Council to act as a legislative body, and Barrett was one of its members. He nominated Pease as the council secretary, and the election was unanimous. Pease, not yet twenty-four, not yet in Texas a year, and not yet a lawyer or a politician, found himself in the company of the men most responsible for the events that were shaping Texas, and his name was spread on the published documents of the council. Full of youthful optimism, he wrote home that it was not possible to know how long the war would last, but his hope turned into fact: "That we shall eventually succeed, there is no doubt." He did advise his father not to come to Texas until the matter was settled.[26]

The General Council had serious differences of opinion with the executive branch over the question of supporting Austin (as most of the council and Barrett did) or Smith and Houston's preference for seceding from Mexico. The council chose to attempt to capture Matamoros in order to encourage a movement against Santa Anna, but that foolish move led Smith to dismiss it on January 9, causing the council members to declare Smith's office vacant and name Lieutenant Governor James W. Robinson as acting governor. Council Secretary Pease wrote in February 1836, "Smith continues to act whenever he has an opportunity, and is embarrassing the Government by every means in his power. Houston aids him so far as he dares."[27]

Robinson nominated Pease to be his private secretary because he was "an efficient person" and qualified to perform the duties of the office. The council chose another nominee, however, handing Pease his first loss in an election. He kept his job as council secretary, although the body could not maintain a quorum after members left to join the army. Pease wrote Wyatt Hanks, chairman of the finance committee of the General Council, "I have thought it my duty to forego my own private interest, for the present to be of some service to the public, for which my reward will probably be kicks and curses ... the reward of public officers in Texas generally." It was a generous but empty gesture, since the provisional government had no funds to pay salaries for its employees. Pease was also putting public service ahead of new personal business. He had received his first land in Texas on February 3, 1836: one-fourth of a league of land in the Mina municipality, under the Mexican colonization law of 1824.[28]

In mid-February 1836, Barrett asked to be discharged from his duties due to health problems that endangered his life. The council declared that "he will leave a void that cannot well be supplied." Barrett then went to Louisiana for medical care, leaving Pease without his first Texas mentor and employer. At that time, Pease joined the council, arriving for the opening of the Constitutional Convention on March 1 in Washington on the Brazos. Claiborne West of the municipality of Jefferson nominated Pease for secretary of the convention that day, but he received only eight of the forty-two votes cast, apparently because of anti-council sentiment. Pease was then unanimously elected assistant secretary, but he declined the office.[29]

The convention adopted the Texas Declaration of Independence on March 2, 1836. Pease fully supported the step because Austin and others had become convinced of the necessity of separation from Mexico. The young man wrote his father two days later, confident of the future of Texas and his own in what he declared to be his home. In a paragraph that opened with his interest in knowing his father's views about emigrating, and an expression of gratitude that he had not yet come because of the war, Pease wrote, without mentioning own role in the event,

> The convention ... has declared Texas *a free and Independent Republic*.
> If we succeed in maintaining it, of which I have no doubt, I would
> not leave Texas for any country on earth. The soil, climate, and other
> advantages which we possess render it the most desirable country in

the world. There is no part of the United States where industry and attention to business of every kind is so well rewarded. I hope at some future day after we have succeeded in establishing our Independence and settled down under a permanent and good Government that you will emigrate to this country to spend the evening of your life. If my life if spared, I know that I can acquire an independence for myself and such of my Father's family as choose to share it.

He noted that his employment had "enabled him to lay up something besides supporting myself." Moreover, he had "many good friends in Texas who would help me if in difficulty. My health is now very good. My love to Mother, brother, and sisters, and all friends and acquaintances."[30]

Pease's task at hand, however, remained with General Council business in the transfer of its archives of official papers to the newly-created interim government. On March 11, the following resolution was entered just prior to the council's final adjournment:

Resolved, that inasmuch as the Convention has assumed to itself the powers of a government, and made a demand for the archives of this body, we deem it a duty to yield to that call, and surrender our trust into their hands ... (E. M. Pease, Sec'ry of Gen. Council)[31]

The work of framing a constitution proceeded slowly. William Fairfax Gray, the visiting Virginian who attended the Convention as an observer and diarist, wrote on March 7 of a draft reported that day: "It is awkwardly framed, arrangement and phraseology both bad, general features much like that of the United States. ... It will have to undergo much alteration ... to make it respectable." On March 9, business still dragged, and delegates seemed reluctant to approach issues regarding land and a loan to the government. "Such miserable narrow mindedness is astonishing," Gray wrote: "There is a great want of political philosophy and practical political knowledge in the body."[32]

The announcement on March 15 of the fall of the Alamo jolted the Convention into hurried, frantic focus. The next day members adopted the constitution, organized a provisional government, and elected David G. Burnet as president, Lorenzo de Zavala as vice president, and David Thomas as attorney general. The officials were sworn in at four in the morning of March 17. Gray wrote that later that morning when they reconvened, delegates realized the seriousness of the situation, "and the awful cry has been heard from the midst of the assembly, 'what shall we do to be saved?'" The Convention adjourned *sine die* with members dispersing "in all directions" in a "general panic."[33]

As the Convention neared the completion of its work, General Thomas Jefferson Rusk called for improvement of the organization and language of the Constitution, and it may have been he who suggested that Pease assist in the work. According to the *Biographical Encyclopedia of Texas*: "Though not connected with the convention ... at the request of General Rusk and other prominent members, [Pease] assisted in framing the ordinance that organized the government ad interim and in putting the Constitution of the Republic into proper form during the last day and night of the Convention." Frank Johnson's *History of Texas and Texans* stated,

> While Mr. Pease was not a member of the convention ... his abilities were so pronounced and his aid and skill in both the detailed and the comprehensive working out of the plans of government were so invaluable that he was called to assist in a very material way in framing the [Constitution], and [he] did much more towards drawing up and perfecting that instrument than many of those who actually sat in the convention as delegates.[34]

It is possible that the first draft of the Constitution was handwritten by Pease. The writing shows variation that may be attributed to haste, more than one pen being used, and probably being written in more than one sitting. The first lines are more elaborate than the body of the text, and there are differences in some letters, such as the letter "A" being in print style at times and in cursive style at other times. It is also possible that some sections may have been written by someone other than Pease, but the handwriting does not differ greatly, and it is very similar to that in his letters. Thus, although there is no conclusive proof, there is a strong possibility that Pease drafted all or most of the Constitution of the Republic of Texas.[35]

Gray documented the flight of the government officials to Groce's Retreat on March 18 and the stay there until March 21. They then left for Harrisburg to be on Buffalo Bayou in case they needed to evacuate to New Orleans. In a letter to his father on March 29, Pease described the movement and what he saw at San Felipe on the way to Harrisburg. He presumed that newspapers had provided information about the war, but nevertheless wrote, "the Garrison of San Antonio has fallen and 170 of our brave men and volunteers from the United States have become martyrs in the cause of *Texian liberty and independence*. While we mourn their fall we rejoice that their end was so glorious. 1500 of the enemy were killed and severely wounded." He reported that there were then "about 1300" in the army, "increasing daily – in fine health and spirits. A few weeks or more at most will bring forth important results." Next he reported, "Our Convention after declaring independence formed a constitution which is to be submitted hereafter to the people ... and organized a Govt to act *ad interim*, more efficiently than our former Provisional Govt could do ... I will send you a copy of the Constitution as soon as it is printed, and send you with this the declaration of independence." He hoped that peace would be restored on land in a few months, and "if we can whip the army now in Texas, they will not be able to send another soon, and the war will then be on the seas." He did not mention his own role in government, nor the source for his optimistic military information.[36]

The following day Pease wrote from Harrisburg to Moses Austin Bryan, nephew of Stephen F. Austin, expressing far more anxiety and distress than he had to his father: "I came to this place via San Felipe ... on our way we met families leaving their homes, with such 'plunder' as they could carry with them, on the banks of the River Brazos at San Felipe. I think there were at least 500 souls camped out. It was really a distressing sight. The individual suffering caused by this war will be immense." He went on to observe,

The great fault with the people of Texas, [is] they have undervalued the resources and power of the enemy. They have supinely folded their arms and rested in the belief that the taking of Bexar put an end to the

war, and now ... convinced of the error, many of them ... are seized
with a panic, and envision the enemy ten times as powerful as they
really are. ... But the panic is passing away and many are returning
to reason. Texas has the physical power within herself ... to maintain
her independence, and dictate terms to her enemies ... confidence in
ourselves will soon free us from our invaders.

Pease also wrote Bryan, "During our short acquaintance, I have formed
quite an attachment to you and should be pleased to learn that it is
reciprocal."[37]

Pease went with Burnet's government to Harrisburg to be on Buffalo
Bayou if they needed to evacuate through the Gulf of Mexico. Still unable to
serve in the army because of recurrent illness, he agreed to be the chief clerk
for the Secretary of the Navy in the interim government, Robert Potter. Pease
went with him in April to inspect the small navy stationed at Galveston to
prevent Mexican vessels from coming into the bay. The potential problem did
not last long. On the afternoon of April 21, the Texas army, led by General
Sam Houston, soundly defeated the larger Mexican army of General Santa
Anna in a battle of "about eighteen minutes" on a pasture at the juncture of
Buffalo Bayou and the mouth of the San Jacinto River. The government,
Pease among them, returned to Harrisburg, but in May they left for the
signing of the treaties of Velasco, which brought an official end to the war
with Mexico.[38]

During the revolution, a younger brother of Pease had come to
Texas. Lorrain Thompson Pease Jr., known as Thompson, was first noted
in Marshall's letters on March 4, 1836, from Washington: "The manner
in which I presume Thompson left must give yourself and mother much
uneasiness, but do not be disturbed on his account. If he needs assistance
I will help him." Soon thereafter, Thompson escaped capture and death
at Goliad.[39]

In spite of telling his father that he would take care of Thompson if
necessary, Marshall was in financial trouble, because the new government
could not pay employee salaries. L. T. Pease was able to arrange credit for him
in New Orleans, and there Pease saw a friend from Connecticut who wrote

that he was "poorly clad, his clothes in rags, an old Campeachy hat on his head, and his feet but partially covered in shoes." Pease told him that he had no money and had eaten nothing for twenty-four hours. The friend fed him and gave him seventy-five dollars in cash. Shortly thereafter, Pease was able to procure $300 from his father's credit line. When Pease returned to Texas from New Orleans, he went to Velasco, where the government had relocated. Potter had resigned, eliminating Pease's clerical position. He became the Chief Clerk of the Treasury Department under Bailey Hardeman, but the government still had no money to pay him. While debating his options, he learned that his brother had become seriously ill.[40]

Thompson Pease died on August 31, 1836, but Marshall postponed writing his parents "because I could not sufficiently compose my feelings ... I scarcely left his bedside ... for three weeks before his death." Marshall felt certain that the cause was consumption, and that death was probably hastened by his exposure during the campaign and by the fever. Marshall regretted that he did not urge his brother to go home after the "massacre" at Goliad. He acknowledged his family's grief, but pointed out they were together to comfort one another. "I am alone," he wrote, and "I feel a loneliness come over me at times such as I never before experienced. I had anticipated much pleasure from Thompson's society here." He then went on to make a major statement about his own future:

> I feel that you will say to me, "come home." I can not, my feelings, interest, all are identified with Texas, and since Brother's death I feel more than ever linked to Texas. I feel as if here ... I can not fail of succeeding and securing an independence in a few years. If my health continues and life is spared I can not return and commence anew for I should be a stranger at home except to my relatives. Here I am known and have good friends. If the war closes, and I succeed equal to my expectations, I shall expect to visit home in a year or two.

Returning to Thompson, Marshall wrote that his brother had regretted not writing the family, and that nothing was left undone to help him. He was buried with military honors by a volunteer company. "I stood alone as mourner." He asked his mother to "imagine one with you that sympathized fully with you" and asked her to "Present my love" to his family," signing himself as he often did, as their "affectionate son, E. M. Pease."[41]

The following month, the Constitution of the Republic was ratified on September 5, and Sam Houston was elected president. The newly elected Congress met on October 3, and Pease was nominated as the Senate secretary but narrowly lost the election. He was nominated and elected as assistant clerk of the House of Representatives, but he declined that job and accepted the position of clerk of the House Judiciary Committee. It would soon be a very important position. Pease biographer Roger A. Griffin writes,

> Pease, though technically only a clerk and not yet admitted to the bar, was well along in legal studies, [and] his mind, his ambition, and his political sense were all uncommonly sharp, and he was willing to work.[42]

During the remainder of the year, Pease was nominated for and lost two other positions. He was nominated in a joint session of Congress in December 1836 for auditor, but he lost on a vote of twenty-three to sixteen, and postmaster general, which he lost on the second ballot. He continued with the Judiciary Committee and went to the newly established capital of Houston when the government moved there from Columbia in early 1837.[43]

Thus, less than four years after landing at Velasco, E. M. Pease had become thoroughly identified with Texas, not as a soldier or exciting political leader, but as a level-headed young man who would contribute immeasurably to the business of establishing a government for the fledgling republic. He could think, and he could write. Soon, he would become a lawyer and combine his work in the law with the acquisition of land to build the financial basis for rising to the top levels of government in Texas.

In the meantime, Lucadia Niles remained in Connecticut. She may have known from family connections about the adventures of her cousin Marshall, but there is no evidence of direct communication between the two after the one letter in 1833. Lucadia, who did not marry as early as most young women did, had a suitor who apparently pressed his case so hard that it was a factor in convincing her in 1838 to take a position as a tutor for the children in a wealthy slaveholding planter's family in Virginia. What she saw and learned there would prove important to her in identifying with Texas when she married Marshall in 1850 and left New England to live in the nation's newest slave state.

Chapter 2

Establishing a Law Practice and Serving in the Legislature, 1837–1853

"My only ambition is to secure an independence."

E. M. Pease

W hile Marshall Pease's roots in Texas were growing deeper, his father in Connecticut maintained an active interest in his son's new home. L. T. Pease proposed an "undertaking" that required recounting the history of the colonial period and the Republic, to which his son responded in a January 1837 letter from Columbia. Marshall mentioned his limited ability to send information that predated his 1835 arrival in Texas. He had collected documents and "old papers" about the early history of the colony, but the enemy destroyed them at Bastrop, and Stephen F. Austin, who could have provided the information, had died. He recommended Mary Austin Holley's book and cautioned against David Barnett Edward's 1836 Texas history, since it contained "little ... that can be relied on except what is stolen from Mrs. Holley." He sent Austin's and William H. Wharton's speeches that were delivered in the United States. His own concise history was composed "in haste," but it was well-written. He omitted his own participation as well as that of his brother in the events of 1835–1836.[1]

L. T. Pease used the material to publish later that year, *A geographical and historical view of Texas, with a detailed account of the Texian revolution and war*. The work was an "annex" in the 1837 and 1838 versions of John M. Niles, *History of South America and Mexico, Comprising Their Discovery, Geography, Politics, Commerce and Revolutions*. The elder Pease presented a highly positive view of the climate and soil of the area of Texas being settled by Anglo-Americans. Overall, it was a testament to Marshall Pease's early commitment to the history of Texas and his father's interest in promoting the Republic.[2]

In February 1837, more than two years after leaving his family in the Northeast, Pease wrote again to his father from Columbia. "It would give me great pleasure to visit home," he wrote, "but I can not leave at this time. ... Since Thompson's death I have at times felt very lonely, but I feel that Texas is my home, and that here I shall spend the balance of my life, with the exception of an occasional visit to the north." Turning to national affairs, he was "mortified" at President Andrew Jackson's special message that rejected immediate recognition of the new Texas Republic, calling it, "unworthy of the head of a great and free people. ..." He went on:

What! The only free government on earth hesitate[s] to recognize a Sister Republic whose government is founded on the same principles, and whose people have shown themselves so worthy to be free ... because the powers of Europe may take offence at it ... the question of our Independence is not considered upon its merits. ... Not one of the various Republics on the continent ever had half the claims to a recognition that we have. Mexico herself was recognized when nearly half her territory ... were in the hands of Spain. ... We do not ask it as a boon, we ask it as a right—but I have hopes that Congress will act on the subject before adjournment. How will your members vote? Will they regard the resolution passed last spring by your legislature?

The young Texan concluded with a request for money and sent love to his family and friends.[3]

After serving as clerk to the judiciary committee through the first half of 1837, Pease was awarded a more important job: Comptroller of the Treasury. A congressional act of June 7 to create the office called for filling it with a person suited to deal with the validity of claims presented by creditors for bonds issued to fund public debt. The comptroller was also to countersign all issued bonds and keep accounts of debt servicing. President Houston appointed Pease to the highly responsible job on June 20 with a salary of $1,500 annually. Many years later, Governor Francis Lubbock observed that Pease's appointment was "quite distinguished for one of his age."[4]

Pease wrote to his father in August, "I have no news to communicate," but went on to say, "Our country continues to prosper." He wrote that he had moved to Houston and announced, "I am comptroller of public accounts for the Republic, an office which is considered next in importance to a cabinet appointment." He said no more about the job, but went on to comment about individuals:

> Houston's conduct, civil and military, has been and yet is severely criticized. Lamar is not alone in the matter ... I do not believe, however, they wish to deprive Houston of any fame that is justly due him. Our politics ... are mingled with much personal feeling in which I of course do not participate, being too young to be an object of jealousy. I remain free to approve or condemn the measures of either. I have many warm personal friends and have experienced much kindness from both divisions.

Pease wondered about the feeling in the United States regarding recognition and asked how the Democratic delegation in Congress would act. "I perceive from Webster's speech ... that the opposition will oppose it violently ... but I hope better things from the democracy of the east." On the same day he wrote his brother, John, that he was convinced that the climate and fertile soil of Texas would make it home to many more immigrants, yet there would be "many difficulties to one unaccustomed to a frontier life." He was looking forward to recognition and wrote that the northeast states should "rise superior to all sectional feelings and jealousy and meet the question fairly on its merits and its ultimate effect upon the prosperity and stability of the Union."[5]

Pease had shown mature qualities of sound judgment, conscientious work, and the ability to make friends across the political spectrum, and those characteristics were paying off. Despite his important new job, he knew that he could never make enough money in public service, and his reason for coming to Texas was to earn a good living. Then, in December 1837, John Austin Wharton, who knew of Pease's work as clerk of the judiciary committee, provided the younger man an opportunity to advance his financial position. Wharton offered him a position as a partner in his Brazoria law office, even though Pease was not yet licensed to practice. It was an opportunity "such as is rarely offered to a young man, and I feel as if I should be making too great a sacrafice [sic] of my private interests to decline," Pease wrote to President Houston. Wharton, who was six years older than Pease, had obtained a law license in Tennessee at age twenty-one and had built a successful practice in Brazoria, the wealthiest area in Texas. In addition to its cotton and sugar plantations on rich soil, the county had valuable river connections to the interior and to the Gulf, and it served as the prime commercial center of Texas. The wealthy mercantile firms of McKinney, Williams and Company and of R. & D. G. Mills were in Brazoria County. Wharton was offering a job with a bright future. His new junior partner likely served as his clerk while he continued to read law from Wharton's books until the spring of 1838. Wharton needed a competent clerk. He had been shot in the right wrist in a duel with William T. Austin and did not regain the use of his hand.[6]

On April 10, 1838, in the courtroom of James W. Robinson, Judge of the Second Judicial District Court then meeting in Brazoria, E. M. Pease stood for examination to be admitted to the Texas Bar. The practice of the time required that he satisfy the court of his good moral character and knowledge of the law. One of the examiners was Don Carlos Barrett, his first mentor in Texas. Court Minutes state the proceedings simply: "On Motion of D. C. Barrett Esqr. E. M. Pease Esqr. was sworn and admitted as an attorney and counsel at law." After paying a $5.00 fee and swearing an oath, Pease officially began a lifelong career. From it, he would acquire wealth and political power. At twenty-six, he had "identified with Texas" by participating in the start of the Revolution in 1835, and he had served in public offices that gave him a variety of experience with the politics and leaders of the time. From the start, Pease's background and intelligence put him ahead of many who were licensed to practice in Texas.[7]

Texas law was never a simple matter when the region was a Spanish province and then a colony of Mexico, nor would it be during the Republic. Spanish (Castilian) law dated to the 1200s. Spanish lawyers required extensive training, and there were none in Texas. One notary in San Antonio had some knowledge but no formal qualifications; few law books were available. During Mexican rule, the situation was a little different. The state constitution of Coahuila and Texas called for courts once state revenue could support them, but meanwhile the law was handled by lay municipal *alcaldes* backed by a legal advisor in the state capital of Saltillo. Mexican law was not as remote as Spanish law, but nevertheless, few trained people were available to interpret and apply it.[8]

With the arrival of Anglo-Americans, two differences soon developed: Stephen F. Austin was allowed to write laws, in English, for his colonists, and lawyers from the United States began to serve colonists, while either becoming acquainted with the general concepts of Mexican law or unlawfully proceeding to practice English common law as developed in the United States. Nevertheless, as legal scholar Joseph McKnight noted, "some rules of Spanish law became established and were maintained by legislators of the republic. Although some of these principles have survived in other areas of Texas law, their chief significance is in family property law."[9] When Austin returned from Mexico in 1823, the Baron de Bastrop (whom Austin had appointed land commissioner) informed colonists that Austin had been given "full powers to administer justice and preserve good order in the colony until it can be regularly organized agreeably to the constitution and laws of the nation." In January 1824, Austin published his Civil Regulations and Criminal Regulations. Diplomat and politician that he was, Austin wisely devised laws that appeared to be aligned with Mexican legal custom (such as no trial by jury) but which satisfied American expectations by creating juries whose verdicts were honored in the seeming decision of the *alcalde* or *Empresario*. Austin, although not a lawyer, thus enabled colonists to begin life in a foreign country by maintaining dimensions of American law. Even then, perhaps most felt that it was just a matter of time before American law would prevail.[10] Only one Anglo-American, Thomas Jefferson Chambers, legally practiced in Mexican Texas. Chambers had worked in Mexico City in the 1820s as a businessman and translator. He was licensed to practice in 1834 and became a legal advisor to the lay judiciary of Texas. Among the men who poured into Texas to practice law from colonial times through the Republic, some had legal training and licenses from American states, but many did not. A few became legendary, such as Sam Houston and William B. Travis. In any case, too many of them were a problem. Thomas J. Rusk, partner of J. Pinckney Henderson in a strong firm in San Augustine, noted in 1845 that practicing law would "barely support a man, owing to the poverty of our people ... and the overstock of young men in the profession."[11]

The unknown author of *Texas in 1837* took a dim view of the status of the law: "Texas presents a state of confusion and uncertainly that almost amounts to chaos .... Each lawyer in Texas has his own system of practice, and each judge his own rule of decision, and it is a matter of little consequence whether the first is inconsistent with commonsense, to say nothing of accuracy, or whether the latter is at war with the most obvious principles of justice." The author realized that Texas needed time to develop its law, but he was pessimistic; "the greatest subject of regret and fear is that Texas cannot hope much from the talents of the men who have taken her destiny into their hands."[12]

A traveler from Virginia, William Fairfax Gray, provided diary descriptions of the court at Brazoria that were less harsh. He observed in April 1837, "The lawyers practicing here are mostly young men, the judge is young, and all the proceedings are loose, and not very ceremonious. Presented my license to the judge, who ordered it to be recorded, and a license was issued to me to practice in the 'District and Inferior Courts of the Republic.'"[13]

From a perspective of more than a century later, McKnight observed that between 1830 and 1840, "a blending of Anglo-American with Hispanic legal elements commenced gradually" and "moved forward with a feverish pace" in the Revolution and the Republic. He noted that during the Republic, legislation was primarily focused on governmental issues, and since issues of defense and government itself were not yet settled, "neither the legislature nor the courts functioned very effectively. Apart from a few civil statutes of the republic and early statehood that perpetuated Hispanic legal institutions, most of the general civil and criminal laws were borrowed from the statutes of various American states."[14]

In this changing world, swirling with a flood of lawyers of various capacities and fed by two different streams of legal tradition, E. M. Pease entered practice. No evidence exists that he was perturbed in the slightest by these realities, nor was John A. Wharton, whose practice he joined, nor was John W. Harris, who also became a partner. Wharton was a Nashville native with a classical education who had been admitted to the bar before he was twenty-one years old. He began his legal practice in New Orleans in 1830 and probably came to Texas in 1833. He fought at San Jacinto and represented Brazoria, where he had established a law practice, in the first Texas Congress. Wharton also served in the Third Congress, but he grew ill with a fever and died on December 17, 1838, at the age of thirty-two. Harris was the executor of his will.[15]

Harris, a Virginian who was more than a year older than Pease, graduated from Washington College (later Washington and Lee University) in law and five other departments before coming to Texas in the fall of 1837 and settling in Brazoria County. By January 1, 1838, he had joined Wharton's firm. When Wharton left his practice to serve in the Third Congress, the two young partners formed the firm of Harris and Pease. It continued until Pease was elected governor in 1853, but the partners worked together at times up to and after the Civil War. They established a reputation for highly competent work, although how they did so at first, with no apparent guidance, is a wonder.[16]

Little documentation of the Harris & Pease firm exists in the Pease Papers. Since Harris continued the practice after Pease was elected governor, it is likely that Harris kept the records of the firm, which he later moved to Galveston. However, various documents do provide information about their work and the times. First is the announcement, dated June 4, 1838, of the opening of the firm in the Brazoria *Brazos Courier*: "John W. Harris and E. M. Pease, Attorneys and Counsellors at Law, Brazoria, Texas, Will attend all the Courts of Brazoria county, the District Courts for the counties of Matagorda, Colorado, Austin, Fort Bend and Harrisburg, and the Supreme Court of the Republic."

Pease wrote his father on July 10, 1838, saying that he had thought of visiting home that summer, but

> since I have embarked in the practice of law my time has been constantly occupied and I could not leave business so long a time as such a journey would require, without a great sacrifice of business and prospects. My prospects in business are greater than I could have anticipated. I believe I told you ... that I was associated with Col. John A. Wharton, brother of our late Minister and a young gentleman by the name of Harris, a Virginian, about the age of myself, both of whom I am well pleased with.

He had suffered a severe attack of fever at Brazoria and gone to Velasco to recover in a large room in a house on the Gulf, where he would spend the balance of the summer. Once again, he was anxious about the United States "politiks," but declared, "I have abandoned political life, believing that my present course of life is the surest road to a fortune if industriously persevered in."[17] After Wharton's death, the partners may have split responsibilities so that Pease stayed in Brazoria, seeing clients and maintaining the office, while Harris worked the district court circuit.[18] Harris and Pease's cases were often in the district court, held in the spring and fall in each of the counties in the district. Other lawyers in the district also had offices in Brazoria, where the district judge was required to live, and members of the bar knew one another well. Courtroom decorum was sometimes informal, and lawyers on both sides of an argument engaged in evenings of storytelling, eating, and drinking. In such comradery, Pease and Harris developed close relationships.[19]

Extant files indicate that Harris and Pease generally practiced civil rather than criminal law. Civil cases included contract law, property law, and probate. Contract law involved drawing up contracts and handling contract disputes in commercial transactions, loan transactions, and debt collection.[20] Loan transactions were particularly important since Texas had no chartered banks until after the Civil War and so private firms issued loans by contract, which required attorneys to handle the paperwork. Property law handled by the firm included land sales, purchases, and land disputes. Probate work included the writing of wills and settlement of estates, which often involved land.[21]

Debt collection was one focus of their work, since both Texas and the United States suffered serious economic problems during the era of the Republic. Edwin Waller (a signer of the Texas Declaration of Independence and the man President Lamar sent to supervise laying out the City of Austin in 1839) was willing to pay Harris and Pease $2,800 to collect on a $5,000 note as well as to obtain his release as endorser of other notes amounting to $10,000. Another example of debt collection, scrawled by Pease, states, "Recd Brazoria April 15th 1838 of Jeremiah Col[e?] on account for collection against McKinney & Williams for the sum of six thousand four hundred and fourteen dollars & seventy five cents, subject to a credit of two thousand nine hundred and sixty one dollars & thirty nine cents as appears by the statement of said account." In 1840, they were collecting for Lewis C. Manson on notes, including two by future president of the Republic Anson Jones for $172.50 each.[22]

Probate featured prominently in their work. Pease was often a legal agent for an estate administrator, or served as one himself. No fee schedules are extant, but the firm received 10 percent of $1,234.47 in acting as agent for John Cumming, according to a receipt signed by Pease on June 1, 1838. Another example of estate work was a notice placed in the newspaper asking that any person having papers belonging to the late Thomas A. Hereford be forwarded to Messrs. Harris and Pease, although the administrator was Peter MacGreal.[23]

Many of the firm's cases involved significant amounts of land, which was being bought and sold in large quantities and created a serious need for lawyers. People often paid debts in land, having little if any cash during the Republic, and land sales required legal paperwork. The partners were also real estate agents on occasion. Litigation involving land titles granted during the Mexican era also had to be resolved. One of Pease's clients with highly complicated land problems was Thomas Jefferson Chambers, who owned vast tracts and was often in disputes regarding them. Harris and Pease took Chambers as a client during his lifetime, and Pease continued work on Chambers's legal affairs for the remainder of his own life. A dispute over whether part of the City of Austin was laid out in 1839 on Chambers's land did not end until a legislative decision in 1925. Another of Pease's clients was James F. Perry, whose wife, Emily, was Stephen F. Austin's sister.[24]

Slaves were listed in property inventories as routinely as was land. "Grayson's Bond with David Smith" (and another man) included an inventory of "ten negroes valued @ [$] 2500" followed on the next line by "1/3 league of land on headwaters of San Bernard [$] 500." William McNair wrote Harris & Pease in 1848, that he was giving them power of attorney in his absence. He listed cash in hand, notes, and a Negro woman valued at $600 with four children totaling $800, followed by land, lots, proceeds from Treasury notes, and more.[25] Pease also served as an agent for absentee owners. For instance, M. W. Chapin wrote from Hartford in 1846, asking that his land be located and enclosing papers for the title. As late as 1866, Pease was still his agent, paying state and county taxes on his 320 acres in Bexar County.[26]

No fee schedules have survived, but scattered examples document the fees Harris and Pease charged. For example, a bill for their client, Isaac C. Hawkins (circa 1840s) shows the following:

writing power of attorney and transfer of stock certificates to E. Andrews	20.00
writing Bill of sale of Negro woman and child to E. Andrews	10.00
writing Petition for extension of time as Adm of F. Johnson	10.00
writing Petition and obtaining order of sale [illegible]	10.00
defending suit of F Adams adm of you in County and District Court No 218	25.00
obtaining Judgmt vs H. M. Pittman	33.00
fee in suit vs E. Henry	50.00
writing Deed from Probate Judge to you	10.00
writing Deed from you to Crane	10.00
Prosecuting suit vs M G. Hill	30.00[27]

Client John Sharp utilized Harris and Pease in the 1840s for the following list of charges:

commission on suit vs Thos. P. Curly in County Court, $176.35 at 10 percent	17.63
comm on suit by Charles Gleason in District Court, No. 335, $168.92 at 10 percent	16.89
comm on suit by Charles Gleason, Mason & Moore in District Court No. 343	56.70
comm on suit by Howard & Ryan in District Court No. 365, $316.20 for defending suit of James G. Powell vs you in District Court No. 434	50.00
comm on suit vs E. C. Hawkins in District Court No. 586, $412.03	41.20
comm on $91.68 collected of Paine & pd to Mills per order	9.16
comm on $75. Collected from C. Bennett in Justices Court	7.50
comm on $50 collected of Logan & pd Carroll per order	5.00
comm for collecting Calding note $333.29	33.32
comm on $48.92 collected of DeBennett	4.89
For defending suit in Justice Court by you & owners SB Amite	16.00
For defending injunction of Howard vs you in District Court	25.00
For defending suit of Pillsbury vs you, Waller & Thompson in District Court	20.00
For drawing agreement for purchase of Goods of Carroll & defending you in Attachment Bond	300.00[28]

Clients were not charged at an hourly rate, but fees for the firm's services as a collection agency supplemented its income.[29]

Public service was often an option. Pease served briefly as interim mayor of Brazoria in 1840. President Lamar offered him the job of district attorney, but he declined. In 1842 he joined Brazoria volunteers in marching to the lower Nueces River to defend Texas from Mexican invasion. (The Mexican troops withdrew across the Rio Grande before the men from Brazoria arrived.) He also let the family know that he had twice been asked to run for Congress, but he knew that public service would not pay as well as the law.

He wrote his mother, "My only ambition is to secure an independence and as I know that it is in my power …. I do not intend to let any considerations divert me from it."[30]

Harris and Pease worked together closely in their practice and on political issues as well. While Pease was in Austin in the Legislature, Harris wrote him, "Be pleased to get from the Land Office and send down the field notes of the Pennington half league of land which Mr. Wharton sold to Mr. Calvert. Two hundred acres have been taken from the tract. What had better be done with William A. Wharton's head-right which Mr. Archer … located … ?" In the same letter, Harris asked if it would be a good to have a law amended "to require a sheriff, when he sold property for taxes, to make a return to the Clerk's office of a list of the property so sold to whom it belonged, who purchased it, and at what price?" Harris inquired in another letter about what Pease thought of his idea to take some undivided land in payment for their legal services.[31]

It is impossible to separate much of the work by John W. Harris and E. M. Pease. They thought highly of one another. Pease wrote his mother that Harris was "a man of strict integrity and very promising talents." James D. Lynch, the author of *The Bench and Bar of Texas*, wrote that the firm was "one of the most noted in the Republic," and he pointed out that their practice in the Supreme Court began in 1840, when the Court first opened.[32]

The firm continued to grow in income and prestige. By the time Texas joined the Union, it was one of the most respected in the state. Frank W. Johnson wrote in his *History of Texas and Texans*, "Probably no firm at the time ranked higher and had a better record of success than this."[33]

Following annexation to the United States in 1846, the first four attorneys general of the state were appointed by the governor, and it was a mark of prestige that Harris was asked to consider the job. He wrote to Pease confidentially on March 30 that he has been asked by Judge Waller and another man if he would accept the office of Attorney General. Harris read the new constitution to see the selection process and how salary and perquisites would be established. Pease had mentioned that the salary would probably be only $1,000 annually. "You request me to come up immediately … [I] cannot, although I will endeavor to write to you in such a manner as to enable you to act ... without embarrassment," and he decided that he would accept the position under some conditions, but not under others. The next day he wrote his partner, "Now remember that in you I have the most entire confidence and were I in Austin I should be certain to follow your advice in the matter." In April he wrote again to Pease in confidence, stating that his friends thought that he should accept the office and that it would increase their practice. He concluded that if the law required him to reside in Austin, he would not accept the office, but if not, he would accept. He commented that he had to go to Galveston occasionally "for business will increase there and the people there seem very much disposed to employ us. It does not suit our business to be absent long." Harris ultimately accepted the position of Attorney General in May 1846.[34]

During the era of transition from an independent republic to a state in the Union, Pease was well-aware of the complex American and international issues that kept Texas a republic. A critical one was the matter of admission as a slave state. Pease received newspapers and letters from the North, and he knew that Abolitionists bitterly opposed annexation because of slavery. Surely, he heard more on the subject when, after eleven years, he was finally able to visit his Connecticut family in the summer of 1845. Pease probably had to entertain sharp questions about the South's "Peculiar Institution," and if so, he had an answer formulated since his arrival in Texas. He agreed with Stephen F. Austin's thinking that slavery was a matter of practical necessity, especially for growing cotton, the Republic's principal crop. Although Pease himself never became a planter, he owned enslaved persons and benefited in numerous ways from their labor as farm workers and domestic servants. He regarded slavery as essential to the growth and prosperity of Texas and for that reason defended the institution throughout the antebellum years.

When Pease went North in 1845, he did so to promote Texas because annexation was nearing. On February 28, 1845, the United States House of Representatives had passed the Senate version of a Joint Resolution to admit Texas to the Union. In the final Senate vote on February 27, the Pease family friend, Senator John M. Niles of Connecticut, voted "yes" in a vote of twenty-seven-yeas to twenty-five nays. On February 28 the House sent a message to the Senate that they concurred with the Senate's vote.[35]

Pease's trip to the North caused him to miss one of the most important events in Texas history to that date—the July 1845 convention in Austin that agreed to annexation and drafted a state constitution. He was still absent in October 1845 when voters ratified the proceedings of the convention, but he did receive a personal and important message about the final step in annexation. On December 17 from "Washington City," L. T. Pease, who had long promoted admitting Texas to the Union, wrote an informative letter to his son, observing that in Washington, "I meet daily some of your Texian neighbors." He was boarding with six members of Congress, including Senator Niles, and he commented that,

> The Texas Resolutions have been up in the "House" & passed in short order. They are now before the Senate and it is understood will occasion very little debate. Probably before the lapse of another week Texas will be to all intents and purposes a State in this Confederacy. I have been and continue to draw great satisfaction from the certain consummation of the measure.

L. T. Pease promised his son that he would write "when the day of final Consummation of Annexation Comes [by] the last of next week."[36] That letter did not survive, but the younger man's response to statehood was clear: He ran for a Brazoria County seat in the House of Representatives in the first Texas state legislature and won.[37]

E. M. Pease had become financially secure enough to afford to return to public service. Perhaps he thought that his legal career would be enhanced, and he must have well known that he could made a meaningful contribution to the laws of the new state. Mail began arriving before he was sworn in. One writer pronounced him "one of the great men of Texas" and promptly asked for a favor; another, client Robert Mills, asked for strict law enforcement.[38]

In the small city of Austin, the first state legislature met on February 16, 1846, in the one-story, frame capitol building that had been constructed in 1839 for the Congress of the Republic. The House and Senate chambers were separated by a dog trot, and a few committee rooms were at the back of the chambers. A porch stretched across the front of the building, which faced east to Congress Avenue. Hickory (later West 8th) Street was on the south; Colorado Street was on the west. The furniture, brought from the capitol at Houston, included tables rather than desks for members.[39] No one had an office. The House had to buy a clock. In this simple place, members conducted legislative business. They met every day except Sunday, and their only special adjournment was on the tenth anniversary of the Declaration of Texas Independence.[40]

E. M. Pease and S. W. Perkins represented Brazoria County in a body of sixty-five members (including replacements) from thirty-six counties. J. Pinckney Henderson was announced as the Governor and N. H. Darnell, Lieutenant Governor. House Speaker W. E. Crump appointed five House members, including Pease, to join the appointed senators "to wait upon His Excellency the President of the Republic of Texas, and Heads of Departments, and invite them to attend the inauguration of the Governor and Lieutenant Governor." The Legislature gathered at "the place prepared for the inauguration" before the Capitol where Pease and others heard the valedictory address of President Anson Jones, who said, "I lay down the honors and the cares of the Presidency with infinitely more personal gratifi- cation than I assumed them," and added his "ardent prayer" that the Union be perpetual. The last line of his speech was, "The final act of this great drama is now performed. The Republic of Texas is no more." If, as is often reported, he said those dramatic words just before or as the Long Star flag was lowered, the moment was not recorded in either the House or the Senate journal. After the governor and lieutenant governor took their oaths of office, Henderson delivered his address, announcing, "We have this day fully entered the Union of the North American States—let us give our friends who so boldly and nobly advocated our cause ... no reason to regret their efforts in our behalf." By the opening of the first legislature, E. M. Pease had been identified with Texas and a part of its history for more than ten years, and he was up to the challenge of having a formative role in its next chapters.[41]

Pease was appointed chairman of the Public Lands Committee and a member of the key Finance and Judiciary committees on the first full day of the session, February 20, 1846.[42] The next day the Legislature voted to make Sam Houston and Thomas Jefferson Rusk the first and second United States Senators from Texas. Pease voted with the majority. He made his first motion February 23 when he offered a substitute for a bill to create two Congressional Districts in the state, and he was appointed chairman of a select committee to work on the topic.[43] He reported that the committee had combined that bill with another and offered a substitute; the bill passed. By February 28, Representative Pease had seen his first legislative success, and this bill became the first law of the first session of the State Legislature when it was signed by the Governor.[44]

The work of the first Legislature fell into several major categories: converting the Republic to a state, organizing state government, managing land, and addressing societal issues. Conversion to a state required not only establishment of congressional representation but also ceding and transferring properties such as custom houses, forts, and armories, as well as recommending needed mail routes. On April 1 the legislature proposed that "the Congressional Delegation be requested and authorized to open negotiation with the Government of the United States ... to enable Texas to pay her public debt."[45] Controller James B. Shaw provided a statement of several classes of debts incurred by the Republic totaling $9,949,007.05. Of that, $8,013,957.65 was domestic, and the remainder was foreign.[46] The Governor signed into law a bill authorizing Shaw to demand monies due to the State by the Federal Government.[47]

Organizing state government required closing offices of the Republic and opening new offices such as the Treasury; in some cases, transferring records was necessary, such as those from the closed War and Marine Department to the new Adjutant General's office. A penitentiary was established. The Judiciary Committee, with Pease as a member, was widely involved in reorganization. It addressed bills that defined duties of state officials from the Treasurer, Comptroller, and Attorney General to district attorneys, county treasurers, notaries public, and more. The Committee also considered the bill that became an act to raise revenue by taxation of property with a direct *ad valorem* tax.[48] Pease was involved in some of this legislation such as the penitentiary and tax bills as a member of both the Judiciary and Finance committees. The new state government required land management legislation, beginning with the conversion of the General Land Office to a state agency. The Judiciary Committee handled legal issues of land ownership arising from the creation of thirty counties plus designating county seats and incorporating cities.[49] Much as Texans wanted to become part of the United States, feelings about the land and retaining control of it ran deep. The mood of the time was reflected in a joint resolution that declared,

> exclusive right of the State to jurisdiction over the soil ... in ... the late Republic of Texas ... [was] acquired by the valor of the people thereof, and was by them vested in the government of the said Republic, that such exclusive right is now vested in and belongs to the State; we recognize no title to Indian tribes; we recognize no right in the government of the United States to make any treaty of limits with said Indian tribes, without consent of the government of the State.[50]

Societal issues received little attention, except for slavery. A bill was recommended by the Judiciary Committee for relief of owners of convicted or executed slaves, but Pease, in the minority, opposed it. The committee recommended a bill calling for trial and punishment of crimes committed by slaves and free persons of color, noting that the matter "ought to receive careful attention."[51] To a bill prohibiting free Blacks from settling in Texas, Pease offered an amendment excepting "such as were living in Texas at the date of the Declaration of Independence, and as such, have been permitted by special statute, to remain in Texas.[52] The committee declared the bill was "demanded by the dictates of self-preservation. It is only *by such means* that we can prevent the immigration of incendiaries, dangerous to the peaceful maintenance of our servile institutions."[53] The report noted dissent in the committee, but no minority report was issued. Pease opposed a bill calling for punishment of persons producing insubordination among the "colored" population.[54] For a bill authorizing a man to liberate certain slaves, Pease suggested an amendment providing "that nothing in this act, shall be so construed as to prevent said slaves to reside in this State, after they are liberated." The amendment was rejected.[55] None of these bills became law. Two others did: one provided for appointment of slave patrols and described their duties and powers, and the other prevented slaves from "hiring their own time, or their owners from hiring them to other Slaves, free Negroes, or Mulattoes."[56]

The topic of public education was also considered in the Judiciary Committee, which noted that creating public schools had been impossible during the Republic on a county-by-county basis, and so they recommended a general fund controlled by a board of school commissioners. The bill did not become law.[57] For the problem of frontier security, the Legislature issued a joint resolution stating, "Texas has merged her former independence and sovereignty in that of the United States with the confident hope that the protecting arm of that great Republic would be fully extended over her citizens ... ." They instructed her United States senators to exert themselves to obtain adequate appropriations.[58] The Legislature also made a $500 appropriation "to send out dispatches for better security of the country."[59] Regarding the "Cochatte" [sic] and Alabama Indians, the Judiciary Committee saw "no evil" in continuing to permit "these poor beings to occupy their lands, their home and only resting place," but the Indians feared ejection, and so the committee recommended indefinite postponement of the bill.[60] Religious affairs received no attention except for a bill passed to protect religious meetings in churches, mosques, and synagogues.[61] Women's rights to hold property (which the Spanish had approved long before) were upheld in a new law regarding conveyance of the separate property of wives and another defining the mode of conveying property in which the wife had an interest.[62]

As a Judiciary Committee member, Pease was involved early in the session in transferring judicial proceedings from the Republic of Texas to the State of Texas and in passing a bill organizing county courts.[63] He offered a lengthy amendment to the bill organizing the county courts; it was adopted.[64] More than one act pertained to county courts, but this primary one contained nineteen sections of detailed law. Thus Pease's role in establishing the county court system was one of his important legislative accomplishments. He served on the select committee to consider establishing county seats in new counties and on another select committee regarding the bill for assessment and collection of taxes, which became a law with thirty sections.[65]

Some bills were Representative Pease's own. One that became law provided for publication of the laws of Texas.[66] Another representative authored an act that provided for the Constitution and "certain laws" to be translated into German and Spanish and included an appropriation to implement it.[67] Pease also introduced a bill to incorporate the counties and another to regulate proceedings in the district courts.[68] The only bill specifically for his constituents authorized the Brazoria County Court to have a duplicate copy made of their deed record book, which had suffered water damage.[69] It is difficult to determine exactly how much direct influence Pease had over most of the legislation that was handled by the Judiciary Committee, both because of the limits of the record in the House Journal and the extent to which subjects under consideration may have been folded into other bills that became law. Considering his grasp of the law and his intelligence, his influence was likely greater than it is possible to prove.

Judiciary Committee reports were usually made by Chairman Peter W. Gray, who, like Pease, authored comparatively few bills but worked on many. One of Gray's bills that became law regulated the practice of attorneys and counsellors at law.[70] One controversial report pertained to a bill to amend the Constitution to provide for public election of judges and district attorneys. The committee majority deemed it "*wholly* inexpedient" to act on the measure because the Constitution, approved by the people, did not call for a vote on the matter, and "in our own State, time has not been allowed for ever a *trial* of the present mode of appointment, and no reason ... [has] ever been given why a change should be made." A minority report on the matter, issued by James Willie and signed by Pease and three others, stated the belief that "the present system is radically defective – [and] .... To acknowledge the existence of a defect ... and to bear the evil, simply from an aversion to change, does not appear ... to be the part of wisdom." The minority report concluded, "it is a matter of much doubt, however, whether the people appreciate the kind intentions of those who are so desirous ... of relieving them of the *trouble and inconvenience of governing themselves*."[71]

The Finance Committee began its work to convert the Republic to a state by considering the organization of the entire Treasury Department and the role of the Treasurer. It was such a complex subject that the chairman withdrew, feeling inadequate.[72] The committee somehow completed its task, and a bill for reorganization was passed. The committee and its Senate counterpart introduced a joint resolution that required destruction of exchequer bills and promissory notes.[73] In some cases, Pease worked on the same bills as they were considered by both the Judiciary and Finance committees, such as the establishment of the penitentiary and the tax bill.

Although Pease was chair of the Public Lands Committee, the topic was relatively minor and caused him more annoyance than time. Two days after the committee received its first petition on February 24 for relief of an individual in a public land dispute, Pease reported that the petition should not be granted because the committee found nothing that required the action of the Legislature, which "ought not to pass special acts for relief of individuals in cases where they have a plain and adequate remedy by applying to the Courts." It was not unusual for people to ask for legislative help in the absence of state or private agencies to fund or provide services, but in this case, Pease disagreed, adding, "the laws of the State afford an ample remedy to the petitioner." The report was adopted.[74] Requests continued to come in from individuals, and Pease must have been greatly relieved when he was excused from service on the committee on April 7 and could devote most of his time to the Judiciary Committee.[75]

In 1846 Texas finances were precarious. Comptroller Shaw reported to the Legislature on May 1 that about $20,240 was in the Treasury. The amount "owing to the late Government" was estimated at $19,500 from custom returns, $12,000 in direct taxes, and $4,500 in licenses.[76] House members, well aware of the state's financial condition, allowed themselves only a three dollar *per diem* and a mileage allotment of three dollars for every twenty-five miles traveled.[77] At the end of the session the Judiciary Committee considered the petition of Thomas F. McKinney for money loaned during the Revolution. They found from records and received from "the Hon. E. M. Pease, who was an officer of the provisional Government, and J. B. Shaw, Esq., the present Comptroller," the information they needed, but they had no money to pay the debt.[78]

Representative Pease showed himself to be a conscientious legislator in both attendance and work output. He was rarely absent for roll call or votes, in spite of the press of committee assignments. Others attended so erratically that a motion was made on April 28 to fine absent members their *per diem* because "it is difficult to keep a quorum to transact business ...."[79] That day another member introduced a resolution to record demographic information about the members and their wives—whether they were "talkative or silent, persuasive or lovely,"—and what they expected upon coming to Texas. The resolution, offered presumably in jest, lost.[80] In spite of difficulties, members passed slightly more than two hundred bills. Even at that, the Judiciary Committee returned bills to the House on May 11, unable to consider them "due to the great press of business before them."[81] The House adjourned *sine die* on May 11.[82] Before they did, the Legislature adopted a Joint Resolution "for safekeeping of Papers and Journals of the Legislature," to which Pease had offered an additional section, "that after the publication of the Journals of the two Houses, the Chief Clerk is hereby instructed to hand over to the Secretary of State, the Journals and all papers and effects of the two Houses." The section was adopted, and with it, Pease, who came from a family of faithful record keepers, made another contribution to the keeping of Texas history.

Representative Pease and sixty-seven other members filled the Hall of Representatives for the second session of the Texas Legislature, which met from December 13, 1847 to March 20, 1848.[83] Conditions in the drafty building were improved over the first session by the addition of a stove.[84] James W. Henderson, whom Pease and others escorted to the chair, was elected Speaker of the House.[85] The Speaker appointed sixteen standing committees on December 15, and the Judiciary Committee was named first. Representative Pease, the first named member, was its chairman, and so just days short of his thirty-sixth birthday, he was the highest-ranking member of a key legislative committee.[86] He was able to concentrate on his assignment, because he had no other standing committee appointments for most of the session. Guy M. Bryan, Stephen F. Austin's nephew and a lawyer, joined Pease in representing Brazoria County. He and Pease had been friends since the Revolution, and Bryan, as Chairman of the Engrossed Bills Committee, usually voted with Pease.[87]

Governor Henderson delivered a message to a joint session at the close of his term on December 15, 1847. He expressed opposition to the Federal government by charging the US Congress with inappropriately questioning the right of Texas to the Santa Fe territory that was about to be taken from Mexico.[88] Nevertheless, he said that the sale of "our unappropriated domain to the General Government will enable the State to pay her debt ... and give to the frontier of our State the most complete protection."[89] Foreshadowing the increased conflict to come between the North and South, he proclaimed, "Those Northern people are the aggressors, and it is our duty to join with the other States of the South, in resisting their efforts with manly firmness."[90] While in joint session the legislature re-elected Sam Houston as United States Senator, with Pease voting in the majority.[91] Days later Pease introduced two resolutions to facilitate the determination of the next governor and lieutenant governor. A joint committee (to which he was appointed) was to ascertain and report a mode of examining votes: with both bodies assembled in the Hall, the committee was to publish a record of votes cast statewide, and tellers were to declare the winners. That procedure was adopted, and hence, George T. Wood and John A. Greer was announced as Governor and Lieutenant Governor on December 18 and inaugurated on December 21.[92] Wood sent a message to the Legislature on December 30 stating that no matter was more urgent than payment of public debt: "Our large and valuable public domain is the only ready resource we have," he wrote, and the legislators must determine how to bring "this immense tract of country into market." He added, "the most suitable and proper purchaser of our public lands is the United States ... inasmuch as the Federal Constitution gives her alone the exclusive right of [dealing with] Indian tribes, she would then be the owner of the soil occupied by the various tribes ... and would then more effectually control them." He suggested that the Legislature should appoint a committee to oversee the sale of Texas's public land to the national government.[93]

The second session focused not on the state's public debt but rather on a number of issues with the Federal government, further development of state government (particularly in the judiciary branch) and the creation of more counties and towns as well as management of the state's lands. Slavery, Indians, education, and transportation were minor topics. Federal relations came up the day after the Governor's address, when State Affairs Committee chairman Lamar introduced legislation that became a Joint Resolution, signed by the Governor on February 2, asking the Texas Congressional delegation to "protest relinquishment of the Mexican Provinces and States conquered by and in the possession of the United States, and also to protest any law which shall be intended to prevent citizens of slave-holding states from taking their property with them ... to said acquired territory." The resolution referred to such laws as an "insult to the southern people."[94] Pease was not a leader in this or other related resolutions, but the rising conflict between the North and South and the role of the Federal government almost certainly was an increasing concern for him.

To begin to address the debt of the "late" Republic, the governor signed a bill calling for documenting the financial obligations involved.[95] It quickly became apparent, however, that Texas had no money to pay its immense debts.[96] That painful fact would remain an issue facing Pease and other leaders for years to come.[97]

The Legislature would soon take steps at least to raise revenue for normal operating expenses. It passed a bill that the governor signed for an *ad valorem* tax of twenty cents on each hundred dollar value of property, real and personal.[98] For collection purposes, another law created the office of county tax assessor and collector.[99] As the population grew and spread, the Legislature created twelve new counties, better defined or made further provisions for others, and located seats of justice and county seats. A general law provided for organization of the new counties.[100] Laws related to land were repealed, written, and amended. Pease had little to do with those laws, but management of complex land issues posed serious problems in early statehood for the people as well as the General Land Office and its Commissioner, Thomas William Ward. Following a legislative investigation, Ward lost the election as Commissioner in a joint session on February 26. Pease was in the minority of those who supported Ward.[101]

In other matters, a law from the previous session was re-written to establish a penitentiary, and legislators envisioned an exchange of books and more with other states and the Library of Congress, as well as creation of the State Library, to be controlled by the Secretary of State.[102] The Legislature was silent on slavery except on the New Mexico boundary question and a bill the governor signed that amended an 1840 Republic law so that "cruel or unreasonable" treatment or "abuse" of slaves was made a misdemeanor with fines.[103] The Education Committee wrote a bill to tax citizens in order to establish public schools, but it did not pass.[104]

The primary focus of the second session was the continued development of the judiciary and related matters. Of the two hundred sixty-one signed bills from the session, the largest number on one topic (forty-three) created a broad foundation of the judicial branch at every level and the administration of law. Judiciary Chairman Pease authored few of these bills, but he and his committee approved, disapproved, amended, or made substitutes for all of them. Their recommendations reflected close attention to detail. The first topic considered was presented on December 21 when Committee member Samuel F. Mosely proposed deducting from the salaries of judges of the Supreme Court and district courts as well as district attorneys if they neglected their duties. The next day Pease reported a more constructive approach: the committee, he said, believed that "public interest requires an increase of salaries in order to induce competent persons to accept those offices" and recommended adoption of a substitute bill.[105] On February 5, Pease called the matter of salary deduction "objectionable in many respects" and asked that the committee be discharged from further consideration of it.[106] The bill to regulate salaries of district attorneys was signed into law without the punitive provisions.[107]

Judiciary Committee work for expanding and reforming Texas courts began with a resolution that the Committee inquire and report on the expediency of revising and amending an act to organize justice of the peace courts and to define their powers and jurisdiction. Later in the session, an extensive sixty-eight section bill to "Organize Justice's Courts and define powers and jurisdiction of the same" was signed into law.[108] Improving the county court system began when Pease issued a long report on February 10 regarding an act to organize probate courts. He said, "[we] have given the subject that attention which its importance demands. The Committee is aware, that the people throughout the state, are anxiously expecting that this Legislature will remedy some of the evils that now exist in our probate system, and they have endeavored to prepare such bills as they think will, in some measure, meet the public expectations." The committee proposed abolishing probate courts and giving jurisdiction to the chief justices of county courts. The other bill pertained to estates of the deceased. Pease said it was "lengthy ... but no part of it could well be omitted."[109] The first bill resulted in giving county courts jurisdiction in probate matters, and it became a 129-secton law.[110] The second bill, relating to county court proceedings in estates of the deceased, was also signed into law.[111] Pease did not agree with certain sections of the Senate version of the county court bill, and a conference committee (which he chaired on the part of the House) worked out differences.[112] Another act regulated proceedings in the county courts concerning guardians and wards of minors.[113] On occasion the Judiciary Committee pointed out instances when existing legislation was sufficient, such as a proposed bill for the support of the poor. Pease reported, "County Courts by existing laws are vested with full authority to provide for support of indigent persons and burial of paupers ... [so] no need exists for further legislation"[114]

The district court system was significantly altered and improved by a bill that originated in the Judiciary Committee and became law as "An Act concerning proceedings in the District Courts.[115] Pease commented that the committee had added amendments to make changes "as experience shows to be necessary."[116] Other bills provided schedules for holding courts in each district, and another named the counties in each district.[117]

Amendments to an 1846 act to organize the Supreme Court were considered by the Judiciary Committee, which recommended a substitute bill for regulation of its proceedings.[118] Pease served on a joint committee that worked out an agreement on the bill, and it became law.[119] The Federal Supreme Court came into consideration in a bill to authorize the governor to employ counsel to represent the state in suits taken to the high court, and the Judiciary Committee submitted a substitute bill; the act became law.[120]

The Judiciary Committee also considered numerous other practical matters. For example, a bill for payment of jurors by appropriating fines and forfeitures was considered by the Committee, which offered a substitute that was adopted.[121] One bill provided for collection of funds and another for paying jurors $1.25 a day.[122] The legal profession came under consideration when Pease issued a report on January 24 recommending an amendment to an act regulating licensing and practice of counsellors-at-law.[123] He reported that the Committee was not aware of any problems arising from the extant law that permitted immigrants from other states to be admitted to practice law after producing a license and evidence of good moral character. The Committee also issued opinions on the work of law enforcement. They thought that reporting statistics on crimes was proper, because the information was valuable and showed the ability and success of law enforcement officers.

The Judiciary Committee issued nearly one hundred reports during the session, most of them in Pease's name and clearly reflecting his thinking. Few minority reports were issued. The topics other than court matters were wide-ranging. For example, the committee considered and recommended against the petition of a free Black man named Nathan Wade to remain in the state.[124] They considered the incorporation of a Union Marine and Fire Insurance Company and recommended the bill, but it did not pass.[125] They considered a bill to enable legal representatives of those who fell at the Alamo to procure land to which they were entitled. The Committee advised that such a law was necessary "on account of the great difficulty in making the proof now required to obtain headright certificates of those ... who fell in battle during the first year of our revolution, many of whom were unknown to the country except to their associates who fell with them ... ." The Committee proposed a bill "more general in its operation ... prescribing the proof necessary for the heirs of those who fell under the command of Fannin, Travis, Grant, and Johnson to obtain their headright certificates ... ."[126] This bill did not become law. On February 14 the Committee recommended a substitute with a bill to define marital rights of parties in regard to common property, and it became law.[127]

Pease served on several special committees. He was a member of the Select Committee on Apportionment of legislative members, which reported March 2 on their agreement that the basis of representation would be one legislator for each 2000 free white males. The bill was made law.[128] Another select committee considered the proposition of Thomas Jefferson Chambers to make a collection and digest of laws of the State of Coahuila and Texas and of Spain, but despite a request from the United States Supreme Court to the Chief Justice in Texas for this work, as well as the Committee's recommendation, no law resulted.

On March 18, three days before the session ended, Pease reported for the Judiciary Committee that the great length of a bill concerning crimes and punishments prevented a "thorough ... examination its importance demands," and therefore the committee was not prepared to recommend it nor to express opinions of merit. However, they presented a list of amendments "as have occurred to several members of the committee."[129] This list resulted in a seventy-four section bill that became law.[130]

The House adjourned *sine die* on March 20, 1849, with Representative Pease having answered at almost every roll call during the session. His highly productive committee had issued more than one carefully considered report for every day of the session, more than three-quarters in his own name. The quality of their work was even more important, because it shaped the Texas court system for years to come.

The Third Session of the Texas Legislature convened November 5, 1849, in the same 1839 Capitol building. By 1849, the structure was so deteriorated that on December 5, pine poles had to be ordered to prevent the Senate Chamber "from falling down until the adjournment of the present session ... ."[131] E. M. Pease returned for the session, then as a Senator from the Eleventh District of Galveston and Brazoria counties. He may have regretted his decision even before his arrival. Taking time to campaign and serve meant delaying his marriage to Lucadia Niles, to whom he had been engaged the year before. Furthermore, a delay in being seated in the Senate cost him choice committee appointments made by the Lieutenant Governor, because on the first day of the session, John B. Jones was present to challenge for the district senatorial seat.[132] Pease sent a petition and documents to contest the election of Jones.[133] The next day, when standing committees were appointed; Jones was named to the Judiciary and Education committees and chairman of Internal Improvements. Pease's petition was referred to the Committee on Privileges and Elections.[134]

Before a decision could be made on Pease's election appeal, the legislature met in joint session and heard Governor George T. Wood's address. Pease likely was present when Wood reported that he had raised a militia to fight "predatory" Indians and that the United States needed to pay the militia. Regarding the public debt, Wood said, "Our situation is so difficult as to forbid any hope of any action ... unless the United States should purchase a portion of our domain." He was deeply concerned about the lack of funding to promote education, which was ever needed in a democracy. "Those who are now children will have grown up ... without being able to read the tickets which they place in the ballot box." In a sign of the times, Wood expressed deep regret that there was no "abatement of the efforts of the abolitionists of the North to agitate the question of slavery ... for its tendency is to foment ... insurrection ...." Finally, the governor announced the report of an 1848 census, which included the disputed area of Santa Fe County, that documented Texas's population at 63,314 white males, 51,187 white females, and 42,455 slaves.[135]

The Committee on Privileges and Elections reported on November 8 their conclusion that in Galveston and Brazoria counties Pease had received 394 votes to 376 for Jones. Jones won Galveston County 288 to 176, and Pease won Brazoria County 218 to 88. The committee explained the problem: the Chief Justice of Brazoria County was absent on the day the returns were counted, and the Chief Justice of Galveston County rejected the returns of Brazoria on the ground that they were not certified by the proper officer; thus the election had been granted to Jones. The Senate committee majority ruled that Pease had won a majority of the votes and was entitled to the senate seat. On November 9, four days after the Third Legislature opened, Pease took his seat.[136] However, he had to accept Jones's standing committee appointments, and the prime leadership position of chairman of the House Judiciary Committee that he had held in the previous session would not be followed by a position of significance in the Senate.

On November 10, Pease's first action was to offer a resolution that the Senate President "appoint a committee of three to report Joint Rules for the government of the two Houses ... and that the House be requested to appoint a like committee to act jointly ...." The resolution was adopted, and he and two other senators were appointed to that committee, whose work improved the legislative process.[137] It would be the first of many committees on specific issues to which Pease was appointed.

Pease authored several bills that became law in the Third Session. His first was for "ceding to the United States jurisdiction of certain land in this State for public purposes," thereby turning over lighthouses, forts, and other Republic property. As chairman of the Internal Improvements Committee, he wrote a bill for incorporation of the Brazos, San Bernard, and Oyster Creek Canal and Navigation Company.[138] Several other bills incorporated railroads, but all of them came to nothing. Pease's most intriguing bill was an early attempt to gather data for the state to meet social service needs. The bill appeared to concern only gathering data on passengers coming into Texas on ships: all were required to be registered by the captain with a record of basic information about each that was to be submitted to town mayors or others in authority. Those who would need care because they were "lunatic, idiot, deaf, dumb, blind, or infirm" were to be noted, as well as who was responsible for them. Penalties were imposed for failure to register correctly, and funds gathered from the penalties were directed to hospitals responsible for the care of such patients. This act, which became law without gubernatorial signature, reflected Pease's awareness of the need for care of the mentally ill, blind, and deaf that resulted several years later in state asylums for them. He was gathering statistical data in the only way he knew.[139]

Some of Pease's bills that became law were necessary improvements on existing law. The first he introduced showed his early advocacy of women's rights: it was an amendment to an 1846 bill, authorizing county clerks to take the separate acknowledgment of married women to deeds they had executed.[140]

Pease generally voted in favor of education bills, including a joint resolution to survey land for two universities and establishing private schools and public schools to teach manual labor. He voted with the majority on slavery issues. However, when a bill arose to prohibit slaves from carrying firearms without owner permission, Pease argued as a Judiciary Committee member who was well-familiar with existing law that the bill was unnecessary, because the subject was covered in an earlier act, and the new bill did not come up again.[141] Various bills that he had authored or had worked on in the two previous legislative sessions concerning the judiciary were ones for which he offered amendments or sat on appointed committees. He recommended passage, for instance, of a bill to organize county courts, first passed in March, 1848.[142] A different sort of bill was important to him personally: he introduced a bill on January 1 to authorize the governor to employ a person to perform the duties of the attorney general when the office was vacant. His law partner, John Harris, had resigned the previous October, and no one was acting in the position. The bill became law January 1.[143]

The Third Session, which adjourned on February 11, 1850, must have been largely an exercise in frustration for Pease. It began with a flimsy challenge to his election victory that probably cost him appointments on important committees and ended with his having achieved relatively little compared to his successes in earlier legislative sessions. The Legislature was called into special sessions in August and again in November of 1850, but Senator Pease attended neither. He left Texas, probably in June, for Connecticut, where the greatest success of his life awaited him: His marriage to Lucadia Niles.[144]

In July, Guy Bryan wrote "Friend Pease" that New Mexico had drafted a constitution and would seek admission to the Union as a free state, thereby creating excitement in Texas that had caused the governor to call a special session. Bryan insisted, "*You must return*" and added, "Your future prospects as a public man require it, & your usefulness ... for the benefit of your constituents require it. We are I fear on the eve of a civil war. If the compromise does not pass before the meeting of the Legislature, I fear for the Union ...." Bryan pleaded, "The necessity of moderate, firm & wise counsels is manifest to you, come home, then at once. Let ... nothing prevent you from helping the state of our adoption & love in her hour of travail."[145]

In spite of the plea, Marshall Pease was determined that he and Lucadia would wait no longer, and they were wed in August 1850. As the second called session began, Bryan wrote to Pease, "first with all my heart [I] congratulate you upon your marriage." However, "Your absence has been of serious injury to you. Had you been here I have scarcely a doubt but that you would be our next Governor. Your friends here (& you have many of them) ... concur in thinking so."[146]

The Peases landed in Galveston in early November, but the newlywed husband did not participate in yet another called session that opened on November 18, 1850. By December 3, when the session was over, Bryan wrote again to "Friend Pease" that chances of his being the next governor were "decidedly the best of all whose names have been mentioned," and "some of the most influential men in the Legislature have assured me that they will do for you all they can."[147]

Buoyed by these reports, Pease decided to run. He soon discovered, however, that his adoration of Lucadia was far greater than his interest in being governor, and the campaign trail was intolerable. By April of 1851, he wrote her, "I have never in my life been so unhappy ... being separated from you ... has given me so much unhappiness that I have pretty much resolved ... to withdraw from the canvass .... "He closed by asking her to accept "a thousand kisses."[148] A month later, Lucadia wrote to her sister, Augusta, that she was expecting her first baby. No wonder Marshall was so anxious about her. Nevertheless, he proceeded, miserably, with the campaign, and the baby, Carrie Augusta, was born prematurely in June, before he reached home. By August, he withdrew from the race, although his friends told him that he could win.[149]

Pease spent the remainder of 1851 and early 1852 happily at home in Brazoria, practicing law, with a few trips out of town. During the summer of 1852, the whole family went to Connecticut and returned in November. By late January 1853, Pease again became a candidate for governor. Lucadia's sister, Juliet, who was visiting in Brazoria, broke the news casually, noting, "he has little expectation of being the chosen one [at a February convention] as he has done nothing to aid in his promotion ...."[150] Following the birth of a second child, Julie Maria, on March 14, he must have felt far freer to campaign, because he spent that spring and summer traveling extensively.[151] The primary reason, however, was that Lucadia wanted him to be the next governor. In her mind, he was simply the best candidate, and so she encouraged him to campaign. The Peases were about to take a major step onto the statewide stage of Texas politics.

Chapter 3

The Travels and Early Married Life of Lucadia Niles Pease, 1837–1853

"[I am] determined to like Texas."

Lucadia Niles

When Lucadia Christiana Niles was twenty-five years old in 1838, she left her native Connecticut, alone, to spend nine months on a Virginia plantation. Reasons for the trip were not stated clearly in her surviving letters, because her family and friends knew about her purpose, but comments hint at some possible reasons and rule out others. Ostensibly she went to teach children of the family on the plantation, but she did not seem to teach regularly. The first implicit reason for leaving appeared in a letter from Clarissa Clark to Lucadia in early 1838: "… I rather mistrust that Cousin Lucadia's eyes were … dimmed with sorrow at leaving Cousin Thomas and by perceiving him with those sorrowful orbs of vision it entered your cranium that his countenance was rather sad … ."[1] Clarissa's letter is cryptic, but she did state that Lucadia had left her cousin Thomas, implying that she was getting away from a suitor.[2] Whatever the reason, Lucadia's trip to Virginia was a highly unusual experience for a young woman in the 1830s, and it would educate her about a part of American culture far beyond New England.

A description of Lucadia's hosts and her journey to the South opened her correspondence about the venture. She began with a description of her planter-family hosts, Burwell Bassett II and his second wife, Philadelphia Anne.[3] During the cool season the Bassetts lived in one of their homes, "Eltham," a plantation in the Tidewater region of southeastern Virginia. "I delayed writing until Mr. Bassett returned [this] evening … that I might give [you] my opinions respecting him, which is that I 'rekon' I shall like him very much." She had only been away from home a week, which "seems as long as a year." Her trip was an adventure in itself as she traveled, partly by ship and partly by train, from Connecticut to Philadelphia, Baltimore, and Washington.[4] She saw Philadelphia, "a city of squares and right angles," and then New Castle, Delaware. She took a steamboat south on "beautiful" Chesapeake Bay, and at eleven that night, arrived in Baltimore, "the Monumental City." She rode a train to Washington, where she saw the Capitol for the first time. It filled her with "questions [and] awe [at] the sight … stupendous, so magnificent … ." She could "find no words to express" her feeling "at seeing the Statue of the Immortal Jefferson, holding in his hand that declaration which proclaims 'all men are equal' … ."[5] After this moving sight, she saw John Trumbull's paintings of the Revolution. She wanted to visit the Library of Congress, but it was closed. Later a porter at the White House showed her and a traveling companion the chandeliers and mirrors of the East Room. Considering the "pomp and gorgeous splendor, I marvel not at the number of applicants for a residence in the President's house." She met "the Secretary of War and the Navy" but which man and what office she meant is unclear. In any case, he was "a fine looking Man, or rather I mean, an intellectual countenance, though I judge his conversational powers were ordinary." Lucadia's parents may have been amused (if not dismayed) that their young daughter, who had hardly ever been away from home, would presume to make such a comment about a cabinet official, but they were an intellectual family, accustomed to intelligent conversation, and Lucadia must have expected more from the man.[6] She sailed down the Potomac River at night, unable to see Mount Vernon. The next section of her journey to Virginia was in a "packed" stagecoach over miserably rough roads, with eight men and herself plus two of her bandboxes, a traveling bag, and a parasol.

At five in the morning, they arrived in Fredericksburg. By three that after-noon, she was at Eltham, "a most charming ... residence" near Leesburg in northern Virginia. It had a "commanding view of Fredericksburg." Lucadia wrote that the "seat" of Mr. Bassett's ancestors was "down country," and that "Mrs. Bassett is a very accomplished lady, frank and agreeable."[7]

"Truth is strange. Stranger than fiction," Lucadia observed upon arrival at Eltham.[8] Soon she found herself "engaged in multifarious employments, alternately attempting to cram ... Virtue into the craniums of my pupils ...."[9] Lucadia helped to move "the contents of wardrobes and drawers into huge trunks which have been in the family from generation to generation, and seem to have stood the test of ages." She was shown "some relics of Genl Washington" – his cane, made from the wood of his carriage, and his coat of oil cloth ...." She felt honored to pack his breeches and felt "satisfied that few of the daughters of New England have seen a piece of the coffin that contained the remains of the 'Father of his country.'" The subject of slavery and abolition arose as Lucadia made her first observation on the growing issue because she had just met Virginians who called Philadel-phians "Northern" and "cold" and "unfriendly "... and who thought that the "overzealous Abolitionists of the North have done much to break the links of friendship which ought to unite all parts of our Union ...."

Lucadia's time at Eltham with the Bassetts included a visit to Richmond, where she found shops "kept by Jews who are here quite numerous and have a Synagogue." She saw the state capitol and its lovely surroundings, but she could not enter to see the statues of the "immortal" Washington. She also saw Chief Justice John Marshall's home. She then went with the Bassetts, the children, and their nurse over fine roads to "Farmington," another Bassett plantation. Lucadia was delighted with the landscape, "where I ... admired the beautiful holly with shining green leaves and bright red berries." The Farmington house was surrounded by rows of trees within view of the Pamunkey River. She saw cornfields, fig trees, box [boxwood] hedges, and perpetual roses in full bloom, but people did not flourish as well as the plants: "few were fortunate enough this past season to escape the fever and ague." She was probably referring to malaria, which caused the Bassetts to flee that property and Eltham every summer.

Lucadia's first observation of slavery came at Farmington. Although her reaction was entirely naïve, the encounter would later shape her approach to her future husband's slaves in Texas. She "called at some of the Cabins to see the servants with Mrs. Bassett and was surprised to witness their affection and exceeding great joy at seeing her. Their attachment to their master and mistress is very great and can arise only from the very kind treatment they receive." At that time, Lucadia had no knowledge of the reasons why slaves at least appeared glad to see Mrs. Bassett. The family left Farmington with "eight whites, four blacks, five horses, two dogs, two guns, and two carriages" to visit a neighboring plantation. From the observatory at the top of the house, she first saw "crops of cotton some of which were not gathered, which in the distance looked not unlike spots covered with snow while all around was verdant." Lucadia looked down at gardens that included "Tea, China, and perpetual roses." In another twenty miles of low, wet land with little variety, she saw the "novelty" of more cotton fields, the New Kent Court House, and the Methodist meeting house, "which we expect occasionally to attend, built of logs ...." She observed, "if they have snow and winds ... (the logs) will be wonderfully convenient for letting them pass through." The family then "came in sight of the Castle of Eltham, which I beheld with mingled emotions of veneration and despond ... at seeing ... one of the oldest buildings in the United States having been built more than one hundred and sixty years [ago] and ... [in] a most delightfully ruinous condition." She wrote that the "Castle" was built with walls three bricks thick, and that it was being repaired. Lucadia stated that Eltham "consists of between four or five thousand acres of land, Eighty slaves, and seems quite too valuable to remain in this dilapidative state, although Mr. Bassett is engaged in ... improvements." The master of the house was "as buoyant as air, making all happy around here! With [that] example before me, I shall hope to escape as I have so far homesickness."

During her visit to Eltham, Lucadia also continued to write cryptically about her "present situation." In a letter to her cousin Maria, she noted that "among the many blessings which I have enjoyed the past year ... none awakened livelier emotions than your "friendly Epistles." She thanked

Maria for her offering of "sympathy for me in my present situation. Yet perhaps I have given you cause (unintentionally) to magnify my need for consolation judging from the tenor of your letter ... ." She added, "I was glad that you approved of my not looking or turning back, and although I left home with the buoyant spirits of youth which delights in anticipating sunshine rather than clouds, and could scarcely fail of experiencing some disappointment of expectation, yet I can assure you I am enjoying this mild clear, bright weather, and basking in sunshine for which you sigh." Maria had built imaginative "airy castles" about Lucadia's surroundings that caused Lucadia to laugh at such romantic notions, compared to the "monotony of my daily employment ... ." While living in the woods, she wrote, her amusement consisted of long walks or riding around the planation, sometimes painting a picture of the old place or a bunch of flowers, or "resort[ing] to an old novel, which may have laid in its hiding place unnoticed and undusted for years," and "perhaps strangest of all ... make it a matter of much interest to see the process of Jenning [*sic*] Cotton, which is the first and all-important, to the further use of the article, as it separates the seeds which are very abundant, and to which the cotton adheres." She was looking forward to good food at Christmas, but she remarked on some differences in diet: Maria would think her "little better than a cannibal" for eating beef heart and hog brains—about which she made no complaints. The subject of Methodism arose: Given the interest she felt in the denomination before she left home, she noted, "you will not be surprised to hear of my riding last Sunday half a dozen miles to attend [a] meeting in the Methodist chapel or log house ... ." The "people who if I may judge from their appearance have surrendered 'worldly pomp and earthly grandeur' ... in the matter of dress ... [are] truly humble." Their clothing contrasted with the ladies of Fredericksburg, who wore rich satins and silks to church. Was Lucadia's interest in the Methodist church counter to her family's denominational preference?[10] The little chapel was no reason to go to Eltham, and the Bassetts were Episcopalians.

Comments about slavery in a letter received from Maria while Lucadia visited at Eltham drew a much lengthier and revealing response than was seen in her first reaction to the institution. "I cannot" Lucadia wrote, "but deem

idle the apprehension you have with respect to an insurrection .... For I find
there is a great deal of affection between masters and servants ...."

> I cannot believe that those who receive from kind masters three things
> which were considered as desirable as to form the [subject?] of a
> supplicant's prayers, 'food and raiment, and pretty good clothes to
> wear,' should lack all feelings of gratitude. You inquire my opinion
> on the agitating subject of Abolition a subject on which our brethren
> have displayed sufficient zeal to ... render themselves obnoxious to
> the South.

She then made an important position statement, with more naiveté:

> For myself I consider slavery as evil to any nation, [and it] is particu-
> larly a blot on our national character holding as we do this truth
> self-evident that all men are created free and equal and contradicting in
> our actions the [words] of our mouths .... yet even [as] I am writing so
> gravely I hear the servants ... singing merrily in the kitchen .... .

Lucadia probably had no idea at the time that singing could mean far more
than being cheerful; the slaves may have been keeping up their spirits
amidst their hopeless reality, bonding over a particular task or shared heritage in their ancestral homeland, maintaining the pace of a dreary job, or
even at times alerting one another to the presence of a master. Lucadia's
observations reflected her first experience with what may have seemed on
the surface a benign institution, yet Jefferson's words about equality also
were firmly established in her young mind.

"Cheerful spring" in Virginia delighted Lucadia.[11] She explored local
plants, and she wanted to send home some roots of a yellow jessamine vine.
She reported that the Bassetts had been visited by the Episcopal priest,
The Rev. Mr. Hodges "and lady" from Williamsburg. It was a major event,
because nearly four months had passed since anyone had called at Eltham.
In one letter, she noted, "I was not a little astounded to find in one of my
packets of newspapers an abolitionist one which ... I handed Mrs. B. to read

who [was] indignant at the interference which some at the north have taken in their domestic concerns ... ." "Her justification of slavery," Lucadia wrote, "she derives from the holy scripture." Speaking of scripture, she noted, going to "Meeting" twice (with the Methodists) where she "listened with profound attention to the learned theologian's expositions. At Eltham the church going bell rings nearly Every Sunday, and we assemble and listen to the reading of the lessons [written] by Bishop Wilson [and] delivered in Mr. B's cleverest style." She also described spring gardening far to the south of Connecticut: "Commencing" had passed: peas had been sown and other vegetables had come up, but they had been planted "with no regard ... paid to the beauty of ... lines and right angles ... ." Lucadia was accustomed to flowers being planted among vegetables, but at Eltham there was not "one simple flower among the celery and cabbages."

In May Lucadia finally wrote to her mother, explaining that she had not intended to wait so long to write, but the reason was "the monotony of my life and lack of occurrences."[12] She noted, however, that she was beginning to anticipate the Bassett family's return to Fredericksburg and the many "fine things I should want when emerging from this retreat." Mrs. Bassett had gone to Richmond to shop for items "suitable for our reappearance in town." Lucadia added,

> I am left housekeeper and mistress pro tem of the establishment, the duties however are not very hard ... consisting entirely ... of being keeper of the keys and taking a general supervision over about a dozen house servants. Col. B. is also absent ... the children and myself might be lonely if we choose .... But I am quite too philosophical for that – and we are all ... merry ... anticipating much delight in going 'up country' and living in town.

A Virginia society wedding in the spring of 1839 gave Lucadia her first view of a world that was wealthier than she had ever seen.[13] She left Eltham on May 30 with the Bassetts, "gentlefolks, servants, carriages, eight horses and about the same number of dogs [and] baggage," heading thirty miles to Farmington. From there the Bassetts went to the wedding of Lucy Oliver and Charles Cary Cocke at a plantation called Chericoke in King William County.[14] Lucadia described the people and setting of this Southern high society event: Chericoke "is delightfully sited upon a hill [with] a commanding view," surrounded by green fields, the Pamunkey River, and the "tastefully arranged" yard and garden.

Lucadia observed that the dinner party made evident "the line between the gentle and simple [that] seems still to exist much as in olden times, particularly among planters." Among nearly forty guests in attendance, the "great display of dress conclusively proved that the company present had explored the idea of beauty being best adorned when adorned the most, which may prove true in one case in a thousand seldom oftener." Lucadia had never seen such a display of wealth, but she perceptively observed that the bride "looked and moved with the consciousness of charms of one accustomed to adulation." That afternoon, guests were served "a very handsome meat dinner" and after champagne, guests entered another dining room where they were served "ice creams of various hues ... custards, ice lemonade, puddings, tarts, and pastries ... strawberries and cream, oranges ... and each dish decked with delicate fresh flowers." The next day, the Bassetts visited another plantation home, where "the style of entertainment was not inferior to that of Chericoke." Lucadia was more pleased with the flowers than the display of clothing, and she may have discovered her dislike of ostentation that eventually would shape her views as a wealthy woman herself.

Following the highly educational nine-month visit to Virginia that extended from 1838 into 1839, Lucadia returned to her home in Connecticut and appears to have spent the next four years in unremarkably quiet fashion. Her usually flourishing correspondence, which generally left such a full record of her life, apparently went dormant. Either the letters that she wrote and received were not preserved, or she was close enough to family and friends that written communication was not necessary. In any case, her historical record resumed in full when she began traveling again early in 1843.

In January 1843, Lucadia went to Philadelphia.[15] She visited friends, met new people, and attended lectures on perspective drawing. Still there in March, she stayed with her Porter cousins, whose house had a furnace in the cellar that made rooms warm at night.[16] She attended Catholic and Jewish services, thus expanding her education. She observed the synagogue lamp that burned continually, men and women seated separately, and their reading from right to left in Hebrew. Historic Chestnut Street, adjacent to Independence Hall, was "all life, noise, and merriment with the jingling of bells and upsetting of sleighs ... ."[17]

Lucadia traveled to Washington, D.C., in December 1844, with her uncle, John Milton Niles, Senator from Connecticut.[18] They saw "Mr. [George M.] Dallas and daughter [Caroline] ...." A crowd gathered "to get a peep at the Vice Pres. Elect" and raised loud cheers for him and for Polk. As they rode on the same train to Washington as the President and Vice President-elect. "Uncle was introduced to Mr. Dallas ... and during some part of the route the Vice Pres. Elect had the honor of occupying the seat next [to me]," she reported with her usual humor. She saw other elected officials and their families on board, including "Mr. Stillwell a member from Lou[isiana] with his beautiful Creole wife." After their Washington arrival in perfect safety they stayed in a boarding house. Lucadia reported, "I have been to the Capitol this morning at the opening of the Senate and looked down from the gallery with curiosity & wonder upon the great statesmen of their nation ... ." Lucadia's interest in lawmaking evaporated quickly, because she wrote the next day that the winter was expected to be "very dull."[19] She observed that the President's message was read by the Senate clerk, while "some of the members [were] occupying their seats while others were walking about and talking." If she was troubled by their lack of attention on seeing it the first time, she did not say so.[20] She made no reports of attending Senate sessions, only of sewing and reading in the morning and having dinner at noon with her friends. She "sadly" missed her sisters, "but I suppose I must content myself till that time arrives by writing." She noted, "Uncle said last night as we were sitting alone by the fire that if Maria had come she would be lonesome ... ."

Mary Jane Welles, wife of Gideon Welles, corresponded from Hartford.[21] She pleaded "Guilty! ... for not responding earlier to your very agreeable and welcome letter ...." Mrs. Pease [Marshall's mother] had called on her, and reported that her daughter Caroline "is so much engaged in her studies she scarce ever takes time to come home at noon," and Mary Jane thought that being confined to a school room as a student all day would result in a loss of health. She knew that the Congressional library would be valuable to Lucadia: "books are pleasant companions and with them, one can while away many an hour ... ."

Although Lucadia did not follow congressional proceedings, she was in the city on February 2, 1845, when the resolution to annex Texas passed. In retrospect, she may have wished she had been present when it happened, but she was not yet being courted by Marshall Pease and knew almost nothing about distant Texas, even though Senator Niles had been persuaded by Marshall's father to vote for annexation. Perhaps the senator mentioned the subject to Lucadia, but she was simply impatient to leave "this city of ... confusion."[22] She made few comments about Polk's inauguration days earlier, but Judge Pease had been there for it. Senator Niles was going to the President's office "almost daily with some of the Connecticut office seekers ... ." Lucadia received a letter from Mary Jane Welles noting, "Judge Pease gave us quite an interesting description of the President's levee"[23] Although Lucadia seems to have paid no attention to political affairs during her visit, she saw lawmakers and experienced Washington as few citizens could at the time.

During 1845 and into 1846, while Lucadia observed life among the nation's leaders, in far-away Texas, Marshall as he turned thirty-four was thinking about marriage. His reasons for waiting to marry may have been rooted in his father's advice about being financially secure before marriage, but also, he had probably not found a lady in Texas who had the accomplishments he had hoped for in a wife. He had been working hard to build a successful law career and had served in the Legislature. In any case Marshall's correspondence in early 1846 paid more attention than before to the subject of marriage. For example, his friend Henry B. Andrews of Galveston wrote happily about his own new marriage[24] and added, "I place more confidence in your judgment, than any other attorney or person in Texas or elsewhere ... ."[25] Marshall wrote his brother-in-law that since Judge Niles's second marriage was to an "accomplished" lady, "I think I need not despair of getting a wife, when the Judge has succeeded."[26] His sister Caroline observed that he had expressed regret at not having married at an earlier age and noted that "John Wharton said something about your admiration of a Texas lady, whose name I do not quite remember."[27] Wharton, who had become a family friend of the Peases, would tell them nothing more, and Caroline wanted to know if "the lady in question was really about to become a member of the house of Pease." She wrote without explanation, "I am surprised at the manner in which you speak of the Texas ladies," and continued, "John represented that they were all angels, fit inhabitants for the earthly paradise of Texas ... ." Marshall's mother informed him, "The Miss Niles's are not married but suppose Augusta is to be ... ."[28] His sister Maria brought up the subject in June with some very direct comments:

> The Niles girls are all well and single tho Augusta is to be married sometime this summer. Lucadia and Maria visited us during Mother's absence. I wish for your sake that the former was about ten years younger for [there] is not one equal in the whole country. She is the most amiable girl I ever saw and you will never find her equal if you search the world .... Read often what I've written about Lucadia & ponder well upon it before you choose a wife.[29]

The Niles sisters and their mother were stricken with grief on June 19 when Colonel Richard Niles died suddenly at the age of sixty-one.[30] Several months later, however, Maria resumed her campaign to convince Marshall to marry Lucadia, writing that Augusta was to marry and adding this heartfelt observation: "Now my dear brother what do you think of Lucadia? She is an angel, and now I advise you as a friend, if you ever mean to marry, you had better take her—she is a rare jewel ... ." Lucadia, who may have been oblivious to the efforts on her behalf, received a proposal in mid-1847 from a J. Booth of Berlin Centre, Ohio, where he had opened a mercantile business. He wrote, "I frequently think of you and of the time pleasantly passed in Town Society ... happy indeed would I consider myself with a companion of your attainments ... ." Lucadia's response is unknown.[31]

By fall 1847, Lucadia was staying with friends Mr. and Mrs. [Amos] Pilsbury (this name is spelled with one "l") in Albany, New York, where he was superintendent of the state penitentiary.[32] Lucadia asked her sisters, "How is Judge Pease? Aunt Jane (wife of her uncle Niles) told me they feared he was in failing health." As for herself, she reported, "I am the very dullest person in the world for society having in the last year or two lost all the life and spirits I once had. In that frame of mind, she saw no reason why the Pilsburys wanted her to stay until Christmas. Lucadia wrote her mother and sisters a week later, hoping "to hear that Judge Pease is much better ...."[33] In her last letter before leaving New York, she mentioned having gone to the State Library at the Capitol, "containing a very extensive and valuable collection of books, and pictures."[34]

Concern about Judge Lorrain T. Pease's declining health was warranted. "Father Pease," as his son-in-law John Robinson called him, was "comfortable" in the spring of 1848, but "low-spirited" and in need of a visit.[35] Pease's younger son, John, wrote Marshall that their father died on April 28.[36] He had waited a month to write the news because he had expected Marshall to arrive: they had read in the papers that he had been on the East Coast for a convention. John also noted that their mother's health "seems to be failing ... O come home then." How hard it must have been for Marshall to learn what had befallen his parents during his long delay, but there is no record of it.

Once Marshall was in Connecticut, he saw that Caroline's and Maria's assessments of Lucadia's qualities were entirely accurate, and the two fell in love. The Pease and Niles families were related through Naomi Griswold Marshall, who was the great-grandparent of both E. M. Pease and Lucadia Niles Pease. Lucadia once wrote to her husband years later that their propensity for hard work was likely because of "our shared Marshall blood."[37] They were second cousins. Intermarriage in families was common and legal, and because many people lived in the same area for generations, people often knew their extended families.

Once Marshall decided to propose, he was so nervous he could not bring himself to do so until the day he left for Texas. Lucadia did not answer him right away. He then wrote to her from New Orleans, and finally she replied, beginning with general comments about weather and the family. At last he turned the page and found the answer he longed for:

> Your proposal to me, the morning of your departure, was so unexpected and surprising, that I might well excuse myself from giving a direct answer. Our long acquaintance and the friendly relationship always existing between our families had given me more than common interest in your welfare, yet I felt unable to decide upon a question of so much importance without longer deliberation. You write you shall be impatient to hear from me, and I am too thankful for your kind regard, too highly appreciate your preference to willingly give you one moments anxiety, or longer delay assuring you of my attachment to you. The esteem and love, of those I love I ever prize above all earthly gifts, and am most happy when so fortunate as to have my feelings reciprocated, and sensible as I am of the worth of your affection, I cannot find it in my heart to cast from me that which you so earnestly offer, but accept the proposal you make to me, with a firm trust that by so doing, I shall secure my own happiness.
>
> I cannot thank you too warmly for the long and kind remembrance in which you have borne me, and if time nor absence have had power to change your feelings, I shall look forward to the bright and confident hope which the future promises with joy and thankfulness. Mother and Sisters desire to be remembered to you.[38]

Lucadia closed, "Yours affectionately, L. C. Niles." Although some of her letter was awkward, it was deeply sincere, and both the future bride and groom must have felt greatly relieved to have found the right life partner at last. He was thirty-eight, and she was thirty-seven.

Acknowledgment of the time required for mail to go to and from Texas was the first topic of Lucadia's initial letter to Marshall once they were engaged.[39] She tried to imagine differences in climate: "the perfection of northern winter weather" with dazzling snow and the merry jingling of bells contrasted with "your summer home, my future home too ... [with] sunny skies ... and bright sparkling waters, luxuriant vegetation ... hardy flowers ... the grassy carpet of green .... Is my picture correct Dear Marshall? For being determined to like Texas, I banish all the desolateness of our winters in my imaginings ... ."

Three months later, Lucadia had joined the Peases in wishing for letters from Marshall. She wrote of both her impatience for mail and her fear of disease, because she knew he had gone to Galveston but had not heard from him. She was happy that spring would be returning, and it would bring them one season nearer to seeing each other.[40] In this letter, Lucadia stopped addressing him as "Cousin." Many if not most women of the time did not call their fiancées or husbands by their first names, but since they were related, the use of first names was normal. In September Lucadia expressed both dismay that Marshall had not arrived as he said he would but an understanding of how the demands of his career kept him in Texas.[41] She did, however, "hope you will write me often, or my sisters will again add me to the numberless victims to the faithless of man's promises."

Caroline Pease wrote her brother in early 1850, expressing dismay about his not coming the previous summer and declaring, "If I was Lucadia I would not marry you at all now, after having been put off a year, for the sake of a political election. Just think of all the trouble it would cause her in her wardrobe to say nothing of other things."[42] Lucadia's support of Marshall, however, only endeared her to him all the more. Although Lucadia had little "village gossip" to report, she filled pages anyway, even to reporting that her goose quill pen (which produced a delicate, fine-tipped result) was poor, since her pen knife had lost its edge.[43] She had spent pleasant weeks in New York, but concluded that she preferred her country home in Poquonock to seeing "striking contrasts" of wealth and poverty in the city.

Lucadia's sister Maria Robinson expressed great pleasure at the thought of being at her brother's upcoming wedding when she wrote in April. "I am really glad you are going to be married at last and to one I love and esteem so much – I think you will enjoy life so much [more] ... . Of course you will name your first boy after our dear departed father." She remembered that he was "so fond of children, and often wished you would marry so he could be surrounded with grandchildren. Lucadia too was the wife selected for you, so my dear brother, you have the satisfaction in knowing your choice was his."[44] By mid-1850, Marshall was not in Texas. Senator Guy M. Bryan wrote urgently that a special session of the legislature had been called, and "No excuse you could make would be [acceptable] .... "You must return. Your future prospects as a public man require it." Senator Pease had other priorities, however, and did not return until he brought his bride with him.[45]

Lucadia Christiana Niles and Elisha Marshall Pease married at last on August 22, 1850, in Poquonock. H. B. Soule, Pastor of in the Universalist Church of Windsor, noted in the town record that the couple "were married by me."[46] No description of the wedding exists among all the documentation of their lives, except for the benediction of Lucadia's Aunt Naomi: "may he who guides the 'winds and waves' guard you in safety, to your distant home, and may the choicest Blessings of heaven be showered on you and yours."[47] In September, Lucadia and Marshall had their "deguerotypes [*sic*] taken" to put in a locket for Augusta, perhaps for little Christina to remember them. The child had declared that "she was going to Texas with Aunt Ca."[48] Lucadia thought that her image "is most horrid looking ... but if it is like me, as is asserted, I suppose I must have nothing to object to." Plans were to go to New York in October to finish her purchases; she had married a man of means, although she would never boast of it. Lucadia's first letter, written to Augusta, began with an outpouring of grief on leaving family and home with such a long journey ahead. "Marshall said all he could to comfort me, and promised our return next summer if I wished ...."[49] She then cheerfully reported on their honeymoon trip. They visited the Pilsburys in upstate New York and went to Niagara Falls. She pleaded for letters to be sent to New Orleans, but the new couple was not entirely without family: Caroline, also known as "Carrie," accompanied them to Texas and stayed with them. After river travel across the country, they arrived in New Orleans in early November.[50]

"I have at length landed on Texas soil," Lucadia announced from Galveston in mid-November.[51] From offshore she first saw the "'towers and turrets' of the City ... the spires of four churches ... a goodly number," she pointed out, considering how young the city was. "Marshall was very happy, at reaching home, and the prospect of seeing his many friends." The Brazoria house he had rented from one of the Mills brothers was not ready, and he left

Lucadia and Caroline at a comfortable boarding house in Galveston while he went to Austin. His first message to his bride showed a fundamental change in his viewpoint and foretold their future: "I have felt so miserably on account of being away from you, and the prospect of being separated three or four weeks more, that I have to day concluded to let the public business take care of itself and consult my own interest and happiness, and have abandoned the idea of going to Austin."[52] He also reported, "We have lost a negro boy about three ... the rest of our servants I found in good health and all anxious for the arrival of their new mistress." He closed his letter, as he would continue to do in slightly varied words, "accept a hundred kisses from your affectionate husband Marshall." Lucadia's next letter home opened with a theme that she would repeat often in the coming years, asking why the family had not written, expressing fear that something serious had occurred, and begging to hear from them.[53] She described her first trip to Brazoria, which was more frightening than others she had made in her life. No boat to Velasco was available, and so they headed out in a carriage on the smooth, hard-packed sand of Galveston Island. After forty miles they crossed by ferry to the mainland and then had to ride in the dark, in high tide, with water "sometimes up to the hubs of the carriage wheels much to the terror and alarm of Carry [Carrie] and myself ...." They made it to Velasco even though the carriage had broken, and eventually drove through the prairie to Brazoria.

A few days later as they were settling in, Lucadia experienced her first "norther as it is here termed" that plunged Marshall's thermometer to an unheard-of sixteen degrees, and a large fire "made no impression on the temperature of the room" because the house was built for warm weather.[54] Lucadia had another surprise when her first visitors came calling in "silks, with laces and undersleeves which looked fresh from [a store] ...." She had presumed that from "the backwoods look of the place, and the small plain looking houses, fashion could not have reached this remote corner." As a practical matter, she was grateful for the rubber boots that she bought in New York; they were "admirably suited" for the heavy Brazoria mud.

As Lucadia began to know her new home, she found the weather "delightfully warm" to her, since the temperature had reached eighty degrees on several January days.[55] She continued to meet neighbors, including

John Woods Harris, Marshall's law partner. She called him a "plain person" with "unprepossessing manners," but his intellect was significant: In 1851 he would got to Washington to argue cases before the Supreme Court. She also met Guy M. Bryan of Brazoria County, who was "very agreeable." As Lucadia adjusted to her new surroundings, she usually described them without criticism:

> Our place, of which Marshall is very fond, is now nothing but woods, no trees, nor underbrush having been cut away – it will require some years to make it look very comfortable according to ones yankee ideas of comfort – but as even comfort is only a relative term, and graduated much by what we see around us, I shall soon I presume become accustomed to things as they are, satisfied to have what the neighbors have.

What the neighbors had were "shabby" houses, badly plastered and without wallpaper, although some had expensive furnishings such as sofas, marble slab tables, and curtains. She described inhabitants more critically: "many of them [are] Dutch [German] and Irish, no [not] very desirable society for the American population." Lucadia was happy to return to Galveston on an "unusually quick" trip of eight hours, and was looking forward to finding *David Copperfield* in the bookstores.[56] Caroline enjoyed parties and "beaux" from the area who called on her, including Dr. Ashbel Smith. While in Galveston, Lucadia sent a description and drawing of the Brazoria house to Maria: it was a four-room, single story structure once painted white. It faced east, with a portico or gallery across the front. The parlor in the southeast corner contained a large fireplace, a cupboard with shelves above it for Marshall's two-hundred volume library, a center table with a lamp, and chairs. Carry's small room was in the southwest corner, and Lucadia and Marshall's adjoining bedroom faced west. It contained a mahogany wardrobe and "fixtures" for hanging clothes on one wall. The dining room in the northeast corner was centered with an oval table. A safe and a secretary from Marshall's office, a clock, and a large world map were also in the room. The pantry in the northwest corner was well-stocked with barrels of pork, beef, and mackerel; staples were flour, rice, sugar, vinegar, potatoes, molasses, lard, dried apples, and cranberries. Soap, candles, starch, loaf sugar, preserves, pickles, "raisons and ketchups," tea, coffee, and chocolate rounded out the provisions. The kitchen was only twenty–thirty feet away, and a large cistern held water for all purposes. A well for garden water was out of order; the fences and premises were "ruinous in their appearance." Plum and fig trees were in the garden, and a little graveyard was in one corner, "remind[ing] us of our mortality." She noted the help of enslaved servants: "Emily is maid of all work & Big Sam, gardener, little Sam errand boy & waiter in general."

By March 1851, Marshall had decided to become a candidate for governor.[57] Lucadia mentioned that as a reason she might not be able to go north in the coming summer; he would not be able to accompany her. She also made telling remarks about the "servants," saying that she had found it hard "to tell black from white – one of the servants [in the Galveston boarding house] is whiter than any of the ladies, with light sandy hair, and yet she is a slave and must associate with real black negroes, an awful feature in slavery." Lucadia's northern youth came through when she noted that Governor Peter H. Bell had issued a proclamation for Thanksgiving on March 6: "He shows his great ignorance of a very necessary part of the Thanksgiving dinner, the pumpkin pies, by his folly in appointing it in March" and not following "the good old Yankee customs."

After Lucadia sent a description of her house to Augusta, she was exasperated to receive a request to be "more descriptive." "I can have but little more to offer," she wrote, but she did say more about the servants and their work."[58] Emily, the cook and housekeeper, was "a quiet and good servant as far as she understands work, she belongs to M." (Lucadia never wrote that a slave belonged to her, but to Marshall or to them both.) Big Sam made the garden, but it only had radishes, onions, and roses at the time. They walked to the "place, as Marshall terms the spot where he intends to build," and on to Tom's to see his family. He directed the other slaves' work. Lucadia bought eggs and poultry from Tom, and his family used the money to buy "finery for Sunday display."[59]

In early April, Lucadia expected Marshall to campaign all summer, and so she could not go to Connecticut for another year. She wrote that he and all the half-dozen candidates were confident of being elected, and she anticipated the enjoyment of staying in Austin. By mid-April, however, Marshall was talking about withdrawing from the race, which Lucadia thought wise, considering the effort of canvassing the state for the chance of election.[60] She was busy at home: Emily had been "confined" with the birth of a boy, "who with her Masters permission she will call John," and the other slave woman, Eliza, was sick, probably with the measles. Marshall wrote from Bellville where he was attending court: "I have never in my life been as unhappy as during the last week. I have dreamed of your every night ... I have pretty much resolved when I return home to withdraw from the canvass ... ."[61]

At the end of May, Lucadia wrote that Marshall had decided to withdraw his name as a candidate for governor and give up politics "forever." She concluded the letter with a shy little essay about how her kind neighbors were sending presents. Only a few days ago she had received

a note and a little parcel containing an infants [sic] shirt which the lady giver wish me to oblige her by accepting, offering at the same time, her experience in all matters related to the expected event. As the fact of my being in the situation 'which women wish to be &c' is obvious to my discerning female friends, I write it to you, with the hope of receiving sympathy – I trust Mother will give herself no uneasiness on my account – Marshall insists upon giving up the prospect of being elected, on my account ... he will be at home all summer – Are you not astonished. I am I assure you.

That was all Lucadia chose to write on so vastly important a topic as the impending birth of her first child, even to her sisters, to whom she was close, or to her mother.[62]

Meanwhile, Marshall, who was still on the campaign trail, wrote to Lucadia from Houston, "I do not think that I ever ... had quite as unpleasant a trip, and I assure you it was not improved any by the reflection that I had parted with you in tears, all my 'ambitious views' are extinguished forever ... ."[63] Nevertheless, he told Lucadia that he planned to finish his scheduled engagements. He wrote next about visiting Huntsville, where he dined with General Houston.[64] Marshall could not know that his baby girl was born prematurely—Lucadia thought by two months—on June 10. Because he had left Lucadia in tears at the beginning of his campaign trip, it must have pained him greatly to learn that he was not present for her when she gave birth. In his message of June 14, he claimed, "a letter from you, assuring me that you are well, would be worth more to me at this time than being elected Governor forty times." Lucadia informed her mother on July 1 of the baby's birth, noting that the early delivery was caused, she supposed, "by overexertion and reaching on my part."[65] "Marshall was absent at her birth, & for two weeks afterwards, but I found very kind friends .... Still one ever wishes I believe for a mothers presence, in these greatest trials of a womans [sic] life ...." She asked her mother to name the baby and sent a lock of her hair. No suggestion of a name arrived, or arrived in time, because the baby's parents called her "Carrie Augusta" by early August.[66] Carrie, named for her aunt Caroline, bore a name that even her parents misspelled as "Carry" and "Cary." In an August 4 letter to her sister, Lucadia noted that she was writing on election day, the "first one for many years that Marshall has not had a personal interest .... His friends said that if he had electioneered through the eastern part of the state, he would have been certain of the election ... but under the circumstances he would not do so ...."[67]

Lucadia and Marshall observed their first wedding anniversary "by inviting about a dozen of our neighbors to tea, or supper as it is called here," Lucadia wrote.[68] "We had some wedding Cake, but too small a slice to serve ...." She had been out little during the summer, because her attention was focused on "dear little Carrie Augusta .... She is now very quiet and so fat and good natured you could not help loving her ...." She observed that the baby afforded Marshall much pleasure. Lucadia was happy to escape fever that plagued many, but "I have not much patience with the insect creation, mosquetoes [sic] being now the most tormenting ... ," Two weeks later she had moved the baby and her sewing to the gallery, where winds blew the "mosquetoes" away.[69] The year-round dampness of coastal Texas created mildew on clothing stored in trunks, and everything had to be hung in the sunshine every few weeks. Recent rain prevented brick-making for their house, but they were not ready to build anyhow. They had a design dilemma: "the one desirable thing here, is to have all the rooms, on the south side in order to get the Gulf breeze, and have no north side ... to avoid having the northers in winter."[70] On the subject of fashion, she wrote in jest, "I am strongly in favor of shorn hair, do describe accurately how your hair is cut, that I may relieve myself at once, of the task of arranging mine, and at the same time become a leader of fashion."[71] In October, Lucadia was enjoying cooler weather, "tho' there has not yet been any frost, yet Marshall thinks it too cool, and is already encased in flannels. Little Carrie seems to have her Papa's aversion to the cold ... when we had what they here term a 'norther' she took a severe cold ... tho' as we intend her to be very hardy we have her taken out to walk almost every day."[72] Little Carrie occupied most of Lucadia's thoughts. She documented Carrie's first tooth, and declared, "Our baby is a jewel in the opinion of Papa and Mamma, and a very good playful baby in the eyes of less partial judges."[73] Her babbling was as understandable to her mamma as Carrie and Marshall were when they were practicing Spanish and translating, together with Mr. Cushing, the teacher in town.[74] "Marshall speaks it pretty well, and translates it rapidly, while I have only learned the morning and evening salutation, baby talk being by me more easily learned and in my vocation more in daily use."[75] When Marshall, an experienced and successful house "doctor," was at court, Lucadia was so uncertain about caring for their little one that she called for a physician to diagnose a hoarse cough, lest it be the croup. He prescribed ashes on her throat and catnip tea. She ended her letter because "Dear little Carrie is waking and I must lay down my pen, her voice is imperative with me, even when I am writing to my dear husband." Since the weather was cold, Lucadia was worried about Marshall in the unheated Austin County courthouse, and she wanted him to keep wrapped in his overcoat. Her letter crossed her husband's; he reported only a slight cold, and expected to be home in days.[76] He assured her, "I dream of you both every night, and wake to be disappointed in not finding you at my side. Give my love to Carrie. Kiss our dear little one for her Papa, and accept for yourself, what you have always possessed, his devoted love and affection."

A severe case of what Lucadia thought was influenza kept her in bed for five or six weeks in the winter of 1852.[77] She believed that flu was the cause of a "most excruciatingly painful" infection in one breast. The baby, who had to be weaned, was so upset, "she learned to speak at once, distinctly and piteously ma ma ma ma." During all her distress, Lucadia's breast was lanced in three places. By March she trusted it was getting well, but "only those who have had a similar [condition] can know how much one suffers." She praised Marshall as "a most excellent nurse, and I know not what I should have done ..." without him. The family went with him to Galveston where he was in court, and Lucadia had more painful medical attention.[78] At least she was able to get fresh vegetables there that she loved, including asparagus, lettuce, radishes, and green peas. Baby Carrie impressed Galveston strangers as "the best baby they ever knew ...." Lucadia signed her letter, "L. C. N. P," noting, "I find my married sisters retain the initial N. & I have resumed it." After returning to Brazoria, Marshall had to go to court in Bellville "with more reluctance than I ever did before .... The business here is not worth the pain of being so long absent from those I love."[79]

In May 1852, Lucadia, the baby, and Marshall's sister Carrie went to Connecticut, and Marshall followed. While in Poquonock he was weighed at 170 pounds, and he noted from New York that friends there remarked on "how fat you are getting."[80] Marshall wrote from Washington in early August, "The proceedings in Congress have not been very interesting, and I have occupied a good portion of my time in visiting the objects of interest ... that I had never had the opportunity to see before."[81] Juliet accompanied the Pease family back to Texas in October. Her first visit began with the observation, "There is nothing of the least interest in going through the whole of the Southern States on the railroad."[82] Her comments were often more critical of the land and people than Lucadia's ever were: She wrote that one woman "must be a good specimen of Southerners easy to become acquainted, wasteful & withal a little 'shiftless.'" In Galveston she saw some "rather pretty places" but "the absence of any large trees ... renders it rather tame & makes you feel that some thing is wanting to finish it ...."[83] Once in Brazoria, Juliet began observations about the Pease slaves that were consistently critical, beginning with "the waste and extravagance of these niggers" in not caring for clothing while the family was away, since "the niggers make it a rule never to do as they are told to do."[84] Marshall and Lucadia did not write in this fashion. That fall, Lucadia asked longingly about Thanksgiving in Poquonock. She also commented, "I fancy Julie [Juliet] finds Brazoria duller than she imagined." Nevertheless, "Marshall's attachment for Brazoria, is so great he is much distressed at the thought of settling in Galveston, while I have less wish to live here than even at first."[85]

Juliet's letters continued her critical observations about the Pease slaves: "L. had enough to busy herself superintending her housekeeping, which is no slight matter … there being four of the niggers to keep in slow motion."[86] She noted, "There is a great deal of sickness among the negroes some belonging to Marshall are sick constantly … ." Meanwhile, Marshall attended the Supreme Court in Galveston, staying at a boarding house where he occupied the same bed as Sam Harris (his secretary), but he wrote Lucadia, "As you may suppose, I do not find him quite as agreeable a bedfellow as you would be."[87] Thinking about home, he wrote in a rare racial comment that he wondered "how you get along with the niggers and the fleas."[88] After receiving a letter from Lucadia, he thought, "some of my clients may thank you for their cases being better argued to day [*sic*] than they would have been if I had not received your letter."[89]

Marshall must have known he was about to spend more time away from his beloved Lucadia, because by January 1853 he had again become a candidate for governor. Juliet mentioned the subject casually in a letter to her sister Maria, noting that "he has little expectation of being the chosen one [by the nominating convention in February] since "he has done nothing to aid in his promotion … ."[90] The convention did not nominate a candidate, and Marshall decided to campaign, so Lucadia decided to spend the summer of 1853 visiting friends in Connecticut.[91] In the meantime, the sisters spent time at home quilting; Lucadia thought that making a cradle quilt "dooms it to too great obscurity." However, she did not mention that she could soon use one, because three days later, she gave birth to another daughter. Marshall wrote his mother-in-law that she was born after Lucadia "suffered exceedingly" for less than three hours, but at his writing, she was "as comfortable as we could expect."[92] He thought the baby "appears healthy, and is very fat." She weighed nine-and-a-half pounds, had dark hair, "and we think dark eyes." Her father wrote, "We think of calling her Julie Maria. How do you like the name?" Since Christiana Niles had daughters named Juliet and Maria, she must have been very pleased. Juliet's response to the name was to ask Augusta, "My name moderned is becoming quite popular – is it not?"[93]

As Marshall campaigned during the spring of 1853, Lucadia's loneliness grew and her devotion deepened even more: "I miss your pleasant smile as you returned at evening ... and now marvel that when I had you with me, I could ever, when you are so kind and loving, be annoyed ... with any of my little domestic trials, even those relating to the sable sons and daughters of the Afric [*sic*] race ... ."[94] She was thinking of staying home that summer, "but should you by any possibility (which I hardly believe) not succeed in your election, then we will remain here a few years ... I will promise you to be right well satisfied in old Brazoria, if you are only with me." She emphasized the depth of her devotion by adding, "as I have often told you, I should be very unhappy, if I thought you proposed doing so against your own wishes, and only to gratify me, for you know that this being a Candidate for Gov. and taking such an arduous electioneering tour entirely to please me I consider a sufficient test of your devotion." Marshall had not received these comments when he expressed his own devotion.[95] He had found supporters in Austin and Washington counties, but "Still I have not entered into the canvass with much spirit, for I cannot sufficiently withdraw my mind from home and all its endearments. My wife and our two little treasures are too often before me, reminding me of my neglect of them, and how much real happiness I am sacrificing to run after a shadow." He was so unhappy it was hard to go to sleep, but once he did, "I was happy for I then had you in my embrace and our little ones by my side." As he began to think he might be elected, he wrote in May, "It is paying dear for [honors] to be so long separated ..., but I cannot back out now, I must go through the race."[96]

Although still "censuring" himself for "having left my happy home to run after such a bubble [bauble?] as the office of Governor," he was heartened by having moved his campaigning farther west in the state. He enjoyed seeing old friends in San Antonio and noted that the city was much more

"Americanized" than it was when he had last seen it when he was "with the Army" during the Mexican army's attack in December 1835.[97]

Lucadia, the children, and Juliet went north for the summer, and Marshall continued his campaign. He wrote in mid-June, "I sincerely believe ... I shall be elected. Do not however set your heart so much on being a Governor's wife ... there are now seven candidates ... and six of course must be defeated ... ."[98] In July he wrote from Tyler, pouring out his heart, full of love for his wife and babies, and concluded, "Kiss Carrie & Julie for papa and believe that you and their health and happiness are the constant prayer of your affectionate husband, Marshall."[99] He must have talked with Lucadia about leaving Brazoria if he did not win, because Lucadia mentioned that she was "so well pleased at the prospect of living at Galveston, that I shall not very much grieve, if my husband is not a Governor."[100] However, she wrote shortly thereafter, "I hope all your exertions have not been in vain, and that the good voters in our State will have sense enough to vote for the best man for the office ... ." She added in jest; "consequently I shall have my ambitious wishes gratified. Should it be otherwise, I fear you will scarcely forgive me, for causing you so much trouble as the electioneering canvass has given you—taken as it was solely on my account, that my aspirations for political honors might be realized."[101]

Marshall was not in a light-hearted mood in late July when he wrote about candidate George T. Wood's attempt to get votes by sending letters statewide claiming falsely that another candidate, M. T. Johnson, had withdrawn in favor of Wood.[102] Although Wood's claim likely brought more voters to Marshall's camp, a letter to Lucadia made his opinion clear: "I am completely disgusted with politiks, and wish that I had never embarked in the canvass." Once the polls closed, Marshall again teasingly wrote Lucadia, "On your account I regret exceedingly that there is a prospect of my being beaten for I know you will be greatly mortified to have your husband beaten ... ."[103] By mid-August, Marshall reported from Austin, "the general impression here is that my election is certain. I think there is hardly a doubt ... . All the other democratic candidates are out of sight behind me."[104]

Once back in Brazoria at the end of the month, Marshall wrote, "I arrived at home last evening—home did I say?—No, Brazoria is no longer home, although it has been for upwards of fifteen years, but my treasures are not here. I found here no wife to meet me with her joyous smile and loving kiss, no babies to fondle and caress."[105] Lucadia had more to think about: both girls had whooping cough, "and little birdie [Julie] has become quite thin."[106] Lucadia had to stay up late every night for about six weeks when their coughing was worst.[107]

On August 26, Marshall wrote Lucadia again: "I would most gladly this evening give up all the honor of being Governor, dearly as it has been acquired, and highly as I suppose you value it, to be at once restored to the society of my dear wife and children." He added comments he had not made before: "I am every day more and more impressed with the obligations I am under to you for having consented to unite your fate with mine, highly as I appreciated you, and much as I thought I loved you before our marriage, I did not then know your value ...." He realized that every day with her "has shown me qualities I did not know you possessed, and has increased my love for you." He concluded with an enormous tribute: "The greatest ambition I have, my dear Lucadia, is to be worthy of the love and devotion that you have shown me."[108] The following day, he wrote, "I think I may now safely assure you that your ambition is gratified and that you are the Wife of a Governor." He asked, "Don't you feel very grateful to your dear husband, for having gone through all the labors of such a canvass, travelling about twenty-two hundred miles on horseback, visiting about sixty Counties and making as many speeches all during the heat of a Southern Summer solely to gratify your political ambition." He also expressed anxiety about influenza in the North, and he urged Lucadia to keep flannel shirts on the babies. He had worn them for eighteen years and remained in good health, despite exposure to many diseases.[109]

Before Marshall's letter arrived, Lucadia sent him congratulations, based on newspaper accounts of the election: "I rejoice exceedingly that you have been appreciated by the citizens of our adopted state—but you are mistaken in supposing I should have been disappointed had you been defeated, or mortified had such been the result."[110] She returned his teasing again: "I am writing away with as little care as if I was not addressing the governor of Texas Elect …. I may learn to be more respectful when you have worn your honors longer, but now I prefer to think of you as my own dearly prized husband … ."[111] The final election results were as expected: in a field of six gubernatorial candidates, E. M. Pease won with 13,091 votes. William B. Ochiltree received 9,178 votes; George Wood, 5,983; L. D. Evans, 4,677; Thomas J. Chambers, 2,449; and John Dancy, 315.[112] As Pease began to envision being the governor, he saw his beloved wife as a partner in his new role. In a letter to her about Army troops being moved to the Rio Grande, "where there is a possibility of there being some trouble with the Mexicans," he wrote, "Wont [*sic*] the responsibility of *our* [EMP emphasis] Gubernatorial administration be greatly increased, if our state is to become the theater of another Mexican War during *our* [EMP emphasis] term of office so soon to commence?"[113]

The couple began to deliberate about the time she could return with the children to Texas once deadly yellow fever abated with cool weather in New Orleans and Galveston, but it was apparent that the governor-elect could not take time late in the fall to escort them by sea from New York to New Orleans to Galveston. Lucadia assured him that he did not need to come: "Remember I am quite a 'woman's rights woman,' and trust us to travel by ourselves … ." This was a remarkable statement to have been made by a woman in 1853. Five years before Lucadia's assertion, the Convention to Discuss the Social, Civil, and Religious Condition of Woman was held at Seneca Falls, New York. It produced the "Declaration of Sentiments" in which Elizabeth Cady Stanton declared, "All men and women are created equal … ." The well-read Niles and Pease families surely knew about that first women's rights convention and may well have heard about it directly from their mutual cousin, Elizabeth Marshall, who lived in Seneca Falls. She visited Poquonock when Lucadia was there in 1853.[114]

The trip to Texas was still undecided in mid-October when Marshall wrote Lucadia, "I leave the matter to your own good sense and discretion … ." He had sent her money for expenses, and was "almost crazy with joy" when he received word that they would be home soon.[115] While Lucadia was in Connecticut, Marshall thanked her for her congratulations on winning office, but confessed that "I have no patience to think of the confounded office, when I am daily reminded that I have obtained it at the dear rate of being separated from my dear Wife and children .... I would most cheerfully, this evening, resign the office and ... remain a private citizen the balance of my life, if that would restore me the society of those whose presence has become so necessary to my happiness ...."[116]

Marshall did not want Lucadia to "mind the expense" when he finally learned the date she and the children would sail. To avoid mosquitoes in Galveston, he wanted them to go immediately to the Wharton plantation, without regard to the cost.[117] He thought that yellow fever had abated, but he could not be too careful. News of Lucadia's impending arrival made him "almost crazy with joy," but he gained sense as he wrote. He thought that if the "girl" (a nurse) Lucadia was bringing did not want to stay with her, "take [young] Sam with you, you know he is quite handy as a nurse." The little family arrived safely in Galveston after a rough seventeen-day voyage.[118] Yellow fever had broken out again, and so they left quickly, going overland to Velasco, and from there to the Wharton plantation. Due to the press of business obligations, Marshall could not meet them.

Lucadia and the girls reached Brazoria in November. By then she had traveled thousands of miles on land and sea since she left Connecticut for Eltham Plantation in 1837. She stated in 1853 that, as a "woman's rights woman," she was capable of traveling unaccompanied, and she did. Her journey to far-away Texas had been necessitated by marrying her life's great love, and she never regretted her choice. She and Marshall had become doting parents of two children by 1853. She had met many people from around the country. She had learned to live with slavery, which she did not like. She had come to Texas determined to like it, and she did. Little could she have imagined that her husband would become governor of the state and refer to her as his partner for "our" term of office.

Chapter 4

Governor of Texas, First Term, 1853–1855

"We have it in our power ... to lay the foundation for ... public improvements and institutions which will hereafter rank Texas as the first State in the American Union."

E. M. Pease

The Pease family jostled along in their Rockaway carriage over very rough roads for eight days in mid-December 1853, headed to Austin from Brazoria. Sam, the slave who was trusted regularly to drive the family, and Maria, a nursemaid recently bought by Marshall, came along on saddle horses. Lucadia thought the country was beautiful and described eating lunches in groves with freshwater springs. Most of the time the weather was pleasant, but two days of rain and sleet soaked them, and Lucadia was afraid they would be bogged in mud. They stayed in public houses except for one night in a private "real log house which admitted of thorough ventilation— and where one could look [through the roof] upon the silvery moon ...." The children traveled well: Carrie, a toddler, sat on the front seat, often singing, and nine-month-old Julie slept. Carrie was "perfectly satisfied with 'chicken fryiars' and 'corn doggers'" [probably fried cornmeal dough known commonly as corn dodgers or hush puppies] on the road. The family arrived in the capital city on the evening of December 19; inauguration day was December 21.[1]

Along the way, the governor-elect must have reflected upon all that had brought him to the office he was about to assume, almost nineteen years after he arrived in Texas and days before his forty-second birthday. He had come from long-settled Connecticut to Mexican colonial Texas in early 1835, fought in the first battle of the Revolution, joined the interim government of the Republic, and served in several governmental capacities thereafter. He had been admitted to the Texas bar in 1837 and begun to practice law in Brazoria, where he developed a reputation for high competence. He had served in the first three Texas legislatures, where his reputation for careful, honest work had grown to include contacts in most every county in the state, and his correspondence showed a network of people who liked and admired him. He had achieved the financial security that was his goal in coming to Texas, and it allowed him to afford to campaign for governor. Pease stood ready to take control of the highest political office in Texas.

The Peases did not leave Brazoria for Austin until mid-December 1853, because legal work had kept Marshall at his desk. Finally, when they reached Austin, the family moved into a large rented room in Thomas W. and Susan Ward's house, where he began that night to write his inaugural message. The house had four rooms downstairs and a three-dormered room upstairs where the Peases must have stayed, because Lucadia mentioned being "called down" to receive visitors. Their residence was three blocks west of Congress Avenue and four blocks south of the newly-built, two-story, domed capitol at the head of Congress Avenue. Lucadia described the Central Texas limestone building as being of "whitish color, and admitting of a polish." The building was so new that the Senate chamber was not to be ready until late in November.[2]

When E. M. Pease appeared before the Fifth Legislature to take the oath of office, its members had been in session since November 7 and had been addressed by Governor Peter H. Bell. Gubernatorial terms were not entirely concurrent with legislative sessions, and neither fell within calendar years. Pease's first term would last from December 21, 1853, through

December 21, 1855. The Fifth Legislature met from November 7, 1853, to February 10, 1854.[3] The official record of the Inauguration in the Executive Record Book described the event:

> The ceremony of Inauguration took place on the twenty-first of December A.D. 1853, in the Representative Chamber of the New Capitol. The Governor and Governor-Elect, together with the President Pro-Tem of the Senate and the Lieutenant Governor Elect, attended by the committee on arrangements of the Legislature and a fine Band of Music entered the Hall of the House of Representatives at eleven o'clock a.m. and occupied Seats prepared for them on the Speakers Stand and surrounded by distinguished official[s] of Texas and strangers from other states.
>
> The retiring Governor having concluded his Valedictory the oath prescribed by the Constitution was administered by the Speaker of the House of Representatives to the Honorable E. M. Pease ... in the presence of the members of the Legislature, and a large and intelligent audience of Ladies and Gentlemen—whereupon His Excellency delivered [his] Inaugural Address.[4]

The chief executive, ever-cognizant of history, must have felt it that day: He had participated in events beginning with those that made Texas a republic, and a longtime friend and neighbor, Senator Guy M. Bryan, a nephew of Stephen F. Austin, had just officially notified him of his election and served as one of his escorts. Now he, E. M. Pease, had a major role to play in shaping the state.

The Governor opened his inaugural address formally: "In appearing before you to assume the duties of the office to which I have been called by the partiality of my fellow citizens, I feel sensibly the magnitude and importance of the trust that has been confided to my charge ... ." He hoped to meet citizens' "just expectations" and would "rely with confidence on the cordial support and co-operation of the legislature, without which my efforts can be productive of little benefit." His mentioned recent Texas history, pointing out that it was the only independent State to come into the Union and that it

embraced territory nearly equal in size to the entire United States at its creation. He acknowledged initial fear "that such a large and sudden requisition
might have upon the peace and perpetuity of the Union, yet experience has
demonstrated the fact that no danger is to be apprehended ... ." He then
elaborated on the potential of Texas:

> Our present attitude before the world is not less interesting; with a
> territory containing more square miles than many of the governments
> of Europe; possessing by nature nearly every element necessary to
> constitute a great and powerful State ... with a large public domain
> unequalled for diversity and fertility of soil, and a climate adapted to
> the production of all the necessaries and most of the luxuries of life, and
> a vast mineral wealth and great capacities for manufacturing purposes,
> we have it in our power by a proper use of all these advantages, and
> a judicious application of our means, to lay the foundation for those
> public improvements and institutions which will hereafter rank Texas
> as the first State in the American Union.

The Governor reminded his listeners, "It becomes us as a people to remember
with reverence that Being who has hitherto watched over and assisted our
progress through scenes of difficulty and trial ... and humbly solicit that he
will continue to us his beneficent care and protection." He closed by saying
that he would not at that point state his views on public policy that should
receive legislative attention; he would submit them later.[5]

Lucadia reported that she was not present for the inauguration but had
heard that Marshall spoke "remarkably well," although he had told her he
had never been so frightened in his life.[6] In spite of speaking in courtrooms,
the legislature, and on the campaign trail, his conscientiousness made him
profoundly aware of the magnitude of the job he was about to assume.
Lucadia did attend the ball that evening, writing:

> There were a great many distinguished persons from various part of
> the Union present. Gen. Green and family from Boston and Generals
> and Ex Presidents [*sic*] and dignitaries without number. There was a
> great display of dress, velvets and satins were as thick as blackberries,

and I formed quite a contrast in my black silk dress, which ... will answer for all purposes, weddings and funerals.

Lucadia knew that women in Texas "wear very rich dresses, at balls, and making calls, a great abundance of jewelry is displayed. It strikes north-erners so oddly to see ladies issuing from log houses, arrayed in such ... costly dress." She was not, as the new Governor's lady, resisting the custom of elaborate dressing; they had only been able to bring one small trunk with them on their carriage, and their other possessions had not yet arrived. She was unembarrassed by her lack of a ball gown, and her husband was proud of her. He enclosed a newspaper clipping in a letter from Lucadia to her sister Juliet, noting that her "diffidence has prevented her from giving you any description of ... the part she played in the grand display."[7]

The same day that the governor delivered his optimistic remarks about the future, the Comptroller of Public Accounts provided a report to the legis-lature that showed the state's financial status at the time. In the treasury, specie (gold and silver) available for disbursement on December 1, 1850, totaled $444,561, and the US bonds given to the state by the federal govern-ment as part of the Compromise of 1850 totaled $3,575,000 in value.[8] Of the $10,000,000 first offered to Texas by Congress in exchange for 67,000,000 acres of land claimed by the Republic, the State received a total of $5,000,000 in US bonds at 5-percent interest after the Legislature agreed to the arrange-ment on November 25, 1850. The remaining $5,000,000 was to pay off the debt of the Republic in cash to creditors. (A complicated controversy concern-ing the border between Texas and the United States would not be settled until early 1856 regarding payment of this debt, and another $2,750,000 was added by the Federal government to the debt payment.) Pease and the legis-lature were focused on the use of the bond money.[9]

The Governor sent his major message to the Legislature two days after his inauguration, describing subjects that were the most important to him. The very first was education. He wanted to "make a suitable and permanent provision for the support of public schools. The highest and most sacred duty of a free government is to provide the means for educating its citizens in a manner that will enable them to understand their duties and their obliga-tions; this, too, is a measure that is enjoined upon the Legislature by the

Constitution." Beyond public schools, the "want of a good University in the State" was on his mind. He advocated a "liberal education" comparable to that available elsewhere in the Union, and asked that it be made attainable without serious inconvenience in Texas. He framed the topic in sectional pride, noting this need "so as to remove the necessity of having to send our youth abroad to be educated among those who are hostile to the policy and institutions of the State."[10]

Second, the governor addressed the need for care of the mentally ill and education for the deaf. His nineteenth century language is jarring more than a century-and-a-half later, but the good sense and knowledge that drove his compassion were far ahead of the thinking of most Texans at the time. He called for "establishment and endowment of an Asylum for lunatics, and an institution for the education of the deaf and dumb ... measures that should commend themselves for your consideration." He noted that census tables showed that Texas had many of "these unfortunate classes, who have a claim upon our sympathy and bounty," but he knew that they had to be sent to distant states "to obtain the means of alleviating and improving their condition." The governor recognized that such institutions could not be established in a state as new as Texas, "except under the care and patronage of the government ...." Pease was probably aware of the needs of the deaf because the Connecticut Asylum for the Education and Instruction of Deaf and Dumb Persons had been operational in Hartford since 1817.[11]

Third, the governor addressed two major forms of transportation— navigable water courses and railroads—that were of great interest to Texans, although past legislation on railroads had produced "little if any benefit." He wrote, "Our large rivers have, without any improvement, hitherto furnished the means of transporting most of our productions," and a "moderate expend- iture of money by the government would greatly increase their useful- ness and add largely to the value of taxable property ...." A bill passed by the previous legislature for river improvements had come to nothing, but Pease thought that an improved act should be passed. As for railroads, "advantages to be derived ... [from their] construction are too obvious to require demonstration ... it is a question of ... policy, by which we can secure their construction at the earliest period." He reminded legislators that constitutional limits prevented the state from building railroads or becoming a part owner of stock in them. For lack of adequate internal capital, funds had to come from outside the state. Pease foresaw a problem for investors, however; they would have so much expense in construction and maintenance for the first five years that profits would be too small to make their risk worthwhile.[12]

The governor wrote that he had intended to present his opinion on the proposal of a railroad to the Pacific, but he did not need to do so since the legislature had already passed a bill for the construction of the Mississippi and Pacific Rail Road. "While the principal provisions of this law are unobjectionable," he wrote, "I think it might have been improved …. It is hoped that this law will accomplish for the State all that is anticipated by its friends." The governor wrote that that he would "cheerfully" carry out duties and responsibilities imposed on the government by the law, and he would "endeavor to execute them in a manner calculated to effect the objects intended by the Legislature." He then wrote more generally about railroad laws, noting that numerous charters had been granted to individuals without designation of routes and no money in capital stock had ever been paid. He regretted that the state had not first located and surveyed routes according to public needs and that charters had been granted to companies that were not capable of paying for their railroads.[13]

Indian tribes in Texas also received attention in the governor's address. "Our situation in relation to this class of the population is different from … other of the frontier States of the Union," he pointed out. "In these the General Government has the … exclusive control of the public domain …" where Indians were assigned territory, and relationships between tribes and whites are regulated. The governor noted that under such policy, depredations had ceased for many years, but in Texas the federal government had no right in the public domain and could not set apart any district for Indian occupation or control their movement. Pease suggested a solution: "a portion of our vacant domain, remote from the settled parts of the State, shall be appropriated for the temporary occupation of these remnants of tribes that properly belong to this State … and a qualified jurisdiction for Indian purposes be ceded to the General Government for a term of years."[14]

Governor Pease wanted certain needs of the Texas judiciary addressed. Beginning with the Supreme Court, he noted that its workload had increased, creating a necessity for more judges. Important cases had to be continued to another term because the three justices did not have time for thorough investigations and preparation of written opinions. Also regarding the judiciary, Pease wrote, "I feel it is my duty to call your attention to the inadequate salaries now paid to the Judges of both the Supreme and District Courts. The duties of these offices are very laborious and they should be filled only by men of stern integrity, and of superior legal attainments." He thought it needless to argue that such persons should be paid adequately, and concluded, "I trust that this subject will not fail to receive your early attention and efficient action."[15]

Next, the Governor expanded on the subject of revising the state's laws. He began with two examples. One was the law regulating appeals to the Supreme Court in criminal, noncapital cases, in which prisoners could be released on bail, even if their sentence was for life in prison. He thought that prisoners should not have this right: "It is hoped that this evil will be remedied without delay." His second example pertained to the "barbarous punishment of whipping" of free persons. Finding it "inconsistent with the general spirit of our criminal laws," he thought that it should be abolished. Much more broadly, he called for a codification of Texas law, a subject with which he had extensive experience:

Our laws, both civil and criminal, in my judgment, require a careful revision. We have adopted, it is true, the best portions of two different systems, but this was not done at the same time, and it was usually effected by crude and hasty legislation; as a necessary consequence, these different parts have never been brought to combine into one harmonious system. Our rules of pleading and practice in the courts are megre [sic] and exceedingly defective. Our statutes concerning crimes and punishments were often passed without reflection, many of their provisions conflict ... and these, more than any other portions of our laws, require ... careful revision and amendment.[16]

Then, in what may have seemed an unlikely topic, Pease recommended "an accurate and scientific geological survey of the State." He was aware that Texas was so sparsely settled that little of its agricultural and mineral capacities were known, and argued that a survey would "disclose sources of wealth and prosperity that would otherwise remain unknown for years." Of course, he had no idea of the oil and gas under the surface, much less their uses, but it was uncommon then even to think about mineral wealth. The governor also suggested that the same geological surveyors could also run and mark the boundary between Texas and the territory of the United States, "from the point where it leaves Red River to where it intersects the Rio Grande." He believed that the state's congressional members would have no difficulty in procuring passage of a US law to "join in the work."[17]

As the population of Texas continued to grow, so did the population of the state penitentiary in Huntsville. Pease, who was willing to spend available money when it was for the good of the people of Texas, was also aware that the penitentiary was an increasingly "heavy expense," and he was convinced that something new should be done to reduce it.[18]

He called attention to land-related matters, pointing out, "laws granting pre-exemption rights to actual settlers upon the public domain are somewhat obscure and …. I think it advisable that they be revised and so changed as to grant to each settler only two hundred acres of land. This is the quantity protected by the constitution as a homestead … sufficient for farming …." In connection with the same subject, he called attention to the law giving aliens the right to hold lands. "We are daily receiving large accessions to our population … from foreign countries. [Their] first wish … is to secure a home and an interest in the soil; but they are now denied the privilege until they have resided here five years—the period required for their naturalization." The governor noted that other states authorized aliens to hold lands immediately, provided they took an oath of their intention to become citizens, and that some states had provisions to give aliens the rights of citizenship even earlier than the time required for US citizenship. Several of these states, he added, have thus "added much to their productions and wealth. If the same liberal policy were here adopted, similar advantages could not fail to result in our State."[19]

The Governor also had a recommendation for the settlement and payment of the revolutionary debt that had plagued Texas for years. He reviewed the situation, writing, "a portion of our creditors have acceded to the settlement of their claims, and received payment therefor; others refuse to acknowledge the right of the State to ascertain and fix the amount of indebtedness to them, and insist upon receiving the face value of their claims, although they were issued ... at rates ranging from twenty to seventy cents on the dollar." Therefore, he wrote, five million dollars of the 5-percent stock that was to have been issued under the Congressional Act of September 9, 1850 [known as the Compromise of 1850] "are still unavailable to the State." He felt that a "reasonable time" had elapsed for creditors to accept the proposed terms and receive payment.[20]

Pease concluded by observing that the late date in the legislative session when he could make recommendations was a result of the "inappropriate time that the Governor enters upon ... his duties." The Legislature and Governor were elected at the same time, but about seven weeks lapsed between the starting dates of the two branches of government. He therefore recommended a constitutional amendment to solve the problem. He recognized that members would also consider other topics, but the time, he thought, "demanded practical legislation." He added, "I trust that all sectional feelings and prejudices will be discarded from our councils, and that every measure will be examined and acted upon solely [upon] its merits ... [for] the interest of the State at large ... ." He noted encouragingly, "Our present condition is a most prosperous one, immigration and wealth are pouring into the State more rapidly than [ever]. A spirit of enterprise and improvement is now abroad ... which if judiciously fostered and encouraged, will at no distant period enable Texas to occupy that position among her sister States to which she is entitled ... . You may be able hereafter to reflect that your labors have contributed much to elevate the moral, social, and political condition of the State."[21]

When the governor described issues that most concerned him as he began his first term, he also proposed legislative solutions. For his primary concern, education, he reminded legislators that the constitutional provision for land donated to counties for public schools had proved to be an unworkable system. However, the only education measure that became law that session, "An Act to Establish a System of Schools," was comprehensive but not feasible. Two million dollars of the 5-percent bonds of the United States were set apart as the Special School Fund for supporting and maintaining public schools, but this seemingly strong plan for a school system did not work. County chief justices and county commissioners were designated as school commissioners and directed to set up school districts "of convenient size" in each of which voters were to elect three trustees. These districts were to have enough "free white children" between ages six and sixteen to maintain a school, and citizens were to provide a schoolhouse. State-appropriated funds were only for teacher salaries. This bill was thought out in detail, down to student roll books. The governor signed it on January 31, 1854, but he may have known that its efficacy was dubious. Since the vast state was largely rural, insufficient numbers of children lived in "convenient" clusters. At least legislators made an effort toward public education.[22]

In the case of higher education, the governor thought that it was time to lay a foundation with $250,000 of the US bonds in the state treasury to be set apart as a perpetual fund. Interest on the money was to be applied to building and supporting a single state university. The Governor wrote that the income from the fund, with the amount realized from lands that were set apart by an act of the Republic, "will, at no distant period, enable us to build up a University fully adequate to all the wants of the State." He knew that the Republic had appropriated land for establishing and endowing two universities, but he thought it would be better to concentrate on one well-endowed institution. He wrote that if such an appropriation was made, it would be necessary to pass laws for the location of the university "at some central point ... as well as for the erection of the necessary buildings and for the organization and government of the institution."[23] His forward thinking came to naught in the Fifth Legislature.

The governor's second major concern, care of the mentally ill and establishment of a school for the deaf, did not result in immediate legislation. He had recommended that $500,000 in US bonds be appropriated and set apart as a perpetual fund, half for each institution, for their erection and support. If legislators agreed, they would need to pass laws for the location, establishment, and government of each institution. He acknowledged that the appropriations he proposed would "absorb a large portion of the US bonds now in the Treasury, but the objects ... are of great practical utility, and will be productive of benefits as lasting as the institutions under which we live."[24] Pease's concern for individuals who may have been mentally challenged or mentally ill is evident in a message to the Sixth Legislature later in his administration. He had granted a reprieve from execution to a man whom Dr. Ashbel Smith, then a member of House, and two other doctors, had examined "to ascertain his true condition." Pease decided that the person should not be executed and granted him a temporary reprieve, submitting his case for legislative consideration. He recommended that a law be passed commuting his punishment to imprisonment in the State Penitentiary, and explained, "I should have no hesitation in doing this myself, if I believed that the authority was vested in me by the existing laws."[25]

The governor wanted the legislature to address the major transportation issues of opening Texas waterways to better navigation and establishing railroads. Lawmakers passed bills to incorporate the Trinity River and Galveston Bay Dredging Company to deepen the river channel at its mouth, and other work was also underway. In August 1855, James B. Shaw, Comptroller, wrote the Governor that the Galveston and Brazoria Navigation Company had completed its work and asked for a commissioner to examine and report on their project.[26]

Establishment of railroads greatly interested the legislature. The Governor knew that vast amounts of capital from outside Texas would be required, and he foresaw that it would be years before any railroad in the state would return 5-percent interest on investments plus the costs of repairs and other expenses. The solution was obvious to him: "we must hold out inducements of ultimate profit. Fortunately, the large extent of our public domain will enable us to do this, without imposing any onerous burden on our citizens." The bill that had recently passed the legislature for building the Mississippi and Pacific Rail Road (not a company name but the end points of the road) was acceptable to him, but "I think that it might have been improved ... particularly in that provision which authorized the company to receive patents for the lands selected … ." Pease's opinion was that in the adoption of any system for aiding companies to build railroads, "we find ourselves embarrassed by the numerous charters … granted … without any specific designation of [their] routes …" and "not a dollar of capital stock has ever been paid." He thought it highly regrettable that charters had been granted to just anyone who applied and that the state did not first locate and survey routes to determine where they were needed before granting charters to companies capable of doing the work. "I think it would be good policy to authorize the school fund, the university fund, and other funds that may be set apart by the state for charitable and benevolent uses, to be loaned out, from time to time, to railroad companies … ." Pease noted that it was nearly time for the bonds acquired from the United States to be redeemed, and "necessity will then force us … to make some investment of them." The Governor thought that if the bonds were used to develop state resources and "contribute to the wealth and convenience of our citizens, it is our duty to make this disposition of them." Thinking about how to accomplish his ideas about railroads, he suggested that a board of commissioners (the Comptroller, Treasurer, and Secretary of State) be authorized, with the concurrence of the governor, to loan these funds at 6-percent interest, not exceeding twenty years, to companies chartered by the State for construction of railroads and other works of internal improvement. The loan amount would not exceed one-third of the cost of the work and was to be well-secured by a lien on the property of the company.[27] In another measure to promote railroads, the Legislature passed "An Act to encourage construction of Railroads by Land Donations," approved January 30, 1854, which provided that any railroad chartered by the legislature and constructed in Texas for a length of twenty-five miles or more would be entitled to receive sixteen sections of land per mile of constructed road, in running order. The governor signed the bill.[28]

Railroad laws of the session amended or supplemented existing acts and incorporated companies such as the Columbus, Wharton, and Austin Railroad, the Tyler and Dallas Railroad, and the Sabine and Rio Grande Railroad. When the Governor felt "constrained" to return such bills without his signature, he noted his objections and made suggestions. The first such bill was a supplemental act to create the Galveston, Houston, and

Henderson Railroad. He reasoned that companies could construct roads within eight years, but "I am not willing that these bounties shall be continued for … forty years, because our past history fully justifies the belief that long before that period, the population and businesses … will induce capitalists to construct all such railroads as may be needed without any bounties of land from the state." He named other objections, stating his unwillingness to grant railroads indefinite power of extension of track. He wrote, "I have felt it to be my duty to make an effort to correct what I deem some of the most material errors of our previous legislation on the subject."[29]

Pease's proposal for stopping Indian depredations was put into effect with "An Act Relating to the Indians of Texas," which called for federal jurisdiction over twelve leagues of vacant public domain to be set apart for the tribes in Texas. This law gave the federal government the authority to establish agencies and military posts, settle the Indians, and then "to exercise control and jurisdiction over [them] as long as the government shall judge necessary for [their] well being …." When land use for them ceased, the land was to revert to the state's public domain.[30] Pease sent a copy of this act to Secretary of War Jefferson Davis, writing that if it was approved by the President, he respectfully suggested that it become law as early as possible, because the public domain was being rapidly filled by individuals.[31] The Legislature passed two other related measures. One increased an appropriation act to defray expenses of three volunteer companies called into service for frontier protection, adding $4,555 for subsistence, forage, and more. The other was "An Act Making Appropriation for the Rescue of Captives … in the Hands … of the Indians." The $5,000 set apart also funded the "restoration of Mrs. Jane Wilson, then in Santa Fe, to her home and friends."[32] The Peases had a personal experience with Mrs. Wilson (then about age seventeen) and her child. Lucadia documented it in a letter to one of her sisters, explaining that their mother should not worry about Indian depredations in Texas: "they seem so far off that I hardly realize their horrors, or had not until last week, when we had as guests Mrs. Wilson and her child." Mrs. Wilson had been with her family on their way from Texas to California when her husband and father were killed by Comanches. After twenty-five days of barbarous treatment while pregnant, she escaped with no food or clothes and nearly starved, but a Mexican trading party found and saved her. The Mexicans gave her a horse to ride and took her to a home where English was spoken; then they went to the Indian Affairs agent in Santa Fe. He took her to his own home, where she delivered her baby. Lucadia wrote that the state furnished the means for Mrs. Wilson to return home to East Texas, but when she reached Austin by stage, alone with her child, the Governor invited her to stay with his family to rest.[33]

Conflicts between Native Americans and white settlers were a far more intractable problem than the legislation of the time could resolve. The subject filled Pease's files with more correspondence than any other. Letters came from citizens all along the frontier who were desperate for protection as well as from federal Indian Agent Robert S. Neighbors, Secretary of War Jefferson Davis, and Commander of the Department of Texas, Army Brevet Major General Persifor F. Smith. A compelling example of Indian problems in South Texas came from District Judge Edmund J. Davis who described the proceedings of a citizens' meeting to Pease. The chairman, Don José M. Gonzales, had made a report of Indian actions of the previous two months. Citizens had been murdered, including Cristiano Bela, "one of the most respected and wealthy of our number ... ." Citizens complained that in spite of the lack of protection, they had to pay taxes to the state as well as a heavy duty to the United States, since they would have to import Mexican corn, "because our Government has failed to protect us so that we may sow and reap from our own fields." They added a devastating commentary:

> Would that those who thus malign us could hear as we do almost weekly the solemn toll of our church bell, telling us that another and another of our Citizens have been murdered, or could listen to the shrieks of the wife and children over the form of the husband and Father brought in a corpse with the arrows still ... in his wounds to the home which he left ... in the morning ... ."

Meeting attendees decided to write to citizens in five counties to organize no less than two hundred men to "carry out civil process" against the "tame pets" of the United States and to require the Indian agent of the Lipan Apaches to monitor them. Davis noted that the report had been read and explained in Spanish and English and concluded that the citizens expected to hear from the governor.[34]

Pease assured Davis that he "deeply sympathized" with the South Texans and would use all the means at his command to relieve them. He had written to those with responsibility at every level, sending copies of their meeting minutes. He also made a legal observation to Davis: Judging the guilt or innocence of the Lipan Apaches properly belonged to the state judiciary, but "I have no doubt that the Lipan Indians as well as other residents of this state may be tried and punished by our courts for robbery and murder, and if upon proper proceedings before our Judiciary warrants should be issued for the arrest of any of them [and if needed] I would most cheerfully call out the militia to aid in their arrest."[35] The Governor also wrote federal Indian agent Robert Neighbors, urgently requesting protection lest citizens had to abandon their land. Neighbors answered that he was not the Lipan agent; furthermore, "our Indian difficulties will increase ... unless the General Govt. will adopt more effective measures ...." He pointed out, "There is no definite treaty [his emphasis] or other regulations for the government of any Indian tribe in Texas, and up to the present time [his emphasis] the General Govt. has not given directions or authority to either of the Indian Agents or the Military authorities to bring them to account for their numerous murders and thefts."[36]

As worried as Pease was about protection of the settlers, he continued to express his legal views on Indian rights, as shown in an exchange with Neighbors about thefts "by the Tonks" (Tonkawas) in Erath County. Neighbors reported that the Tonkawas were guilty and the chief had delivered them over to the military at Fort Inge, where nine of them were in close confinement. Neighbors asked how to proceed.[37] Pease replied with a legal observation on Indian rights under state law: "It will be nearly impossible to identify them as the Indians who committed the offences, and I presume that the admissions they made will be held by the courts to have been made under duress, and excluded in the trial." He suggested that they be held by the military "for some time" and not be allowed near settlements.[38]

As spring turned into summer in 1854, conflicts with the Indians as well as with the US Army did not cease, and Pease was at the center of these difficult issues. He was addressed by San Antonio citizens who declared that since the "General Government" had failed to protect life and property, "which as good citizens they have the right to expect ... it has become absolutely necessary to have recourse for aid to the Government of Texas." An appeal to the Commander of the Department of Texas, General Persifor F. Smith, resulted in no help. Davis and others reported that he was not calling out troops, although the Secretary of War had authorized the General to do so. Smith refused since the Secretary thought that only a large Indian invasion would constitute an emergency.[39] Texans knew well that small invasions of fast-moving Indians were deadly. South Texans made the important case that since the close of the war with Mexico, settlers had been promised US protection. Then, "the inhabitants who had been driven out could return—It was this hope ... which reconciled our population of Mexican birth to a government of strangers ...." Yet repeatedly their settlements were disrupted. E. J. Davis and others claimed that it was "ridiculous" to think that four or five hundred mounted troops could control land from the headwaters of the Colorado River to the mouth of the Rio Grande; five hundred more were needed to exterminate or remove the Indians. Smith then relented, and allowed Pease to, "feel authorized ... to call out six companies of mounted volunteers, to be mustered into the service of the United States, at the time and places indicated by you, for twelve months ...." He concurred that careful troop selection was needed. Pease issued a proclamation about Smith's request. Companies of eighty-eight men would be mustered in on November 1 for twelve months. Each man was to supply his own horse, equipment, rifle, and brace of pistols; the Army was to supply ammunition, forage, and subsistence.[40]

The Governor seized control when, despite seeming progress, the military situation worsened. With five companies ready and a sixth forthcoming, Secretary of War Davis ruled that militia could only serve for three months. Then, while General Smith was on the frontier, the Department of Texas Headquarters postponed the order. Pease responded by publishing a circular stating that the problem would not have arisen if Smith had been available, and that the Adjutant General would muster the troops into state service. Pease, who had had only a few weeks of military service in the Texas Revolution, trusted his own judgment. He ordered troops where to go and promised them supplies. If Smith refused to receive them, the Governor would ask for legislative support.[41] Summarizing events for Smith, Pease stated that he was in an embarrassing situation and added frankly, "I cannot believe that you will refuse to receive these companies ... [when] you [stated that] you need them in protecting the frontier from Indian invasion." [EMP emphasis].[42]

During the second year of Pease's first term in June 1855, an unusual event transpired that again forced him to call up a company of troops due to inadequate federal responses. Indians murdered settlers including William R. Jones of Comal County, whom Pease had known as a "valuable ... old citizen of the State and as highly respected as any man we have ... ." Eighty-four area residents petitioned the governor, citing a year of depredations during which the General Government had done nothing to remedy the "evils."[43] Pease told Smith without his usual courtesy that a company was required.[44] The governor then wrote to revolutionary soldier and frontier fighter James H. Callahan that a mounted force was needed, and "since the United States Government has failed to notice these depredations ... I [will] authorize you ... to raise a Company of Mounted men to serve for three months ... ." Pease could not furnish supplies but would depend upon "the justice of our Legislature." He told Callahan, "I rely with confidence upon your good sense and prudence to avoid attacking any Indians ... that are peaceably disposed." Callahan replied from Camp Enchanted Rock in Gillespie County that he was keeping some of his company "on the Scout all the while ... ."[45]

September began with Bexar County citizens reporting still more outrages and calling on the Governor for aid. Smith was unreachable, and Pease's frustration with the general increased when he went to San Antonio to consult him and found that Smith had left. He wrote Smith, "My situation is a very embarrassing one. Our citizens are entitled to protection from the General Government, but not receiving it, they appeal to the State authorities." Pease acknowledged the danger of calling up volunteers, who "may in their zeal punish the Indians [and] interfere with the efforts ... by the

General Government to settle the Texas tribes at the reservation on the upper Brazos."[46]

The governor's anticipated fear became a reality in a surprising way: Callahan himself, who Pease trusted, gave him ample reason for alarm. Callahan and his troops crossed into Mexico in early October while pursuing Indians, and although Pease felt that the men were justified in following the raiders to punish them and recapture property, he admonished Callahan: "you had not the right to take possession of or to occupy Piedras Negras or any other village or property of Mexican citizens; ... you should have returned immediately to this side of the Rio Grande, and I trust that you have already done so." He praised Callahan for the defeat of so many Indians, and expressed the hope that "no acts have been committed by your command, against the Citizens of Mexico which will give them any just cause of complaint against you."[47] Pease wrote to Smith, "if this leads to a border warfare between the Citizens of this State and the Mexicans and Indians, no one will regret it more than myself, but the fault lies with the US government, where neglect to furnish protection to our settlements against the repeated ... depredations ... during the past year, rendered it necessary to call into service volunteers of this State, for our protection."[48]

When Pease sent volunteers into service, he was careful about meeting their needs. A letter at the close of the year described how a paymaster was to be bonded, where he was to go, and when he was to make payments. The paymaster would earn only one hundred dollars, which Pease thought inadequate but acceptable due to the circumstances.[49] As the governor's first term came to a close, no solution to Indian depredations was at hand despite his best efforts. His opinion about the Indians continued to reflect conflicting views. He had recognized their civil rights while believing they should be prosecuted for harming settlers, but he also wanted peace. He wrote to the Secretary of War that Indians "must be furnished by the Government with the means of living until they are taught to support themselves by agriculture." This position, little different from the Spanish of two centuries earlier, sought to teach the natives how to grow crops and lead sedentary lives. Obviously, mid-nineteenth century whites had still not learned that most Indians did not wish to lead such lives and relinquish their own culture. Nevertheless, in the midst of Indian murders and thefts when Pease called out the military to protect white citizens, he was not calling for the extermination of native peoples, as did others around him.[50]

Changes in the judiciary that Pease proposed in his first address to the Legislature were straightforward. First, he suggested a constitutional amendment to increase the number of Supreme Court justices from three to five. If the Legislature concurred, he suggested another amendment giving to the Governor the power to fill all vacancies that might occur in the Supreme and District courts, as well as the offices of Attorney General, District Attorney, Comptroller, Treasurer, and Commissioner of the General Land Office. These appointments would be in effect until the next regular election. Such an amendment would remedy the problem created by the Constitution that required offices to remain vacant until an election could be held. The Fifth Legislature did not increase the number, nor pass the governor's request to permit vacancies to be filled prior to regular elections, but it did pass legislation to amend an act to organize the Supreme Court of the State. The new legislation called for one Supreme Court session a year in the cities of Austin, Galveston, and Tyler.[51] Pease's request for increased judicial salaries met with no success in the same session.

The governor's ideas about the need for codification of the state's laws were based on his legal and legislative experience as well as intelligent thought. He wrote that the defects in Texas law could not be cured by "hasty legislation" and recommended that the Legislature form a commission of three gentlemen who were "learned in the law, whose duty it shall be to prepare a code of civil and of criminal procedure, and also a code of general laws or rules of decision, and that all these be reported for action of the next Legislature." He thought that if a code was developed with ability and care, justice would be better served, and that rather than having to deal with an almost endless number of sources, Texas law could be contained in a single volume that would be accessible to everyone. The Governor concluded, "it is evident that there is a stronger necessity for a revision and codification of our laws than those of any other State in the Union. Besides, we should receive aid from the lights furnished by the successful experiments of several of our sister States." He expressed "entire confidence" in his recommendation, which would produce a vast advantage to the State.[52]

The Legislature concurred and passed an act to have the civil and criminal laws "amended, revised, digested and arranged." The governor signed the bill on February 10, 1854. It called for three commissioners, appointed by the governor, to present a report before the next legislative session. They could borrow records from the secretary of state's office and books from the Supreme Court library; the commissioners were to be paid $1,500 annually.[53]

The governor's request for a geological survey must have seemed so far-fetched that the legislature made no response, but Pease's suggestion that surveying be done at the same time did motivate the legislature to pass a bill to provide for "running and making the boundary line" between Texas and US territory. It was signed on February 11, 1854, and called for gubernatorial appointment of a commissioner, surveyor, and clerk to act in conjunction with officers appointed by the federal government to do this task between the Red River and the Rio Grande.[54]

Pease's idea for generating income for the penitentiary was to put convicts to work once the prison buildings were complete and workshops were erected. Convict labor could be made available to the highest bidder, he thought. The Legislature agreed and passed a bill to establish "Cotton and Woollen [sic] Factories" in the Penitentiary." Convicts were to build, within the walls, a place for fifty of them to make coarse cotton and wool cloth. Proceeds of the sold cloth were to go to the institution.[55]

Legislative response to unclear laws granting pre-emption rights to settlers on the public domain came in the form of a supplemental act granting relief to certain pre-emption claimants by extending the time they were required to have the land, including their improvements, covered with valid certificates. Pease signed the bill on January 7, 1854. He then signed an act donating to actual settlers on vacant public domain one hundred sixty acres of land on February 13, 1854. It reduced the size of such grants by forty acres.[56]

As for aliens who were coming into Texas, a bill to define their civil rights was signed on February 13, 1854. It defined aliens as free and white and gave them the right to hold property, real or personal, so long as they declared their intention to become US citizens. No time limit was placed on them.[57]

The problem of revolutionary war debt that Pease mentioned in his message had to do with differing opinions about the actual value of debts in 1836 versus their value in US currency nearly twenty years later. He therefore suggested that a law be passed "designating a time within which all holders of recognized claims against the State of Texas shall present them to the Treasury, accompanied with releases of all claims against the United States ... in the form ... [as] prescribed by the Secretary of the Treasury, and approved by the President of the United States ... ." Otherwise, he argued, "such claims shall be forever barred and the holders no longer recognized as creditors." The Legislature promptly passed a bill to extend the provisions of an act to provide for ascertaining the debt of the late Republic of Texas, and Pease signed it February 11, 1854. It allowed an extension of the Act of March 20, 1838, to August 1, 1855. All claims that were not presented to the Auditor and Comptroller on or before that date would be forever barred. The same state officials were to give notice of the extensions in Texas newspapers and other US cities.[58]

A broad range of other matters occupied the governor during his first term, and he dealt with them evenhandedly, even when they involved favorite subjects such as education. For example, Pease's logic and legal advice were spelled out in his return message to the House concerning a bill to incorporate Tyler University. He objected to a tax exemption for a specific school; exemptions must apply to all similar institutions, he argued, because the Constitution declared that taxation should be equal and uniform. Pease noted that since a law of the Second Legislature, forty-eight colleges and literary institutions were only exempt for certain property. "Were there no other objections to this provision but the fact that it grants a privilege which is denied to forty-eight other institutions ... it would be sufficient to induce me to withhold my approval from it." He then added another point: "I think it will probably be held by the Courts that this provision conflicts with that section of the Constitution which directs that "no law shall ... embrace but one object and that shall be expressed in its title." As for the Tyler University tax exemption, Pease stated, "No one will contend, for a moment, that the provision is necessary for the incorporation of the University … ." The Legis-lature went ahead and approved the bill on February 11, 1854.[59] The governor, who favored an equitable tax base, vetoed another bill that he explained was flawed, but the legislature overrode him. The bill relinquished the state tax of 1854 and 1855 to the counties. Pease wrote that he would have no objection "if relinquishment has been made to the counties in which the property is situated, upon which the taxes are assessed … [but] you are aware that … an individual has the privilege of assessing all his property in the state, in the county where he resides … ." He knew that the bill was to enable counties to pay their debts, erect courthouses and jails, and make other improvements, and he thought these were proper uses of the funds, but he did not consider it just to tax property in one county and have the money expended in another, and the practice was particularly unjust to frontier county citizens.[60]

After adjournment of the legislature in early February 1854, Pease's gubernatorial duties shifted. The largest issue was the proposed creation of the Atlantic and Pacific Railroad in response to the Mississippi and Pacific railroad act of 1853, which sought to encourage the building of a transconti-nental line through Texas along the thirty-second parallel. Pease had said in his first address to the legislature that he was not entirely satisfied with the law but would work with it. The law set aside land as a building incentive; a reserve along each side of the proposed line allowed the railroad to take alternate sections along each mile of road after they had built the first fifty miles of track, and the company would receive right-of-way through public lands. In order to prove financial capability, the company was to provide a $300,000 bond in gold or silver that would be forfeited if a road at least fifty miles in length had not been built in eighteen months.[61]

United States Senator Thomas J. Rusk wrote Pease in April 1854 about Robert J. Walker (former Treasury Secretary under President Polk) and T. Butler King (ex-Congressman from Georgia), noting that he knew they were planning to submit a proposal to Texas for building the railroad. Rusk stated, "Of the good intentions of Walker and King I have no doubt as to their talent and capacity … ." The men's intentions had been denounced the previous November, when an editorial in the *American Railroad Journal* described the first set of directors from various states for the "Pacific Railroad" (including Walker and King): "There is not ... a first class name, in the whole lot, nor a person calculated to command the confidence of that class of men who are to build the road." They were "politicians and speculators [who] throw doubt on the real intentions of the parties and lead to the belief, that they have a very different object from the one set forth." The journal called for half the directors to step aside before capitalists would cooperate; "under the present lead, the company will simply make themselves ridiculous, and will be equally powerless before the country, and Congress."[62] This weekly publication covered national railroad business news, reports on developing roads, and mechanical engineering. Pease may well have known about the article and been uneasy about the men, but the Atlantic and Pacific Railroad Company was the only bidder for the Texas road. They submitted a certificate of deposit to the governor of $300,000 on the Farmers and Merchants Bank of Memphis. The governor awarded a certificate in August for building the road, and by then the Atlantic and Pacific Railroad, still led by Walker and King, had new directors who were prominent Texans. They were led by M. T. Johnson and included H. P. Bee, George Hancock, John Hancock, John W. Harris, J. Pinckney Henderson, and even high state government officials, James H. Raymond and James B. Shaw. Pease stated that, in his judgment, the proposal met "all the circumstances of the case, offers the strongest assurance and guarantees that the road will be promptly and substantially built, in the whole length according to provisions of the act."[63] However, the $300,000 deposit failed to arrive in Austin, and Pease's tentative confidence in the company evaporated. In September, Walker and King wrote Pease about the Memphis bank stock, noting their awareness that Pease did not think the evidence was sufficient but assuring him of full payment. They also claimed that the route had been surveyed "at great expense through Texas to the Pacific."[64] Leaders around the state sent comments to the Governor, supporting him and questioning Walker and King. B. F. Benton, copublisher of the *Redland Herald* in San Augustine, congratulated Pease on his "firmness" and alluded to the fact that Senators Houston and Rusk did not have much confidence in Walker and King. He added, "Rest assured that your action ... will be sustained by the people of the State, and that it will be fully endorsed, should your name ever come before them at any future election." Former governor J. Pinckney Henderson wrote Pease of his determination to withdraw from the railroad deal. Texas Senator Guy M. Bryan wrote the governor that he hoped there would be no called legislative session on the matter: "You know what our Legislature is, and there is no telling what would be done were it assembled .... I know you are a man of your own mind, and act from its promptings." He did not think King or Walker "had the confidence ... of the community," and he "felt rejoiced that you did not let the N. York Company have the contract."[65]

Walker and King persisted. They sent Raymond a certificate for $300,000 of preferred stock in the Sussex Iron Company of New Jersey for deposit on behalf of the railroad; the stock was assigned to the Governor of Texas. Articles of incorporation for the iron company were enclosed. Walker and King wrote to Raymond, "We cannot close this letter without desiring to present to his Excellency the Governor ... our congratulations on the brilliant prospects of the speedy completion of this great work, fraught with such inalienable blessing, and benefits to our state, and the whole country."[66] Pease was not impressed. He wrote Raymond that as chief executive officer of the state, "whose duty it is *to take care that the laws are faithfully executed* (his emphasis) I feel that it is my duty to give you my opinion ...." He declared that the bank stock and the iron company stock were not what the law required to be deposited, and he used his own mathematical calculations to show that the actual value of the stock was insufficient; also, he noted that projections made about expected profits were not the same as real money. The governor then officially inquired in writing of Raymond if $300,000 in gold or silver had been deposited by the railroad in the state treasury. Raymond's answer two days later was inadequate, since Pease had to press him about "what the deposit consists of."[67] The answer did not satisfy Pease. He wrote Raymond on November 8, "I consider that it is my duty to declare that said contractors have failed to deposit with the Executive ... $300,000 in gold or silver ... within sixty days after entering into said contract, and the term of this contract ... is null and void ...." Considering what to do next, he noted that under the existing law, he was "authorized and required to enter into another contract with any other company or individual for the construction of said road ..." if, of course, any could qualify.[68] Pease's position continued to be supported around the state. Memucan Hunt, active in Texas public affairs since the Revolution and a recent legislator, sent his congratulations to Pease on the stand he had taken "and the very able manner in which you have vindicated your position." Hunt had disassociated himself from the railroad.[69] The governor issued a proclamation on December 1 declaring that the Walker and King contract had become null and void, and he gave notice that proposals from other companies or individuals would be accepted until May 1, 1855. No further proposals were submitted, and thus ended the hope of a transcontinental railroad through Texas for the time being. Bryan wrote the governor that he regretted Raymond's and Shaw's involvement with the company, "And to you I say well done good and faithful servant ...."[70]

Since railroad issues were largely unresolved, a group of Galveston's powerful business leaders led by M. B. Menard, a founder of the city, wrote Pease to inquire what his proposed solution was, due to his "anxious solicitude for the relief of the State." Their letter and Pease's response were published in the Austin newspaper.[71] The Governor told them that since his previous ideas about railroad development had proved unworkable, he had concluded that the best approach was for the state to construct railroads. Interest on loans would be paid largely by an internal improvements tax, and he laid out his plans for this approach. "In order to give capitalists confidence in our internal Improvement fund, as a security for loans, it shall be created by a constitutional provision, and placed beyond the reach of repeal until all loans contracted ... are paid." This plan was not widely appreciated across the state, and citizens may have felt that Pease had drawn a hard line on a policy statement rather than a proposal.[72]

Other thorny issues continued to arise for the Governor; one involving protection of a US citizen in Mexico and another involving military versus civilian jurisdiction in a murder case. A petition by Antonio Manchaca for the release of Carlos Rios, a US citizen then in Matamoros, was sent to Pease from San Antonio by citizens who thought it best for Pease to forward the request to the President of the United States or the Secretary of State. Pease wrote to the President, endorsing Manchaca's petition, which was supported by an affidavit showing that Rios had been forced into the military service of

Mexico. Pease stated that the petitioner Manchaca was a native Texan with whom he had been acquainted for nearly twenty years, and always found him a man of veracity. He asked that the matter by investigated.[73] In other business, issues that involved Federal relationships came up for the Governor; one that involved military versus civilian jurisdiction in a murder case is a good example. Texas authorities and the US military came into conflict when Army Assistant Surgeon J. M. Steiner killed a man in Waco Village and ended up in civilian jurisdiction. Pease wrote a lengthy letter to Brevet Brigadier General William Harvey, providing his own legal opinion in the absence of the Texas Attorney General. Pease stated that the matter was of "great interest, involving ... important constitutional questions ... I have given the matter much examination and reflection." He was disposed to "always give full effect to the constitution and laws of the United States within Texas," [but] "I think that, in the case of Dr. Steiner, the jurisdiction of the State Courts was rightfully exercised in the first instance ... . Unless the offence of Dr. Steiner be one which the authorities of the United States have exclusive jurisdiction, it is certainly arguable in the courts of the State ... ." He called it a "well established rule of law that where courts have concurrent jurisdiction over the same matter, the court that first takes jurisdiction retains it. In this case ... the first prosecution against Dr. Steiner was commenced by the State Court ... ." Pease continued: "The claim of exclusive jurisdiction in the United "States [is], I do not think warranted." He argued that if the site of Fort Graham had been purchased by the federal government, Texas would have no authority. "But I cannot assent to the proposition that because Fort Graham was occupied by United States troops, where the offence was committed, the authorities of the United States have exclusive jurisdiction over it ... ." With no evidence that the Federal government had bought the site, Pease said he must "presume that offences committed there are subject to indictment and trial in our courts."[74]

Relations with Mexico remained mostly calm during Pease's term, except for the Callahan excursion, but a request for archival records annoyed Adrian Woll, Governor of the Mexican State of Tamaulipas. Attorney Pryor Lea of Galveston wrote Pease that he had learned that the "Archives of Goliad" were in Matamoros, subject to control of the Governor Woll who was willing to surrender them to Texas. These land records, perhaps a cart full, were necessary to sustain proper titles, and Lea was worried that the records could be modified. Pease wrote to Woll, explaining that these archives were removed from Goliad when it was abandoned during the war between Texas and Mexico, and that because the records contained evidence of titles, they were of great interest to many Texans. Pease asked if Mexico had these records, and whether they could be delivered to Texas authorities. Woll answered that a part of those archives were in the City of Matamoros, "in proper custody, and perfectly Secure, consequently persons interested who may desire to obtain any evidence of property may have recourse to this Government under my control to request 'testimonies' of the evidence they may wish … ." He added, "in conformity with our laws … the originals cannot be extracted …" and concluded, "This is all I can say to you."[75]

The accomplishment that Pease may be best remembered for is the building of the Governor's Mansion. Legislation initially provided for the erection and furnishing of a residence for the Governor and called for a $14,500 appropriation for "suitable" structures and $2,500 for furnishings. The bill required the governor, comptroller, and treasurer to act as commissioners. The buildings were to be constructed with stone or brick, but the size, plan, and furnishings were left to the commissioners' discretion. Abner H. Cook of Austin won the contract. The house was to be located where the General Land Office was later placed, southeast of the capitol and on its grounds, but the house could not have had the east-facing front that Cook required to provide afternoon shade on their front porticos, and so the commissioners settled on the block immediately southwest of the capitol so that the house faced east on Colorado Street. The purchase of the lot and financing of the residence was through sale of state-owned lots in Austin, not state taxes or US bonds in the state treasury. The Governor was surely delighted to sign this bill on February 11, 1854.[76] By the time Cook was chosen, he was building the large, two-story Greek Revival-style homes of Commissioners Raymond and Shaw. Cook was called a "master builder," a nineteenth-century term for someone who had apprenticed with masters of carpentry or other trades. He was not an architect; few buildings of the time were designed by anyone other than the builder. Cook's draftsman drew plans for the exterior of the governor's mansion, based on the elegant designs of the Shaw and Raymond homes. Each of these three houses were described as "a great squarish flat-roofed block, made of brick with six two-story Ionic columns supporting a full entablature and cornice." They were built of Bastrop pine and caliche brick from Cook's kilns on Austin's nearby Shoal Creek.[77]

The design for these houses came from carpentry books showing the perfect proportions of columns in an ancient Greek temple and other features. These books apparently provided a guide for Cook's simple, equally elegant millwork in the house. The distinctive signature of Cook's design was an X-and-stick balustrade of slender wood slats forming a narrow X with a vertical bisecting slat, appearing to tie the X in the middle. This feature was a popular Federal design element elsewhere in the country, but it was new in Austin. The Peases had seen Neo-classical buildings in the North, Washington, and New Orleans. The style pleased them, or else the Governor's house would not have been built as it was. Greek revival elements of columns across the front of these symmetrical two-story homes with large porticos were not exclusive to Southern plantations; the design had originated in ancient Greece, spread to Europe, and was already in use in the American North, Midwest, and South when Cook built in Austin.[78]

Until the house was completed, the Peases remained in the Ward home, which probably had been built by Cook for Ward in 1846. It stood on one-half a block at Lavaca and Hickory (later West 8th Street) with ample space for vegetable and flower gardens as well as cows. Lucadia reported that they were able to rent and occupy the entire house in April 1854 once Susan Ward left Texas. They bought most of her furniture and refurbished the story-and-a-half, colonnaded house. The property had two unusually large cisterns, one holding 40,000 gallons of rainwater that the Peases shared with neighbors. Lucadia, who loved flowers and was a fine gardener, took care of Susan Ward's roses and noted, "I have given cuttings of roses enough if they grow to make the whole town a bed of roses."[79]

In this house, the couple's third and last child, Anne Marshall, was born on November 28, 1854. Her parents debated for months on a name for her, and although Marshall wanted her named for her mother, Lucadia was "decidedly opposed." Anne finally bore her great-grandmother Clark's first name and the Marshall family name. The couple's love of one another and their children only grew with time. Marshall wrote Lucadia from Houston, weeks after their new baby arrived, "I shall pass my time as pleasantly as it is possible ... when away from my dear wife and children."[80] A letter of Lucadia's crossed his in the mail:

> We have now a severe norther and I hope you are comfortably protected ... as myself and our little darlings are .... a good fire [is] blazing ... our eldest our dear Carrie sleeping so sweetly on papa's bed, having given me ... scores of kisses for her papa, then loving, and impulsive little Julie on Mama's bed, who goes nightly to sleep on Mama's arm, after vainly exclaiming at every noise she hears "papa's come" .... now comes our third treasure in the very morn of her existence, sleeping in her cradle bed with her unspoken claims upon your love .... And dear M—if you were only in our midst, in your now unoccupied chair, the picture would be complete, for you and they are such treasures and blessings to me, that I wonder I can ever find any objects with which to be dissatisfied.[81]

After two years in Austin, the Peases were comfortable in the busy little city while they awaited completion of the governor's house. Lucadia received a letter from her husband that must have pleased her greatly when he admitted, "Each visit I make here [to Brazoria] I return to Austin much better satisfied with the upper country."[82] Until then he had preferred Brazoria's mild winters and cooling Gulf breezes in the summer. Lucadia had fallen in love with the Austin area right after their arrival. In mid-January 1854 she wrote, "We have Big Sam here, and I often ride in the carriage around the Town, and there are beautiful drives in every direction. The roads are excellent, rocky and hilly, but smooth and dry, and the scenery is very pretty." Considering Austin's inland location, she was surprised by its improvements, including "a few good blocks of stores on the principal street," but it had only been "eight or ten years since Indians came into the centre [sic] of Town and in the daytime took off several children." She noted that churches were small and hotels were uncomfortable. Marshall was unable to go with her at first to sightsee or return social calls, but she hoped that once the legislature adjourned, they would go to San Antonio, "a town of more interest, (having been an old settlement of Spaniards) than any other in the state."[83] As her first spring in Austin progressed, she went to Mount Bonnell,

> the great resort here—The road there is very pleasant, and the view from the mountain magnificent, at our feet the Colorado, breaking its way through high rocky banks, its waters clear and beautiful, and the woods covered with cedar brightly green—and on the mountain a shrub which they call mountain laurel—an evergreen with a purple flower.[84]

She saw more bright wildflowers in May, when she wrote about taking the children on evening carriage rides with her husband's private secretary Sam Harris, who was staying with them while Marshall was away. She was delighted to see the "much praised prairie flowers, and find them more gay and abundant than I had imagined," and she noted "very beautiful cactus" in bloom.[85]

After adjournment of the Legislature, Pease began going back to Brazoria and Galveston periodically to attend to his law practice. He would have depended on Harris to handle correspondence, which Lucadia described as "a score of letters in every mail." When Pease arrived in Brazoria in mid-May after a "fatiguing trip," he reported to Lucadia that his office looked the same, and he was sleeping there. He closed his letter by asking her to "remember me to Harris, and accept the assurances of the undiminished love of your devoted husband, Marshall." In February 1855 he reported that he was "happy to learn my treasures at home are all safe," and was eager to return. He had not been able to close all his business in Galveston, but he had finished with some "that [have] annoyed me for years, and which could not have been closed by [John] Harris ... ." Come May, he was preparing cases for court in the fall for others to try and had rid himself of more annoyances. Thinking ahead about being able to stay in Austin, he wrote Lucadia that the children would soon be of age to need education. "Your duties and responsibilities to them are increasing every day, and I wish to be with you and them constantly so as to lighten your labors."[86]

Marshall Pease, deeply loved at home, was respected and appreciated widely as Governor E. M. Pease. Early in his first term he had received congratulations by a friend from Hartford who observed wryly, "I hope none [of the people of Texas] will ever regret the choice they have made." Apparently, most of them did not. While there were inevitably those who disagreed with him at times, most of his papers show appreciation. One letter from Galveston, where Pease was well-known, began, "Entertaining the highest regard for the dignity of your office and of your integrity and ability to perform the duties thereof, it is with much pleasure and great respect I make this address." Attorney Richard Coke, who wrote from Waco that he needed a new copy of his notary public certificate, added: "the people of this County and as far as I know the adjoining Counties most heartily approve your action in regard to the Pacific Railroad …. I regard your arguments in support of your position as perfectly conclusive."[87] The governor was in a strong position to run for re-election.

Governor E. M. Pease. *Courtesy of State Preservation Board.*

E. M. Pease. One of the youngest available images of Pease, perhaps painted when he became governor at age forty-one. PIC B 06774, Austin History Center, Austin Public Library.

Another portrait of Pease as a young man. ART 00002, Austin History
Center, Austin Public Library.

E. M. Pease dressed as a proper Victorian gentleman. AR-A-001-1006,
Austin History Center, Austin Public Library.

An aging Governor Pease. AR-A-001-980, Austin History Center, Austin Public Library.

A photograph of the Governor in his later years. PIC B 10311, Austin History Center, Austin Public Library.

The youngest available image of Lucadia N. Pease, showing a rare smile for a nineteenth-century photograph. PIC B -06782, Austin History Center, Austin Public Library.

A full-faced image of Lucadia N. Pease in middle age. PIC B -06775,
Austin History Center, Austin Public Library.

A photograph of Lucadia N. Pease, wearing a full-skirted antebellum dress, about 1860. AR-A-001-1589, Austin History Center, Austin Public Library.

A picture of Lucadia N. Pease, perhaps in her seventies. AR-A-001-981, Austin History Center, Austin Public Library.

Julie M. Pease, the second of the Pease's three daughters and a graduate of Vassar College. PIC B 06790, Austin History Center, Austin Public Library.

Most likely Sam Barber, a freedman who was formerly a Pease slave.
This worn photograph is in a Pease family album. AR-A-001-1572,
Austin History Center, Austin Public Library.

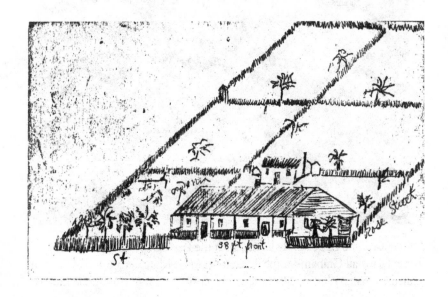

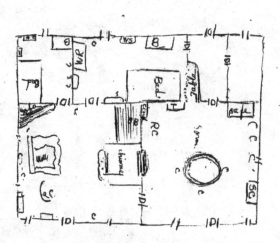

Pease home in Brazoria, drawn by Lucadia Pease and dated December 1850. It was sent in a letter written by Lucadia Pease to her sister Maria Niles on February 12, 1851. Austin History Center, Austin Public Library.

Woodlawn, the Pease family home, with the Pease grandchildren on the lawn: Marshall Graham on the pony, and Carrie Margaret and Niles Graham seated in chairs. PICH 02200, Austin History Center, Austin Public Library.

First National Bank, Austin. Governor Pease, a wealthy lawyer and land owner, was an officer of the First National Bank in Austin, created after the Civil War. It stood on the prominent corner of Congress Avenue and Pecan Street (now West Sixth Street). PICH 04107, Austin History Center, Austin Public Library.

Chapter 5

Governor of Texas, Second Term, First Year, 1855–1856

"I have labored harder than I ever did in my profession."

E. M. Pease

Lucadia Pease summarized her husband's campaign for re-election as governor in 1855 by observing, "there seems [to be] every prospect of his being re-elected" in the midst of what she called, "an unusual degree of political excitement here, meetings, and speeches almost every night ...." She pointed out that the excitement was largely due to the rise of the American Party, commonly called the Know-Nothings, whose candidate for governor was David C. Dickson, then-Lieutenant Governor.[1] Former Governor Henderson wrote to Pease in June, asking for a statement of his position on the "Know nothin [*sic*] party" and pointing out, "A very large majority of us in this region [East Texas] ... differ with you in regard to your railroad policy—but that difference is a small thing compared with the questions of 'Know Nothingism'—we think that the Legislature will not agree with you in your railroad policy ...."[2] In San Antonio, the *Western Texan* reported a strong endorsement of the Governor from state senator

Sam Maverick. "Texas either as a Republic or a State, has never possessed a person better qualified for the Office of Chief Magistrate than E. M. Pease ... a thorough constitutional lawyer, a tried and reliable man ... entitled to the suffrage and support of the citizens of Bexar." Maverick did not entirely agree with the Governor in his projected improvements, but he believed that "a better and safer man, or one upon the whole, of sounder and more practical views, could nowhere be found." Maverick noted that the manner in which Gov. Pease had exercised his veto powers, "reflected the utmost credit upon him."[3]

Pease was re-elected on August 6, 1855, by a vote of 26,336 to Dickson's 18,968.[4] A. P. Thompson of Houston gave a revealing summary of issues in the election writing: "It certainly is not, from all we learn here by Telegraph and otherwise, premature to congratulate you on your election, by a splendid majority. Your friends here did the best for you they could. And when you reflect that a large railroad interest in this place was directly brought to bear against you ... I say you will think we have done well. After the Walker and King swindle ... people about here lauded you to the skies and declared you should be our next United States Senator." Thompson expressed indignation at having to remind voters about Pease's stand on issues that were for the benefit of themselves and the state.[5] Another tribute arrived after eleven one night at the Pease's home in Austin, although the couple had already retired. Lucadia wrote:

> The German band came upon the gallery and gave us a delightful serenade. They brought their music and lights, and the music was very fine ... We have not received Election returns from the whole state—still enough have been received to render it certain that Marshall is reelected—The election has been an unusually exciting one, the Know-Nothing party seeming determined to elect their candidate by fair means or foul, while the democratic party were many of them opposed to the views which Marshall had advanced, with regards to state improvements &c.[6]

Pease would not be inaugurated for his second term until December 21, and political activity continued into the fall. Lucadia described "a great Democratic Barbacue" [*sic*] on a warm day in early November:

> The procession formed on the Avenue the principal street—when the Gov and staff rode ... to the Grove prepared for the barbacue—I went in a carriage with our lady visitors. There were bands of music, and firing of cannon, and waving of flags, and cheering of the speeches, and feasting and great rejoicing over the downfall of Know-Nothingism—Came home, had tea, and then witnessed the torch light procession, which was very beautiful. They stopt in front of our house and called upon the Gov. to make a speech which was loudly cheered—Then we dressed for the Ball which was largely attended .... Had a very handsome supper, cold meats and turkeys, cakes and confectionary, coffee and tea .... Next day, the procession and speeches were continued ....

Lucadia knew that the Know-Nothings would have a "barbacue" with their hero Sam Houston present. She also wrote, "M. will probably invite him to dinner, and I shall have an opportunity to see him—We hear that the Know-Nothing women are to ride in their procession on horseback, ladies have taken strong sides on politicks [*sic*]. Some right amusing things have been said—some declaring that Marshall must be a foreigner 'he looked so much like an Irishman.'"[7] Houston accepted the invitation to dine with the Peases, and Lucadia described the occasion:

> We wanted to invite a few gentlemen to meet him, but were sadly at a loss who to ask as ... a Know-Nothing he would not like to see his former democratic friends, and M-would not entertain his new Know-Nothing ones. So we invited Dr. Ashbel Smith who is not much of a partizan [*sic*] [and two other men]. I think you have seen Gen. H.—His figure is very dignified, and he was very social and interesting in conversation— He addressed me as lady, and I have since

learned it is his universal practice to bestow that title upon his feminine acquaintance—But what bemused me a little, is that Doctor Smith has adopted the peculiarity—Dr. Smith has a fund of conversation upon every subject, and you are not left long in ignorance of his having traveled in Europe … . He speaks French as well as a native, and was here a few nights since with a Frenchman, who could speak but little English, and was interpreter for us unlearned.[8]

Lucadia also wrote with a touch of her subtle humor, "The Inauguration of the Gov. and the Inauguration ball are to be next week, and I shall probably go to the ball arrayed in my new dark silk, tho' I think it will not probably receive as much notice as my black silk did and that rare head dress two years ago." She had asked Susan Ward, then in New York, to send a dress, cloak, and bonnet. The dress and black velvet cloak were "handsome," but no plain bonnet could be found, and so Lucadia took bows and flowers out of the "ridiculous" white velvet creation she received.[9]

Inauguration Day was "mild as May," Lucadia observed. She made no mention of attending her husband's swearing in or his address. "At night I attended the ball and although I did not dance I enjoyed it very much. There was a great display of fine dress and an elegant supper."[10] The governor's inaugural address was brief but significant. He began by saying, "The proof of the confidence of my fellow-citizens, manifested by my re-election … fills me with emotions of gratitude which I find it difficult to express." He thought it appropriate to mention politics, "since our late election … is the first that has been decided by our citizens upon political issues alone." Because of Know Nothing opposition to immigration, Pease focused on it, saying that "the sages of the [American] revolution" had encouraged it, and in the most recent election Texans had shown "their devotion to these great democratic principles … discarding the heresies of the new political party … ." From there, however, Pease began to move away from broad American principles toward distinctly Southern sensibilities: "The rise of this party has given new vigor to the … abolitionists of the Northern and Eastern States … whose dangerous and disorganizing attempts to resist the execution of the laws of Congress, threaten the peace and permanency of the Union." He said he trusted that the "good sense" of people all over the nation would "extinguish the hopes of these fanatics who, for the fancied advantages of freedom to a race who are incapable of appreciating or enjoying it, would put at hazard the existence of a government upon which rests the hopes of the friend of the rights of man throughout the world." This statement placed him squarely on the side of Southern slaveholders. Pease's inaugural address came more than six weeks after the Sixth Legislature had convened and received a major message from him as the incumbent governor.[11]

The Governor had worked hard to prepare for the opening of the Regular Session of the legislature. Lucadia noted, "Marshall has very sore eyes, nearly used them up, in writing his message …. He had so much company in his office during the day that he was obliged to write it at night, and until late hours."[12] Pease's lengthy message was read to the legislators on November 6, 1855, the day after the session opened. He began, "It gives me no ordinary pleasure to welcome you to the capital, and to congratulate you upon the present condition of the State. We are receiving large acquisitions to our wealth and population; our citizens are in the enjoyment of a healthful season and abundant harvest … and our inhabitants are prosperous and happy in a degree unexampled in our former history." He told members that he believed that Texas would soon be "allotted that high position in political importance among the States … to which she is so justly entitled … ." He then laid out the issues he thought the legislature should address, some of which he had named two years before, and he proposed specific solutions to those issues.[13]

The first item on the Governor's list for the regular session involved the most immediate and financially immense topic, payment of the long-standing debt from the Texas Revolution. Although the Compromise of 1850 had made settlement possible, for five years Texas had rejected federal proposals for methods of paying the debt and claims. Pease invited members' attention to the Act of Congress of February 28, 1855, that proposed a final adjustment to the public debt of Texas and all claims against the United States. Pease pointed out: "In lieu of the five millions of United States five per cent stock still due to this State, under the Act of Congress of the 9th of September, 1850, the Act of the 28th of February proposes to pay the sum of seven millions seven hundred and fifty thousand dollars to those creditors of the late Republic of Texas, for whose debts the revenue of the late Republic were pledged, to be apportioned *pro rata* among them." The Governor provided members with copies of the act and made it clear that the Federal law could not take effect until the Texas legislature agreed to it and passed a law "withdrawing and abandoning all claims and demands against the United States growing out of Indian depredations or otherwise." He then went on to detail the financial and legal issues involved. He was so adamant that the legislature pass the requisite bill to grasp the greatest good for Texas ever offered by the United States that he recommended overriding a popular vote in a referendum. Pease noted that the acceptance or rejection of the act had been submitted to citizens in the most recent election, when only 25,427 of about 45,000 who voted "felt interest enough in the subject to vote upon it" with 11,609 for its adoption and 13,818 against it. But, he added, "under the circumstances, I do not consider the result ... any test of the opinion of the people ... upon the merits of the Act, and do not think it should exercise any influence upon our action in regard to it." The Governor emphasized that the Act provided for payment of all of the debt of the late Republic that had not been paid at par from the Texas Treasury and would pay to creditors about seventy-eight cents on the dollar of the "ostensible value" of each claim on July 1, 1850. He advised legislators that to accept or reject the Act they had to bear in mind the legal issues of the final settlement of the debt had to "be assented to by the United States, the creditors, and Texas." Pease made the conditions clear:

Texas alone cannot prescribe the terms on which it shall be settled, for she has already ... consented that the United States shall retain the five millions due under the Act of Congress of the 9th of September, 1850, until those creditors, for whose debts, the duties of the late Republic on imports were specially pledged, shall first file at the Treasury of the United States, release of all claim against the General Government for or on account of those debts, in such form as shall be prescribed by the Secretary of the Treasury and approved by the President of the United States."

The Governor continued: "The construction given to this provision by two Secretaries of the Treasury and approved by two Presidents, requires that all those creditors who hold any of the bond or promissory notes of the late Republic ... shall file such releases at the Treasury ... before any portion of the reserved five millions of stock can be issued to Texas." He reminded legislators that the state had objected to this construction and passed a law in 1852 with specific requirements that the United States and some creditors had refused to accept. Thus, he wrote, "I do not think any reasonable hope can be entertained that this debt will ever be settled, either under ... the original Act of Congress [September 9, 1850] or under the [1852] law of Texas." Nevertheless, he firmly believed it was a matter of interest to creditors and Texans that the debt be settled: "It was contracted in establishing and maintaining our independence, and every principle of honor and justice requires that we shall discharge it as soon as possible, since we now have the ability to do so." The debt was $4,435,638.78 on July 1, 1850. If paid with interest, Pease specified, Texas would have $705,459.32 remaining from the $5,000,000. By acceding to the Act, Texas would "receive of the five millions, the sum of $179,163.93 after paying creditors according to its provisions ... so that in a pecuniary view we lose but $526,288.39 by accepting the Act, instead of paying the debt in accordance with our own laws. This is a small consideration compared with the great importance of having this troublesome business settled upon terms satisfactory to our creditors." Additionally, Pease stated that Texas had withdrawn and abandoned all its claims and demands against the United States that came from Indian depredations during the Republic era, even though the Indians were the responsibility of the United States. He continued:

Upon a deliberate review of this subject ... I am satisfied that we ought to accept this Act. We shall never settle our debt on better terms, and it seems to be the only mode by which it can be discharged in any reasonable time. I, therefore, recommend the passage of such a law ... concurrently with another law appropriating out of the amount we are to receive under its provisions, such sum as will be sufficient to pay those creditors whose *pro rata* will be less than we owe them, the difference

between their *pro rata* and what we admit to be due them, which will
be about $118,901.42.

Pease concluded, "If this debt were settled, Texas would be in better financial
condition than any other State in the Union."[14] The Legislature followed
the Governor's lead and passed a bill giving assent of the state to the
Congressional act of February 28, 1855, and Pease signed it, surely with
enormous relief, on February 2, 1856.[15]

Another financial matter involved taxes. The Governor stated that on
November 1, 1855, the State Treasury held $1,582,742.68, plus the school
fund of more than $2,000,000. In addition, Texas had "a public domain the
value of which can scarcely be estimated." Taxable property was increasing "with astonishing rapidity"—the increase from 1853 to 1854 was about
27 percent, and from 1854 to 1855, about 17 percent. The state tax of fifteen
cents on each hundred dollars of the assessment for 1854, plus a poll tax of
fifty cents on free white males aged twenty-one to fifty, yielded $209,481.46,
and in 1855, $245,632.35. Additionally, business, occupations, and sales
taxes for 1854 came to $37,030.65, and in 1855, $27,570.60; the reduction
was due to a law regulating the sale of liquor. These revenues resulted in
"a few thousand dollars surplus" since the operating expenses of the government in both years was about $357,041.40.[16] Pease thought that taxes could
be reduced from fifteen to twelve and a half cents on the hundred dollars,
which would still produce an "amply sufficient" amount for appropriations
needed for 1856 and 1857. In the previous four years, he reminded legislators, taxes had been relinquished to the counties (largely for the purpose of
building courthouses and jails) and during that time government expenses
had been paid from the bonds received from the United States in the settlement of the Northwest boundary. The amount of bonds then remaining in the
Treasury was $1,575,000. That amount would pay for another eight years of
state expenses, but "these bonds having been received as the consideration
for the relinquishment of the right of soil and jurisdiction over a portion of the
territory acquired by our revolution, ought not to be expended for temporary
purposes; they ought rather to be husbanded and used for objects of public
utility, permanent in their character," Pease declared. Because state taxes had

been returned to counties for building purposes, that need had largely been met, the Governor opposed future relinquishment of state taxes.[17]

Public education remained a high priority for the Governor, who was disappointed that little progress had been made in the previous two years, although he knew that the existing law was seriously flawed. It required more effort than most of the ninety-nine counties had put forth, but Pease believed that amending the law would improve education for Texas schoolchildren. He suggested two possible ways to amend the public education law to make it more acceptable to the public. First, he recommended heavy penalties on county assessors and collectors who failed to report on the number of school-age children in their counties in the time required. Second, rather than dividing counties into districts, the law should allow county courts to disburse funds to teachers whom parents and guardians might choose to employ. He recognized that with changing times, the law would need to be changed. The treasury had then about $124,000, accumulated from the one-tenth of annual revenue set apart by the Constitution for school support; of that, $53,000 had been invested in the US bonds. Pease recommended that the funds be added to the $2,000,000 school fund, and that thereafter the tenth, plus income from the fund, be annually distributed according to the school law. Thus, Pease reasoned, the annual amount applied by the state for the support of schools would be about $120,000, and it would increase as tax revenue increased. For the further sake of public education, Pease believed that the school fund could be greatly increased by "judicious use" of the four leagues granted to each county for financial support of the schools. He did not think the value of these grants would be maximized if left with the counties, since thirty-eight of the ninety-nine had made no land selections and twenty others had made only partial selections; therefore, he did not expect them to take advantage of the opportunity and realize the full value of the land. He regretted it had not been set apart and managed by the State in the first place with a general fund for the benefit of all. Pease noted that in states where school land was managed by the state, the results were more successful than those in which the matter was left to local control. He projected that in a few years at least $3,000,000 would be added to the present school fund. If his suggestions were unacceptable, he recommended a constitutional amendment to authorize counties to sell their lands at not less than a minimum price, keeping the proceeds as a fund, and applying the income to school support.[18] The Legislature did not address these issues until its adjourned session.

Also for the second time, Pease invited legislators' attention to "the importance of establishing a State University, which shall afford to our youth all those opportunities for obtaining a liberal education, that are to be found in any part of the Union." He reasoned, "We cannot appreciate too highly the advantages of educating our children within the reach of parental authority, where they can daily witness the practical operation of our government, its institutions and laws, and become familiar with the habits and sympathies of the people with whom they are destined to associate ...." Pease was concerned that a portion of the University lands had still not been selected, and he suggested a "sufficient appropriation" be made to pay the expenses of selecting and surveying them. He also recommended that $300,000 in US bonds, then in the treasury, be appropriated as a permanent fund. The fund would be increased by proceeds of a gradual sale of University lands, and the income applied to the building and support of such an institution. In this way, the state would also be able to employ professors "in every branch of literature and science, and place the institution on a sure basis for future prosperity and usefulness."[19] No action was taken on the matter during the regular session.

Again, Pease called attention in his address to "the necessity of establishing an Asylum for Lunatics," because such an institution would allow those "afflicted with insanity [to be] restored to reason." Texas still needed a school for the deaf, and he added the blind to the same institution. He recognized that such an institution would make "these unfortunate classes ... useful members of society." He knew that, "Institutions of this character are necessary in every community," and he reminded lawmakers that they could not be founded and operated without the care of the State. Pease recommended that $250,000 in US bonds, then in the treasury, be appropriated as a permanent fund for each institution, and that provision be made for the erection of these institutions as soon as the income of these funds would permit. He wanted legislators to recognize that it would be good to furnish people at home with all the facilities "for improving and ameliorating their mental, social and physical condition, which are to be found in other parts of the world."[20] No legislative response was forthcoming during the regular session.

The ongoing matter of establishing railroads was the Governor's next topic. Although much of the settled nation had railroads, Texas lacked the essential benefits of the Industrial Revolution to make them possible. As the state grew ever more agricultural products, especially cotton, hauling by cumbersome ox carts was slow and expensive. Pease opened the important topic with a review of the troublesome reasons why a contract could not be made with the Atlantic and Pacific Railroad, a company that had never been organized, and he pointedly observed that all of those involved were Texans except for Walker and King. The Governor then suggested that it was up to legislators to continue or change existing laws for building and running railroads. He could foresee great advantages in having a railroad across the state, but he admitted that until it should first be built from the Mississippi River to Texas, "the uncertainly and expense [of transporting] iron and other materials to its point of commencement [in Texas] would be so great as to deter any company from undertaking even this part of it." He thought that a company might be found to undertake construction "from the head of permanent navigation on ... some of our bays, up to the line which is proposed that the Pacific road shall run, and then ... to the eastern line of the State, and west to the Colorado River."[21]

The Governor thought it was a good time to revise railroad legislation. Thirty-seven charters had been issued with "greater inducements for their construction, than were ever before offered by any government." Nevertheless, only one road of about thirty miles operated from Harrisburg on Buffalo Bayou to near Richmond on the Brazos River, and two others, the Galveston and Red River and the Galveston, Houston, and Henderson railroads were being built. Since so many charters had failed, Pease thought that it was inadvisable to renew them or to give relief to companies organized under them unless they were working on a road, could show that they had expended significant sums, and could complete the number of miles needed to be entitled to land under existing laws. He advised that no new charter be issued over a route where another road was being built or was near enough to

decrease its value. Also, every company should be required to conduct its
business in Texas, a majority of its directors should be state residents, and its
principal office should be in the state. New charters should be held to rules:
routes should be selected according to public need, books should be open for
subscription of stock, subscribers should elect officers, subscribers should
become a corporation, and charters should not be issued to speculators. Pease
thought that pursuing such a course would prevent "paying a premium to the
persons who have induced the Legislature to pass [their charters.]" As for
the three companies then building roads, Pease stated that it was not generally supposed that they would be able to build twenty-five miles a year after
January 30, 1856, and thus secure a sixteen-section bonus unless they were
assisted by a state loan. He reasoned that little progress could be made for
many years by private corporations unless such loans were authorized, or
by repealing the provision of the act that required companies to construct
twenty-five miles a year, because they would not presently yield enough
profit for capital investment without the advantages of land bonuses.
The Governor recommended passage of a law, similar to one attempted in
the previous session, authorizing loans of $8,000 a mile to enable the three
companies to extend their roads about seventy-five miles in three years. Such
a development would be a relief to those sections of the state, even though it
still left most of the state without railroads, he wrote.[22]

Governor Pease wanted more than railroads: "What our citizens need
is a general system of ... railroads, river improvement and canals, that will
extend its benefits to every section ... and give them cheap transportation of
their productions to a market." He thought that possible to accomplish within
fifteen years by "judicious use of our public domain, aided by a moderate
internal improvement tax; which will never be onerous to our citizens, and
for which they will be repaid tenfold ...." He described how the unappropriated public domain, estimated at one hundred million acres, could by its
gradual sale accomplish his plan. He projected that Texas might spend
twenty-five to thirty million dollars for internal improvements in fifteen
years, at the end of which all improvements would have been paid by sales
of the public domain and the internal improvement tax. The state would own
the constructed works, and the whole state, except for its northwest region,

would be furnished with railroads. Pease thought that this idea would have to be made permanent policy and built into the constitution, "beyond the reach of legislation." He projected that the entire state and county tax would be thirty-seven and a half cents on each one-hundred dollars, which was less than that currently being paid in three-fourths of the states. Even better, the increase in taxable property values statewide would enable reduction of taxes for government expenses, so in a few years the total state and county tax would not exceed twenty-two-and-a-half cents on one hundred dollars—the same paid in 1855.[23]

Pease then returned to his focus on railroads, stating that he was "well satisfied" that the interior would not have their benefits in the present generation unless they were built with state credit. If such a plan could not be adopted, he was willing to see certain routes designated for which the state would furnish the iron after the road bed was prepared by corporations; alternatively, he was willing to see the state become a subscriber for half of the capital stock needed to construct them, with the other half from individuals. "By adopting either of these plans, the same constitutional provisions would be necessary to establish a proper basis to sustain the credit of the state and to guard against its improvident use, as if the state were to undertake to construct them herself." He tried to convince legislators that they should keep in view "not only the present moment, but the future, when it will be inhabited by thousands where it is now has hundreds, and when its exports shall have increased a hundred fold." He concluded, "I have dwelt upon this subject at length, because my views in regard to it have been misunderstood by some and misinterpreted by others, and I felt that it was a duty I owed to myself, to place them properly before you and the people of the State." The Governor honored his felt duty, but most lawmakers disagreed with all or many of his policies on railroads, as evidenced by the fact that they passed more than twenty railroad laws during the session; most amended or supplemented existing laws for specific railroads and five created new companies.[24]

Another difficult subject, liquor sales, was on Pease's list for legislative consideration. An election had been held in 1854 on repealing a law permitting sales of liquor in any quantity less than a quart, and a large majority voted to abolish such sales. He pointed out that although he had signed the 1854 bill he knew it was defective, because it did not provide a penalty against selling alcohol without a license. He also knew that no simple law was a solution: "A close observation of the operation of such laws and their effect upon society and upon the evil which they propose to remedy, has produced the conviction with me, that their influence is anything but salutary." He observed that it was "extremely difficult" to confine liquor sales to specified purposes. "and in attempting to do this, it has been found necessary to establish ... a system of espionage into the affairs of individuals inconsistent with the proper enjoyment of personal liberty ... [resulting in] ... penalties and punishment entirely disproportional to the offence committed." He knew that these "extraordinary" means did not stop drinking nor prevent intoxication, judged by criminal court records of states with such laws. He thought that many of the "evils" caused by the use of intoxicating liquor could be prevented by a judicious law regulating its sale. Since most problems arose from selling it in small quantities in public places where most of the personal encounters produced "so much misery in society," he advised legislators to pass a law closing all "drinking shops." The Legislature passed a bill granting licenses for retail sale of liquors in quantities of less than a quart, and imposed a license tax. Sales to minors under the age of sixteen, school students, and slaves were prohibited, and no games were to be permitted where liquor was sold, but "drinking shops" were not closed. Pease signed the bill.[25]

The Governor then reviewed matters of frontier protection, especially Captain James H. Callahan's October 1855 punitive expedition against Indians in South Texas and Mexico. Pease provided the Legislature with a review of Callahan's activities, beginning with the need to send the company to protect citizens on the Guadalupe River in Comal and Bexar counties and on the upper Blanco River. If necessary Callahan's force was "to pursue any marauding parties of Indians ... in which case, he was author-ized to follow them up and chastise them wherever they might be found." The company had skirmishes in which they killed Indians and recaptured horses. The Governor stated, "Their services were unremitted and efficient ...." Depredations continued, however, in Bexar, Goliad, and other counties, "distant from the operations of the company," so Callahan had pursued the Lipans across the Rio Grande, where "a large party of Indians assisted by many citizens of Mexico" killed four of Callahan's men, and Callahan's company killed a number of Indians and Mexicans. Callahan had occupied Piedras Negras opposite Eagle Pass, and when attacked by Indians and Mexicans, had set fire to the town and retreated to the United States. Pease informed the legislature, "His report shows that he crossed the Rio Grande, in pursuit of Lipan Indians who were escaping with property stolen from our citizens, and I think he was fully justified in doing so, by the laws of nations." He added, "It appears too, from this report, that the Mexican authorities favored and assisted his crossing; with the knowledge that it was his intention to attack the Lipans." Pease described his letter to Callahan that justified the latter's conduct, except for occupying the village, and ordered him to return at once to Texas. "It is much to be regretted that it afterwards became necessary for him to burn that village ... but the fact that the Mexican authorities made common cause with the Indians against his command ... excused his conduct in this regard." The Governor stated that Callahan was selected because of his frequent service on the frontier, and "his known prudence and discretion ... ." Pease added,

> His high character for integrity forbids the idea that he had any other object in entering Mexico, than that avowed, which was to recapture from those Indians the stolen property that they carried with them in their retreat from the State, and to punish them for the wrongs they had done to our citizens. It is also a sure guaranty, they he would never have authorized any wanton destruction of the property of citizens of Mexico.

Pease's comment about Callahan's character and his not having entered Mexico for any purpose but to recapture stolen property raises the issue of Callahan's purported intent to capture slaves. Although slaves were property, it seems that Pease's standard of honesty would have required him to mention slaves to the Legislature if Callahan had indicated that slaves were involved. The term of service of the company had expired on October 20, 1855, when they were discharged, and Pease wanted the men to be paid promptly. Likewise, a bill for supplies for Captain Callahan's company needed to be paid. The fourth bill of the session promptly appropriated funds to pay the Callahan company expenses from the State Treasury, and the Governor was authorized to request repayment from the federal government. Shortly thereafter, a bill was passed to pay the six companies of mounted volunteers for three months of service plus $50.00.[26]

On what he must have regarded as a more positive note about the Indians, Pease reported that twelve leagues of Texas land had been selected and surveyed for the benefit of Indian tribes in the state under the law passed in 1854. One tract was near Fort Belknap on the Brazos River and the other was on the Clear Fork of the Brazos. The legislature set aside five leagues of the state public domain for tribes residing west of the Pecos River, and it was left to the federal government to select and survey the land or to purchase it from individuals. Jurisdiction was also ceded to the federal government to regulate trade and relations with the Indians on that land.[27]

Pease then turned to an earlier recommendation he had made for a constitutional change to increase the number of Supreme Court judges from three to five. The Fifth Legislature had not acted on the subject, and Pease was convinced that the ever-increasing work load of the court would result in appeals remaining undecided for years. He also advised increasing the salaries of Supreme Court judges. He argued, "Should a State, with a large surplus capital, be willing to avail itself of labor, of learning and of talent, and give a return what only amounts to a bare subsistence? Can Government expend its treasure for any object more laudable than ... to secure a wise and a just administration of laws?" Pease's attempt failed in the Sixth Legislature. Members were at least willing to pay judges a good salary of $3,000 annually (equal to the governor's salary) and to see that they had the library they needed, but the number of positions was not increased and caseloads remained too high for them to work expeditiously.[28]

On another matter of importance, Pease explained that he had "matured a plan for the issuance of head right, bounty, and donation certificates for land, different from that heretofore pursued, under which it has been discovered that numerous frauds have been committed, but the recent burning of the office of the Adjutant General has destroyed most of the original evidences upon which bounty and donation certificates were issued." Nevertheless, he hoped to present information to the Legislature at a later date. The fire in the Adjutant General's office was a major problem, since it destroyed the military archives of the Republic. Pease, who submitted a message from the Adjutant General, told legislators, "This great loss should impress upon us the necessity of providing suitable fire proof buildings for the security of remaining archives of our government." He warned legislators that the papers of the State Department were in an unsafe wooden building, and that the General Land Office was no longer adequate for its increased business. The Legislature responded, first with a bill to erect and furnish a large, fireproof General Land Office building, for which $40,000 was appropriated. The bill also made the Governor, General Land Office Commissioner, Treasurer, and Comptroller responsible for seeing to the construction and furnishing of the structure. The designated location was a half block at the southeast corner of the Capitol grounds. Once built, the offices of the Secretary of State, Governor, and Attorney General were to move into the safe building vacated by the General Land Office.[29]

Pease concluded in his November 1855 address to the Sixth Legislature that he had presented information that "I thought would be useful, and [recommended] such measures as seem necessary to remedy the defects that exist in [the state's] administration—to promote the moral and social welfare of our people, and to develop and improve our internal resources." He recognized that they would "originate others which you may think likely to secure the welfare and happiness of our citizens."[30] Thus, when it became obvious that more time was necessary to address a number of topics of major concern to the Governor, an Adjourned Session was called for July 7, 1856. At its opening that day, the Governor sent a short message to legislators recognizing that "extreme heat renders this an unfavorable season for legislation" but trusting that they could do the work the public interest demanded. He wrote that most of the important questions before them had been fully discussed in his previous address, and he urged their adoption.[31]

Because no legislation had yet been presented regarding codification of the state's laws, the Governor addressed members on that subject: "I have examined all the reports [of the commissioners of the code] with much care, and while I find some objections to them, I believe they are a great improvement upon our present very defective laws ...." There were codes for civil procedure, criminal procedure, a penal code, and a revision of general statute laws. Pease reported that "their adoption with modifications, will give us a basis ... to erect as good a system of laws as is possessed by any state in the Union." He added observations on lawyers:

> It is to be expected that the reports will meet with opposition, for no great reforms in the principles or the practice of the law, have ever been introduced into any country without encountering strong opposition from a large class who are always adverse to any innovations upon established usages, and I regret to say, that a majority of the legal profession are generally to be found in that class.

He trusted that a majority of legislators would not be influenced by such considerations, but that they "will, in obedience to what I believe to be the public sentiment of the State, give to these Reports a careful examination, and adopt them with such amendments as may ... be necessary."[32] The Governor knew that every lawyer would greatly benefit from having Texas law available in an orderly, single source, since from the state's chaotic beginning laws had never been fully codified. Once the legislature took up this extensive subject, the Senate concluded that due to time limits, only the Code of Criminal Procedure and the Penal Code would be considered; the Code of Civil Procedure would be postponed to the Seventh Legislature. The result was "An Act to adopt and establish a Penal Code and a Code of Criminal Procedure for the State of Texas," signed by the Governor on August 28, 1856. An appropriation bill that included a line item to pay for "printing of the laws and journals of the Sixth Legislature, including the code of Criminal Procedure and Penal Code ... and other printing for the adjourned session of the Sixth Legislature" was signed by the Governor on September 1, 1856.[33] The Governor then had to choose commissioners for the difficult task of fulfilling the law for "amending, revision, digesting, supplying, and arranging the Laws, civil and criminal of the State." Pease selected lawyers whom he well knew were capable of the task and whom he could trust: James Willie, then-State Attorney General and a former legislative colleague; John Woods Harris, former State Attorney General and Pease's longtime law partner; and Oliver Cromwell Hartley, Supreme Court reporter and compiler of a digest of the laws of Texas in 1850. Willie wrote in a preface in the published code book that the legislature adopted the penal code with "very material amendments" and the code of criminal procedure with "slight amendments." He compiled the necessary index. This book (in spite of the lack of civil law codification) must have become indispensable to Texas lawyers and judges, and they had E. M. Pease to thank for his leadership in bringing it about.

Pease's address to the Adjourned Session next described "a measure of acknowledged interest to the entire State, which I consider it my duty to press upon your consideration. This is the adoption of some system for the survey and sale of our public domain, which was heretofore prevented, on account of the lien hanging over it, for the security of our public debt, which is now happily extinguished." He wrote that it had occurred to him that a system similar to that used in the United States would be the best: the minimum price of land would be a dollar per acre (one-fifth less than the minimum price of inferior lands in the United States), and settlers should be protected with the right to take, at their option, a quarter or half a section, including their improvements at the minimum price established by law. Pease advocated that proceeds of sales of the public domain should be placed in a fund for educational and internal improvements. Also, a law should be passed with a time limit on location and survey of those lands.[34] No law regarding sale of the public domain was passed.

Pease mentioned that most of the important matters for legislative consideration were so fully discussed at the beginning of the regular session that, "I trust that you will be able to speedily perfect those measures which the public interest demands … ." He assured members he would "most cheerfully cooperate with you in all measures calculated to promote the welfare of our common constituents."[35] The Governor had both successes and failures as the session progressed. For example, the Legislature disagreed with his view that counties should no longer receive diverted state taxes. They passed a bill to relinquish the state tax for 1856 and 1857 to the counties to fund public buildings and gave county courts authority to divert the funds if public buildings had been constructed. Pease vetoed the bill and wrote to the Senate that if the bill became law, government expenses would have to be paid as they had in the past five years, out of bonds received from the United States, leaving the Treasury with about $600,000. He declared that nothing had changed his mind since the start of the session on the topic and added, "This policy has ... lead to extravagant and imprudent appropriations, both on the part of the State, and the different counties." He noted that appropriations had more than doubled since the beginning of paying them with bonds, and "I see no means of checking this ... except to return to the system of paying the expense of the Government from the proceeds of our State tax, when the appropriations will generally be limited to the amount to be received from that tax." Pease further expressed concern that the state should be using the bonds to establish a lunatic asylum and for education of the deaf, because "It is the duty of the State to provide such institutions, and it will have to be done sooner or later. If we fail to secure them now by the use of these bonds, we shall have to do it hereafter by resorting to taxation. The Legislature proceeded to override the Governor's veto.[36]

The Legislature passed a bill for improvement of the public education law, but the bill had nothing to do with Pease's vision. Support of schools first required the state treasurer annually to transfer specie held in the School fund (received from one-tenth of paid state taxes) to US bonds, and those funds were to be added to the $2 million Special School Fund. Interest from the bonds was then to be appropriated to the counties "for the use and benefit of the children of said counties, between the ages of six and eighteen years ...." County tax assessors and collectors were to list all the "free white population" of school age, and counties were to administer funds for "free public schools." The state treasurer became the ex-officio superintendent of schools. Legislators tacked on one final thought: "No school shall be entitled to the benefits of this act unless the English language be taught." The legislature also passed a bill and an amendment to it in the Adjourned Session that provided for investment of the Special School Fund in the bonds of railroad companies incorporated by the state and made the governor, comptroller, and attorney general a board responsible for withdrawing the school funds. Pease did not sign these bills, but he let them become law without a veto.[37]

For supporting university education, the Legislature responded with three bills that Pease signed. One authorized disposition and sale of university lands by having the fifty extant leagues set apart in 1839 surveyed and divided into tracts of one hundred-sixty acres each in six hundred and forty-acre sections, to be sold in alternate sections. The proceeds would then constitute a university fund. The second bill authorized the governor to have surveyed vacant or unappropriated lands belonging to the state with 22,250 acres or the un-located balance donated and set apart by the late Republic for endowment and establishment of the two universities. A third bill provided protection of land that had been or would be granted for educational purposes with no statute of limitation.[38]

Legislative response to Pease's requests to help those with special needs was not as far-reaching as he had proposed. First, an institution for education of the blind was established with a $10,000 appropriation and a directive for a board of trustees. The school was to be located in Austin, and the governor was to see that a "suitable" building was rented and a superintendent was appointed. The school was not to spend more than $5,000 annually. The Governor approved the bill on August 16, 1856. Second, an institution for the education of the deaf and dumb was also established with a $10,000 appropriation and the same directives that established the school for the blind. It was signed on August 26. Third, the bill for the erection and support of a lunatic asylum appropriated $50,000 in US bonds plus interest to erect a suitable building and the governor was to appoint commissioners to select a site between fifty and one hundred acres. The governor was responsible for appointing a "skillful physician, experienced in treatment of lunatics," as the superintendent. Ten thousand dollars was set apart for operating expenses until the next legislature convened. The bill, signed August 28, did not specify where the facility was to be built. A fourth bill set aside 100,000 acres each for the benefit of these institutions, and the governor was responsible for employing a competent person to locate and survey the land. The bill was signed

August 30. Even though these bills were not made law until the last few days of the session, and even though they were not as well-funded as Pease would have liked, he had to have felt relief that these first steps had finally been taken in Texas.

Railroads continued to be a contentious subject. When the Adjourned Session opened, legislators found veto messages awaiting them, including one for the Senate that was a firm rejection of another bid from Walker and King to charter the Texas Western Railroad. The Governor declared that the bid failed to meet his criteria for charters and asked directly, "Is there anything in the previous management of this company to entitle it to peculiar favor?" He summarized the earlier failure, adding that after Walker and King's attempted imposition upon the state and attempts to defeat its policy and interest, the current bill should be rejected.[39] The veto did not fare well in either chamber. The House Internal Improvements Committee reported that the bill and veto had been "duly considered" and recommended its passage, "the objections of the Governor ... no[t] withstanding."[40] The episode did not end there, however, as the Governor reported to Lucadia:

> I have just returned from the House of Representatives, where they have had a most exciting debate upon one of my vetoes of Walker & King's Pacific Railroad humbug. Of course I came in for a good deal of abuse from the friends of Walker & King, but the friends of the veto were lavish in their praise of me. There was great excitement when the vote was taken, the lobbies were crowded. It was generally expected that the veto would be overrided [sic] as it had been previously in the Senate, but to the utter astonishment of myself and every body [sic] else the veto was sustained by a large majority. The power of honesty and truth were for once an overmatch for corruption. The honesty of the House on this occasion will excuse them from much hasty and imprudent legislation.[41]

Pease's delight was short-lived, however. Legislators reversed their vote, and the bill became law.[42]

Pease fared better with a veto of a bill to incorporate the Trinity Valley Railroad, writing to the Senate:

> I mentioned rules [at the opening of the session] I thought should be adhered to in granting railroad charters ... Subsequent reflection has strengthened my conviction of the soundness of these rules .... The incorporation of the Washington County Railroad Company passed at this session contained all the provisions [I] recommend, and it was approved by me. This Act contains none of them. I feel unwilling to sanction any more charters of this character; I therefore return it to you for your consideration."[43]

This railroad bill was not re-submitted for his consideration.

Other transportation improvements interested the legislature. The most important bill that passed promoted improved river navigation, which Pease advocated. In addition to a $40,000 appropriation, the public was responsible for raising a minimum of a thousand dollars by subscription to support work on any given waterway, and a collection system was set up, requiring reports to the Governor on both finance and work progress, particularly on dredging shallow areas and breaking logjams. The legislature also incorporated the wondrously named Terraqueous Transport Company. Thomas Jefferson Chambers reported that he had "a new manner of vehicle for the transport of freight and passengers ... travelling equally on the land and the sea, and passing from one to the other." This vehicle would not require the expense of iron required to build railroads. The Governor joined legislators in their hope and approved the bill.[44]

Laws concerning slavery were a minor subject in this legislature. One bill created a small exception to the rule that free persons of color could not live in Texas without legislative approval, and another made it unlawful for slaves to carry firearms without a written permit. Pease vetoed the first of these bills, designed to permit three freed slaves to live for two years in Harrison County. He wrote that while that would seem to do no harm, "I fear at the expiration of that time, the fact that they have been allowed to remain ... will be urged as a reason for their longer stay ...."

This veto message began with a review of legislative history of slavery in Texas, followed by a position statement: "I think the policy heretofore pursued by the State, of excluding free negroes and mulattoes, is a wise one, and should be adhered to, for it is well known that their intercourse with slaves, tends to corrupt them and make them dissatisfied, and ought by all means to be avoided."[45]

The summer of the Adjourned Session was especially busy—and difficult—for the Governor. Lucadia's absence at that time and during the fall resulted in an exchange of letters that well-document the period, including Pease's earliest days in the Governor's House, their personal observations on the Legislature, his health, the family, and the couple's abiding love. The summer began with Pease's move into the official residence for the governor. Although long under construction, it remained unfinished. The house had been funded by the Fifth Legislature and was under construction by Abner Cook when the Sixth Legislature added $6,000 for fencing the grounds around the house, additional furnishings, and digging a well, all under the authority of the Commissioners of Public Buildings headed by Pease.[46] Cook was so busy building large homes at the time he contracted for the governor's residence that he could not meet deadlines there. Lucadia wrote in early 1856 that the house was to have been finished the previous September.[47] In late February Commissioner Pease wrote a letter, also in the name of Raymond and Shaw, informing Cook, "It is extremely unpleasant for us to call upon you so often in regard to the slow progress made with the work about the Governor's house." The Commissioners found that day that nothing had been done about the cistern or cellar, and "we are now notifying you that unless you proceed forthwith to have the cistern cleaned out and cemented so that it will hold water, and also to clean out the cellar, we shall employ some one [else] to do this work …." Furthermore, Pease warned Cook that he would have to pay a year's rent of $900 on the Ward's house if the Peases had to stay there past May 1.[48] Lucadia had thought the house would be ready in May before she left town, but it still was not.[49]

The Governor finally began moving in to the house on June 9, and that evening he described his placement of furniture to Lucadia, assuring her that he would move pieces wherever she wanted. He said he expected the next day to "take my supper and sleep in *the Executive Mansion*" [EMP emphasis]. He was able to do as he planned, and wrote Lucadia about it while sitting in their chamber. He asked wistfully, "How long will it be before my dear wife is here to sleep upon my arm again, and our sweet darlings to say their prayers and good night to papa?" The next day he reported,

> I still continue moving to day, but shall not get through, it will take about one day to remove our corn ... I am heartily tired of moving and wish you were here to divide the labor, or rather ... to consult and encourage me [and] the labor would be nothing. I find the house much cooler than the old one, the cistern water is excellent ... The heat is so oppressive that for the last week I have drunk at least two gallons a day.[50]

His next letter, written on a Saturday after a nap in their room, mentioned the fine breeze there, although there was none on the ground. Fortunately, the house was built on a small rise. Work was still not entirely finished. He reported, "I almost had a quarrel with Mr. Cook about the stable. I refused to receive it, and told him he must take out all the inside work, and do it over again in accordance with his contract or he should not have a cent for it."[51] On June 16 he wrote his wife, wanting to

> devote a few moments to one who has contributed largely to my happiness in life, and whom I fear I shall never be able to repay for all the love and kindness bestowed on me. Every days [*sic*] separation reminds me more forcibly how much I am indebted to you, my dear Lucadia. I had spent a good part of this day at the office writing letters and preparing for the meeting of the Legislature [the Adjourned Session would begin on July 7]. I suppose I shall have to give them a short message, but the spirit has not yet moved me, and it is useless for me to commence until just before the meeting, for any thing I might write now would not suit me .... You know my habit. This evening I have resumed the reading of Macauly [*sic*] ... I should enjoy it much more if you were here to listen to me [read it aloud]. Cleaning up the house progresses

> very slowly, and the carpenters work about the place [is] slower still,
> I think I am too easy and that your presence is needed to infuse some
> spirit into all hands.

The letter resumed the next day with condolence because he had learned
that Lucadia's uncle, Senator Niles, had died May 31. "I know how much
you all loved him, and I sympathize with you most sincerely," he assured
her. "Few men have ever served in such exalted stations and retained such
a simplicity of character and integrity of purpose as he possessed." He also
expressed concern that it would be two more years before he could visit his
own mother.[52]

The Governor regretted that duty required him to remain in Texas,
and he suffered once more with the long separation from Lucadia and
their daughters. Besides visiting (mostly with Lucadia's large extended
family) Carrie and Julie went to class, and their papa, writing in the third
person to them as usual, promised, "He hopes Carrie will be able to read
when she comes home, and if she is, he will have a nice present for her.
He hopes Julie has not forgot her knowledge of geography, and that Anne
will talk quite well when he meets them." He added, "They shall all have
nice presents ... ." In Connecticut the family delighted in abundant fresh
fruit including cherries and strawberries, and Carrie was certain that she
could send to her papa the strawberries she had picked.[53] He wrote Lucadia,
delighted that Carrie "makes herself agreeable, and sorry Julie is so bashful,
for if [not], she would be equally agreeable with Carrie. Though they are
our own, few ... will accuse me of partiality ... two of the most interesting
and better behaved children cannot be found, and dear little Anne too is
not far behind ... God bless and preserve them and their dear Mama, and
restore them to my arms safely."[54]

The physical labor required for moving into the new house as well as
household and garden work was carried out by the enslaved persons the
Peases called "servants." The Governor wrote to Lucadia about them at
the time of the move to the new house. Her excellent maid, Emily, would
be put to work cleaning the house for the first time on June 13. Although
Lucadia generally cooked for her family, Emily sometimes substituted.

When her master received a "fine mess of peas" from Mrs. Sam Harris, "I told Emily how to boil them with a small piece of the pork that you prepared so nicely and made an excellent dinner."[55] The Governor did not mention who moved furniture, but he spent June 18 "reading, writing, and giving directions about the arrangement of the house, as usual ... but I cant see that I make much progress. I am satisfied you would have accomplished more and with half the trouble in two days, than I have in ten." After a rain in July, he reported, "the boys all engaged in setting out Bermuda grass, that which I had set out the last rain is looking finely and I hope to have a fine grass plat in the front yard before you return." He mentioned, "Emily often enquires when you are coming home, she expressed great anxiety to see the children. She does very well this summer, though her health is not good. Together with Sam, Tom, and Dave they cleaned house after the enormous public housewarming party, and "it looks quite decent now— It was an awful sight the morning after the party."[56]

As the Adjourned Session of the Legislature approached, the Governor had been "compelled" to write most of June 21, although he had a severe toothache and "fevre." The day before, he had been able to arrange all the family's books in two cases, and he thought they looked good. During the summer, the Governor had such pain and fever from abscessed teeth that he was miserable and even incapacitated at times. He took quinine for pain, although it made his head "too flighty to write."[57] In early July, he reported that he was well, and although weak, worked most of the day. He remembered Carrie's birthday, promising her a large party the next year in the Executive Mansion, "if we all live." Arriving legislators called on him, although he did not feel like entertaining them.[58] He wrote after the Legislature reconvened on July 7 that he was unwell but working. He skipped "two picknicks [sic] and a barbeque" on the Fourth of July, although friends joined him on the Mansion gallery for a choice view of "brilliant" fireworks on the Capitol grounds.[59] Two months later he finally had two teeth extracted and admitted to Lucadia he wished that he had removed them early in the summer and "saved much suffering." She wished that he had filled rather than pulling the teeth, and she may have been in a position to know. Early in the summer she had all her upper teeth removed "*all in one setting*," [her emphasis) and although she did not complain about that experience, she noted with her usual self-deprecating humor, "you can imagine what a beauty I am ...." Her appearance was so changed, she did not know herself. She reported to her husband that on meeting a cousin she did not know, the woman exclaimed, "Is this Lucadia, been to Texas, and lost all her beauty and grown so old?" Lucadia intended to have some temporary teeth put in that week. Her husband asked that she not be troubled about her cousin's exclamation, "for to me you are more beautiful now than before we were married."[60]

Governor Pease struggled to produce the quality and quantity of work he demanded of himself despite physical pain, his family's absence, and his displeasure with the Legislature. In the first week of the session, he must have been annoyed in a new way when he received a letter from House Clerk H. H. Haynie: "I find the Executive office situated in Room 13. Will your Excellency please state by what authority this room is ... taken possession of." This inquiry followed a House attempt to find enough committee meeting rooms and to determine their occupants. Pease answered the clerk promptly: "For the information of the Honorable House ... by a law, approved 13th February, 1854, all the public buildings, furniture, and grounds ... are placed under the charge and general supervision of the Governor and Comptroller ... none of the rooms in the Capitol have ever been appropriated by law, for any specific purpose." Pease explained that since "the public Archives of the Executive and Secretary of State offices were becoming seriously injured" where they were held, he felt it was his duty to preserve them. He and the Secretary of State found rooms 13, 14, and 15 unoccupied, and he directed that "the Office of the Executive and Secretary of State should be removed into these rooms." In any case, the office of the Governor of Texas remained in Room 13.[61]

A week into the legislative session Pease expressed his unhappiness with the state's lawmakers in a letter to Lucadia:

The Legislature keeps me very busy, and it is probably well for me, that I am compelled to exert myself and keep about, or I should feel no disposition to do any thing—I gave them but a short general message, indeed I suppose I might have excused myself from giving them any, as this is but a continuation of the former session. I had to send them six veto messages of acts passed at the former session. I send you a copy of the general message and one of the veto messages ... .

Lucadia, worried that his fever was caused by hot weather or overwork, felt selfish to have left the move to the new house to him alone, and she also declared, "I have no patience with the Texas Legislators who meeting now in the heat of summer will compel you to work night and day ... I hope you have not written a message ... I fear that has kept you so long sick. You have never been sick so long when I have been with you ... ."[62] A week later, Pease was able to go to a ball given by the House speaker, "not for pleasure, but because I thought my absence would be ascribed to some improper cause." The Governor had so much to write that he worked at night by candlelight, affecting his eyes. As August began, he made a major declaration to Lucadia:

This summer has completely extinguished all desire for political distinction if it is to be procured at the expense of being separated from my wife and children. I might now be happy with you in Connecticut if I had not consented again to accept an office, in which I have labored harder than I ever did in my profession, and for which few will ever thank me. The question is often asked me, if I will be a candidate for Congress at the next election ... to do so, would require me to be absent from you, canvassing all next summer. My answer is No .... [63]

On an evening at seven when the thermometer read ninety-seven degrees in the library (the southeast downstairs front room) he wrote his wife, concerned that he had not heard from her about the health of the children, noting that the state election the previous day was calm, and finally making another definitive statement about his work:

I am in constant turmoil with the Legislature. I have already vetoed more bills, than all the Presidents and Governors of Texas who have preceded me. I think they will call me the veto Governor.

They occasionally sustain one of my vetoes, but the outsiders say
I am right, and that all of them ought to be sustained. I will be
known hereafter that I have been the Governor of Texas, and that is
more than can be said of some of my predecessors ... .[64]

The Governor felt redeemed the next day when he watched an exciting debate
in the House of Representatives on his veto of the "Walker & Kings Pacific
railroad humbug," but days later he was fed up again: "After being annoyed
all day by the foolish, improvident, and corrupt legislature which is going on
here, and which I have not the power to stop, it is a relief to come home and
read your letters before going to bed." The temperature had been as high
as one hundred degrees every day for the last ten and most of the cisterns
in town were dry, but he had a good supply of water and the "coolest house
in Town, so that I do not suffer any when at home."[65]

Although the Governor admitted, "I shall rejoice when they are gone,"
he wrote that he was giving the legislators a party—which he dreaded.
He was not fond of large social events, especially with politicians, and he
would not have the help of his gracious wife. Anxiety made him unable to
eat the day of the party, but during the event he had made himself "as agreeable as possible ... ." However, he wrote Lucadia that his "great party" was
called the "talk about Town ... the best one ever got up in Austin." An estimated five hundred people were present during the evening, and over three
hundred "staid to supper. The table was the finest I ever saw set in Austin."
He noted that the table included all of the brandied fruit and most of the
preserves she had made and stored. He assured his wife, "every thing was
arranged with the best of taste, for which I am indebted to Mrs. Sam Harris,
Mrs. Jack Harris [and two other ladies]. "They arrived on Saturday morning
and worked hard all day .... . They all wished that you were here, but I wished
for you much more ... ." He reported the next day, "I knew it was expected
of me, as the first occupant of the new Executive Mansion. It was the first
Public party ever given by a Governor of Texas, and I felt anxious that it
should be a creditable one, as it is the standard by which others ... will be
measured. The result has satisfied me, and I believe my friends were proud
of it."[66] The legislature, with only a week more in session, passed bills at a

furious rate. The Governor wrote Lucadia, "I hardly have time to read them, and then it takes time to write the vetoes that I have to send them. I have sent three in one day. If I did full justice to the state I should veto two-thirds of all that pass. I shall be through with them next Monday when I intend to go somewhere in the Country and stay a week or ten days."[67]

The Governor's vetoes including not only topics of vast importance such as railroad legislation but simpler matters of common sense. For example, the Senate bill to incorporate the Austin City Bridge Company would have permitted bridging the Colorado River within five years, anywhere within city limits. Pease wrote, "I think this company ought to be required to designate the site ... within one or two years ... it is by no means improbable that long before the expiration of five years, a company may be organized [to construct] a bridge within these limits for the privilege of charging half the rate of toll that this company is authorized to charge." (He expected tolls to decrease over time.) He objected to a fifty-year charter at a set rate for the same reason. He added, "These matters may be thought by some, not worthy of consideration ... but [if] this company shall select the only suitable site ... and acquire the right of extracting tolls for fifty years ... the question will then be asked why proper restrictions were not placed ... to protect the public from ... extortion." The bill was changed, largely according to Pease's recommendations, and he signed it.[68] Another bill fell to the level of unconstitutionality when the legislature voted to pay themselves *per diem* and mileage in their Adjourned Session, even though the Governor cited the constitutional limits of such payments to once each session. They overrode his veto.[69]

Pease's frustration notwithstanding, the Adjourned Session of the Sixth Legislature did pass the bills that the Governor most wanted and that had a lasting impact on the state: acceptance of the Federal law that made it possible for Texas to pay its debt from the Texas Revolution, creation of state institutions for the deaf, blind, and mentally ill, setting aside land in the public domain for education, and codification of the law.

With the Legislature gone, Pease's workload changed. The most far-reaching topic was his involvement in resolving Texas debt claims. Comptroller Shaw was in Washington in September, fulfilling a Legislative act of February 2, 1856, "to detect and prevent the payment of fraudulent acts of public debt and to provide for the collection of certain money due by the United States." He wrote Pease that he would have a final report once all the securities had been filed at the Federal Treasury. He included a letter from James Guthrie, Secretary of the Treasury, written to Shaw on September 11, asking him to return to Washington. Because the Joint Resolution of Congress of August 18 extended the time of presenting claims under the Congressional Act of July 28, 1855, and the act of acceptance by Texas on July 1, 1856, to January 1, 1857, Guthrie wanted Shaw present in December to examine the claims. Shaw asked the Governor's advice about returning, since "Mr. Guthrie is extremely anxious" that all claims be presented and examined by January 1; the Governor agreed that Shaw should go.[70]

In other follow-up to legislation, Pease accepted applications from a number of men who wanted the contract to survey land for the state's various asylums. All three institutions were located in the Austin area on vacant land. Administrative work for the Lunatic Asylum began with Pease's appointment of O. T. Branch as its first commissioner.[71] In a smaller but important topic following legislation, Pease received a proposal to have an artesian well dug to replace the cisterns that were filled with barrels of Colorado River water. Sam Maverick wrote the governor from New York about boring artesian wells, describing technology used at nearby paper mills, and he suggested their equipment inventor and operator to Pease.[72]

All sorts of other needs called for Pease's attention such as that for English translators as European immigrants moved to the state. The Governor received a letter from Jno. Twohig of San Antonio, who asked that the postmaster of Panna Maria in Karnes County be appointed as a notary public. Twohig explained, "Pana [sic] Maria is … settled by 180 Polish families, only three of which have title to the lands they occupy. Not one of them understands English …. You can plainly see that those poor people will be put to great hardship in going [seven miles to a translator in] Helena with their Titles for Record without the Same Being duly authenticated." He wanted his signature acknowledged before the notary, who would also be able to explain the contents of land-acquisition documents to the immigrants.[73] A number of other needs were met by private relief (payment) bills that went through every legislative session, some of which were signed by the governor and others were not. A few of these bills still involved the Texas Revolution. One bill named the governor. Amaziah E. Baker claimed the loss of as much as $7,500 in merchandise when San Felipe de Austin was burned at the approach of the Mexican army in March 1836. Baker's loss was "satisfactorily established by testimony of Gov. Pease," but relief was not granted to him. Although the Legislature continued to grant land to veterans and others, the Committee on Claims and Accounts thought that the monetary claims of citizens could not be paid.[74]

Governor Pease spent most of the first year of his second term on legislative issues. When he raised a topic that concerned him, he always made one or more practical recommendations for resolving it. He had the legal and legislative experience, business ability, and deep sense of civic responsibility to direct his high intelligence toward enabling legislators to grasp highly complex topics. He was not afraid to veto legislation, and he wrote careful messages explaining his reasons and what he thought would work better. Inevitably, lawmakers, the press, and citizens did not always agree with him, but his lasting accomplishments were impressive.

Chapter 6

Governor of Texas, Second Term, Second Year, 1856–1857

"The welfare of the citizens imposes high individual responsibility."

E. M. Pease

he second year of Pease's second term began quietly on December 21, 1856, with a reminder of Texas's Spanish foundation that was recorded in the Nacogdoches Archives. The Governor received a letter from H. H. Edwards asking for boundary information from the old Spanish Archives to help settle a lawsuit; an indication that citizens felt free to write the Governor to request almost anything they wanted.[1] However, the matters that drew most attention during the second year of Pease's second term centered on military responses to frontier protection from Indians, and a new problem, later called the Cart War, that was rooted in the attitudes of white Texans toward Texans of Mexican heritage and Mexican citizens. Work on improving river navigation also progressed, and advances were made in developing institutions to care for those with special needs.

Indian affairs came to Pease's attention in December 1856 when John R. Baylor, Indian agent to the Comanches on the Clear Fork of the Brazos River, wrote concerning newspaper reports of depredations; Baylor identified the Indians as "Northern Comanches," whom he said were receiving government funding. He wanted them punished, writing that, "war partys [*sic*] of Kansas Comanche are continually going to Mexico and [are] on our frontier for the purpose of robbing and killing." Baylor added, "The Indians on the Reservation frequently ask, why is it that those Indians are permitted to roam at large when they are confined to a small Reservation ...."[2] By mid-1857 Brevet Major General David E. Twiggs had assumed command of the Department of Texas. He first suggested a treaty with the Indians, because "carrying on a war like the present [one] is exceedingly annoying and harassing to the troops, and no good permanent results can be looked for." He quickly changed his mind and noted that "I am convinced a treaty with these Indians would be worse than useless ...."[3] By Spring 1857 Pease began receiving requests from local groups wishing to arm themselves for frontier protection and wanting rifles, not muskets, for that purpose because rifles were far more accurate at long range. John A. Wilcox of San Antonio began correspondence with the governor in April, stating that he had been elected captain of the Alamo Rifles and asking for arms and equipment that were not in the state arsenal. The company had adopted a gray uniform with silver trim, and, clearly proud of their patriotic eagerness to serve, Wilcox expressed hope that they could pay an in-person visit to the Governor. In May Wilcox wrote several more letters criticizing antiquated muskets, but he then found in the San Antonio Arsenal "a very neat, new-style percussion Musket, which the Alamo Rifles would be willing to adopt ...." Pease apparently agreed because in August Wilcox wrote that in light of continuing depredations in Goliad County, the Alamo Rifles tendered their services.[4]

Also during the mid-1850s, a serious frontier disturbance of another type arose. Texans of Mexican descent and Mexican citizens transported items, sometimes for the US government, by oxcarts from Indianola on Matagorda Bay inland to San Antonio. They moved food and other goods more quickly and for less cost than Anglos in the same business, and this situation apparently contributed to the anger of whites toward Tejanos and Mexicans. The prejudicial attitude of the Anglo-nativist Know-Nothing Party and the supposed sympathy of Mexicans for black slaves contributed to growing tension. The conflict began when white Texans wrecked Mexican oxcarts and stole merchandise. A notarized statement of Antonio Flores and others on July 27, 1857, from Bexar County specified that Flores, Gavino Brito, Francisco Martinez, Francisco Moralo, and Juan Flores had been fired upon on Saturday, July 18, while encamped in Karnes County with their five carts on their way from Powder Horn (an Indianola port depot) to San Antonio. Between three and four o'clock in the morning,

> about fifteen or twenty men, some on foot and some on horseback, approached their carts, and without any provocation whatever, fired their guns into the Camp of affiants, upon which affiants retired to a distance for personal safety, during which time the said fifteen or twenty men took, stole, and carried away four sacks of corn from their carretas, ...

The affiants further stated that the corn they were conveying was for government agents.[5]

No government protection was immediately forthcoming, but it is unclear if the official report was promptly received by either Pease or Twiggs, both of whom were focused on Indian depredations. The Governor wrote the General in August, stating his concern on having learned that Colonel Albert S. Johnston had been ordered elsewhere in the Union, possibly leading to the transfer of his regiment or a portion of it. Pease claimed that transfer of the troops would leave the frontier with even less protection and added encouragingly,

> Your high character and energy gives assurance to our citizens that you will leave no means untried to give them protection, but without a sufficient military force at our command ... no force but a mounted one will be of any service ... and even a mounted force, to be efficient, should be composed of men who are familiar with the situation and county. A regiment of such men could easily be raised ... I am well satisfied that under your skillful direction it would soon put a stop to the depredations ....

Twiggs replied that he did not know that any troops from Col. Johnston's cavalry regiment were to be removed, and in fact he (Twiggs) had already applied for an increased force for protection of the Texas frontier. Twiggs assured Pease, "The necessity of more troops here is most imperative, and if an additional Regiment of regulars cannot be sent, I am strongly in favor of having one of mounted volunteers raised. This regiment, if raised, should be mustered in for twelve or eighteen months, with field officers from the Army and company officers elected by its members.[6] Twiggs sent Pease a "sketch" of a bill for raising an organized regiment of mounted Texas volunteers, to be submitted by the Governor to the Texas Congressional delegation. He wanted troops to serve for a year, or for two if practicable. Pease duly submitted a bill and informed Twiggs.[7]

Meanwhile, J. A. Wilcox informed the Governor that cart men had been attacked again, and "Old Man Delgado, an aged and respectable citizen ..." was murdered near Helena in Karnes County. He added, "This is the third attack. I regard these men as public enemies, as outlaws ... as evil ... as insurrectionists [emphasis his] .... As an humble citizen, therefore I would beseech Your Excellency to act promptly and effectively ...." The same day, Nicandor Valdez and others from Bexar County wrote to the Governor, telling of being attacked by up to forty men who shot and killed one of their fellow cart men.[8] United States protection of the Mexican cart men carrying goods for the Federal government was assured on September 19 when Twiggs sent the governor a copy of Army Special Orders No. 122, which called for a military escort for cart trains. A detail of a subaltern, two sergeants, and twenty privates was to escort trains from San Antonio to Powder Horn and back.[9] Apparently, the troops did not arrive fast enough, because Pease, writing to Twiggs from San Antonio, announced, "Circumstances have rendered it necessary that I shall call out a company of mounted volunteers to suppress certain outrages against the Public peace ... in this vicinity, and the State is without arms at this place. I have taken the liberty of applying to you to obtain them from the Ordnance Depot in this City. The emergency is great ...." Pease asked for seventy-five rifles and one hundred-fifty pistols to be issued to Captain G. H. Nelson, who was to be the commander of the company. In response to Pease's written request, he received a letter from the Captain of Ordnance, J. M. McNutt, stating that General Twiggs still required a written request "setting forth the necessity."[10] McNutt received the required paperwork from the Governor, and the captain wrote Pease four days later with the news: "General Twiggs directs me to say in reply that there shall be no delay in issuing the arms and equipment to Captain Nelson …." Meanwhile, the Governor still had to deal directly with matters such as rations.[11]

Cart War troubles continued in mid-October when Pease received a letter from the Adjutant General's office at the Department of Texas Headquarters in San Antonio stating through sources that "Lieutenant George Bell, First Artillery commanding the escort to the train … from Powder Horn to this place … will undoubtedly be attacked between Goliad and Cibola [according to] an old and respectable citizen …. A body of at least sixty men are organized for that purpose."[12] Meanwhile, Captain Nelson stated that he was having more difficulty in raising the company than anticipated because local opposition intimidated and dissuaded men from joining. He still expected to have troops soon, and added,

I thought it best not to send any detachment until I could go with it myself, a miss step on first going into those counties would make difficulty [which he would prefer to] avoid. [General Twiggs] said that he had promised to give the company arms in direct opposition to a positive order from the war department but that as he promised he would take the responsibility of letting them go.

As Nelson was recruiting, the Army fortunately issued another special order that substituted rifles for muskets.[13]

The Mexican government was alarmed by the treatment of its citizens in Texas and issued a protest that added to Governor Pease's difficulties. On October 14, Manuel Robles Pezuela, Mexico's minister to the United States, wrote to Secretary of State Lewis Cass complaining about the treatment of Mexican nationals in the San Antonio region. Pezuela "presumed" that the United States would investigate and take all such means demanded by justice. The Minister sent another letter to Cass days later, stating that he did not doubt that the United States had already directed an investigation, but he could not refrain from suggesting that the outrages were a matter of public notoriety, and he cited newspaper articles including one from the San Antonio *Ledger* pointing out,

> The Constitution of the State does not discriminate between its citizens. The Mexican citizen, however humble he may be, has as much right as the proudest American, to the security of life and property under our laws …. We moreover object to the "resolution" because it works … against a class of our citizens (the Mexicans) who … respect laws …. To compel them, like slaves to carry a pass in their pocket is repugnant to our notions of constitutional liberty.

The article specified that the resolution was one adopted in Uvalde County prohibiting all Mexicans from traveling through that county unless they had a pass signed by some American. Similar outrages against Mexicans in other Texas counties are also "guilty violations of its constitution and laws and especially an infringement of the treaties of peace existing between the two countries."[14]

Cass immediately passed the problem on to Governor Pease on October 24, enclosing Pezuela's correspondence and stating,

> I have expressed to General Robles [Pezuela] my entire confidence that Your Excellency's best efforts would be [directed] for the protection of those who are exposed to the <u>indignities and maltreatment described</u> [Cass's emphasis] and I beg that such an investment may be made as will enable you to communicate to this Department the exact nature of the evils complained of, so that in its relations with Mexico the Government of the United States may be fully informed upon a subject which is likely to be productive of unpleasant consequences.[15]

Captain Nelson wrote Pease from Lavaca on November 8 to update him, first noting that with a full company, he went to Medina while court was in session and heard the sentiments of the people. "I assure you I was never more surprised in my life than I was to find as much prejudice and disregard for law and order," he wrote; adding that his own observation convinced him that the

> head and front of the difficulty: was in Medina, because in going through there with the train, "considerable taunts ... were thrown at us, and rowdies congregated ... drew a pistol on one of the cartmen, but Mr. Sternes happened to be near and ... prevent[ed] his firing ... calling out to me to wheel the company, which I did immediately letting the company remain halted in town until the whole train passed.

The captain assured Pease he had no doubt that "if the train has been without escort, some of the cart men would have been killed." Once the company passed through Medina, they met with no more hostility. Captain Nelson added in postscript, "The Company has acted in most orderly and circumspect manner, no member ... has ever attempted to argue or dispute any of the people, but in reply to all attempts to draw them into dispute have replied that they did not come to argue, and all they desired was the privilege of traveling the road unmolested."[16]

A deadly attack on a cart train belonging to C. L. Pyron was reported to Nelson by Lt. E. A. Stevens from the camp on the Cibolo on Nov. 24. "While getting up oxen," Stevens wrote, two men were killed, and two fled. The bodies of the two dead Mexicans were taken to Camp Cibolo and buried. An inquest was held on the bodies in Helena, but "the verdict amounts to nothing ... they ... seem to ... wish to exterminate the Mexicans and intend to do so even if they have to commit murder." Nelson wrote the Governor on Nov. 28, pointing out that those in charge of the carts had made the decision to go without military protection.[17]

Nelson reported again to Pease from San Antonio on December 17, noting that a lieutenant with twenty men was escorting a train of carts, "and I gave him instructions not to leave them until they reached this side of the Cibolo on their return." The term of the service of the company was nearly over, and Nelson hoped the men would be paid for their extra time. He informed Pease that the "balance" of the company had been discharged and company equipment placed in storage, subject to the Governor's orders. Pease wrote a brief reply, naming the paymaster, the paperwork needed, and instructions for returning equipage.[18]

In his address to the Seventh Legislature in early November 1857, the Governor noted that he would send information about the Cart War, and it was delivered on November 30. By then the two Mexicans in Pyron's train had been murdered. Pease described that event and told lawmakers, "No blame whatever attaches to Captain Nelson or [his] company as Mr. Pyron did not apply to them for an escort ... ." The Governor's sense of justice and his humanitarian values spilled over:

> It is painful to have to record such acts of violence and a subject of deep mortification that the law places no means in my power to prevent them. Such outrages cannot occur and pass unpunished in a county when the officers and the mass of the people entertain a proper respect for the laws. And it becomes a matter for your consideration, whether the citizens of a county that permits such acts to be done with impunity, should not be compelled to pay a heavy pecuniary penalty, this would, without a doubt arouse them to the necessity of preserving the public peace.
>
> It is now very evident that there is no security for the lives of citizens of Mexican origin engaged in the business of transport, along the road from San Antonio to the Gulf, unless they are escorted by a Military force. The term of service of the Militia now employed will expire on the 8th day of December, and unless some direction is received from the Legislature, to continue their services, I shall feel it my duty to discharge them on that day.
>
> It will require an appropriation of about $14,500 to pay the service of the company and for their subsistence and forage.[19]

As Pease's term came to a close, his final letter to Cass on the subject reassured the Secretary of State that prompt measures had been taken to arrest and punish the offenders and to put a stop to such outrages. He sent Cass a copy of his message to the Legislature detailing what he had done and assured him, "Laws will doubtless be passed … that will prevent such offenses for the future."[20]

On a more positive note in Pease's last year in office, the program of internal improvements for the state he had advocated began to advance. William Fields, the State Engineer, began sending Pease progress reports in February 1857 on the 1856 law for improving rivers. In addition to state spending, individuals were required to subscribe to that work for the water-way on which they owned property. Fields sent a subscription list and reported the amount subscribed for rivers and bays totaling $71,250, added to the state appropriation of $285,000. He reported from Galveston in April that he had been busy "fixing up contracts for workers upon the bays" who were then at work. From the central section of the coast, Fields planned to go to east, ending with "a long and tedious trip down the Sabine." Costs of needed, expensive machinery had not been considered by the Legislature, and Fields was concerned that contractors could not get advances against their costs. The engineer's next report in June declared that the Colorado River "has given me much trouble. The Raft is a terror to everybody … ." Consequently, he received no bids and finally awarded a contract of thirty to forty thousand dollars with little positive result. Fields reported in September that a channel had been cut through Cloppers Bar at the mouth of the San Jacinto River, ahead of schedule and "deeper than the Bay for a mile or two below, and we hope it may remain so, but of course it is impossible to say what will be the result." The next month, a rise on the Brazos River prevented scheduled work on the large $50,000 contract for it; otherwise, workers would have completed the first section between Columbus and Richmond. Pease's term expired before the river clearing project was completed.[21]

Frontier concerns doubtless took most of Pease's attention during his last year in office, but he also maintained a continuing interest in creating institutions for the education or care of those with special needs. Locating and surveying land for the new state institutions took months, and land surveyor Robert Cruzbar's June 1857 report announced that he had fully completed all the field work in locating and surveying the Asylum and University lands. Wanting to a good job of the maps and field notes neces-sary, he asked for three months to complete his work, and submitted a bill

for $9,000.[22] Apparently, some Texans were growing anxious for the prom-
ised facility for the mentally ill. Pease received a request from Huntsville
inquiring if the State "has anyplace at the Capitol … for keeping Lunatics.
Our county has one such man, he is docile … at times some rationality—let
out to the lowest bidder the man goes into the hands of a man who cares
nothing … for him …." York Rite Masons in Washington (Texas) wanted
to know when preparations would be made for the reception of lunatics.[23]
When the Seventh Legislature convened, Pease submitted a summary of
the status of state finances, and noted that the small annual appropriation
of five thousand dollars made by the last legislature for the blind and deaf
asylums was been sufficient to put them in operation, but that delays in site
selection for the Lunatic Asylum had occurred. The Commissioners realized they lacked knowledge about the care of patients and had to find help
before proceeding with building.[24]

Many topics of less general importance demanded attention during the
last year of the Governor's term. He continued to receive inquiries about
land. For example, William Crain of Illinois wrote, stating that his wife's
father, James A. Long, had died in Texas in 1827. Crain thought that Long
had received "a league and a labor on the Brassos [sic] river in San Felipe—
is supposed to be worth something." He wanted an answer from Pease.[25]
Texas still had land that had not been explored by white settlers. B. E. Tarver
returned from a lengthy tour of the state north of the Red River, an area "nearly
equal in extent to … Ohio … comparatively unknown …." He was referring
to the Panhandle. Tarver wrote the Governor, "Knowing the interest you feel
in all that concerns the material interests and property of our state … I [call]
your attention to the character … of this interesting region." He continued,
"The question naturally arises why should this immense territory in our own
state be virtually closed …? It seems that the great government of the United
States has for years labored in vain to subjugate a few thousand half naked
Comanches!" Apparently, Tarver had not encountered them.[26]

Pease had much work and little staff to help. On at least one occasion
the Governor, rather than his secretary or a clerk, had to serve as a meeting
secretary. The Minutes of the Board of School Commissioners of March 21
show that the subject was not education but the relation of the Special

School fund to railroad financing. Pease was so accustomed to writing his own messages of all sorts that it may not have seemed unusual to him to be taking minutes.[27]

The subject of cotton, the crucial Texas cash crop, came across Pease's desk in two ways. The "Office of Cotton Weighter" [sic] established by the Sixth Legislature resulted in applications to Pease from port locations named in the act for the job. The Governor could add other places if he chose; for instance, Jefferson citizens asked for appointment of a suitable person, and Pease directed a clerk to make out a commission for someone they named. The global importance of southern cotton was illustrated by a prospectus Pease received for a proposed journal, *Cotton Supply*, from R. Adeane Barlow in Manchester, England. Barlow proposed a journal focused on issues in areas that supplied the growing British cotton manufacturing industry. He was interested in "the great Negro question now threatening to inflict such distress ... so long the only element of discord in the American Union, the permanency and prosperity of which are desired by every intelligent European." He was opposed to slavery, but he sought answers from leaders in the Southern States by correspondence with planters.[28]

Toward the close of Pease's term, his clear memory of the Texas Revolution and early statehood combined with his eloquence in a memorial on the death of James Hamilton, a former governor of South Carolina and a financier of the Texas cause. Pease praised Hamilton as "one of the first who raised his voice in our behalf at the commencement of our revolutionary struggle, and his services and means were freely given to our cause both before and after he became a citizen of the Republic. His high standing and influence in the world, contributed much to the successful issue of our Revolution."[29]

The Seventh Legislature opened about six weeks before the beginning of a new gubernatorial term, and so Pease made a biennial address to the session on November 4, 1857, with only a little more than a month left in his term as governor. His message began with this observation: "The pleasure experienced in meeting you on this occasion, is somewhat alloyed by the fact, that our usual prosperity has been interrupted, in some sections of the State, during the past two years, by a failure of crops caused by a

drouth unexampled in the annals of the country." Texans were then farming (or attempting to farm) farther west than ever before, and they may
have found themselves in land that was better suited for ranching rather
than for farming. Still, Texas had "abundant cause for congratulation, in
the bountiful supply with which other sections have been favored" as well
as remarkable public health, a population increase, and rapid extension of
settlements. He believed that "These blessings should fill our hearts with
devout gratitude ...." Pease thought that many factors made the session
unusually interesting. One was "financial embarrassments" in other parts of
the country due to the rapid increase of banks, "whose improvident issues
of paper money have led to reckless speculation and an extension of credit
beyond the reasonable demands of business." Since Texas had been only
slightly affected due to its prohibition of banks, he added with a broad
hint, "It is hoped that the present financial crisis and the causes that have
produced it [the Panic of 1857], will not be disregarded by those who are
seeking to change our policy in regard to Banking."[30]

The Governor provided information on the financial condition of the
state, gratified by "a very considerable" increase in the value of taxable
property over the past two years. The value of the assessment for 1856 was
about $284,213.79, an increase of nearly 8 percent over 1855. In addition
to property taxes, poll taxes and taxes on occupations and merchandise
sales contributed to state income. Net revenue after deducting expenses for
assessment and collection, as well as the 10 percent set aside for the schools,
was $229,289.53. The total valuation for 1857 improved even more: the
amount of $327,662.88 showed an 11-percent increase, with a net revenue of
$255,044.05. Net revenue for the two years was about the same as expenses,
including support of the insane asylum, schools for the blind and deaf, and
the penitentiary. On November 1, the state treasury, exclusive of the school
fund, held approximately $1,230,000, but $470,000 was subject to existing
appropriations. The Governor told legislators that expenses for the next two
years would be greater because of additional judicial districts for the frontier counties and costs of criminal prosecutions, which under the Code of
Criminal Procedure were to be paid by the State to clerks and sheriffs. Pease
noted that the treasury had the funds for these expenses, but if it continued

to rely on those funds alone while returning to the counties the taxes of the two ensuing years (as had been done during the previous six years), "we shall find ourselves with an exhausted Treasury in 1860 and 1861." He stated plainly, "It has, therefore, become a matter of necessity that we shall now abandon that practice." He projected, however, that the *ad valorem* tax could safely be reduced from the rate of fifteen cents to ten cents on the hundred dollars, and the poll tax from fifty to forty cents. He emphasized, "*A thorough investigation of this subject has satisfied me that this reduction may be made and that we shall still have ample means to meet all appropriations here recommended, and all others that justice and sound discretion may dictate.*" [EMP emphasis.][31]

Next, the Governor wrote that he could not omit calling attention to the fact that some creditors of the Republic still had not received payment. In particular, the loans of Samuel Swartwout and others during 1836 had not been repaid justly because of a legislative mistake that Pease explained, concluding, "I feel that the honor and the reputation of our State require that they should be paid."[32]

He then turned to the subject of the public schools, noting that the principal of the School Fund had increased to $2,200,000 since two laws of the previous session added to the $2,000,000 designated by the Constitution. One law set apart 10 percent of state revenue for the fund, and the other added sales proceeds of public land in the Mississippi and Pacific Railroad reserve. Pease recommended a bill to add proceeds of public land in other parts of the state, thus increasing the fund by more than $100,000 annually. Nevertheless, given the increasing numbers of students, this fund could not begin to pay for public education statewide. He commended the report of the State Treasurer, Ex-Officio Superintendent of the Common Schools, for serious consideration. Once again, the Governor called attention to the importance of establishing a state university and wrote: "No country was ever better situated to commence such an undertaking. We have ample means in the Treasury, not needed for other objects, with which to erect ... buildings ... ." He pointed out that 221,500 acres was already set apart, and with properly managed proceeds for an endowment, it would allow for employing "the ablest professors in every department of learning."

A remaining fifty leagues of university land had been selected and surveyed according to the act of the previous legislature, but some of the land had not been properly surveyed and divided into quarter sections with alternate tracts to be sold. Therefore, Pease did not advise selling any of the land until all of it was ready for sale.[33]

Pease delivered the first progress reports of schools for the blind and deaf as well as the lunatic asylum to the legislature. He noted that the two schools opened during the year with the "small" annual appropriation of $5,000, but that the trustees of each encountered many difficulties and that much credit was due to them for their efforts, which were uncompensated. He continued, "The education of these unfortunate classes of our population is no longer an experiment in this State." The school for the blind had seven pupils in the previous month, and the school for the deaf, eleven pupils. The Governor praised the trustees and superintendents, stating, "Few establishments of the kind have been as successful in the first year of their organization ... ." Pease then recommended purchase of permanent sites and erection of buildings.[34]

The lunatic asylum did not get off to such a rapid start. After a delay in site selection, fifty acres in the Austin area was chosen. The cost of the land was $2,500, but only $250 of that amount was paid by the state; "the residue by the citizens of this place." The unusual comment that citizens of Austin paid $24,750 for the land raises the question of who they were. The number of those who had enough interest in this matter, plus the means to contribute, would have been few. Perhaps one was William Fields, the state engineer; another may have been Thomas Jefferson Chambers, who had owned at least part of the land and who resolved a title problem when he signed a release for it. Two others might have been state controller James Shaw and state treasurer James Raymond, both of whom had been drawing good state salaries for years. The most likely person was Pease himself, who had both the commitment and the means to make a significant contribution. However, Pease's personal financial records do not indicate a contribution to the state for this land. After acquiring the land, the Commissioners found that they lacked knowledge about running the institution. They needed someone familiar with institutions for the treatment of insanity, and so they hired a qualified superintendent to guide their first decisions on building the facility.

Pease noted that the 400,000 acres appropriated by the previous legislature for the three institutions and an orphan asylum were all within the Mississippi and Pacific Railroad reserve. The area was settling rapidly, and the land should soon be sold for good prices, Pease thought.[35] The railroad reserve was a strip of land thirty miles wide on both sides of the proposed route along the thirty-second parallel, available for the company to select twenty alternate sections of land for each mile of railroad completed after it had built fifty miles. The bill that set up this plan was passed in December 1853, but since the railroad company failed to meet the original contractual agreement, it remained for the state to sell the land.[36] Pease then continued with a detailed analysis of how the state could make the sales while respecting the interests of those who had already settled on that railroad reserve from late 1853 to mid-August 1856. The whole message was a good example of his attention to the needs of a rapidly developing state.[37]

In another land matter, running and marking the boundary between Texas and US territory from north of the Red River had been authorized by the Fifth Legislature, and Texas asked Congress to pass a law for the Federal work as well. Pease noted that he knew of no law subsequently enacted by Congress, but Texas settlers were then surveying that land, and the cooperation of the United States should not be delayed.[38]

Pease also submitted the first annual report of the Board of School Commissioners that was created by the act to provide for investment of the special school fund in railroad company bonds. Only two loans had then been made by the board, both of them to the Houston and Texas Central Railway. One loan was for $150,000 the previous April; the other for $60,000 on October 28. Meanwhile, the Buffalo Bayou, Brazos, and Colorado Railway Company had applied for a $150,000 loan. The governor stated that the law authorizing these loans had not proved to be as good for the companies as their advocates had promised. Amounts loaned were not enough to give them much relief, and they could not get a second loan after their road was mortgaged to the state. The problem, Pease wrote, was the cost of iron. Moreover, people in Texas who had money "find more certain and more profitable modes of employing it than investing it in railroad stock ... ." Still, Pease did not feel disposed to recommend any other system of providing state aid and was in favor of retaining the constitutional restrictions on the legislative support for internal improvements: "The present system was adopted after mature deliberation, and seems to be satisfactory to a great majority of our citizens ... ." After covering more details on railroad laws, he wrote, "It is much to be regretted that we did not at first, adopt the principle of granting to all our railroad companies, similar powers and privileges, if we had, there never would have been any inducement for besetting the Legislative halls with applications for extraordinary favors." He suggested removing that inducement.[39]

Pease's knowledge of railroad building at the time came notably from correspondence with Paul Bremond, President of the Galveston and Red River Railroad, founded in 1855. Bremond wrote Pease in April 1857 about progress on the line, which had become the Houston and Texas Central Railway in 1856. It was one of the few that actually graded a road, and he wrote Pease to ask for an examiner to certify work so that state funding for it could be made available. Bremond documented the massive amount of human physical labor involved in road building, noting that planters would soon be able to take hands from the fields and make from three to five hundred men available for hire. Iron for the rails was being ordered from Europe, and 20,000 of the wooden ties had been cut for one section. More than a year later, Bremond wrote again, to report that 350 hands were working on grading and 500 in all were engaged in getting timber, building culverts, and more. Five miles of iron for the Hempstead Road "is now all afloat" direct from England.[40]

Pease then moved on to the penitentiary report, noting that affairs appeared to have been well-managed there. For more than a year, a large number of convicts had been manufacturing cotton and woolen goods that found a ready market. Officials expected that the penitentiary would, with convict labor, be self-supporting and even profitable instead of requiring the usual $20,000 appropriation.[41]

The penal and criminal procedure codes that Pease had envisioned and that became law in 1856 came under the Governor's review. He noted that the Penal Code, in force for nearly a year, had shown some omissions and points that needed correction, but in general he thought that the code should be favored by the public. He argued that, "The most salutary changes in the law often meet with opposition, until the community, for whom they are designed, become[s] accustomed to their operation ... ." The Governor submitted the report of the Attorney General, containing suggestions for amendments to both the Penal Code and the Code of Criminal Procedure.[42]

Pease reminded lawmakers that they were responsible for providing for the census of free inhabitants and electors in preparation for a new apportionment of state senators and representatives. He suggested that county tax assessors and collectors could do this at the same time they counted children of school age and suggested imposing a penalty for failure to make legislative apportionments, which at times had previously been estimated for lack of information. He also advocated gathering information on the amount of land in cultivation and the value of agricultural, mechanical, and manufacturing productions. Then for the third time, he emphasized the importance of a geological survey, and added weight to his insistence, stating, "Public opinion demands that this measure shall no longer be delayed."[43]

Next, Pease noted, with his usual attention to detail, that a constitutional amendment proposed by the previous legislature that would have authorized the governor to make temporary appointments to fill vacancies in state offices until the positions could be filled at a general election had failed. "You are aware," he observed, "that to adopt an amendment to the Constitution, it must receive a majority of the votes of those who voted for Representatives." In the previous election, that number was 48,700, but several counties failed to make any return of the votes for Representatives. Therefore, he concluded, counting those who voted against it with those who failed to vote, the total "no" vote was 29,944 while only 18,756 voted for the amendment. The Governor thought that the indifference of voters on such important matters made it difficult ever to adopt any amendment and led to the conclusion that the legislature should ask electors to consider making it easier to amend the Constitution:

The situation of the State has changed so materially since our Constitution was framed, [in 1845] that in many important particulars, it requires radical amendments to adapt it to our present wants.

Then we had but thirty-six counties, with only about a hundred and fifty thousand inhabitants—now we have one hundred and sixteen counties, with a population of more than half a million, scattered over nearly three times the extent of country they then occupied. Greater changes have occurred here, in a period of twelve years, than usually happened during several generations in older communities, where it is found necessary for each succeeding generation to revise their Constitution.[44]

In various other matters, Pease noted that the report of the State Engineer regarding navigation improvements was pending. The governor subsequently reported that the State Engineer's report showed spending totaling $24,900 on the Colorado, Brazos, San Jacinto, and Guadalupe rivers.[45] This very large expenditure of money and labor likely alleviated river transportation in some places for only a fairly short time, given that Texas rivers have naturally shallow gradients and little continuous flow for lack of constant rainfall. Logjams were not pushed out by the force of rapidly moving water, and the mouths of rivers naturally silted in, creating sandbars that boats and ships could not readily cross. Therefore, Texas remained without any adequate means to move heavy cargo, most especially cotton.

The Governor reported that frontier counties had been subject to some Indian depredations during the previous two years, but less than before. He commended General Twiggs for doing all that he could to protect citizens, but commented that his force was simply too limited. If no additional troops could be sent, Twiggs wanted a regiment of mounted volunteers to be called into service, and he would communicate with Congress accordingly. Pease added a comment on the Cart War, promising a special message on the subject and how it had been handled.[46]

The Governor then delivered a chilling commentary on a far larger topic:

Our relations with the Federal Government and the states composing it, are a subject of deep anxiety to every patriot. The rapid strides in the last few years by a party in the Northern States, organized with the avowed object of endeavoring to effect the abolition of slavery as it now exists in fifteen States and some of the territories, has very justly excited fears for the perpetuity of the Union. Such movements tend inevitably to destroy that harmony which should exist between different parts of the same nation, and cannot fail, if preserved in, to produce the most disastrous results. The people of Texas are attached to their domestic institutions; they ask nothing from them, from the Federal Government, but those rights guaranteed by the Constitution, and any infringement of these rights will never be submitted to.

Although he took a hard position with such a statement, he then softened it a bit by pointing to the election of the Democratic candidate James Buchanan as President in 1856:

The threatening aspect this subject assumed during the last year, has been changed by the result of the late Presidential election. We have every reason to expect that during the continuation of this administration of our present Chief Magistrate, the rights of the South will receive the protection guaranteed by the Constitution, since his policy, thus far indicated by his official acts, conforms to the principles upon which he was elected.[47]

Pease then mentioned the deaths during the past year of Judge James Webb of the Fourteenth Judicial District, Judge Abner S. Lipscomb of the Supreme Court, and Senator Thomas Jefferson Rusk. Once again, his memory of Texas history and his own values were evident:

The two former had occupied high judicial stations before they removed to this country. They participated largely in the public affairs of both the Republic and State of Texas, and enjoyed a high degree of public confidence. ... Their virtues and their public services will ever keep them in grateful remembrance.

Gen. Rusk had been an important actor in all the prominent scenes of the eventful history of our Republic. Often called to places of high trust in the field and in her councils, he proved himself equal to every emergency. When called to a more extended field of usefulness, he established for himself a reputation in the councils of the nation that placed him in the first rank of statesmen, and reflected lustre [*sic*] upon the State whose service his life had been devoted.[48]

The Governor concluded his message by noting that although his remaining time with the lawmakers was short, he would be pleased to cooperate on measures that the welfare of the citizens demanded. Protecting the great future of Texas, he said, "imposes a high individual responsibility upon those who are intrusted [*sic*] with the direction of its public affairs. It is my ardent prayer that we may, under the favor of Providence, be able to acquit ourselves of that responsibility ... ." He tendered to the people of Texas, "my sincere gratitude for the many evidences ... of their confidence", and concluded somewhat cryptically, "In retiring from the responsible station with which they have twice honored me, the only regret I shall feel, will be, that I had not the power to serve them as my inclination prompted."[49]

The Governor had done all he could under difficult circumstances in four years. His largest accomplishment, leading the legislature through the process that resulted in payment of the Republic's debt, not only paid the state's creditors $7,500,000 in cash, it also provided $5,000,000 in US bonds to the Texas treasury. Those bonds enabled payment of governmental operating expenses for both long and short-term purposes. On more than one occasion, it was necessary to cash bonds.[50]

Other major goals of the Governor's, such as a system of public education, simply could not be accomplished in the 1850s, but in addition to working toward that goal as circumstances allowed, he made a unique and lasting inroad by making knowledge available for legislative members and state employees. He had noted in his message at the opening of the Seventh Legislature that a state library was being created by a Sixth Legislature appropriation of five thousand dollars. The Governor had discretion over state library expenses; hence, for purchases. He wrote, "In the selection of books, care has been taken to order [those] useful to the Legislature and those engaged in other departments ... ." Another appropriation was made for "fitting up the Library room" and for a librarian.[51] Months before the library bill was signed, the Governor had talked with E. H. Cushing of the Houston *Telegraph*, who wrote that he had complied with Pease's request for back copies of his newspaper for the State Library. Pease corresponded for months with S. S. Nichols, a Philadelphia bookseller, who provided catalogs of public libraries, Boxes from Nichols began arriving in July, containing *The Americana Almanac* (twenty volumes), the *Encyclopaedia Britannica*, George Bancroft's *History of the United States* (six volumes), *Niles' Register* (fifty-one volumes), and Henderson K. Yoakum's *History of Texas*. The thirty-three-title invoice totaled $348.94. A $207.00 invoice included William H. Prescott's *History of the Conquest of Peru*, John Lord Campbell's *The Lives of the Chief Justices of England*, and a botanical history. More boxes contained Plutarch's *Lives*, a chemistry text, a history of Spain and Portugal, and other works totaling $278.19. In the absence of an appointed librarian, Bird Holland, acting librarian, deposited these books in the library.[52] Pease received a list from New York publisher Wiley and Halstead that included a volume on bookkeeping and accounting as well as Rev. George B. Cheever's *Windings on the Waters of the River of Life*. Toward the end of his years as governor, Pease may have had long thoughts on the windings on such waters, indeed.[53]

Pease's devotion to education was further evidenced by a small receipt in his files, written by Nichols and dated December 11, 1857: "Received of E.M. Pease Governor of the State of Texas, the sum of Five hundred [dollars] as an advance to be used in the purchase of books for the Texas State Library." Although it is not clear whether this was a personal or state treasury advance, the receipt does not indicate it was from the state, but rather, from Pease himself. If so, he was the first donor to what began as a one-room library and has become the Texas State Library and Archives Commission. Three days after Pease left office, he wrote a statement certifying that he had drawn five hundred and five dollars from the treasury on July 17, 1857, for the purchase of state library books from Nichols. Therefore, the last item in Pease's papers as governor pertains to education for legislators and state employees through books that he chose for the new state library.[54]

Another example of Pease's values had deep roots in his New England heritage, which his wife shared. As Governor, he issued proclamations for the observance of Thanksgiving on the third Thursdays in November, just as it was kept in Connecticut. His 1854 proclamation read,

> It is no less a duty of communities, than of individuals, to acknowledge their accountability to God, and to receive with gratitude the dispensations of his favor, while they bow with resignation to the chastenings of his Providence. Not therefore, that the People of this state may unite in rendering devout acknowledgements to Almighty God for his numerous blessings ... during the past season, I do hereby recommend that Thursday the 26th day of November next be observed as a day of Public Thanksgiving and Prayer.

Pease's second proclamation, less stern, called for clergy of the various denominations to meet with their congregations "and unite with them in Thanksgiving and prayer to Almighty God for ... numerous blessings ...." Lucadia described the day, November 29, 1855:

> We had Thanksgiving here the same day as yours in Conn't . I went to church in the morning (after making pumpkin pies, and a big old fashioned chicken pie) and heard an excellent sermon from our Episcopal minister, and at dinner we had some gentlemen to help us eat our Turkey, and other good things. There were horse races, on that day, which were better, or more numerously attended than the churches I believe.[55]

Pease's proclamation for Thursday, November 27, 1856, named causes for thanksgiving: abundant health, peace "within our borders," and the "fruits of the earth" in spite of an "unexampled drouth." The Governor felt that "advantages of education and the gospel have been more widely diffused among us than at any former period" and all those blessings "demand from us an acknowledgement of our gratitude to their author." He urged clergy to unite with their congregations in thanks and praise, and in "imploring a continuance of his beneficent protection to our beloved State." In 1857, Lucadia wrote about the holiday:

> Last Thursday was Thanksgiving with us as well as with you—
> We intended to have a good deal of company, but as Anne had not
> recovered from [influenza] we did not, only Marshall invited four
> Legislators to take dinner with us, and he and Carrie went to Church,
> while I stayed home ... making Yankee chicken and pumpkin
> pies .... There were services in all the Churches in Town, & [sic]
> generally well attended.[56]

On the Governor's last day in office, December 21, 1857, he delivered a valedictory address to the legislators and others assembled for the inauguration of his successor, Hardin R. Runnels. Pease finally felt free to make a few comments to legislators that he had not expressed before. He began by observing that during his time in office, "many difficult and vexed questions of public policy have been disposed of, among them, the settlement of our Revolutionary debt was the most important." He noted that it had been discussed for years in the legislature, and how delays in its resolution only complicated matters "and left it to the action of those, who having not participated in the scenes out of which it grew, could not feel the same obligation to see it justly arranged, as the generation by which it was contracted." He added for emphasis,

> I was familiar with the nature and origin of that debt, and all the diffi-
> culties in the way of its settlement. While there were many and strong
> objections to the act of Congress, by which the United States proposed
> to pay it, I felt it would be a less[er] evil to accept it, then to have the
> questions open and thereby embarrass our Legislature and retard the
> progress of all plans for Internal Improvement; these convictions
> induced me to recommend its acceptance, though apparently in viola-
> tion of the public sentiment of the State, as expressed by the partial vote
> of the people in regard to it. Now that the subject has been disposed of,
> and the effect of its payment upon the reputation and credit of the State

abroad and its prosperity at home, has been seen and appreciated by our citizens, I am happy to believe, that few can be found who would recall the act.[57]

Next the Governor said it was his fortune to differ frequently with legislators regarding the merits of the laws which had been passed. "On such occasions, I did not hesitate to exercise the veto power, and with few exceptions, my action was sustained by them, when they came to reconsider the questions." He noted that his vetoes subjected him to

> censure from many who seemed to think that the veto should only be used to correct ... measures that are repugnant to the Constitution. That instrument, however, imposes no such limitation ... and an Executive who would avoid the responsibility of making use of it to arrest what he deemed improper and unwise acts of Legislation, would be as faithless to his trust, as the representatives would be, who might shrink from recording his vote against them.

Pease then put his other achievements into his own perspective, saying that he would not review everything in which he had a part,

> but there are some whose influence will be as lasting as the government itself. I refer to the creation of the school fund, the establishment and endowment of a Lunatic Asylum, and institutions for the education of the Blind and the Deaf and Dumb. It will ever be a source of gratification that I aided in the adoption of these measures, and if nothing else had been done during my official term, those alone would be sufficient to mark it as an era in the history of the State.

Then, as conscious as ever of time—past, present and future—he said,

> Although my official connection with the State has ceased, my interest in its prosperity and progress will remain to be undiminished. Having been identified with the country since the days of its colonial

independence, and having passed with it through all its vicissitudes and trials and contributed to the formation of its institutions and its laws, I cherish for it no ordinary attachment and shall never cease to fill the most ardent desire for its welfare.

He concluded with an observation to legislators that they were in a "most interesting period" of the state's history, since Texas was "free from debt, has an overflowing Treasury, a rapidly increasing population," and ample means to develop its vast resources. He thought that with all these advantages at the command of the Legislature, by a wise and liberal policy, Texas ought, at no distant period, to occupy a proud position in the Union.[58]

E.M. Pease had his share of difficulties as Governor of Texas over four years, and he was limited by a constitution that vested greater power in the legislature than in the governor's office. For example, his power to appoint was limited to the secretary of state, a private secretary, and minor officials, including notaries public who had to be confirmed by the legislature. Reading hundreds of letters of recommendation for notaries must have been tedious, but it did give Pease a way to maintain loyal contacts in every county. He was sometimes inundated by letters from citizens who either had no one else in government to address about their problems or who did not know whom to address. His salary was only $2,000 annually when he took office and $3,000 beginning in 1856. Pease had told his wife that he had worked harder as governor than he ever did as a lawyer, and considering his frustration and annoyance with the legislature on a number of occasions, it was, in many ways, a thankless task. He did not want to be separated from his family to run for office in 1853, and experience had shown him in 1855 how difficult the job was, yet he ran again. The reasons are evident throughout his messages: he was willing to work for the people of Texas as a public servant, not because he wished to be a politician. As an experienced lawyer and a three-term legislator, he understood how Texas government functioned, and his own words showed his vision for the state. He was willing to work hard to make that vision a reality. Some of Pease's ideas that were enacted by the Legislature shaped the future of the state, particularly his leadership in eliminating the debt of the Republic, making the best use of public land, laying a foundation for public education at all levels, and creating state institutions for those with special needs. At the end of his two terms he was still as "identified with Texas" as when he was an idealistic young man.

During Pease's second term, people began to suggest him as Sam Houston's successor in the United States Senate. It would have been a job with the prestige his friends felt that he deserved; he could have kept his family together in Washington and placed the children in good schools there; and most of all, he could have continued to work for Texas. Pease did not seek the job. The principal reason was likely his weariness with the political realm; he had told Lucadia quite firmly that he was finished with politics, and he certainly knew his own mind. Perhaps he could see that a grave national crisis was coming, and he knew his position could not be easily explained. Although he had complained about Abolitionists, considered himself a Southerner by choice, and was a slave owner, he was a moderate, not a fire-eater. During 1857, then-supreme court chief justice John Hemphill was being considered for the senatorial position, along with former Republic of Texas president Anson Jones, Pease, and others. By the time the Legislature elected a new senator on November 7, Pease had been heard from a few days earlier in his gubernatorial message, but it may not have been sufficient to meet the demand for ever-stronger southern sentiments. Additionally, Pease had angered a number of the legislators over the steadfast principles that he had expressed in his messages, including his vetoes. Finally, it was clear that Pease did not seek the job of senator. Although it may have been embarrassing and disgusting to those who were loyal to Pease, the legislature elected Justice Hemphill. After December 21, 1857, the Governor would soon be free to return to Connecticut to visit his family and then to resume his law practice in Texas and spend more time with Lucadia and their growing daughters. Having fulfilled his duty to the people of Texas, he wanted nothing more than what would bring him satisfaction—income as a lawyer and a measure of personal peace.

Chapter 7

The Pease Family in Secessionist Texas, 1857–1865

"Pease, I tell you we are on a volcano."

Guy M. Bryan

When Texas Senator Guy M. Bryan foretold the Civil War in 1857 by writing, "Pease I tell you we are on a volcano," he stated more than his vision of a secessionist future: He also warned the sitting Governor of the personal political danger already at hand. Pease received this ominous observation in a letter from Bryan at the time he was being discussed as a possible United States Senator during the May, 1857 Democratic convention in Waco. Bryan informed the Governor that the delegates regarded him as "not sufficiently Southern in your feelings." He advised Pease to use his upcoming legislative message to address the problem:

> You can't take ground too high provided you base it upon feeling and conviction. Go back to the time you came to Texas, your long residence here and in the South, your interest being here, your children born here &c &c. I tell you the truth ... there is a deep deep feeling growing

in the minds of men to oppose at all hazards the slightest encroach-
ments upon the part of the north. Confidence in the perpetuity of the
Union is fast leaving the Southern mind, & one of these days we will all
wake up and find ourselves in ... a revolution. Pease I tell you we are
on a volcano – I have rarely been mistaken in my views .... We must
settle [the question of slavery] or this government is doomed.

Bryan wrote as a close friend and Brazoria County neighbor, noting that in
public life, "You and I have climbed together, and never Pease, have I failed
to defend & sustain you when I could do so ...." He wrote to Pease "truly &
frankly" and "to yourself alone," and he asked for a like response.[1]

Pease's answer in mid-June did not begin with addressing Bryan's alarm
but instead spoke to another matter of political and personal importance:

In regard to the office of United States Senator I feel much indifference. I am not unmindful of the responsibility of the station, and the
honor it would confer on a man who filled it .... I would not again
enter on an active political canvass for that or any other office in the
world. Still I always expect to take a strong interest in all political
questions and shall never withhold any [thing] to secure the success
of the Democratic party.

While I would not refuse the office ... I do not feel sufficient
anxiety for it, to electioneer for it, and if I receive it, it must come
without effort on my part.[2]

The Governor's response affirmed his position on politics: "I never
did have any ambition for any office but that of Governor, and that, under
the present circumstances .... I would not again take if I were eligible ...."
He wrote Bryan, as he had written Lucadia earlier, "I have always labored
harder for the public while in office, than for myself in private life. The only
reward I have ever received or ever expected, is the satisfaction of knowing
that my services have been appreciated by a large majority of my fellow citizens." "I have a family warmly attached to me and to whom I am devoted,
in their society I am happy, and I shall never under any circumstances again

take an office [in which] I cannot take them with me." He acknowledged that he could take them along if he became a senator. "If it is given to me I shall accept and cherish it as an evidence of the confidence of my fellow citizens, but if it is conferred on another I shall feel no regrets ... ." Despite Bryan's warning, the senatorial issue was uppermost on Pease's mind, and he wrote in the context of a calm and normal time. It was certainly unusual for a successful officeholder to state that he was willing to accept the office of United States Senator only if he did not have to work for it.[3]

On the issue of slavery, he seemed more annoyed with Bryan's questions than worried about the topic, and yet he answered as clearly as he could:

If there exists in the minds of any of my friends an apprehension that I am not sufficiently "Southern in my feelings" I know not how to secure it. If my past history is not a sufficient guaranty of the soundness of my views on the great question of slavery, it would be idle for me to make any public declarations of these views at this time, when it may be said that the declaration was induced by a desire to obtain office.

I came to this country nearly twenty-three years ago and have ever since looked upon it as my permanent home. I have not a dollar in the world and never expect to have, which was not earned in Texas .... At a time when I had no political aspirations and never expected to enter political life, when I did not own a slave and had not a dollars [sic] interest in Texas except my right to land if I remained in it, I drew the clause of the Constitution of the Republic of Texas which first legalized and established slavery in this country, and urged upon the members of the Convention the importance of its adoption, this was done at a time when I was not a member and in no way responsible for the action of the Convention. I could not therefore be presumed to have any other object in view, than the establishment of such institutions as my experience had taught me were demanded by the situation of the country and the interest of its inhabitants.

Having laid claim to his role in the very act of legalizing slavery in Texas at its beginning, Pease concluded, no doubt perturbed, "If having assisted in fact [in] establishing the institutions of our State, and devoting much time and labor through a long course of years to their perfection, does not furnish sufficient evidence of my devotion to them, then I can offer nothing that will."[4] He was not taking into consideration the enormous growth of the state's population from 1836 to 1857 and all the new Texans who had no first-hand knowledge of the Revolution and the early days of the Republic, much less Pease's role in it.

Obviously, Pease had no regrets about slavery in Texas, and no regrets about his role in making it possible. Although he had been only twenty-four and a clerk for the Convention of 1836 that hastily wrote the Constitution of the Republic of Texas, he was able to "draw" the section of the document that guaranteed slavery. He did so because he was influenced by the prevailing view that it was "practical" for slaves to supply the crucial physical labor necessary for white citizens to make money in an agricultural economy based on cotton. He was motivated then, as he was for the remainder of his life, to do what he thought was best for the citizens of Texas—and slaves did not count. Like the Texans around him, most of whom had southern roots, he had come to view slaves as incapable of being educated and of having civil rights. In 1836, Pease was following the lead of Stephen F. Austin and others on the necessity of slavery. Nearly twenty years later, as abolition was ever more widely advocated in the North, Sam Houston would say to a Boston gathering: "It is necessity that produces slavery; it is convenience, it is profit, that creates slavery."[5]

Bryan pressed Pease again in September, 1857 for his "real view" on "the Southern question and State Rights." He wanted to know Pease's position on the powers of the states and on the federal government, whether slavery was right in itself or a necessary evil, and what he would do if a "Black Republican" were to be elected president in 1860. Pease prefaced his reply by stating that if he did not believe Bryan's sincerity "in your professions of confidence, I should be led to think that your questions implied a doubt in regard to the soundness of my opinions on those great questions which are of ... interest to our section of the Union." He wrote, "I shall answer them frankly, and you are at perfect liberty to speak of my opinions, for I entertain none upon morals, religion, or politics, which I do not act upon, and avow publically [*sic*] on all occasions ... but I do not wish this letter made public ... because it might seem ... that I was catering for the office of Senator." He went on confidently, "I am well satisfied that no one will question the soundness of my opinions in regard to our institutions, except he does so as a pretext for hostility ...." Pease then made a significant statement about his background and how it led to his opinion:

> My coming to Texas was neither a matter of shame or necessity, but of deliberate choice, with a full knowledge that slavery then existed here under the sanction of the public opinion of the Colonists and with the belief that whenever they had an opportunity to establish a government for themselves, they would legalize it: Neither is my present residence here a matter of necessity, for I can readily realize enough from my estate, to live anywhere I may desire to go. Now if I had any scruples about the morality of slavery, I certainly would not be the owner of one, and if I regarded it either as a social or political evil I would not remain here one day longer than would be necessary to sell my possessions and remove.
>
> I should regard the election of a Black Republican for President as one of the greatest evils that could [come] before the Country, and believe that it would lead to a dissolution of the Union. Should such an event take place, I shall be prepared in conjunction with my fellow Citizens of Texas to unite in any measure required for the protection of our institutions.[6]

When the Governor sent his message to the Seventh Legislature on November 4, 1857, he stated that Texas would never submit to infringement of its constitutional rights regarding slave property.[7] His position did not convince the lawmakers to elect him as the next United States Senator, although factors other than slavery were involved. Pease had made his pro-slavery positions known, especially in his second inaugural address, in which he expressed his trust in "the good sense of the people of every part of the country" who would "forever extinguish the hopes of those fanatics" who held "fancied advantages of freedom of a race who are incapable of appreciating or enjoying it ... ."[8]

Bryan's concerns about Pease reflected how Texans were becoming more extreme on the issue of the rights of states, especially regarding slavery. In 1857 the Supreme Court's Dred Scott decision, which declared the right of slaveholders to take their slaves with them into Federal territories, galvanized many anti-slavery northerners, and that resulted in a strong southern counter-response. Perhaps Bryan and other Texans who were then or were becoming fanatical as "fire-eaters" raised doubt about whether Pease was still a Yankee at heart. At the end of April, the lawyer and editor of the Austin *Southern Intelligencer*, George Paschal, pronounced his friend Pease "an astute lawyer—a well-informed scholar, and a national conservative politician of the old school."[9] Paschal meant his words as a compliment, but others were no longer in favor of such conservatism. Pease's career as a politician seemed to be over, although he was elected to the Texas Democratic Party's executive committee in January, 1858. Pease may have hoped that he could finally be at peace once he left politics when he departed from the governor's office, but the gathering storm would not leave him in peace for long.

Once free of office, Pease immediately returned to his legal practice. While governor, he had gradually closed cases when the legislature was not in session, but in January 1858 he resumed his profession full-time with John Harris. Law was a field in which his intelligence and judgment made him highly successful, and in which he could begin producing a substantial income again. He was at work in Galveston by January 8, 1858, there again in court in February, and on March 14 noted, "The case against Mills was argued for three days last week, and our other important case was commenced yesterday." The brothers Robert and D. G. Mills, leading Galveston merchant-importers and financiers, were defended by Pease and Harris when they were fined $100,000 for an alleged illegal banking operation. They won the case in the Texas Supreme Court in 1859. The Mills brothers could have afforded to hire any lawyer, and so it is a testament to the ability of Pease and Harris that they were chosen.[10] The family spent the summer and fall out of the Texas heat in an extended visit to their families in Connecticut and in Janesville, Wisconsin, where Pease's mother was living with another of her sons. Because the family was together, no correspondence exists, but Pease's Austin friend, merchant S. M. Swenson, wrote him about local matters and noted, "your servants are all well." Pease did write to Lucadia from New York in October, suggesting the possibility of a return to Texas by a land and river route through St. Louis or Chicago.[11]

Pease returned to the realm of public policy and politics in 1859 when he could no longer tolerate the extreme views of John Marshall (an Austin newspaper editor and Democratic Party leader), Runnels, and others who were agitating to reopen the African slave trade, although it had been outlawed by Congress more than fifty years earlier. Pease believed that the issue was not about the need for more slaves to expand westward, but that the agitation was for the purpose of creating a sectional crisis. He and others wanted the issue to go before the voters in the 1859 governor's race. The editor of the Galveston *Union*, Ferdinand Flake, wrote to Pease in May "on behalf of my democratic friends" in the belief that the Democratic convention "did not fairly represent the Democracy ... [in refusing] to endorse the General features of the administration of James Buchanan .... We believe that our Standard bearers should be [Democrats], not by virtue of a Platform [but by their] feeling and by their acts." Flake continued, "We believe that your administration has given general satisfaction and that your Democracy is undoubted," and "we prefer to support a man who will oppose sectionalism whether it comes from the north or the south." He then asked Pease to allow his name to be placed in nomination as governor in the August election. Pease declined. Instead, he supported Sam Houston as a candidate.[12] Although Pease previously had opposed Houston for supporting the Know-Nothing Party, he now thought that Houston's support of Buchanan's administration and his opposition to all disunion measures made him "far more acceptable to all conservative democrats" than Runnels.[13]

Pease, who was actively involved in Houston's campaign, may have been uneasy among his former Know-Nothing opponents, but unionism had been a major issue for their party and preservation of the Union was of primary importance to Pease. Prominent Democrats including M. T. Johnson and Samuel Maverick joined Pease in supporting Houston. Although Pease did not like to make speeches, he worked for Houston. He received an invitation from Thomas Stribling to visit San Antonio, assuring him of the "high esteem in which you are held by our whole community both as a man and as a Statesman." Pease replied, "The generous support and confidence I have always received from the citizens of Bexar County imposes upon me an obligation to serve them .... I assure you it will give me great pleasure to visit them as soon as I can dispose of some business in Court ...."[14] Pease also wrote a lengthy public letter to Hamilton Stuart, editor of the Galveston *Civilian*, fully stating his views on the proceedings of the recently completed Democratic Party convention in Houston. He began by calling it "amusing" to "witness the attention of the presses in service of some of the nominees ... to excommunicate and read out of the party those Democrats who are so obstinate as to refuse to support the African Slave Trade ...." His choice of the word "amusing" indicated underlying disgust, if not anger, because he went on to state, "The Editors of these presses, being new converts, seem, in their zeal, to think that Democracy had no existence in Texas, independent of Conventions. They entirely overlook the fact, that every administration of our State government has been democratic, and yet that no one but the present had the aid of a convention." He then schooled readers by stating, "Conventions are useful as a means of uniting a party ... but when they fail to express the sentiment of those whom they pretend to represent and present candidates whose opinions ... are repugnant to the mass of the party, their action is entitled to no respect." Pease hammered in his point:

It may be asserted without the fear of contradiction, that more than three-fourths of the Democracy of this state are and always have been devoted to the support of the Constitution and the Union, and believe that the laws prohibiting the African Slave Trade [are] both constitutional and right; yet we find a large majority of the delegates to the recent convention at Houston were open and avowed advocates for re-opening that trade, and entertained the opinion that the laws prohibiting it are not only unconstitutional but that it is disgraceful for the Southern states to submit to them; and as a necessary consequence, that Texas must go out of the Union unless they are repealed.

Pease argued that this position was "fully sustained" by debates during the convention as well as the refusal to pass a resolution declaring "that to make the renewal of the African Slave Trade a party test at the time, would tend to establish a sectional issue calculated to produce a dissolution of the Union." In his usual lawyerly approach, he noted that every nominee of the convention seeking or in political office was in favor of re-opening the trade, and thought that laws prohibiting it were unconstitutional: "If proof is wanted ... it will be found in ... interrogatories ... [in] which they answered other questions [but] they refuse to disclose their opinion on the subject. Their silence is a confession of the charge."

Pease then provided background on the issue: "This is not the first instance in which those who controlled the ... party have gone astray in disregard of the sentiments of the masses." He noted that in 1850, the Legislature decided that citizens should elect delegates to the sectionalist convention that year in Nashville, "but the people gave them a rebuke at the polls, which had a salutary effect for several years." In 1855, the State Central Committee and its chairman, plus most of the leading Democratic editors, "deserted to Know-Nothingism, and endeavored to carry the rank and file with them; but they, true to their principles, rose in their might, discarded those who had control of their [party], and achieved a glorious triumph without ... any party machinery, and they will do the same at the next August election."

Pease noted that the prohibition of the African slave trade "has always been considered a Democratic measure. The laws on the subject were recommended by those Fathers of Democracy, Jefferson, Madison and Monroe; they were matured by Democratic committees and enacted by Democratic Congresses." He asked rhetorically, "What is Gen. Houston's present position? The only safe test by which to try politicians, is their acts and votes. Their declarations are worth but little." Pease stated that during the last two sessions of Congress, Houston had done nothing to support restoration of the African slave trade. "On the contrary, he has, during that time voted with the national Democracy for the admission of Minnesota and Oregon .... [and] he has enjoyed the confidence of Mr. Buchanan and his administration as fully as any member of the Senate." Pease pointed out that the Texas convention at Waco refused to endorse Buchanan. In his open letter to citizens, Pease had more to say about the failures of the Houston convention to represent rank and file Democrats. "It was expected that an effort would be made ... to introduce economy and reform into ... our State government, the appropriations for which have increased from about $156,000 [in 1846 and 1847] to about $1,227,000 for the years 1858 and 1859." He provided the example of public printing expense, which rose from about $8,000 in 1846–1847 to about $150,000 in 1858–1859 with no corresponding increase in the workload. He charged the convention with leaving the control of the party "to those who have been the largest recipients of these improvident expenditures." Pease expressed displeasure that the issue of internal improvements, "which has proved so acceptable to our citizens," had not been addressed, and that "the means of establishing a more perfect and general system of education" were "ignored or neglected ...." Pease also expressed disgust about the reason for this neglect: it was "for the paltry object of securing candidates for the political offices, who would use [their] patronage ... to indoctrinate our citizens with the beauties and advantages of the African slave trade, and to prepare their minds to look upon the revival of that trade as more important to our future welfare than the preservation of the Constitution and the Union." He pointed out that the promoters of the slave trade "are filled with declarations that the measure is not an issue ... and falsely charge those who are opposed to the measure with having originated the issue. Who, but the friends of the measure, introduced it into our late Legislature, and ... embodied the arguments in its favor into a book of 88 pages, which was published at a cost of about $3,500 ... [?]" He also asked, "Why is it that every Democrat, who refuses to support these ... nominees is denounced and vilified ... as a traitor to the party ...?" The governor concluded,

> surely no democrat who believes the laws prohibiting the African slave trade to be Constitutional, ought [no] longer to hesitate what course to pursue in this election. It is his duty to lay aside all differences of opinion upon minor subjects and unite heartily in support of those candidates, whose success will save them from the disgrace of being considered as favorable to this disunion measure."[15]

This letter was strongly supported by Flake in his newspaper:

> The plain, frank and unimpassioned letter of Gov. Pease ... should be read by every Democrat of Texas ... [he] was never a Know-Nothing ... or any thing but a true National Democrat. He has made his mark upon the history of Texas, both as a legislator and as her chief executive officer. He has stood and will stand, the strictest scrutiny. His warning voice has never been raised without cause, nor have his counsels ever been disregarded without detriment to the public interest. He is not only a strict constructionist of the constitution and laws, but in favor of a rigid economy in the public expenditures and a strict accountability in public servants.

Flake also pointed out that Pease was not motivated by personal ambition, since he refused to have his name brought before the Houston convention and did not want to run for office as an independent. Flake concluded, "Whether the reader may coincide in his views embraced in the letter or not, he cannot fail to be satisfied of the sincerity of the writer."[16]

Pease's position angered other Democratic newspaper editors. The Huntsville *Item* asked him to remember that although they had not agreed with the former governor on his railroad position in 1855, they had been loyal during his re-election campaign to keep Texas out of Know-Nothing control. Now, however, he was not standing up for the Democratic Party: "No, like the land to which you owe your birth, intolerance [is] in your nature .... Shame on you, Elisha; this act of yours is a deed of ingratitude to a people who have freely trusted you ... ; it is a crime which will stick to you to your grave ... ."[17] Pease's former supporter, Democrat John Marshall of the *Texas State Gazette*, criticized him dramatically and bitterly—and without the ability to rise to Pease's logic. His long front-page response to Pease's letter began, "as he enters upon the stage, he grins a ghastly smile at the Democracy with the unnatural exclamation, 'It is amusing!'" Following an argument on what actually happened at the Houston convention, the editor wrote, "when E.M. Pease, who now stands charged with betraying the Democracy which has done so much for him, asserts that the Democratic party and its nominees and presses *conceal* their sentiments on the foreign slave trade ... he simply unveils the deformity of his own character for cunning and duplicity" and is a "traitor." Furthermore, "Mr. E. M. Pease exfoliates from the Democracy just at the time that a contest is likely to arise with Black Republicans, and when he can feel more congenial sympathies with Sam Houston than with the good State Rights Democrats." The editor wrote that it was Pease's opinion that Sam Houston had "uniformly acted with the National Democracy during the last two sessions of Congress. "We deny it." The editor concluded, "we have said enough to satisfy all candid men of his treachery and his false accusations against the Democratic party on betaking himself to the camp of the enemy."[18] None of the anger expressed in the press or on the stump prevented Houston from being elected. He, much like Pease, did not oppose slavery but was eloquent in his defense of the Union.[19]

Unionists who wanted to believe that Houston's election meant they had gained control of the state suffered a setback when John Brown raided the federal arsenal at Harper's Ferry in October, 1859. Texas secessionists were invigorated by the act, and the legislature elected "fire-eating" Louis T. Wigfall to the United States Senate in December after Henderson's death. Pease and other unionists decided to promote Houston as a candidate for President in 1860. The former served as chairman of the platform committee at a meeting for that purpose and presented resolutions opposing sectionalism and agitation of the slavery question and advocating the formation of a new party focused on the Constitution and the rights of the States. Pease was named chairman of the committee to correspond with Houston's friends in the Union.[20] This effort resulted in Harris and others writing to Houston in 1860 to ask if he would allow his name to be put forward. Houston agreed to run if he was nominated by the people, but he lost the nomination of the new Constitutional Union Party to John Bell of Tennessee. Texas unionists continued to organize, and Paschal, A. J. Hamilton, M. C. Hamilton and others asked Pease to serve as a Constitutional Union Party elector. He declined, but he worked to organize the Travis County Union Club, and then served as chairman of its Executive Committee of Correspondence for statewide promotion.[21] Pease was the lead author, joined by A. J. Hamilton, W. C. Phillips, and John Hancock, as the Union Executive Committee prepared a lengthy document addressed to the people of Texas advocating the Union Electoral Ticket headed by John Bell. They expressed the need for national unity to defeat Lincoln, reasoning that conservatives of the South and North must unite.[22] In the November election, however, Texas overwhelmingly voted for the southern Democrat, John C. Breckenridge, rather than the Constitutional Union party. Abraham Lincoln won the presidency.

With Lincoln's election, more and more Texans began to favor leaving the Union. Lucadia explained the situation as she understood it in December 1860:

Gov. Houston ... like all Southerners regrets exceedingly the election of Mr. Lincoln. You have seen by the newspapers during the summer, that the northern abolitionists or black republicans have caused a great deal of trouble here, by their interference with the negro's [sic] tho'. many of their statements were greatly exaggerated—which appeared in the papers—I ... now begin to realize what some of the terrors, would be, were the Union divided, and the North fighting against the South, like members of one family, as indeed many of them are."[23]

Secessionists successfully demanded a convention, although it was extra-legal; only the legislature could call for one, and Houston would not convene a special session for the purpose. The Secession Convention assembled in Austin from late January to early February, 1861. It began the process of removing Texas from the Union, which was put to a vote of the public. Once Texans approved secession by a wide margin, the Convention reconvened on March 5 to make Texas part of the new Confederate States of America. Houston disapproved. The Convention then required Texas officials to swear allegiance to the Confederate States and ordered Houston to appear before them on March 16. The night before, he paced the floor of the Governor's Mansion and concluded that he could never swear such an oath. He went to the Capitol on March 16 but stayed in the basement governor's office. When he did not appear before the Convention, the office was declared vacant, and the Convention appointed then-Lieutenant Governor Edward Clark as the Governor. Ironically, Clark's political career had begun with Pease's appointment of him as Secretary of State in 1855. It was another political loss for his mentor. Lucadia's opinion about the situation in mid-February began, "There is scarcely anything talked about here, but the distracted state of the country ...." She mentioned the timing of the vote for secession and added, "Although the South has been driven to this measure by the Black Republicans of the north disregarding the Constitution of the U.S. in respect to Slavery, yet it will be a most grievous thing particularly for Texas. Marshall who is ever sanguine, still has some hope that the people of the state will not vote for the Ordinance ...." Sanguine though he may have been, he was "so firm in his opposition to immediate secession that he is called by the fanatical seceders a submissionist, and one who is still willing to be trampled upon by the north ...."[24]

Pease and others worked hard against secession. In addition to all his unionist arguments, he pointed out that leaving the United States would result in the withdrawal of Federal troops, thus exposing frontier settlements to Indian attack. No argument worked. Texans voted overwhelmingly for secession, although Travis County and a few others did not. Pease and other unionists hoped to use the Union clubs to gain control of the state government by an election in August, but the plan could not be carried out, because war erupted at Fort Sumter, South Carolina in April. As Pease's friends fell in line with the Confederate cause, he stood firm in his belief in the American Union. He faced a grave dilemma: With little he and others could do for the Union in the capital city of one of the Confederate states, and with the possible mortal danger they faced if remaining, should he and his family abandon their Texas home and go to Connecticut? He concluded that if he left Texas, he would lose all his property, and so he would take his chances and stay at home. Lucadia wrote, "Marshall would send us north but he cannot go ...." Anticipating the mail blockade, she explained, "I should not be able to hear from him .... It will perhaps be best for us not to go." Also, she wrote, "Marshall like many other Union men here has all his life long hard earnings invested here, and at the ruinous depreciation of property, at this time, is obliged to remain."[25] Travis County Tax Records for 1860 show that Pease owned one hundred-ninety acres of the Spear tract (on which Woodlawn was located) valued at $12,000. Austin lots 6, 8, 9, and some portion of 7 (the land bought in 1855) were valued at $3,000; other land in the city was valued at $647.00. Seven slaves were valued at $5,200.00. Horses and cattle were valued at $500.00. His total taxable value was $24,147.00[26]

When the war began, Pease and other Unionists in Travis County created a militia unit, the Home Guards. They conducted drills and had the support of the fine German band.[27] The purpose of the Guards is not clear, but the *State Gazette* was of the opinion that their criticism of the Confederacy should be stopped. The Marshall *Texas Republican* accused Pease of being a "traitor" for his involvement in the group.[28] More and more unionists gave in to the Confederate cause, and Pease lost friends in the process. The Home Guard dissolved. A general election in August, 1861 showed the depth of the change in public opinion. People in Austin who had voted against secession in February became Confederates by the summer.

Pease and others who remained loyal to the Union faced major problems; among them, the dangers of being called traitors or at the least, being harassed. Fellow Unionists and Austin residents, John Hancock and A. J. Hamilton, both fled to Mexico for a time, but Pease chose to remain in Austin. Practicing law was another matter. Lucadia wrote that because her husband refused to swear an oath of allegiance to the Confederacy, he could not practice law in its courts, and therefore he stayed at home and farmed. It was true that no Unionist could practice in Confederate courts, but Pease did not practice at all, while some unionist lawyers, including Hancock, apparently practiced before local and state courts.[29]

Pease must have felt more and more alone. Years later, when the war was over, Lucadia wrote to her family that he suffered "almost every species of tyranny, which desperate man, engaged in a desperate course could inflict was resorted to against him."[30] He was required to show a pass issued by the Travis County provost marshal, even for short trips, and he may have even spent one night in jail for failure to carry it.[31] He had a more serious legal issue to contend with caused by the Confederate Sequestration Act of 1861. Land in Texas owned by enemy aliens (US citizens living outside the Confederacy) was confiscated by the Confederate Government and sold. Although Pease was not an enemy alien, he represented northerners who were, and he was ordered to the Confederate District Court for the Western District of Texas (in Austin) to appear as a defendant. Pease presented papers showing the names of owners (and heirs) and locations of five of his clients for whom he had paid property taxes through 1860. The last person he listed was his brother, Lorrain T. Pease, who was granted land posthumously for his Army service in the Revolution. Governor Pease did not state that Lorrain was his brother, or that the heirs were his and Lorrain's sisters. In answer to the court inquiry of their residence, he wrote dutifully, "when last heard from, they resided in the Town of Janesville, state of Wisconsin." While he could have last heard from them the day before, the court was apparently uninterested in any of the information; they simply wanted the land. It was taken from the owners in this and every case but was restored by the United States after the war.[32]

Because Pease did not practice law during the war, his income was severely restricted, if not eliminated, for its duration. Lucadia wrote afterward that if the war had gone on any longer, ever-higher Confederate taxes on their property would have ruined them. To make matters worse, Pease had loaned at least $47,184.61to individuals as of May 20, 1860, and since most people had nothing like the resources that the Peases did, those loans could not be collected during the war, if ever.[33] Pease's life apparently was threatened at least once. No mention of the matter seems to have been recorded locally, but the threat was mentioned in the biographical account of him published after his death in *Memorial History of Hartford County, Connecticut*.[34]

The Peases spent the war years at Woodlawn. It was a large house with a working farm and surrounding woodland of 190 acres located one and one/ half miles west of the Capitol. Pease had bought the property in 1859, but at the time he already owned a large tract adjoining it to the east. On Christmas Day, 1855, four days after beginning his second term as governor, he bought 97.41 and 2/3 acres for $2,000 in all or part of City of Austin Outlots six, seven, eight, and nine. The land was bounded on the west by Shoal Creek from generally what is now West 12th Street, north to West 24th Street, and west to property then owned by James M. Shaw.[35] On January 14, 1856, Lucadia announced to her sister Maria that Marshall had purchased land on which they would build a home during the two years they would be in the

Governor's house. Three days later Lucadia wrote her sister Juliet that the day after the inauguration,

> We took a drive to our new place, as Marshall calls it .... he has bought about eighty acres of land, not a mile from town, where we are intending to build a house and settle down permanently—It is a very pleasant situation, commands a view of the town, and is diversified with hills and dells, and a brook, or as it called a creek, but unfortu-nately it is dry most of the year—Marshall will commence to improve the land .... We have commenced drawing plans for the house and shall begin it soon, as mechanics here are slow about their work.[36]

The exact location of the intended house is unknown, but since the town was visible, it would have been atop the tree-filled bluff just west of Shoal Creek. The street that was laid out as Parkway in 1914 is parallel to the creek on the east and at the foot of this bluff. Lucadia's note that the creek was dry most of the year, which is typical of creeks in Central Texas, disproves the legend that the creek ran constantly.

Plans were drawn for a house with "bow windows, and unlike the square regular house Marshall used to plan," Lucadia wrote. He paid A. H. (Abner) Cook for 10,548 feet of cedar lumber, had land plowed, and planned to plant corn. His 1857 account book notes "expenses for farm" on land "purchase[d] from Moreland"—$2,056.57 for "771 cedar posts and lumber for fence, harness, plow."[37] A year after their first plans for the house were mentioned, Lucadia was thinking about a house with three rooms on each floor, but no house was built. They debated whether to live there or in Galveston. They were still renting the Ward house after leaving the Governor's Mansion, but they spent time in the north in 1858 and so the matter of a home was not critical. In April 1858 they had "some intention" of choosing Galveston because of better travel connections, year-round fresh food, and available seafood, but yellow fever epidemics were a deadly danger. In May they thought they might live in Galveston "a few years" until Austin had railroads. Marshall wrote Lucadia that he had looked at their Galveston lot and would urge her to live there if it had a house on it. His law partner was "exceedingly anxious" for his return to Galveston, but Marshall told his beloved wife, "I shall leave the matter up to you." She chose Austin.[38]

Marshall Pease received a letter from his former secretary, Samuel Harris, in December 1858 with surprising news: James Shaw, the former state comptroller who owned the largest house in Austin on land west of and adjacent to the Pease's undeveloped tract, had made his home available for rent because he was leaving town. Harris relayed the information that if Shaw did not return, he would sell the house "at a lower price than you can afford to build." In March 1859, Shaw wrote Pease that he would sell his estate. The offer came in a letter while Pease was away, and Lucadia let her husband know that "Mr. Shaw [writes] that he will sell you his place .... The price is fifteen thousand dollars without the furniture ...." Later she added, "I am longing to know your decision and whether that is to be our future home."[39] Shaw's offer positioned the Peases on the cusp of good fortune, for they would soon own the elegant mansion, but Shaw made the proposal because his child had died and his wife was ill and needed to move. In spite of the tragic circumstances, Shaw was fortunate to be able to sell his home to the only person in Austin who could afford it and who needed a house. In offering it to Pease, he said, "I have ... offered it to you at a much lower price than it cost me—fully 33 per cent. You can take it as it stands, exclusive of furniture, for $15,000. With the furniture, glass ware, silver ware, kitchen utensils $17,000. (The furniture, etc., cost me fully $3,700.) For the cattle, hogs and poultry you can pay whatever you please." Pease paid for the estate in two installments. His Swisher and Swenson account shows the first payment of $6,686.59 on January 11, 1859. Pease's promissory note of August 10, 1859, stated his intention to pay $6,000 plus interest on January 1, 1860. Shaw confirmed the first payment from Galveston on January 11, stating, "Your draft on R & DG Mills for $6,246 was this day paid." The payment for the estate, plus interest, and the payment for the livestock and equipment totaled $12,932.59.[40]

The Peases' new home was (and still is) located on a tree-filled, slightly elevated plateau about a mile west of Shoal Creek and about one and one-half miles west of the Capitol. It was likely the largest and most expensive home that Cook built, and it is the prototype for the Governor's

Mansion. It faces east. The original plan placed two adjoining parlors and the dining room on the south side, separated by a wide hall and stairwell from a library on the northeast corner, thus forming an ell-shape with the base of the ell as the front of the house. Four bedrooms were upstairs. The kitchen and quarters for the house slaves were behind the house. Part of the house rests on a limestone foundation. Exterior walls are three bricks thick and interior walls are two bricks thick. The yellowish-beige bricks, made of caliche, are likely from Cook's Shoal Creek kilns. (Caliche is, like the limestone Central Texas hills, calcium carbonate; it has a clay-like consistency that permits firing it into sturdy brick.) The capitals of its six elegant, two-story columns across the front are designed after the ancient Greek Temple of Illyssus, a drawing for which is in a nineteenth century carpenter's guide book. Three two-story Doric columns frame the south portico off the dining room.[41]

Lucadia was as "elated at having a home of her own as a child with a new toy." She called it "handsome" and located on "the most beautiful" site of any near Austin. It was a remarkable improvement over the shabby little house in Brazoria she had come to as a bride only nine years earlier. Lucadia invited her mother and sister Juliet to visit. She and Marshall considered naming the property "Windsor Lawn," but Marshall felt that name had pretentious overtones of Windsor Castle in England. By November, "We call our place Wood Lawn though it is subject to change, when we can think of a name we like better." She and her daughter, Julie, wrote the name as "Wood-Lawn," but gradually the name became "Woodlawn." (Julie mused later that it could have been named "Elmhurst" or "Elmwood" for its prevailing tree type.) Preparing the house for occupancy took months. Lucadia expected to move in the first part of November. She observed lightheartedly, "Our moves have been so frequent that once would almost suppose that the [furniture] would become animate and walk off without assistance to their new destination, but on the contrary everyone has had to be toted … ." She discovered a practical problem after moving in: "our house though abounding in pillars and galleries, was entirely deficient in closets [and] pantries …. We are now having a nice pantry or butlery with a window in it made, and a sink room which I shall prize more than all the columns."[42] The sink that Lucadia prized was a "dry sink," commonly used before the advent of plumbing. It was a cabinet with a recessed top for holding a basin and water pitcher.

Only part of the Pease estate was farmed. The Agricultural Schedule of the 1860 US Census showed that Pease owned forty acres of improved land and two hundred seventy-five acres of unimproved land with a total worth of $12,000. He paid $500.00 in wages during the year. He owned six horses, eight milk cows, six oxen, and fifteen cattle; all together valued at $600.00. The land produced nine hundred bushels of Indian corn. In November 1865 when the whole family went north, Pease leased Woodlawn to F. S. Schieffer for a year, to use the land and outbuildings but not the house. He could use the kitchen and smokehouse, mule and two yokes of oxen, small wagon, and farm tools, and he was to keep fences in good order. He had charge of the flock of goats plus the cows and calves. Pease left fifteen bushels of wheat which, with the corn in its crib, Shieffer was to use and replace. He was to receive half the value of the crops he produced, and was free to cut wood for use but not to sell.[43]

References to the farm are infrequently found in modern descriptions of Woodlawn, but the farm is described throughout the Pease records. Lucadia mentioned Marshall's farming and gardening at Woodlawn during the War; noting that he farmed with his slaves and was proud to wear home-spun pants.[44] He wrote in 1866 that he sold his wheat and barley to US Army officers, noting, "Mr. Schieffer has made a fine crop of wheat growing on the lot next to Mr.[Confederate General Nathan George] Shelley's, and has just commenced planting corn on the lots where we had wheat and barley last year. He has part of the garden spaded … ." This letter documents that culti-vated fields were west and south of the house. Ten years later, a deed record noted Pease's arrangement with the International and Great Northern Railroad, which laid tracks though the west side of his property. A cedar plank fence was to be built to contain stock, as well as

a cut under their track, a short distance South of the Log Cabin that stands near the Southwest corner of my cultivated field, which shall be at least twelve feet in width and high enough … to permit a full load of hay to pass under the railroad track, and the end fences shall close on the sides of said Culvert, so as at all time to offer an open passage way ... for stock of all kinds to pass ... without any hindrance from my pasture on the East side of said railroad track to my pasture on the West side ... .[45]

The Pease farm garden grew vegetables, including green peas in years with enough rain, and watermelons, a dependable summer fruit staple that provided rind that Lucadia pickled. Peach and fig trees were in the orchard when they bought the estate; more peach trees and plums were added. Julie wrote later while in school at Vassar, "I am reminded of our room at home when the orchard was full of blossoms." The room she and Carrie shared faced south and west. She mentioned the smokehouse; a drawing of the barn is extant. An 1872 map depicts the garden to the north, a stable across from the house, and the orchard to the south. Pease's handwritten inventory accompanying his will included livestock and farm equipment.[46]

Woodlawn was never a plantation, although it has widely been so-called. This misperception is due to the size of the estate and style of the house. Architectural historian Kenneth Hafertepe explains, "Although scholars have long been aware that the Greek Revival [style] began in Europe and that in 'America it started in Philadelphia and spread north, south, and west, in the public mind [it] is indelibly associated with the antebellum South ... .'" If Woodlawn had been a plantation, cotton would have been grown there, which it was not, and Pease would have been called a planter, which he was not. (He did not have the twenty slaves that would have defined him as a planter.) Cotton was not cultivated at Woodlawn for good reasons; most of the estate is on relatively thin soil with a limestone base rather than the rich, deep soil needed to grow cotton, and annual rainfall was usually insufficient. (The 1916 *Austin City Directory* noted, "Rainfall for the city is 37 inches. This is sufficient for growing crops ... with the exception of cotton ... .") Cotton needs full sun, but most of the estate was wooded; furthermore, most of it is not level enough for cotton plantation fields. It is not known if Shaw or Pease cleared any land for cultivation of farm crops or if they farmed in natural openings along Johnson Creek. Most of the tree cover and other native plants remained as long as Julie lived (until 1918). Countless large old oaks and elms, junipers, and other trees still stand, many of them far more than one hundred-fifty years old.[47]

Life at Woodlawn just before the War involved attempted gardening, the constant maintenance of the large house and the farm, and the effort to educate the children. During the second growing season at Woodlawn, Lucadia reflected on gardening since moving to Austin: "we are now engaged in making our garden but have had so many things for years past to prevent our having success ... ." She admitted that she had "very little hope," but "Marshall is as hopeful as if he had never failed, in raising fruit, flowers or vegetables—when in fact the grasshopper or drought or something else has prevented us from having much any year." Apparently nothing was irrigated by hauling river water up to the garden at Woodlawn until a well was dug years later.[48] Fresh fruit and vegetables were always in short supply, and she noted that she had cooked some dried apples that her mother had sent her. Served at tea, they were proclaimed "the best ... ever." A cask also arrived in the box, and she supposed it was cider brandy.[49] Lucadia was always physically involved with housekeeping as well as cooking; she did not merely direct the slaves. She wrote, "We have begun house-cleaning, which is a great job, in a large house, with a surplus of large windows." Two weeks later, she was repairing old carpets. This letter was among the last before the blockade began.[50] Educating the children without schools and good teachers was impossible on a regular basis. When the Peases had no teacher for the girls, Lucadia noted to her mother, "Carrie [then age eight] is beginning to write a little on a black board—but she has more fondness for housekeeping than for her books. Last week ... she made bread twice, and was very proud of its being very good. Anne [then age five] promised to be the best scholar, and if she was at school I think would learn fast."[51] In February 1860, Carrie was taking piano lessons, and her teacher reported that she was making good progress, while Anne is "sewing fast on a patchwork quilt." In March 1860, Marshall's mother was visiting, and she served as a teacher. Seven-year-old Julie, who was "very quick and impatient," had failed to study and could not recite her lesson to her mother. Lucadia wrote Marshall about the incident, and Julie became determined "at once."[52] In May 1860 Lucadia wrote that Marshall's mother was going home, and the children "will lose their teacher as she has been in the habit of hearing them read and spell every day."[53]

While the farm produced some food during the War (mostly corn and wheat), it and the surrounding land provided raw material that replaced goods that became unavailable because of the blockade. Lucadia wrote, using ink made at Woodlawn from boiled sumac berries, about making bonnets and hats from corn and rye husks or wheat straw; and making gloves from fabric they spun, knitted, and dyed. They also cobbled shoes. They made soap and candles, and coloring candles became, she noted, "the great art of arts, the leaves, berries, bark and roots of every tree were tried ... and when we called upon our friends, instead of discussing the merits of the latest published novel, we talked of some practical matter, such as experiments with dyes."[54] This was not as frivolous a comment as it might seem. Rather, it was an example of Lucadia's life-long ability to be cheerful and to make the best of a situation, and perhaps it was also meant to keep her New England family from being too upset about what had been endured in Austin. She did write about the anxiety of not being able to stay in touch, especially about their greatest loss during the war. "Our darling Anne who was such a good, loving, unselfish child, has been taken from us, and has left a void in our hearts and home which can never be filled." In a letter that Lucadia thought was undelivered during the war, she wrote that Anne, "our flower girl," died of typhoid fever in July 1862. She was seven years old. Lucadia had observed that when Anne was little more than two, she was "the smartest of the lot" and when she was not yet five, she was promising "to be the best scholar" of the three. This little child was the first of the family to be buried in their large family plot at the Austin City Cemetery (now Oakwood Cemetery.)[55]

During the entire war, the Pease's former landlady and Lucadia's friend, Susan L. Ward, was their houseguest even as her husband, Thomas William Ward, was elected mayor of Austin for the third time in 1864. She had sued him for divorce in New York because on his cruelty to her. She had asked for alimony and won, but she had to divorce him in Texas to be awarded a property settlement on Texas land. Because she would not employ a Confederate lawyer, no one could give her legal help with divorce proceedings. Lucadia wrote that Mrs. Ward was not awarded enough money, and Ward "has put his property out of his hands ... they have not been able to get it for her ... ." Mrs. Ward lived at Woodlawn until Lucadia could take her girls north, and the house was closed.[56] Miss C. E. Townsend of Massachusetts, the girls' teacher, also lived with the family during the War. She had asked Pease in May, 1861 about getting to Galveston and New Orleans safely, but it was too late.[57]

Because of the mail blockade, few letters were written. One of Pease's to Carrie states, "The heat has been so oppressive during the last week that I have not felt like doing anything, still I have read a little every day, besides riding to Town to learn the news about the war, which has been unfavorable to the cause of the Southern Confederacy."[58] After the war, Lucadia's resumption of correspondence with her northern family provides glimpses of their war experience. At the close of the war, she wrote about the Confederates, whom she called "Secessionists": "Everybody here are anxiously expecting the Federal troops, most zealously the former Secessionists, as there have been many disturbances in town since the disbanding of the Secession troops, and some lives have been lost by them, and all classes hope for order from the presence of the Union troops among us," Reflecting on what had happened because of the war, she wrote, "Confederate taxes, and tithes and impressments upon every species of property seems as if it would ... deprive us of everything ... and yet I cannot complain, when so many have ... [been] stript of all their wealth, widows and orphan depended entirely upon themselves."[59]

Pease's fears about leaving the Union had been realized. He was most fortunate to have survived with his life, and the family was most fortunate that they did not lose nearly as much as many others did whether they were Confederates or Unionists. However, the hard years of Reconstruction were ahead, and Pease would bear a heavy burden in that era, a burden he did not want as the result of a war he did not want.

Given that slavery was at the root of the war that tore the nation asunder, and since the Peases owned slaves, it is important to review their attitudes toward their own in particular, as well as acknowledge, to the extent possible, the enslaved human beings who worked for them involuntarily.[60] Little could Marshall Pease and Lucadia Niles have imagined as natives of New England that they would be so deeply involved with slavery in the South, much less that they would defend the institution. Marshall had come to Texas in 1835, aware that slavery was practiced in the Mexican colony, and as a young man he was quick to conclude that slavery was necessary for agriculture, particularly for the production of cotton. Lucadia had ventured to Eltham Plantation in Virginia in the 1830s, and there she saw slavery for the first time. She struggled to comprehend the institution, considering American principles, but began to conclude that her hosts, the Bassetts, treated their slaves so kindly in meeting their human needs of food, clothing, and shelter, it was not a serious problem. After all, she heard the slaves singing "merrily" in the kitchen. By the time Marshall married Lucadia and brought her to Texas in 1850, he owned slaves, although he had very little agricultural business. Most of his 10,000 acres in Brazoria County was undeveloped; but he had a small hog-raising and corn-growing operation and a garden for growing food for himself and his slaves. His first mention of slaves in a letter to Lucadia was in a report on the condition of the house and furniture after returning from Connecticut. He noted the loss of a "negro boy about three years old ... the rest of our servants I found in good health and all anxious for the arrival of their new mistress." Lucadia's first mention of "servants" was casual; in January 1851 she referred to "sable people." She noted in March, "'the niggers are not so black' as [expected.] I have been puzzled almost every day to tell black from white—one of the servants in the house here is whiter than any of the ladies, with light sandy hair, and yet she is a slave and must associate with real black negroes, an awful feature of slavery."[61]

When Lucadia's oldest sister, Juliet Niles, visited, she made tart comments in letters to their family about slaves. She referred to the "waste and extravagance" of the slaves in not protecting clothing from moths "as the niggers make it a rule to never do as they are told to do." She observed that Lucadia was busy superintending housekeeping, "there being four of the niggers to keep in a slow motion."[62] Juliet's use of the "n" word was common. Marshall used it in wondering how Lucadia was getting along with the "*niggers and the fleas.*" Juliet wrote about the financial advantage of growing sugar cane ("better than hoeing corn in the north") but added, "there are two sides to the question of Slavery a subject which I shall not discuss at present & one side is very *dark* indeed." She thought that Texans "are very fond of 'niggers' & are not completely at ease without one or two at their elbow .... " Furthermore, "many here think the only use of money [is] to buy negroes."[63]

Lucadia successfully supervised the family "servants," as she called them, although she was "annoyed" by them at times. Marshall wrote her, "you would have accomplished more with half the trouble in two days than I did in ten."[64] When she went to the North, the house servants were hired out. Lucadia occasionally made defensive comments concerning slavery. In mid-1856 she wrote her husband about people in Connecticut, specifically a "very zealous Republican woman" who was "questioning me closely with regard to your opinion respecting the Sumner outrage and the Kansas riots, and expresses her regret that you are on the *wrong side*. [she] is a most violent antislavery woman making the Hartford [newspapers] her gospel ...." If it were not for the Hartford *Times*, Lucadia wrote, "I should not know while here, that there are two sides to the question." She later wrote in 1856 about an absorbing "proslavery" conversation she had with friends in New Hampshire.[65]

The letters of the Peases during the years of slavery reflect relationships with their slaves that seem in most instances more like those with trusted free persons than enslaved ones. However, it would be misleading to come to such a conclusion: no matter how kind an owner was to a slave, a slave was never his or her own person, never free. Furthermore, no record of the Pease slaves' own comments was probably ever recorded, except by the Peases.[66]

In order to make clear the Pease's attitudes about their slaves and to do justice to as many of the enslaved persons as possible, they are named in family groups or singly in alphabetical order of their first names, following the two slaves that were most frequently mentioned, Emily and Sam. Notes about their lives as free persons are in a following chapter.

Emily was the slave most often mentioned by the Peases. Shortly after Lucadia arrived in Brazoria, she wrote that Emily was her "maid of all work." Marshall had bought her and her mother, Mary, from Brazoria County Sheriff Robert Calder when Emily was about seventeen. Lucadia next wrote, "we have Emily in the kitchen and for all general housework. A quiet and good servant as far as she understands work; she belongs to Marshall."[67] This was the first of several instances in which Lucadia pointedly referred to slaves as belonging to Marshall, not to them both. Emily was "confined" and gave birth in April 1851, "to a fine boy who with her Masters permission she will call John." That only left Eliza, who did washing and heavy work but who possibly had measles, Mary, who was a young girl, and Sam to do all the house work when Lucadia's first baby was due two months later.[68] Over the years Lucadia and Marshall mentioned Emily frequently, noting her being hired out, her illness, and what she said and did. She could tease Lucadia (and Juliet in abstentia): Lucadia wrote to Juliet that Emily "wished you would come and stay with us, but she supposed you were thinking about getting married."[69] Emily's major illness came in the summer of 1856 when Lucadia was in the North. The doctor prescribed cold water baths for "falling of the womb," and Marshall fretted that she would "be worth but little" if she did not improve. He reported weeks later that Emily inquired often about Lucadia's coming home.[70]

While Emily was ill, she was in her room on the second floor of the Governor's Mansion. Lucadia mentioned that Emily was the only person upstairs; "the house seems very large for one family," she wrote soon after she returned from Connecticut the summer that Marshall had moved into the Mansion. Emily was the first person to clean the big house, and "does very well, better than others," their master reported. He also told her how to cook the "fine mess of peas" (likely black-eyed or field peas) that Sam Harris sent him, although Marshall's instruction for Lucadia's method was probably well-known to their cook.[71] Emily was first quoted two years earlier when Lucadia thanked her sister for sending a "thin," cool dress that she wore often: "'Miss Cady, what do you wear that dress so much for' [?]"[72] In 1857, recently returned to the Ward's house, the Pease family servants had a Christmas party with a "handsome supper" for other servants in town, serving turkey, ducks, chickens, roast beef, cake, biscuits, and coffee; they sang hymns and "others tript it on the fantastic toe." The Pease servants "went to several parties which were almost as genteel, Emily told us, as white folks parties." As usual, the servants' Christmas social season was active, and Emily and Maria each attended two weddings and several balls.[73]

Sam Barber, also called "Big Sam" and "Uncle Sam," was first mentioned in Lucadia's letters as the gardener in Brazoria; he had belonged to Marshall before she arrived. Lucadia wrote, he "points out to me daily how *beautiful* the radishes and onions look." Juliet reported that he went there daily, about a half-mile from the house in town, to grow sweet potatoes. She also wrote that Sam asked her if she had ever seen firecrackers, which were a novelty in Brazoria: "He told me he was going to buy some and then I should hear something worth hearing." Sam continued to be the gardener in Austin, producing "common garden vegetables" and melons.[74] Soon after the family moved into the Governor's Mansion, he and the other "boys," as the Governor called them, set out Bermuda grass for a lawn. Sam was also the regular coach driver and was one of the two slaves who accompanied the Peases to Austin. Lucadia reported his taking her on drives to see Austin when they arrived, and in 1855 he drove Lucadia's sister, Maria, and her husband to San Antonio and apparently returned to Austin alone—doubtless, with written authority from his master.[75] Sam, who complained of "rumatiz," seemed to have been ill more often than others. The Governor thought that since there was nothing visibly wrong, Sam must not have had a physical problem. He was, however, a servant who showed pride in his station at the Governor's Mansion: "Uncle Sam will put on more dignity I think than any member of the family," Lucadia wrote.[76] The Governor observed once that in the absence of a nurse maid, "Sam is quite handy as a nurse" for the children. While in Austin he married "a very smart likely girl according to his own statement," Lucadia reported. Years later, Sam had been sick for a week or more, Lucadia wrote, and "not able to do anything, thou' Sunday he drove the horses to Church for us—to night he is some better and has gone to see his wife."[77]

Tom Hawkins was "director of the Negroes" and person "in charge of the farm" in Brazoria; Eliza was his wife. Their five children included Little Sam, Carline, and Lina. "Every Sunday they are dressed cleanly and come up to see their Master and mistress," Lucadia wrote. The Peases bought eggs from Tom for 18 ¾ cents a dozen, turkeys, and chickens, and the money "furnished them with a quantity of finery for Sunday display."[78] Carline, "who lives in the house" with the Peases had the croup when "a great many of the negroes some belonging to Marshall" were sick, Juliet mentioned in early 1853.[79]

Marshall assured Lucadia that Eliza and her family were well that summer. He noted later, "Tom Hawkins, Eliza and Big Sam enquire every day about Missis, and appear to be almost as anxious for your return as their Master is. They are much delighted with the prospect of going to Austin."[80] Weeks later, Eliza miscarried, and Marshall wrote Lucadia that she had been very sick but was recovering, although it would be "some time before she will be strong again." He reported her to be recovered two weeks later.[81] Little Sam had first been the errand boy who also waited on the table. He contracted yellow fever in Galveston, but recovered.[82] Before moving from Brazoria, Lucadia noted, "Tom Hawkins and family are to be in the Governor's suite at Austin," but she did not make clear what that meant, since the Mansion was not yet built; perhaps they would all live upstairs in the Ward's house with the Peases when they first moved in. Lina went with Lucadia and the girls to Connecticut in 1853, where she had the croup and was quite ill. Lucadia wrote, "[I] fancy Tom and his family [were] right glad to see you. Tell them Lina has grown quite fat, talks about them all at the place [Brazoria], but is quite contented here, and will have a great deal to tell them when she gets home of the sights she has seen here." She later instructed Marshall, "Tell Lina's Daddy and Mammy she is a very good girl and very well & happy."[83]

Other slaves were mentioned in the Pease letters and a few in financial records. For example, there was Charley, "who belongs to M −& has just married a girl on Mrs. Whartons plantation [has] brought his bride to show to his Master and Mistress. She was dressed in a white muslin, with a profusion of red ribbons, and both bride & groom wore white cotton gloves, which made their hands ... conspicuous ...."[84]

Dave played the violin in the Ward's house on the night before the Governor moved to the Mansion. Pease mused, "if the children were here tonight they should have a farewell dance in the old house." Dave had helped with the move. Later that summer, he cooked for the Governor when Emily was ill, and still later, Emily, Dave, Sam, and Tom all cleaned up after the Governor's large party at the Mansion. Dave proved so trustworthy that the Governor sent him alone, riding one horse and leading another, to Richmond where he would get their new carriage that had been shipped to Galveston. The Governor wrote Lucadia from Galveston, asking her to give him "about ten dollars" in silver for expenses. "Tell Dave to enquire about the ferries, whither [*sic*] they are fordable and where to ford them." In another capacity, Dave provided music for Carrie's seventh birthday at the Mansion, the first year she had a party, when the children had such a fine time running around, eating, and dancing to the music that Lucadia's "greatest enjoyment was when it was all over."[85]

Dow (whose first name may have been Lowery, but he was called "Dow") was first mentioned by Lucadia when he was ill, but quinine made him "nearly" well. Several years later Marshall sold Dow for $1,000, "a half on cash and half on credit with ten percent interest. I found that he would do nothing unless I was on the place to watch him all the time, and I got out of all patience with him. He has a kind and good master, who wanted him merely for a body servant, he lives some eight or nine miles from town."[86]

Esther (later known as Easter), an "old woman" and "Hard Shell Baptist" with "many good qualities," was purchased by the Governor in 1857. She had belonged to Edward and Rachel McDonnell of Travis County, was "about" forty-five, and was bought for $450.00.[87]

Maria, "a black girl M bought," had been the property of Clinton Terry of Brazoria. The 1853 bill of sale reads, "in consideration of $800 paid by E. M. Pease ... a certain negro woman slave named Maria aged about thirteen years old ... ." Maria, the children's nurse, was "nigger like, full of laugh and songs and gets sissy [sister Carrie] in a frolic very often," Lucadia wrote.[88] Later, however, in commenting on various illnesses among the slaves, Lucadia observed dryly that Maria was "a good deal diseased with obstinacy." The Governor noted that she was hired out "at a good price," but a month later, she had been doing badly, "and I have made up my mind to sell her, as soon as I can get what she is worth." Five months later, she was still hired out and had been ill with pleurisy and "felons [inflammations] on her fingers." When Lucadia gave a party the following spring, Maria was still at the Peases, too ill to cook. That summer Lucadia wrote, "I am quite out of patience with Maria, and her many derelictions of duty ... it will be quite a relief when we can dispose of [her]. Maria is really a very capable servant— sews well, but has so many vices ... she will never be worth anything except on a plantation." She was quite a sight the Sunday that Lucadia inquired of one of her sisters, "Are hoops worn with you. I was quite amused to see Maria dressed for Church ... with hoops in her skirt which actually came from an old hogshead—I believe she did not find the fashion a comfortable one, for I overheard her say 'she would never wear them again if they were all the fashion.'"[89]

Mary Ann Pruett appeared importantly in 1855 when Lucadia wrote to her sister: "Mary Ann Pruett is very desirous to go with me (to Connecticut) and I shall probably engage her." Her arrival with the Peases is documented: J.M. Pruett wrote in 1856 from Brazoria County,

> I hereby deliver to E. M. Pease my slave Mary Ann daughter of Aunt Minny and authorize him to take her with him to any part of the United States, it being understood that I take upon myself all risks of her returning or not returning to Texas, and that the said Pease shall not be responsible in any manner for her return, and that said Pease is also authorized to bargain with said slave for her services and to pay her for the same such sum as said Pease and Mary Ann may agree upon and that said Pease is not to be responsible to me in any manner for her services.[90]

Only one Brazoria field slave was mentioned by name in the Pease family correspondence. A man named Osho had the daily chore of grinding grain by hand to make corn meal.[91]

If Pease had runaway slaves, no records are in his surviving papers. Sam Harris had one, and he asked Pease to be on the lookout for the runaway.[92]

As Governor Pease's second term came to a close, and before the threatening storm clouds of secession began rapidly rolling in, Lucadia made an observation that was as honest as ever when she wrote, "For the last month we have all had influenza ... none of the family white or black have escaped except Carrie ... ." She referred to the family, black and white, as singular. She and the Governor had documented their honest opinions and feelings about their slaves (generally called "servants" but at times characterized with racial epithets) on whom they depended for daily life. Both were annoyed with them at times, but a number could be greatly trusted and were clearly appreciated. Lucadia's references to "Marshall's slaves" (not servants) may indicate that she did not believe in buying human beings and would not do it herself, but she had no choice in the matter in the time and place in which she lived. She had come to believe, and said plainly, that there were two sides to the matter. Marshall, who believed in the practical necessity of slavery and had written it into the Texas Constitution, was convinced that the subject need not destroy the Union. It took a brutal war to decide the matter conclusively: he could not have both the Union and slavery.

Chapter 8

Return to Leadership in Post-War Texas, 1865–1867

"I am convinced he is the man who can do the most good."

Genl. Charles C. Griffin

When Texas officially surrendered to the United States on June 2, 1865, the way forward was not clear. There was concern over whether occupying Federal troops would provide public safety, which Lucadia had expressed a need for in mid-June; but there was also the matter of who would play leading roles in the next government of Texas. Even a month before the surrender, Leonard W. Groce, a friend of Pease since the 1830s, wrote that "all sensible & moderate persons" in his Hempstead area wanted Marshall to become the governor if the Federal government permitted an election.[1] Newspaper editor E. H. Cushing wrote from Houston that he and John Hancock wanted Pease to be the governor, but noted that others preferred Hancock because of his reputation as a strong Unionist. Some tended to support Hancock because they did not know if Pease would accept a nomination; Cushing thought Pease was hoping for a seat in the United States Senate.[2]

The role that Pease would play in reconstructing the state did not go according to the assumptions of these Texans, however, because it depended first on Andrew Johnson, the unionist Democrat who succeeded Abraham Lincoln in the presidency in April 1865 and adopted Lincoln's idea that the president should direct the way states would return to the Union. Civilians appointed by the president would run Reconstruction, and the military would support the process. Reconstruction began in Texas on June 19 when Major General Gordon Granger arrived in Galveston and issued an order making the Emancipation Proclamation effective for all slaves across the state. The announcement of the end of bondage resulted in an immediate, joyful response from the Freedmen, who came to call the day "Juneteenth." Granger added the solemn advice that they were to stay with their previous owners and sign labor agreements while waiting for assistance from the Freedmen's Bureau. The Peases immediate reaction to emancipation and how they told their former slaves the news is not known, but they likely welcomed it while wondering what freedom would mean for former slaves. In a letter to her sister later that summer, Lucadia rejoiced in the "blessing of peace" but expressed concern about "the trials and troubles the result of the war has brought upon the freedmen and women, who had no part in bringing on the war, but upon whom the evils of it will fall most heavily."[3]

A month after Granger's announcement, Andrew Jackson Hamilton was appointed by Johnson as the provisional governor of Texas. Hamilton, a Unionist who had been in Texas since 1846 and gone north during the war, arrived in Galveston on July 21, 1865. His first task was to register voters who could take an oath promising future loyalty to the United States and to supervise the election of a convention that would write a new constitution – one without mention of slavery. A following election would approve the constitution and choose state officials as well as a state legislature and United States Senators and Representatives. With Johnson's approval, Presidential Reconstruction then would be complete. At least, that was the plan.[4]

Hamilton, who arrived in Austin on August 2, was greeted by a number of supporters. Pease gave him an official welcome at the Capitol and engaged in some wishful thinking when he stated that those who had supported the

Confederacy were ready to "acquiesce in the result of the war and cheerfully accept the consequences that legitimately flow from it." Pease report-
edly called Hamilton a fellow Texan identified with others in sympathy and
interest. Hamilton, however, soon had a problem when Texas Unionists split.
His group had maintained loyalty to the Union and believed that they should
be permitted to lead Texas in the future. They wanted Freedmen to have basic
human and legal rights, but most did not favor enfranchisement. The other
faction, including James W. Throckmorton, had opposed secession at first but
then had supported the Confederacy. They wanted Freedmen to have freedom
but little more. Pease favored the more liberal Unionists and became Hamilton's
advisor. He wrote Carrie, "I meet with Gov. Hamilton every day."[5] Pease did
not advocate vindictive policies, worked to get pardons for his old friends,
and even appealed to Johnson for the release of former postmaster general of
the Confederacy John H. Reagan from Federal prison after Reagan advocated
cooperation with Federal officials and acceptance of suffrage for Freedmen.[6]
Pease's sympathy for the former rebels had decreased by the end of August,
however, when he suggested to Hamilton that a constitutional convention
should not be called right away because of unrest around the state. He saw
that a number of newspapers claimed to accept the situation but were actually
promoting discontent with Federal policies.[7]

One of Hamilton's first acts was to adopt Pease's recommendation that
the status of the State Treasury, which had been broken into and robbed in
June 1865, should be investigated.[8] Hamilton had come into possession of
106 US bonds that had been in the State Treasury, and he wanted an investigation of both the Treasury and the financial condition of the state, so he
appointed Pease and fellow Austin resident Swante Palm to examine the
contents of the Treasury vault and financial records kept during the war. After
a three-month investigation, the two issued a detailed report on October 30.
It began with an overview of the State Military Board, the agency created
by the Texas Legislature in January 1862 composed of the governor, comptroller, and treasurer and given responsibility to provide arms and ammunition for state military defense. The Board had the power to use $500,000 in
8-percent bonds or coupons that were in the Treasury. Another legislative act
approved at the same time authorized the Board to issue any bond or coupon

not exceeding one million dollars, and in January 1862, the legislature appropriated another million dollars for military purposes. During its existence, the Board's members changed several times, although the report referred only to the first and second boards; the second was created in April 1864.[9] Pease and Palm opened their report by pointing out that the records of both boards were in total disorder and confusion. From the controller's books it appeared that $1,651,621.85 had been withdrawn; the largest single amount of $634,000.00 came from US 5-percent bonds. According to the report, "they"—presumably the Board—had returned to the Treasury $315.55 in specie and $543,958.28 in Confederate Treasury notes. Most of these funds were drawn during the year 1862, and most of the Confederate notes were returned in October and November 1864, when they had lost all value.[10]

The purchase and sale of cotton was documented. The old board had purchased 5,736 bales of cotton, for which they paid $544,438.23, mostly in Confederate notes. Proceeds from selling the cotton went for weapons, ammunition, clothing, medicine, and ordinary needs. The funds were also used to create a state foundry and percussion cap factory, outfit a ship, and more.[11] The sale of US bonds and coupons was described next. The Board had received from the Treasury 634 bonds valued at $634,000 and interest coupons valued at $132,700, making a total of $766,700. The bonds and coupons were placed in the hands of several agents for sale or exchange. The report named various sellers but focused on two of them:

A contract was made in January 1865 between the new Board and George W. White and John Chiles ... to give W & C [EMP's abbreviation] 135 of these bonds with coupons amounting together to $156,275. ... W & C were to deliver to the board at Austin 25,000 pair of cotton cards at five dollars a pair and the balance in Medicines, ... For the other 76 cards and coupons, W & C were to pay the board one half in cotton cards and one half in medicines at the same price ....[12]

The report described events from March 12 through June 1865, when White and Chiles claimed that they had shipped the cards and medicines from Matamoros to the board in Austin. Pease and Palm summarized the situation: "There is nothing in the office of the board to show that White and Chiles ever delivered any of the Cards or Medicines under this contract, or that they ever made any settlement for the bonds and coupons." Regarding contracts for exporting cotton to Mexico in the name of the Military Board, the report stated, "Cotton could be exported for the State or for the Military Board, but the military Confederate authorities permitted no other exportations, unless an equal quantity was delivered to them by the exporters."[13] The subject of cotton cards arose again when Pease and Palm reported that the "old" board kept records of goods they bought: "There appears to have been goods on hand in April 1864, when the new Board was organized, amounting to $24,788.81. But with the exception of one article, cotton cards amounting to $4,957.81, only a few hundred dollars' worth appears to be accounted for by the new board, and it is impossible to ascertain from their record, what became of them."[14]

The report covered related subjects, including Gov. Murrah's cotton operations and cotton exported to Mexico by directors of the penitentiary. Pease and Palm also noted such things as Governor Frank Lubbock's withdrawal of specie from the treasury and the state debt to the School Fund ($1,137,406.65) and to the University Fund ($283,514.22). The largest debt of more than $3 million was for Confederate soldier pay and supplies, pushing total state indebtedness to $8,714,065.67.[15]

It must have been painful for Pease to see in stark monetary terms how much the rebellion against the Union had cost Texas, including what it had done to the School Fund and the University Fund, which he had initiated. Little could he have anticipated that the actions of White and Chiles as detailed in the report would raise legal issues that would result four years later in a landmark United States Supreme Court decision, *Texas v. White* (1869). The legal tangle would unfold as follows: In 1866 an ordinance of the Presidential Reconstruction Constitutional Convention in Texas gave the governor authority to recover the state's bonds, so when James W. Throckmorton was elected governor that year, he tried unsuccessfully to negotiate with White. Then, once Congress took over Reconstruction in March 1867, and Pease was appointed governor in late July, he appointed the highly capable Austin lawyer, George Washington Paschal, as the legal agent of Texas in recovering the bonds. Paschal sued, and the case, styled *Texas v. White*, went directly to the United Sates Supreme Court because the court had original jurisdiction in cases involving a state. Paschal served as the principal lawyer for Texas. The decision in April 1869 found that the contract signed by the Military Board with White, Chiles, and others was null and void, primarily because it had been drawn up to further the Confederate cause.

Texas v. White was far more significant, however, than simply a decision about a Confederate business transaction. The Court ruling found that "The Constitution, in all its provisions, looks to an indestructible Union, composed of indestructible States." This statement by the highest court of law in the land meant that secession was unconstitutional from its beginning. However, the court also ruled that the states themselves were indestructible, and so the acts of state legislatures during the war were not necessarily null and void. Such acts could be overturned on other grounds, as was done in the case of the Texas bonds contract, but they were not automatically null. Pease must have been deeply gratified by the Supreme Court ruling. He had wanted to see secession declared unconstitutional and had, of course, remained true to the Union at all costs. At the same time, he certainly wanted the White case decided in favor of Texas. He must also have also been delighted that his good friend George Paschal, who had moved to Washington with this case, had argued it so successfully.[16]

As soon as the Treasury investigation report was completed in October 1865, the Peases went to the North to see their families for the first time since 1858. Carrie and Julie, then ages fourteen and twelve, were placed in good schools at last, and they would receive three years of education before the family came home in the later part of 1868.[17] Soon after they left Austin, Brevet Major General George A. Custer came to town with Federal troops in November 1865. Custer and his wife stayed at the vacated Blind Asylum by invitation of Governor Hamilton. Custer's troops camped along Shoal Creek, and when some of them died in an epidemic, they were buried on the Pease's side of the creek.[18]

While Pease was in the North soon after the war, liberal Unionists, without his knowledge, put his name up as a candidate to oppose John Hancock for a seat in the 1866 constitutional convention. Pease lost, probably because of his absence as well as because of Hancock's popularity. He returned to Austin alone on February 7, 1866, the day the convention opened, and attended sessions as an observer and as a participant in the caucuses of the liberal Unionists. He wrote that no more than a third of the delegates were "really union men."[19] This must have been evident when the conservative majority removed slavery from the state constitution but would not ratify the Thirteenth Amendment. They recognized that the secession ordinance was null and void, but they refused to state whether it had been so *ab initio* (from the beginning) as the liberal Unionists insisted. They agreed to repudiate state debts created during the Confederacy but refused to declare void *ab initio* acts of the state since secession. The election date for approving the constitution and electing officials under it was June 25, 1866.[20]

The liberal Unionists were so disgusted with the convention results that they came forward with a slate of candidates. Thirty-one Unionists including Pease petitioned Hamilton to head the ticket, but he declined. Pease was then drafted to run for governor, and he wrote on April 9 that, against his own wishes, he had agreed to join the race because "it was thought that without the use of my name, there was no chance for the Union Men to Succeed."[21]

Pease's key campaign document was a circular published in the Austin *Southern Intelligencer* on May 1, 1866. Although it was only a single sheet of small print, its words cast a bright light on the darkness of the time. Pease laid out the status of Texas after the war, what had to be changed and how, and what the consequences would be if Texas left its future to the same people who led it into secession. He stated what the war had really cost Texas, and, in his usual grasp of broad issues, he named subjects that needed to be addressed to move forward. Whether people wanted to see the reality he described was another matter. He began with something that the defeated Confederates did not want to hear: "We all profess to acquiesce in the abolition of slavery and the reestablishment of authority of the United States government over us. If we are honest ... there should be no great ... difference of opinion among us in regard to the course we ought to pursue." He immediately laid bare the truth: Slaveholding had ended forever, and "Our future happiness and prosperity ... imperatively demand that we shall as early as possible adapt our habits, our laws, and our institutions to the great change that has taken place in our system of labor." Every inhabitant of Texas is now free, he continued, and all are entitled to the same civil rights. It is "our duty to secure these rights by our own laws .... If we fail to do this, it must and will be done by the United States government, under ... the recent amendment to the United States Constitution."

Pease was specific about Freedmen's rights, stating that justice and humanity demanded that they be treated justly and kindly. Since Texas was largely dependent on them for hired labor, it was necessary to "encourage and assist them in improving their moral and physical condition, and in seeing that they and their children are educated. We have now no alternative but to make this trial." Furthermore, when Freedmen could have the same protection in the courts as the white race now enjoys, they will cease to regard the latter as hostile to their interests. Suffrage had been settled by the Constitution, Pease stated, and could not be an election issue. However, he made a significant statement of his own opinion at the time:

Some of the Union men of Texas favor qualified negro suffrage, the great mass of them do not believe that the Freedmen of Texas are at present intelligent enough to exercise the privilege properly and in this opinion I agree with them freely. Neither the President nor Congress have required any such concessions from us as a condition to our reconstruction. Should they hereafter do so, I am free to admit that I would concede suffrage to such as them as can read and write understandingly, rather than have Texas remain in a provisional or territorial condition.

The next section of Pease's circular gave the cause of the problem Texas faced: "Unfortunately, the majority of [the members of the Constitutional Convention] was composed of those politicians who were instrumental in bringing about the present order of things ...." That included denying full civil rights to Freedmen, failing to declare the Ordinance of Secession null and void from the beginning, denying Freedmen any benefit from the School Fund, and other similar failures. Pease reiterated, "If we continue to submit the work of reorganizing [to] those politicians who were most active in its destruction, I fear that we are going to suffer further disappointment and delay. Is it asking too much of human nature to require the same politicians to undo and repair [their] errors [?]" Apparently, his answer was "yes."

Pease's address then described the situation in the other Confederate States that had made more progress than Texas. He asked,

> How shall it be in Texas? Are we prepared to leave the work of reconstruction to those who declare that they will only keep good faith towards the United States government so long as it is morally and legally obligatory ... that their faith in republican liberty is waning in consequence of the recent war ... and that the present temper of the South is incompatible with any other settlement than an admission of the correctness of the political doctrines for which she contended, and that and unless these doctrines are admitted the civil war will have to be fought over again? [EMP emphasis]

He pointed out that widely circulated newspapers were urging the return of state government to the hands of those who would repeat the "horrors of the late unhappy civil war," and wrote, "I do not believe that you desire again to peril your dearest interests to any such contest." He reminded Texans that the United States government controlled their future, writing "Our past conduct has placed us in a position where we can exercise no power in deciding what the action of the Government shall be towards the State ...." "The fact that no one of the Southern states has accepted all the measures of reconstruction recommended by the President has caused Congress and the people of the north to distrust our sincerity" and hence, "Southern Senators and Representatives ... have not been permitted to take their seats in Congress." Pease noted that some in Congress favored confiscation of rebels' property and that some proposed governing the former CSA states as Federal Territories. However, the Republican Party had not sanctioned either action, so it is "therefore unwise and unjust to denounce the majority of Congress or the Union party of the North as hostile to our interest and unworthy of our confidence."

He then turned to an attack on his opponents, arguing that they had learned nothing from the previous four years.

> The chief sponsors ... of the Conservative Union ticket use the same politicians who deposed General Sam Houston, and overthrew our State Government in 1861. They then promised us a better government, with larger liberty and a higher degree or civilization. They also assured us there would be no war, and ... during the days of the Confederacy, that we should have the intervention and aid of the great European powers, in establishing our independence ... instead ... they subjected us to martial law, conscript laws, tithes, imprisonments, cotton agents, and ... military despotism ... and no citizen had any security ... .

Pease also pointed to the loss of money from the School Fund and the University Fund as well as the robbery of the state treasury. And if all that were not enough, he said, by "following the counsels of these politicians, our people have sacrificed upwards of $100 million of property in slaves, almost the entire product of labor ... for four years, besides a vast amount of other property." It would take years of "patient industry and economy" in peacetime to repair such loss, but "the loss of life and indescribable mental anguish and suffering" [of] the bloody war "and the humiliation of defeat can never be repaired." He asked again if Texans had forgotten these "calamities" and were still willing to follow the counsels of those who had created them.

Pease then made a conciliatory statement: "I do not remind you of these transactions ... in any spirit of bitterness, but in order that we may avoid similar errors in the future." He then described what needed to be done once the civil government was reorganized: first, judicial system reforms for "speedy and certain administration of justice," and second, executive and legislative department reforms to "establish economy ... and a rigid accountability ... of those entrusted with the collection and disbursement of public moneys." Third, the tax system required a thorough revision because at the time, "no less than twelve million acres of patented lands escape taxation entirely." Fourth, Texas needed a system to encourage immigration, both from the North and from Europe, for a labor pool to cultivate land and develop resources; fifth, railroads were needed to facilitate travel and transport products to market. Sixth, "Our education system has been entirely neglected during the war, but our amended Constitution secures us a magnificent fund ... if honestly and judiciously administered ... to educate every child ... ." Seventh, and finally, protection of the frontier from Indian forays would be possible "if our government acts in harmony with that of the United States."

Pease stated that he did not wish to be a candidate for governor, but he had been asked to run. "These are times [in] which ... all candidates for public office should speak manfully and truthfully and call things by their right names. Those who ... endeavor to keep alive sectional strife and bitterness ... are not loyal citizens ... ." He concluded, "There can be no permanent peace and prosperity until kindly feelings ... are resumed between the different sections of the country, and those who contribute by their counsels and example to produce this desirable result will deserve the respect and confidence of our citizens."[22]

In spite of the clarity, logic, and foresight expressed in Pease's campaign circular, it made little difference. Many people had no access to the document; moreover, how many of those who read it were favorably disposed toward the liberal unionist argument, given the temper of the times? Certainly, Pease's campaign had serious problems. He freely admitted that he did not want to run and barely campaigned. Political problems abounded. Cushing warned him that unless the radicals were to discontinue their loyal Union Leagues, many of Pease's pre-war friends would not vote for him. Hamilton stated his conviction that African-Americans were in many respects equal to whites, and the Crockett *Sentinel* declared, "Pease is a Hamilton man and Hamilton is an unequivocal negro equality man, and the people of Texas cannot be forced to swallow this damnable doctrine."[23] The *Huntsville Item* attacked Pease: "If the radicals could effect the election of Pease, whose money we presume buys their support, they would not hesitate to send him to the Senate, though he can't get off a sentence which does not make you shudder ... ." The paper expressed wonder that radicals made such a strategic error in nominating "a born Yankee."[24]

Pease knew that he could not win, and although he addressed some rallies, he campaigned very little. He told his family he had done his duty "in trying to redeem Texas from secession rule, but the people clung to the old politicians." He predicted the vote would be about the same as the vote against secession in 1861, and he was correct. Throckmorton won, 49,277, to Pease's 12,168. Pease carried only 11 counties of the 114 reporting. The amended constitution also passed by a large margin.[25] Voters had been made to believe that Pease and his followers were sympathetic to northern radicals. His position on the Freedmen was regarded as proof of his northern sympathy. The result of the constitutional convention, the differences between Johnson and the Congress, and his opponents' campaign tactics, as well as the outcome of the election, would move Pease toward a more radical position.

Once the election was over, Pease left for Connecticut for nine months, where he could conduct business and engage in political affairs more easily. He became involved in the on-going issues of Reconstruction and tried to have a major impact on the process in Texas. During the summer of 1866 in Washington, he visited with his longtime Connecticut friend Gideon Welles, who was then Secretary of the Navy. Welles's diary entry for August 2, 1866, outlined their talks:

I have had two interviews with Governor Pease of Texas. He is earnest and honest, and gives a deplorable account of affairs in that State, where he has just been defeated in a gubernatorial canvass. There is, he says, no toleration of Union men; five sixths of the people are hostile to the Federal Government, and they persecute those who do not agree with them. The only way by which Union men can live there, he says, is under the protection of Union troops, and the Federal Government, he claims, is bound to protect loyal men in person and property.

I inquired whether the remedy he proposed was practicable and consistent with our system of government. If there is danger to person and property in any State, the person aggrieved ... must look to the local ... and State authorities for protection. But it is claimed that the authorities will not do this and that five-sixths of the people approved their course. This is unfortunate and wrong, but ... would it not be better to remain passive and quietly and patiently strive to modify public opinion ...?

Welles added that that the Federal government "cannot attempt to control the elections in the States, and that by military force, without overthrowing free government – thus destroying free elections." He inquired of Pease if he was not asking too much. Welles noted that Pease's "good sense made him appreciate the case, though he said that if this was the policy he would be compelled to leave Texas and so would every Union man."[26]

By mid-1866 Pease had become convinced that Texas would require both military rule and suffrage for African-Americans.[27] A new opportunity to promote his views arose when a meeting of Texas radicals in Houston in early August 1866 chose him as a delegate to the Southern Loyalists' Convention in Philadelphia in September. Pease was elected one of the vice presidents of the convention, which declared that Reconstruction was the responsibility of the legislative branch of the Federal government and supported the proposed Fourteenth Amendment to grant citizenship to African-Americans. Pease, who presided over a session that denounced President Johnson for his course during the previous year, stated that the majority of southerners were no less rebellious than they had been during the war and declared that a way to save the Unionists from "death itself" and save Freedmen from a return to a coercive labor system was "for ... national ... legislation, enforced by national authority .... [to] confer on every citizen in the states we represent the American birthright of impartial suffrage and equality before the law."[28]

Pease kept abreast of conditions in Texas during the remainder of 1866 and knew about the terrible state of affairs under Throckmorton's adminis-tration. Black Codes passed to keep Freedmen in conditions close to slavery included apprentice and vagrancy laws as well as year-long labor contracts. Unionists, both Freedmen and white, were terrorized and murdered where Federal troops were lacking, postmasters tampered with unionist mail, and Unionists could not get justice in state courts. Pease's friends wanted the rebels removed and replaced. They favored Congressional disfranchisement of everyone who voted for secession in 1861. Radicals also wanted to keep former secessionists from acquiring power by dividing Texas into two or more states; one would be the western counties including Travis and Bexar, where unionism was strong. Pease likely objected: he always saw Texas as a whole, and Brazoria, where his old Texas roots were, would not be included in the western side of the state.[29]

In mid-December Pease returned to Washington, where he tried again to impress upon Welles the urgent need for Federal troops and to make the case for Army control of elections. Welles reported in his diary,

> He [Pease] says that fully three fourths and he thinks four fifths of the people of Texas are still Rebels at heart ... that they hate the Union men ... and would trample them under their feet.
>
> I asked ... if there were organizations or armed rebellions in any part of the State. He said there were not, but the feelings of the people were hostile to the Union .... He said the Federal Government must send troops there to control the Rebels ....

Welles then framed the situation by asking,

> You think that one fifth should govern the four fifths; that it can only be done ... by force, and you would have Federal bayonets control the Texas election. This Union was not established by such means or on such principles, nor can it be sustained by such remedies.
>
> On his asking me what, in the meantime, the Union people of Texas and the South were to do, I replied, "Be patient, be forbearing; submit to the majority. Do not argue against them .... It may be hard to submit to wrong, but it will be temporary .... You have been right in the past, continue in the future.

Pease must have strongly disagreed with Welles and thought him unable to see the real situation, but he did not argue, because Welles wrote, "Without controverting ... my views, we parted, he promising to call soon and see me."[30]

Pease probably felt relief when on March 2, 1867, Congress passed the first of four Reconstruction Acts. The South was divided into five districts under military commanders with power to exercise control over elected civil governments. The law established steps for restoring states to the Union. Delegates were to be chosen for a constitutional convention based on universal suffrage except for those ex-Confederates who were disqualified from holding office under the proposed Fourteenth Amendment. Once a majority of registered voters ratified the new constitution and elected state officials, the legislature would have to ratify the Fourteenth Amendment. Those elected to the United States Congress could then be seated. The second Reconstruction Act was passed three weeks later, detailing procedures for district commanders to supervise the election of delegates to constitutional conventions. These steps provided specific means for the secessionist states to be governed until Reconstruction was completed.[31]

Texas and Louisiana comprised the Fifth Military District that was commanded by General Philip Sheridan, appointed in March 1867 by President Johnson. Hopes in Texas among Unionists were that Pease would be appointed governor. Pease's friend E. P. Hunt noted that Galveston Unionist editor Ferdinand Flake had talked with General Charles Griffin, commander of the Sub-District of Texas, and the chances looked good that if Throckmorton was relieved, Sheridan would name Pease. Pease wrote on April 6 that he planned to return to Texas "to contribute something towards the early organization of the State."[32] These plans did not materialize. Griffin asked Sheridan to remove Throckmorton and to replace him with Colbert Caldwell, a district judge. Pease did not know about Caldwell when he headed for Texas. Lucadia thought that her husband was going south to confer with General John C. Robinson, his sister's husband, who was then in North Carolina, about the possibility of establishing residence there.[33]

In June, Pease called on Gideon Welles again, as the latter recounted:

We had a very earnest talk on the condition of the country. He attempted to justify or excuse the Reconstruction bills, but, [found] he could not .... He preferred despotism, if it would give security to persons and property, rather than a continuance of the condition of things ....

The Union people have undoubtedly suffered greatly. I asked if he could not peaceably enjoy his property in Texas if he remained passive. He admitted he could, but said that was despotism. He could not freely express his opinions and have open discussion.[34]

Pease re-entered public politics on July 4, 1867, in Houston at the first state convention of the Republican Party of Texas. As much as anyone else, he was responsible for the founding of the party. The "Republican Union men" (Freedmen and whites) of Travis County had been called together at Pease's request the previous April "to restore peace and harmony to our country upon the broad basis of equal justice for all … ." Twenty-seven counties sent delegates, most of whom were Freedmen. Pease was president of the convention. It endorsed Sheridan's and Griffin's policies and advocated free public schools for all children. Predictably, the conservative press referred to it as a "mongrel" convention and declared it a failure, but Pease wrote that the delegates showed good order and the speeches by all were "fully equal."[35]

Once Pease arrived in Austin on July 10, he received a letter from fellow Texas Unionist James H. Bell stating that if Congress authorized military commanders to make removals, Pease would be asked to become provisional governor.[36] Travis County Republicans met on July 12, advocating removal of Throckmorton and appointment of Pease, who let Griffin know that even though he did not want to be governor, he would accept the role if it was offered because it "would be acceptable to the Union men of the state generally."[37] A week after the meeting in Austin, Congress passed a third Reconstruction Act, making it possible for Sheridan to remove Throckmorton. Griffin had reported to Sheridan on July 20 about Texans' hostility to the Federal government, and he wrote that the cause was disloyal civil officials at all levels. All would need to be removed, he thought, but at the time he only advocated the removal of the governor. He withdrew his nomination of Caldwell and recommended Pease, stating, "I am convinced that he is the man that can do the most good." On July 3, 1867, Sheridan made the appointment, and E. M. Pease would soon begin service as provisional governor.[38]

Welles made a diary note that Sheridan had appointed "my old friend E. M. Pease ...." He thought that the choice was a "good selection" but expressed concern about how well Pease's Republican views would be accepted in Texas. He continued:

In a contest between Throckmorton and Pease ... some twenty months since, the people of Texas elected T. by a vote of six or seven to one over P. This was then the voice of Texas. This is probably about the present position of affairs with the legal voters .... Pease is the best, wisest, and safest man, but the public whom he is to govern are of a different opinion. He has, from the Rebellion ... become warped in mind .... but he will, I think, commit no imprudent or oppressive act."[39]

Pease, knowing he was to be appointed, wrote General Griffin on July 22, recommending "proper persons" for appointments, and stating, "I do not want the office of Governor, and would much prefer that someone else should be elected, but the indications seem to be that my appointment would be acceptable to the Union men of the state generally, and this makes it incumbent on me to take the place if it is tendered." He requested a personal interview and noted, "The general intent I feel in the success of the reconstruction measures of Congress has induced me to write you with much more freedom than our slight acquaintance would justify ... ."[40]

Pease began his service as provisional governor on August 8, 1867. He broke the news to Carrie, then sixteen, first writing casually about the weather and telling her that ice was being made in Austin, which had two well-patronized "ice cream saloons." He had not yet visited them, although "one of them is in our building on the [Congress] Avenue." Then he wrote,

On Thursday last ... we had a telegram from New Orleans, announcing the removal of Throckmorton and appointment of myself. I know this will not be very pleasant news to Mama as it will prevent me from going north this fall. I cannot well decline .... The same night the Union men got up an impromptu demonstration and came down to Mr. Morrell's

with a torch light procession and a band of music. We had several short
speeches and some good singing – about forty ladies and six hundred
or more males were present, altogether a pleasant time. It will be some
days before we get the official order of Genl. Sheridan when I shall
take possession of the office.

As usual, writing to his daughters about what interested them, he added that
a baby had been born during the cannon fire and procession, and that the
"young folks are to have a grand inauguration ball next week: Don't you
wish you were here to take part in it?" He then noted that voter registration
was progressing, although the number of those disfranchised was greater
than anyone expected. He thought that a third of the registered whites
would vote for the Union ticket, plus nine-tenths of the Freedmen, adding,
"The knowledge of this fact is having a wonderful effect on the Rebels, who
are behaving much better."[41]

Texans began corresponding with Pease right away, some offering
support. For example, J. M. Burroughs of Milam in Sabine County thought
that as a previous governor, "your acts and conduct would compare
favorably with the most enlightened Governors …." He noted, "Your
Publik life is a just [and important part] of the history of Texas …. I can
not call to mind a single act of yours, that is repulsive, or unfriendly to
the people of Texas … you have proved yourself to have been a wise law
maker and law adviser." Judge C. B. Sabin of the Third Judicial District
in Houston wrote, "The people of the country are partial to you." From
Houston, newspaper editor E. H. Cushing wrote to Pease, "Your appointment [is] approved by the best citizens. Throckmorton could do us no good
in the thankless and laborious position – civil affairs will be administered
with prudence and reason." Jasper Starr, editor of the *Bosque Beacon* in
Meridian, informed Pease that, "You made the best Governor Texas ever
had, save Sam Houston."[42]

Before initial pleasantries were over, the governor began receiving
letters about serious problems around the state. He had to spend a significant amount of time answering Texans who had no one else to contact
in a government that lacked a lieutenant governor, state representatives

and senators, and local officials. Many of them knew him from his public service of more than thirty years, or they had voted for him. Many were desperate for help. To handle correspondence, he had only his so-called "private" secretary, a state employee who served as a clerk to write his letters and make copies of them.

Pease's primary task was to make recommendations for removal of ex-Confederates from local, county, and statewide offices and for their unionist replacements. Throckmorton's departure had opened the door wider for removals of those in office who could not swear the Test Oath of 1862 that they had never voluntarily supported the Confederacy, and Pease's presence gave Griffin a valuable resource: The Governor had countless connections across the state and could often confirm information about who should be removed or appointed. When Griffin asked for recommendations, Pease sometimes responded on the back of an incoming letter, referring him by date to suggestions he had already made.[43]

Filling positions began immediately. The day before Pease took office, Judge Sabin wrote to him about James Green, "one of our colored citizens formerly of Brazoria County" who wanted to be a justice of the peace in Galveston. This is a very early instance of a Freedman's expression of interest in holding public office. After only a week on the job, citizens of "undoubted loyalty" in Williamson County petitioned the new governor to appoint Dr. Beriah Graham as superintendent of the state Lunatic Asylum. The Austin physician and his family were well-known to the Peases, and the appointment was made on August 20.[44]

The official notice regarding replacements came by United States Military Telegraph to Griffin in Galveston from Sheridan in New Orleans on August 28, authorizing the latter to remove disloyal county officials throughout Texas. The notice was followed the next day with the order, a copy of which was sent to Pease.[45] The order was followed by another that removed all five justices of the Texas Supreme Court and named replacements that included Edmund J. Davis who would soon become a leading Republican in Texas.[46] Davis declined the appointment with regrets, explaining that, "engagements ... as a practicing attorney ... prevent my acceptance of any Judicial Office."[47]

On September 15, Pease received a telegram from Galveston with a stark announcement: "General Griffin died this morning." The yellow fever virus had taken his life during a rampant epidemic. The Governor wrote Lucadia ten days later that General Joseph J. Reynolds would replace Griffin and had permission to move his headquarters to San Antonio or Austin due to the epidemic on the coast. He presumed that Reynolds would move to Austin, which he did. Pease called Reynolds "very acceptable" but thought that "he would not fill the [place] as well as Genls Sheridan & Griffin, who had become familiar with their duties and the people as well as our laws." Pease, however, was unhappy with his personal situation: "I am in for it and must go through. Matters will come right in time, though none as in times past. If I could go home at night and meet my wife and children, I should for a short time be able to forget the troubles of life."[48]

Removals and replacements did not always go smoothly. For example, an Austin notary public, J. B. Morris, refused to surrender his papers. Pease wrote the Austin post commander, "The remedy ... by the civil authority is somewhat uncertain .... I therefore respectfully request that Mr. Morris may be arrested by the military and held in custody until he shall comply with the law ...."[49]

In many places the operation of routine government functions became impossible when offices were vacant due to the lack of Loyalists who could perform as officeholders. Justice of the Peace W. B. Caraway wrote, "there is not now ... within the County of Shelby ... a Sheriff, Constable, or Coroner ... to execute the process issued from my court." Charles Russell, Karnes County Judge, wrote the Governor that Griffin's order requiring all jury members to swear the "Ironclad Oath" of 1862, needed modification: "Under that order it is impossible to obtain a jury in this county" because a majority of the population could not swear that they had not voluntarily aided the Confederacy. A Bryan citizen wrote to ask if mayor and a council could be appointed and police to protect them "against all manner of depredations committed during the dark hours of the night ...."[50]

By October 28, thirty-three officers had been replaced in sixteen counties. Removals and replacements continued for months more. Some people were prominent, but others were not; some had appropriate experience for a position, but others did not. In San Antonio, James P. Newcomb and others recommended George W. Brackenridge, National Bank President, and Theodore Hertzberg, Registration supervisor, as aldermen because they were "gentlemen whose standing in the community and loyalty to the Government it is unnecessary to endorse as none stand higher." From Boston in Bowie County, the Governor received a request from a man of no prominence but deep sincerity who wanted to be the County Clerk: "I once hird [sic] you deliver a speech in Sherman when you were Canvassing ... and gave you my vote ...." He added, "I have ever loved the Union never way Disloyal .... My foot was broken off ... and am crippled for life ... I am 48 years of age ...."[51]

Another problem statewide was the number of people who did not know how to handle the transition to new officeholders. A Denton County Tax Assessor and Collector wrote that he had been removed but since his successor had not qualified; what should he do? Pease instructed him that it was the duty of the County Judge to give such notice, and when he was notified, he would forward the recommendation to the commanding General for appointment.[52]

The number of those who documented problems and sought solutions from Pease between August and December 1867 must have seemed an unending stream to him. Many inquiries came to him from the military occupiers of the state. He found it necessary to provide explanations of legal and other matters to commanders who were unfamiliar with Texas in every way, who had no training as lawyers, and who had no experience in the civil government of any state. For instance, military control created dilemmas when no provisions were made to accommodate previous legislative actions. Judge W. F. Baylor of Wilson County presented one such dilemma: He had written General Griffin, noting that the Eleventh Legislature provided for election of school board members, but Sheridan had declared all elections were forbidden, and so what should be done? Griffin referred the question to Pease, who answered thoroughly with a more far-reaching answer than Griffin expected. He pointed out that the 1866 Texas act provided for whites-only schools, a provision that violated the Federal Civil Rights Act of 1866. Therefore, no school board elections should be held, and the school fund should not be spent until state legislation provided that it would be used for the benefit of all Texans.[53]

Native Americans remained active on the frontier, and Pease received letters from white settlers pleading for military protection. The problem of the best placement for limited numbers of troops was ongoing. Griffin wrote Pease that he would send "an additional agent to the frontier to protect against Indians ... ." The General thought the loss of property taken by the Indians was a small consideration compared to the loss of life and suggested that local settlers organize for home protection.[54]

The late months of 1867 were filled with increasing anxiety over inadequate military protection as lawlessness escalated against white Loyalists. For example, Pease received a letter from Lampasas Judge W. B. Pace regarding threats to citizens and hopes that troops would not be removed: "At present I am of the opinion that I will have to Leave until times change hear [sic] the Loyal men hear [sic] have had to stand many hard times ... ." Pace wrote again soon thereafter, "lawless men are getting away with it and troops need to stay ... ." Pease then wrote to the Austin Post Commander, forwarding a copy of Pace's letter and requesting, "very respectfully, that you retain the present command at Lampasas if it [is] within your power to do so."[55]

Freedmen were often in desperate danger of starvation. Henry Cheatham of San Marcos, addressing the Governor as "Dear Friend," pointed out that Freedmen did not have enough to eat. This was no isolated case when many newly freed people left or had to leave the farms on which they had lived and had no steady employment or land on which to grow food. Pease was made aware of the problem early in his administration when he received a copy of a congressional resolution calling "for the relief of the destitute in the South and South Western States ... to prevent starvation and extreme want to any and all classes of destitute or helpless persons where a failure of crops and other causes have [occurred]."[56] Exactly what he was to do about the situation was not clear.

Freedmen were also in mortal danger from violence. For example, members of the Board of Registrars in Fort Worth wrote urgently about increasing violence toward themselves: "We have been compelled to suspend

Registration in this county until we can procure more troops we have but 6 soldiers our lives are threatened, and from reliable information an attack is contemplated on the Board by 25 or 30 ... today .... The whole cause of our troubles can be traced to the Responsible leading men of this place who furnish young Bloods with whiskey and Spur them on while they themselves stand behind the scene .... " Days later, the Board wrote to Griffin that a Freedman had been shot and possibly killed.[57]

Judge Caldwell of Jefferson addressed grave and growing problems there:

> The spirit of bigotry and intolerance is as rampant as ever, and with few exceptions all state officers use their influence in opposition to the call for a Convention. He who has the moral courage to speak on behalf of the Republican party, and in the advocacy of reconstruction under the military bills, is at once met with distraction as to make the stoutest wince.

Caldwell added, "The Colored voters are told, if they vote with the rebels, all will go on smoothly – if they vote with the Yankees they may look out for danger. They are further threatened with being discharged from employment if they do not obey the behest of their employers." He felt certain that, "There is a remedy for that, and Gen. Sheridan has inaugurated it – displace the office holders." Caldwell concluded that for the time being he would remain silent, but yet he was "somewhat encouraged. I know we have the strength – The white and colored voters in this District will be about equal. There will be no difficulty in our securing the negro vote, if they can be informed of their interests, and have protection guaranteed them."[58]

Two weeks later, Caldwell wrote, "I tell you Governor a majority of the White voters are with us if we could only emancipate them from the awe in which they stand of rebell [*sic*] denunciation. In this & Davis County [formerly and later Cass County] where we did not receive 30 votes last year, we would now get at least one third of the White vote .... " He asked Pease to publish "an address in the nature of an inaugural" to "Arouse the non-slave holding element & show them how they are [were] domineered over during the rebellion by the aristocracy .... The Negroes should be distinctly informed that all their future hopes for prosperity and protection depends upon our Success." Caldwell reminded Pease, using round numbers, that in the previous year, 60,000 men voted, with Pease having received 12,000 and Throckmorton, 48,000. Since 8,000 of Throckmorton's voters are disfranchised, Caldwell wrote, and "none of ours, now under more enlightened and liberal views you would receive 24,000 to Throckmorton's 28,000. There will be 34,000 Negro votes, of which you get 30,000." Thus, Caldwell reasoned, Pease would have 54,000 votes and Throckmorton, 34,000. "Let the rebells [sic] do their best & we can defeat them."[59] Nevertheless, safely getting Freedmen to the polls was no easy matter. A letter from Huntsville asked the governor to use his influence to provide "some protection at the Ballot Box for the Freedmen of Polk County. If something isn't done in their behalf, and they are permitted to be run off and [be] intimidated as they are at present, Polk cannot send a sound man ... to Congress."[60]

Letters for Pease documenting a need for troops seemingly everywhere continued to arrive. General James Oakes wrote the Governor, acknowledging his request for forty or fifty troops at Cameron to enforce the law, where the "disloyal citizens of Milam County, who are a majority of whites, are almost in a state of insurrection ... I am fully satisfied of the necessity of having troops ... but unfortunately I have not the force disposable."[61]

A public health crisis caused by yellow fever also attacked a wide swath of the Texas population in 1867. During the late summer and fall, an epidemic swept through Texas from the coast as far inland as La Grange and Brenham in Central Texas to Henderson and Anderson in East Texas. People were unaware that this disease, with its high mortality rate, was transmitted by mosquitoes but was not contagious. Livingston Lindsay, Associate Justice of the Texas Supreme Court, wrote Pease at the close of September about vacancies of clerkships in Fayette County due to the "trouble and distress from the ravages of the Yellow Fever." Lindsay wrote again to Pease on Oct. 9, telling him that their friend, Dr. M. Evans and his daughter, "both departed this life last night" and that three members of his own family had been sickened. It seemed that the fever "has proved more fatal here than it has ever been anywhere in the South ... one hundred seventy deaths in ... a little over four weeks, in a population ... of not more than fifteen hundred and more than two-thirds have fled their homes!"[62] R. W. Kennon, Chairman of the Board of Health in Chappell Hill, documented conditions there, writing the governor, "We are suffering at this place terribly from the yellow fever" with "seventy-three deaths of white persons and about twenty among the Freedmen." The community was "in need of almost everything ... Can you not interest yourself and procure us some assistance among the good people of Austin, especially in behalf of the Freedmen." Pease's response is not of record, but he may well have been moved to action. This public health crisis also had financial costs. In 1868, vouchers totaling a thousand dollars were forwarded from Brenham for expenses of the "sick and poor in this county during the Epidemic raging ... last Summer."[63]

Two other crises in 1867—a crop failure and a hurricane—gave the Governor even more worry. Both had humanitarian and financial implications. A writer from wealthy Brazoria asked Pease for suspension of payments of taxes for about ninety days, explaining, "Many of the planters here have not the money to pay their taxes ... and commission merchants will not advance it to the best man in the County." S. W. Perkins, Brazoria County Judge, wrote, "In view of the almost total failure of the cotton crop in Brazoria County the past season," he asked for "suspension of payment of property taxes until the Epidemic now raging in Houston and Galveston ceases." To make matters worse, a hurricane slammed into Galveston, the state's largest city. E. P. Hunt wrote the Governor, "We have had a tremendous hurricane here and great damage has been done ... ."[64]

Two land issues also occupied the Governor's attention. Acts of the legislature during the war affected land certificates and scrip. General Land Office Commissioner Joseph Spence wrote Pease, acknowledging that "you are unwilling that any patents shall be issued from the General Land Office with your signature ... upon any Certificate or Scrip of any land that has been issued or sold under any law of the State ... passed by any pretended or so-called Legislature since ... the Secession Convention of the year 1861 ... ." Spence assured Pease that he would refuse to issue any such Patents upon Certificates or Scrip. Another matter of payment of taxes on land showed widespread rebellious attitudes toward state government that had enormous financial repercussions. The issue arose when Comptroller M. C. Hamilton wrote Pease regarding the propriety of suspending sales of lands on which taxes had not been paid. Pease wrote to Reynolds that he did not concur with Hamilton, because those who had failed to pay taxes were, "generally speaking, large Landholders who hope thus to escape taxation." He observed that an increasing number of people were not paying taxes, and in his most recent examination, he found that "there were some fifteen million acres not then rendered ... mostly ... by the most ardent rebels ...." Pease advised Reynolds that it would require much labor and some expense to carry out the law fully, but that would be a "small consideration when compared to the importance of securing the taxes upon fifteen million acres ...." Reynolds replied that suspension of sale of lands not rendered for taxes would not be ordered. This topic shows the breadth and depth of Pease's grasp of an issue that the military commanders lacked.[65]

The issue of Freedmen's education reflected resistance to the changing times. Little progress was made for or by former slaves, but Matthew Symington and forty-eight others in Galveston signed a petition stating that they "and all our colored citizens" wanted E. M. Wheelock to be named the Superintendent of Freedmen's Schools.[66]

In addition to all of Pease's problems, Morgan C. Hamilton, the brother of Pease's friend and political ally, A. J. Hamilton, created another difficulty by refusing in his role as Comptroller to pay the Governor's salary for a time. Pease wrote, "The reasons you assign for not drawing a warrant for my salary for the month of November 1867 are not warranted by the facts as disclosed by the Books of your office," and the matter was resolved.[67]

As the year drew to a close, reports of violence continued to add to the litany of lawlessness in the state. For example, Sophia Wilson of Pine Grove in Cherokee County wrote the Governor, without explaining her relationship to those named in her letter, "I feel it is my painful duty to inform you, sir of one of the most cold-blooded murders that has ever been committed by a demon in human form ...." Half-brothers J. H. Wilson and R. W. Wilson and their brother in law, J. M. Lewis, had eaten supper when a man "by the name of McCann, who lived on the place," was knocked down with a six shooter by J. H. Wilson. Lewis died in the incident. The writer hoped for arrest and punishment "according to the laws of the country." She signed herself, "A friend of peace and Harmony."[68]

At times, something more normal and less stressful was evident in the Governor's papers. Because he chose to live in a boarding house rather than alone at Woodlawn or in the Governor's Mansion, he made the Mansion available to the commanding general. Pease wrote to his wife in October, "the law requires [furnishings] be purchased," and since Lucadia was close to New York, he asked her to shop for carpets, light fixtures, and curtains. He preferred her taste in selections, but S. M. Swenson would make the purchases. Swenson, Pease's friend, former Austin resident, sometime banker, and supplier of goods at Swenson, Perkins & Company in New York, noted those purchases in December. Swenson wrote, "Mrs. Pease will leave this evening in company with William R. Baker Esq. of Houston. The weather is very inclement but moderating and if they get through the Snow drifts they will soon be in a warmer climate." Everything for the Governor's Mansion had been shipped, except for the lamps and the chandeliers that had to be made.[69]

Swenson, a Swedish emigrant who resided in Austin when the Peases arrived in 1853, remained interested in Texas after he left town during the war. He wrote another letter to Pease in mid-December 1867, observing, "I never had any fears that Texas would be governed by the colored race, and if patience could be exercised for a few years, all present annoyances would pass away. Thus far it seems to me that the negroes have all the time behaved better than the whites, but it is natural that they should now be tenacious of their rights and easily led astray by ill advice ... ." Regarding immigration, he stated, "I am very glad that you feel an interest in an influence of European Emigrants ...," and he hoped that Texas would encourage them. He added, "My brother in Sweden ... is beset all the time to aid people to go to Texas. They all however lack means."[70]

As the year came to an end, Pease's difficulties increased because Genl. Winfield Scott Hancock, who had become commander of the Fifth Military District in New Orleans on November 29, allowed his personal politics as a Democrat to interfere with congressional (and hence, Republican) mandates for Reconstruction. Although military commanders were supposed to remove those who opposed Reconstruction, Hancock appointed Democrats to office. Later, the General rejected a request by Pease for a military trial in a case that did not suit his politics, and he ignored the reality of conditions in Texas with an amazing statement: "At this time the country is in a state of profound peace." Apparently, Hancock's reference was to the northern reaches of the nation, without regard to lawlessness in Texas. Pease's letters as Provisional Governor certainly had not reflected profound peace in the Lone Star state.[71]

Back in October, Pease had written to Lucadia, "There is no probability of Genl Hancock removing me or any other of Genl Sheridan's appointees – Personally I should feel it to be a great relief to be rid of this office ... nearsightedness [on the part of the military] is a great misfortune ...." Ten days later, Pease wrote to his wife again, expressing disappointment that he had not heard from her or the children, "when I so much needed something to soothe my temper, which has been greatly ruffled by the conduct of ... the former Atty Genl and the late Comptroller, who have taken up some strange notions in regard to what laws are to guide us under the Reconstruction laws ...."[72] How very ruffled he must have felt after Hancock declared that the country was in a state of profound peace.

Chapter 9

Governing Reconstruction Texas, 1868–1869

"It is necessary that peace and good order should be enforced."

E. M. Pease

On January 17, 1868, Pease answered what he called Hancock's "near-sighted" view of the situation in Texas with a well-focused review of the Federal law governing Reconstruction and of conditions in the state. This reply, addressed to an aide, was an open letter, printed for circulation to the public. The Governor began, "I dissent entirely from the declaration that 'the State Government in Texas, organized in subordination to the authority of the United States, is in the full exercise of its proper powers.'" He summarized conditions in the government of Texas for Hancock and concluded that point by writing, "I am at a loss to understand how a government, without representation in Congress and without any organized militia force, with such limited powers ... can properly be called a state government ... in full exercise of its proper powers."

Pease also dissented from Hancock's declaration about the condition of life in Texas:

> Texas cannot properly be said to be in a state of profound peace. It is true that there no longer exists any organized resistance to the authority of the United States, but a large majority of the white population who participated in the late rebellion are embittered against the Government by their defeat in arms and loss of their slaves, and yield to it in an unwilling obedience only because they feel that they have no means to resist authority. None of this class has any affection for the Government, and very few of them have any respect for it. They regard the legislation of Congress ... as unconstitutional and hostile to their interests, and consider the government now existing here ... an usurpation upon their rights. They look upon the enfranchisement of their late slaves and the disenfranchisement of a portion of their own class as an insult and oppressive.

Such feeling "by a large majority of [those] who have heretofore exercised the political power in Texas ... renders it extremely difficult to enforce the criminal laws" where the state is densely occupied, and "often impossible" where it is not. This "induces many to redress their fancied wrongs and grievances by acts of violence." Pease called it "lamentable" that more than one hundred homicides had occurred in the previous twelve months and that not a tenth of the perpetrators had been arrested, and less than one-twentieth had been tried. Army officers and soldiers had been killed, and none of the perpetrators had been tried or punished. In civil cases, officers could not function without citizen support. Offenders escaped from insecure jails, and indicted parties remained at liberty. When sheriffs did their jobs, grand juries and petit juries often failed to convict offenders. The result was that "there is but little security for life in Texas ... by law."[1]

Hancock responded to Pease's reasoned, organized letter with a rambling twenty-five-page commentary. He began tartly, noting that Pease's letter was not received "until it had been widely circulated by the newspaper press. To such a letter—written and published for manifest purposes—it has been my intention to reply as soon as leisure from more important business would permit." He did not dispute Pease's review of state governance, but wrote that if Pease thought Texas should have more powers, he should direct his complaints to Congress. Regarding his explanation of the opinion of Rebels toward government, Hancock was unsatisfied that "this is all you have to present for proof that war and not peace prevails in Texas, and hence it becomes my duty (so you suppose) to set aside the local civil tribunals, and enforce the penal code against citizens, by means of Military Commission." Also, "My Dear Sir, I am not a lawyer … but I must lay claim … to some poor knowledge of men, and some appreciation of what is necessary to social order … and for the future of our common country, I would devoutly wish that no great number of our people have yet fallen in with the view you appear to entertain." Hancock then made remarks on history and wrote, "That the people of Texas consider acts of Congress unconstitutional, oppressive, or insulting to them, is of no consequence for the matter at hand …. At the end of almost two years from the close of the war, we should begin to recollect what manner of people we are, to tolerate again free, popular discussion and extend some … consideration of opposing views." Pease "might as well deny that profound peace exists in New York … where a majority of the people differ with a minority … or … in the House or Senate … or in the Supreme Court, where all these questions have been repeatedly discussed …. It is rather more than hinted in your letter, that there is no local State Government in Texas and no local laws outside the Acts of Congress, which I ought to respect, and that I should undertake to protest the rights of persons and property in my own way and in an arbitrary manner."

The general became agitated as he wrote, declaring that Pease would put him in a position in which "I am now to protect all rights, and redress all wrongs. How is it possible for me to do it?" He declared, "There has not been a moment since I have been in command … when the whole military force in my hands has not been ready to support the civil authorities of Texas in the execution of the laws." Pease should not "indulge in wholesale censure against the civil authorities" when he was the chief among them, and many had been named at his suggestion. "Now it is against this local government, created prior to my coming here, and so composed of your personal and political friends, that you have [made] the most grievous complaints" of not doing their duty, maintaining justice, and punishing crimes. To Hancock the situation was a "profound mystery," and he believed that Pease was "in very great error as to facts."

Finally, the General concluded, "I have found little else in your letter but indications of temper, lashed into excitement by causes which I deem mostly imaginary, a great confidence in the accuracy of your own opinions, and an intolerance of the opinions of others; a desire to punish the thoughts and feelings of those who differ with you, and an impatience which magnifies the shortcomings of officials .... ." He closed by saying, "If I have written anything to disabuse your mind of so grave an error, I shall be gratified."[2]

Pease had no need to reply. He no doubt happily welcomed the news when Hancock transferred from command of the Fifth Military District on March 18 in a disagreement with President Grant on a Louisiana matter. Pease thought that Hancock's successor, General Robert C. Buchanan, was no better about appointments, but the two did not argue openly.[3]

The majority of the extant letters written to Pease in 1868 documented escalating lawlessness and violence and asked—even begged desperately—for Federal troops. In East Texas, where white plantation owners no longer held slaves, high numbers of blacks remained, and tension ran especially high. Whites feared that blacks could dominate society because they had the right to vote, and many whites had been disfranchised. In much of North, Central, Southeast, and even South Texas, deeply entrenched white racist attitudes about Black inferiority also led to open hostilities. Federal troops in insufficient numbers across Texas could not maintain peace, and Freedmen were in constant, mortal danger. Throughout the year Loyalists' questions of Pease formed a troubling litany: Are we to remain in subjugation to rebels? Are we to be killed one by one? Does the United States intend to protect us, or not? If not, why will the government not say so? These fundamental questions and more filled the Governor's letters for months.[4]

The first letter of the year 1868 for Pease, written on January 2 by Judge Colbert Caldwell, documented the volatile situation in East Texas. Caldwell called this event the Marshall "Riot," although no one was physically injured. He wrote that in the town of Marshall, "the pent up wrath of all rebeldom culminated and exploded" when, on December 30, 1867, he and other radical leaders went there to urge voter turnout in the upcoming election of constitutional convention delegates. Unable to use a court room, they gathered about three hundred supporters, mostly Freedmen, in a court house basement hallway during a snow storm. "I addressed them for about five minutes," Caldwell wrote, and "there was no incendiarism." A Black man, Scipio McKee, began singing the Union song, "Rally Round the Flag," and "the song moved [the Rebels to] indignation." Freedmen fled when the Marshall Chief of Police fired his pistol into the ceiling. A deputy sheriff arrived to maintain order, but Caldwell thought he was supporting the police chief and said that the two had ordered him out at gunpoint. Caldwell went to the Federal post commander, to whom the Sheriff and Deputy Sheriff also went, to explain the incident. An ensuing argument in the Freedmen's Bureau office made matters worse, and Caldwell accused the deputy sheriff of sympathy with assassins. Caldwell feared for his life and claimed that an armed Freedmen's Bureau attaché saved him. The Army officer had the civilian officers arrested, but the district judge released them. The police chief and deputy sheriff forbade radical speeches in town, where everyone must "cuss Congress and damn the nigger." Caldwell hoped that the county delegation to the convention would be in the hands of the radicals if troops protected them during the election, yet his hope was tempered by the fact that blacks are "so cruelly wronged and outraged that humanity itself is beginning to manifest some of its animal instincts." They had no protection, and he feared that "on some trying occasion they will take the matter in hand ... and then, of course from a rebel standpoint they will be in the wrong and ought to be exterminated." Nevertheless, "the last one of them will vote if he can." Caldwell knew the potential price of his beliefs: his own life was in danger.[5]

From Jefferson, Unionists Donald Campbell, B. W. Gray, and C. T. Garland documented conditions the spring of 1868. Campbell and Gray wrote that since the Presidential Proclamation of the previous September, "insubordination and the spirit of persecution have ... alarmingly increased ...." They sent a copy of the "filthy" and "incendiary" *Jefferson Times*, promoting "the necessity of a war of races" and trying to "strike terror into the minds of loyal men." Campbell and Gray wrote, "We are no alarmists: but society here is on the verge of eruption." Days later, Campbell wrote that he had searched for replacements of officials, but "men are absolutely afraid to accept office—they are loyal enough at heart—but feel that the moment they accept office under the 'Yankee, nigger equality government'" their lives would be endangered.[6] C. T. Garland wrote about desperados going un-arrested, and how the outlaw Cullen Baker, long the "terror of the county," walked the streets. Garland expected the murder of Loyalists. The Ku Klux "stick up their grotesque devices" with messages written in blood. He declared, "If our Country cannot protect us, it is time for the world to know it. If freedom of speech and of the press is not to be permitted because it does not agree with the 'white men's party' it is time for us to know it." He had written an article "appealing to the laboring men of Texas not to act politically with the men who dragged them from their peaceful homes into Jeff Davis' army to fight for a slave holding Aristocracy who staid at home to hunt down Union men with dogs .…" He observed, "It hurts the feelings and dignity of the gentry here wonderfully for Union men to use argument against them." He antici-pated that Union League meetings would have to be suspended.[7]

William Phillips of San Augustine wrote on February 10, the first day of four in the election for constitutional convention delegates, that polling had been quiet until armed rebels assaulted the polls and decreed that no more votes should be cast. The Sheriff did not keep order. "Is there no remedy, is there no punishment to be meted out to such villains? Are we the loyal Men of this Section of the Country to remain in Subjugation to the Rebels? If so Loyalty is a very great burden, Treason would be honorable and easy to bear." He wanted an answer to his letter, but there is no copy of a reply in Pease's papers.[8]

Writing about the Panola County delegate election, J. K. Williams lamented that it was his "painful Duty to give you the foul proceedings of Some of the Disloyal men of my County. On Monday morning … about 400 Freedmen were present and fifty white voters .… W. D. Anderson Sheriff of Panola County (who is a vile Fire Eating Anti-Conventionist) was one of the [Election] Board .… " Williams urged Freedmen to vote, but they thought they should not. Later Williams informed Pease that in Panola County the sheriff, his deputy, and others attacked him with arms drawn and said he was "a Damned Radical the Negroes friend" and he must flee or denounce the Republican Party. "I thought it best to compromise on that occasion ... ." He asked, "What can civil law do ... ?"[9]

Other letters from northeast Texas documented brutal conditions. J. F. Johnson telegraphed Pease after a Freedman was shot in Mt. Pleasant, where troops were leaving. "The freedmen will leave because of fear—the Farming interest will be ruined and many Loyal men forced to leave—Can you not have the order countermanded—see Genl Reynolds at once—help us now or our friends are ruined. Please answer."[10] From Quitman, B. W. Musgrove described outlaws "stalking ... at noon day in defiance of Law who swear that they have not yet Surrendered as Confederate soldiers to the US authorities and that they will not do so." He continued, "Their business is to kill negroes and terrify Union men off their premises ... Josh F. Johnson [who had just warned Pease of the possibility] has been compelled to leave the state throwing open his whole Farm." Musgrove offered to become a deputy sheriff.[11]

Pease noted to himself that H. E. Scott had reported from Grayson County: "People are generally well displeased [with] certain orders from Head Quarters" and "relapsing into indifference regarding the negro ... defrauding him, swindling him out of his pay ... the county is in no better hands" than it was earlier. Later, he had a letter about deaths and injuries there: "[t]hey are playing high havoc below Pilot Grove" in Grayson County.[12] From Denton County, John L. Lovejoy described two "outrageous and unprovoked" murders. He "thought it was the duty of someone to inform your excellency ... and request you to offer a reward ... ." One murder involved stolen hogs; the other, a "trifle."[13]

In Southeast Texas, men were cutting timber on an absentee owner's land, and "a man's life is not safe if he interferes with them," attorney Robert McMann in Chambers County wrote. He called it "nonsense" to seek protection since no one would be the sheriff. He and Judge Chambers had tried for a year and applied to Genl. Reynolds. "If we cannot get protection from Austin we must try higher authority at Washington. I think that what few of us that was loyal through the war should be protected."[14]

Central Texas had similar problems with lawlessness. In Bastrop, three men were killed and the murderer went un-arrested, Jeremiah Hamilton wrote. G. Schutze appealed for troops, writing that almost within a week five murders were committed, "not counting other outrages .... What frontier county can show such a bloody record from the hords of radical savages? Can not the government spare us a file of men?"[15]

Disorder also occurred in South Texas. Republican leader E. J. Davis wrote that he would look for men in Refugio County to fill vacancies despite a shortage of unionists. He noted, but did not elaborate, that Bee County, "is probably the most completely rebel county in the State ...."[16]

Statewide, other issues arose that put additional demands on the Governor's time and energy. For example, Cameron County Judge Jeremiah Galvan wrote from Brownsville that after an 1867 tornado destroyed the court house and jail, they had not been able to rebuild and pay expenses of a temporary jail. He asked that General Reynolds be impressed with the need for help. Hays County Judge P. D. Alexander sent recommendations for positions, and "as Genl Hancock refused to appoint a freedman [as] Commissioner, I have now recommended Mr. Armstrong (white) ...." T. S. Anderson recommended officers for Orange County, where all positions were vacant "or filled with men utterly incompetent .... The county is intirely destitute ...." J. M. Kammheimer of Houston stated that he was made tax assessor but the city council prevented him from work. Soon thereafter, Reynolds asked Pease to nominate four aldermen for Houston.[17]

Official copies of Pease's outgoing correspondence that began in mid-June 1868 provide additional insight into his thoughts and work. Many of his letters were to General Reynolds. On June 19 he transmitted a statement of A. R. Hall, Harris County Sheriff, to the general regarding Freedmen and city officers in Houston. Pease believed that police action under the city marshal was "wanton and unprovoked' in killing a Freedman who was not charged with an offense, and Mayor A. [Alexander] McGowen was "inefficient and unfit." Order was restored by the "efficient" conduct of the sheriff, whom Pease knew as an army officer during the war. "I have taken much trouble to ascertain the truth in this matter," he wrote Reynolds, and recommended men for mayor and marshal who "enjoy the respect of all classes." He felt certain that no more riots or other troubles would take place.[18]

Days later the General received a letter from Pease, describing conditions for the people of Falls County, where "the peace, order, and security of their society ... and all they hold dear, are placed in great jeopardy by the presence among them of a number of reckless, desperate men, who perpetuate assassination and violence [on] unoffending people."[19]

As Governor, Pease also had to correspond on myriad other topics in the first half of 1868. Because Texas eleemosynary institutions were founded during his earlier governorship, he may have been especially interested in a letter from Galveston mayor Isaac Y. Williams about a young, blind man from Virginia who wanted admission to the Asylum at Austin: "I appeal to you for such friendly aid as you may be able to grant him." In another Blind Asylum matter, State Comptroller M. C. Hamilton, feeling none too charitable toward that institution or Pease, created an annoyance by refusing to authorize payment of a routine expense; Pease referred the matter to Attorney General E. B. Turner, who ruled that the Comptroller had no power over the Trustees."[20]

"Old Texans" and acquaintances continued to write to the Governor. A Pennsylvanian claimed that his wife spoke warmly "of yourself and Mrs. Pease," and asked to become State Engineer and Geologist. A. G. Moore wrote from Limestone County, reminding the Governor that he had known him in Bastrop when Pease was "acting clerk for D. C. Barrett." He wanted an appointment. This reference to three decades earlier when Pease first arrived in Texas must have brought a smile to him as he reflected on his youthful confidence in Texas."[21]

Letters from Pease to his daughters in school in Hartford, dated from January to October 1868, show that his ever-affectionate self was not lost in the tide of awful correspondence that regularly surged across his desk. In January, when Carrie was sixteen and Julie was fourteen, he wrote to express his pleasure in Julie's wise choice of an opera glass rather than a croquet set for a Christmas gift and offered twenty dollars to buy a good one for their use in classes. On January 25, he announced a move from the Merrill's boarding house to Mrs. Beal's, "closer to the office. It would be dull work keeping house without our dear children at home, and it would greatly increase Mamas cares ... so I do not think we will keep house ... until we are all together ... ." The next item was politically important: Hancock was in town and had a reception on January 24 at the Governor's Mansion. "Mrs. Merrill and Mama went with me, there were few Ladies present, but the parlors were filled with gentlemen. More of the Rebels however [were present] than ... Union men. The former expect great things from him. They confidently predict that he will remove me, but he dare not do it, since the indications are that Congress will soon pass a law, putting the Rebel states under the orders of Genl Grant ... ." In the couple's room at Mrs. Beal's, they planned to hang Julie's drawing of Niagara as well as pictures of Lincoln and Sheridan. As for the convention delegate election, he thought that if the state did as well as Travis County, Texas would be back in the Union within months. In March 1868, Pease expressed the belief that he would be "kept here until next Fall, for I do not suppose we can get a new government organized before Sept or Oct next and I shall be compelled to hold on until that is done, unless I have the luck to be removed."[22]

Pease wrote to his daughters on May 7 about an officer camp "near the River back of our place ... fitted up [with] a tent with a floor" for dance parties. "[Few] rebel ladies attend, they are as bitter as they were while the war was going on." He mentioned a new theater production, and in spite of the dreadful condition of Texas, still thought "Austin has been gayer this Spring than I ever knew it before." "Mama" was soon to leave for the North, and he promised not to let work prevent his writing weekly. "[L]etters from my daughters are my greatest pleasure. I watch in them the growth of their minds ... ." On June 7 when Carrie was almost seventeen, he recalled his dark-haired firstborn. It had been three painful years of separation since he had seen his girls, but "I wished you to have ... an education, which could not be procured in Texas." He wrote Carrie on June 24, urging her to acquire good knowledge of history and to take notes as a means of remembering it. She had asked him about presidential candidates, and he thought that Grant's election was certain. Democrat success "would place the old Rebels again in power all over the South, and all the great sacrifice of men and money to suppress the Rebellion would have been ... in vain."[23]

On June 1, 1868, while lawlessness and violence ruled the state, ninety delegates assembled in Austin for a constitutional convention. Ninety-three men were delegates at times: eighty-two were Republicans and eleven were Conservatives; eighty-four were white and nine were black. Lucadia wrote that Blacks had been "as quiet and orderly in their demeanor as if this was not the first time their manhood had been acknowledged by the Whites," but many former rebels were "like madmen in their indignation" that black people could vote.[24]

Some delegates paid a price for their beliefs. C. T. Garland wrote that a Harrison County delegate left secretly for the convention; another started out but was warned that desperados were watching, and so he returned home. A third man rarely slept in the same place two nights in a row. D. M. McAdoo of Brenham sent Pease a letter about one of the Black delegates, Oliver Waters, "a very sensible freedman and good man …." He was a Union League member "out of a sense of duty" and local council president who was subjected to complaints by delegates. McAdoo asked Pease to confirm that the Republican Party accepted "all good men who … see fit to enter it. Am I not right?" Waters carried the letter to Pease but did not know its contents. Since he was worried by what people were saying, McAdoo asked Pease to see and talk with him. The Governor must have been glad to do so.[25]

Republicans comprised a majority of delegates, but they split into factions that made progress difficult. The largest faction was led by former Interim Governor A. J. Hamilton and included Pease. The two men were longtime friends, and Pease favored of Hamilton's leadership in the Republican Party and at the convention. However, Pease was not a delegate, and his chief role was to serve as liaison between the convention and the commanding general.[26] As Interim Governor he may well have had contact—even extensive contact—with delegates, but little of that is part of the record. Edmund J. Davis, leader of another Republican faction at the convention, was elected presiding officer over Colbert Caldwell, the Hamilton-Pease faction's nominee. Davis was elected in an open vote on the floor, but from the beginning he apparently had little control over delegates.[27]

When the Constitutional Convention opened in Austin on June 1, 1868, Pease sent delegates a message with recommendations concerning the new fundamental law. Among them were free public schools for all children, homesteads for all, land grants to encourage immigration, and state encouragement of railroads. He also recommended the temporary disfranchisement of a certain number of men who had participated in the rebellion, in order to place political power in the hands of those loyal to the United States Government. He told the delegates that the constitution must "secure equal civil and political rights to every inhabitant of the State, regardless of race."[28]

The *ab initio* question that occupied the delegates had grown from one of nullifying state actions during the war to a broader question of including the convention of 1866 and acts of the 11th Legislature that followed. Pease recommended that the new constitution declare "the pretended act of secession and all laws that have been enacted in aid of the late rebellion, repugnant to the Constitution and laws of the United States … null and void," and he wanted repeal of "all laws that made any discrimination against persons on account of their color, race, or previous condition." However, he could not recommend a blanket renunciation of laws as called for by *ab initio*, and that issue remained controversial until settled later in 1869 by the US Supreme Court's ruling in *Texas v. White*. Pease thought that the idea of dividing the state was a mistake and asked delegates not to consider it. It was driven by serious, competing economic and political issues, but he pointed out that Texas would be weakened economically by a split and that division would increase taxpayers' burdens so that public education and other functions would suffer. He also reminded delegates that division would require congressional approval, and the issue likely would delay Texas's rejoining the Union. The issue was finally laid aside in mid-July. Pease did make a surprising land-related suggestion that Texas sell to the United States the area west of the mouth of the Pecos River to the southeastern corner of the Panhandle.[29]

Republicans knew that statewide violence had to be stopped, and delegates created a committee early in the convention to study the problem. They issued a report documenting that 509 Whites and 468 Blacks had been killed between 1866 and mid-1868. Republicans thought the rise in crime was related to the appointment of Hancock, but the larger question was what they could do about ongoing murders of Freedmen and Loyalists. They decided to send a commission to Congress with their report and also asked that Pease be given the right to remove and appoint public officials. They also decided to ask for permission to establish a state militia, since the military was obviously not providing enough support.[30]

Convention debate was suspended in August 1868 while a state Republican convention met in Austin. The Governor was a Travis County delegate. He served on the platform committee with George Paschal, A. J. Hamilton, and E. J. Davis. They issued a report approving Congressional Reconstruction, the work of Republicans nationally, and the choice of Grant as nominee for president. They proclaimed that only the Republican Party could rebuild the economy of the South and called former Confederates "misguided" but still invited them into the party, asking only for support of its principles and an "earnest declaration that they will demand no rights for themselves, which they are not willing to accord to any other citizen of the United States."[31]

When the convention resumed work after the Republican convention, delegates finally voted on *ab initio*, which Pease and A. J. Hamilton opposed. Republican Radicals argued that the issue was not only one of principle but also that citizens had to be protected from unscrupulous railroad developers and others. Legislation during the war had allowed railroad companies to pay obligations to the permanent school fund in state warrants, which were worthless at the end of the war, and the fund thus lost several hundred thousand dollars. Other wartime legislation permitted some public land that was reserved to benefit a future university to fall into speculators' hands. Nevertheless, *Ab initio* lost by a nearly two-to-one margin in late August.[32]

Radicals who opposed Pease and A. J. Hamilton thought that the latter were supporting railroad companies in which they had too close an interest. Hamilton had pushed an ordinance through the convention that permitted the Houston and Texas Central to get a favorable loan and cancel its previous obligations. Pease, as state agent, had to complete the transaction by December 1, and he asked Reynolds to approve the ordinance, noting that the H. & T. C. was the only company that had demonstrated the financial ability to build a road in Texas since the war ended. Reynolds refused, but permitted Pease to make a new loan agreement with the company, contingent upon approval of the first legislature to meet after Texas returned to the Union.[33]

The convention recessed at the end of August for lack of funds, and money for another session had to be raised by taxes. The lack of progress on creating a constitution was due to strongly held conflicting opinions, unwillingness to compromise, and lack of adequate leadership. Historian Carl Moneyhon speculates, however, that "the most likely explanation ... was that the Republicans were delaying, trying to keep the state from seeking readmission before the national elections that autumn." He notes that a Grant victory was likely, but with the rapid buildup of the Southern Democratic Party in Texas that victory would have been even more likely if the Lone Star State remained out of the Union. Since Johnson and Hancock had deterred Republican progress in local Republican Party building, Texas Republicans did not know if they could ensure Grant's win.[34]

During the second half of 1868, while delegates debated issues that were not leading to a constitution, Pease received constant reminders that lawless conditions still prevailed across the state. For example, Pease wrote "Outrages" on an August letter from C. T. Garland in Jefferson, who informed the governor that six white Union men had been driven out of town since July 4—two had made Republican speeches and one was teaching in a Freedman's school. A Freedman was lashed three hundred times, and others were threatened with death if they refused to get membership tickets to the Democratic club. "We are afraid to publish accounts of these outrages for fear of assassination. We must suffer in silence until protect[ed]."[35]

Also from Jefferson, Donald Campbell wrote about a near-riot in August. A Ku Klux band had threatened to burn the "Negro" church. In response, the Freedmen armed themselves and waited. "They interfere with no one ... but if their church is attacked, [they will] die defending it .... Last night a party of Ku Kluxes went out to attack them, but through efforts of Lt. Smith and several others, it was prevented." Horsemen ran from the church while the hall bell was rung, and horns were blown to warn

Loyalists and Freedmen. "It was feared that the troops would be attacked [but] they stood with their guns in their hands … everything passed off without injury." Campbell thought that even if a hundred troops came as expected, that number would not help, since rebels would be quiet only until troops left. Campbell wrote that his own life was endangered. He could not safely leave town nor telegraph Pease privately. "I will continue to keep you posted should my life be spared."[36] Campbell wrote later to Pease that an infantry company of a sixty men had provided "comparative quiet," but the Klan continued to meet. The situation deteriorated still further. Judge N. V. Board wrote from Marshall about murders in Jefferson and the lack of help by the military as well as by Longley. "Is [there] any way to keep the county peaceable and quiet?"[37]

Judge A. B. Norton notified Pease from Stephenville that in Hood and Erath counties, "officers were either drunk or totally incompetent," while "scores of men say to me that they dared not take office … ." The judge later reported from Weatherford in Parker County that people said, " 'You had best get some of the d——d Yankees to help you' and laughed loudly. Some of them called the officer a 'd——d radical.'" Norton wrote Pease, commenting that he was, "greatly grieved at the removal of Genl Reynolds for I believe that he … was honestly endeavoring to discharge his duties. I trust that the change will not affect … reconstruction in Texas." Norton added, "Since the election of Genl Grant there has been a change for the better in public sentiment in this portion of the state."[38]

Conditions to the south were equally bad. "It is with a bursting heart I address you," Judge E. P. Upton of Refugio wrote in July. "My Son Wheelock H. Upton has been fouly murdered by a band of miscreants in Brazos County." His life and those of two other sons were also threatened. "I pray to GOD that something may speedily be done … or else a civil war will follow as sure as day follows night." He asked for an answer, since many postmasters were rebels who interfered with mail. The judge's son, R. A., had written his father of Wheelock's murder, and the judge sent Pease a copy of the letter, stating that the murder was "in cold blood by the d——d arch fiends of Texas. No Union man's life is safe out here on the Brassos—they … tried to hang me … . GOD help us, are we to submit to [being] murdered one at a time in cold blood? GOD forbid is my earnest prayer." Wheelock's wife was robbed, and she and her child were destitute. In October Upton acknowledged a "kind" response from Pease.[39]

At the end of December 1868, General Canby wrote Pease that it was "impractical to send troops everywhere," but that he would establish positions throughout the state. He did not specify how his plan differed from the location of existing posts.[40] The letter probably amounted to one more frustration for the Governor.

Pease's outgoing correspondence between June and December 1868 showed that his frustration and disgust rose as he received ever more distressing news. Routinely respectful letters to Federal commanders became more forceful, starting on July 1 over naming the Jefferson mayor. Aaron Grigsby was recommended by Judge Caldwell and George P. Smith, and Pease knew Grigsby as a moral man with a good education. To the governor's "great surprise," he received a copy of Gen. Reynolds's orders appointing W. N. Hodge. "I know not upon whose recommendation this appointment has been made, but I must respectfully protest against it as unjust to the loyal inhabitants of the City of Jefferson ...." He had received a petition for the appointment of Hodge, "signed by Rebels ... now active in endeavoring to defeat the reconstruction of the state." Pease then took a bold step, considering the polite interpersonal relations of the time: "I transmit herewith a letter directed to Genl U. S. Grant, in regard to this case, which is signed by Judge C. Caldwell and Geo. H. Smith, two of the delegates to the Convention from the District, and also by G. W. Whitmore and Geo. H. Slaughter, two delegates from the adjoining District, which I request may be transmitted with this letter to Genl Grant."[41] Since Grant was the Army general in chief, a personal friend of Reynolds, and a West Point classmate, this move must have made the Texas commander uncomfortable and perhaps angry.

Pease continued, however, to write forcefully to Reynolds. In transmitting a letter of Judge R. G. Shields of Falls County, he referred to the murders of two "unoffensive" Freedmen by lawless white men. Pease declared, "White men who would have justice done, dare not say or do anything for fear of being assassinated themselves. To kill and rob Black people, especially the best and most thrifty class of them ... is getting to be a practice tolerated by society. No effort is made .... The law is a dead letter."[42]

E. J. Davis wrote a letter forwarded by Pease to Reynolds that protested removal of John McClure, Sheriff of Nueces County. Pease was "greatly surprised" by McClure's removal after a high character reference. Pease knew McClure as "a gentleman of integrity [and] fine intelligence" who seemed to be one of the best sheriffs in the state, and "this action will be hailed ... as a triumph of the lost cause. In accordance with the request of General Davis, I ask that his letter, with a copy of this, may be sent to General U. S. Grant." Another request to go above Reynolds must have set his teeth on edge.[43]

The Governor's clear understanding of the law came before Reynolds yet again when Pease forwarded a letter of John H. Reagan with a memorial of citizens of Anderson County, asking for removal of W. V. Tunstall as County Judge due to his absence from the county. Pease wrote, "It is objectionable that the County Judge should be absent ... for so long a time, yet such cases do often happen, and the law contemplated that they will happen, for it provides that any two of the county commissioners shall have the power to do and perform all the duties of the county Judge when [he] is absent from the county." Pease sited *Paschal's Digest* and the article number, and provided references to laws prior to the 1866 Constitution. "When the County Commissioners are competent officers, no injury results from the absence of the County Judge; for the County Judge is hardly ever a lawyer, and the County Commissioners are usually as well qualified to discharge the duties as the County Judge is." Pease wrote that he would protest the removal of Tunstall and then made a strong statement:

> Their whole movement is gotten up by John H. Reagan, E. E. McClure, and Thomas J. Johnson, all of whom are personally known to me. They have been for years the prominent politicians of that County and section .... They were and still are the most violent rebels in the State, and are moving heaven and earth to defeat the reconstruction of the State.

Pease believed that the causes alleged for Tunstall's removal were a pretext. "From the long and intimate knowledge I have of all these men, I feel certain that neither of them would recommend the appointment of any man who is honestly working for the reconstruction of the State ... even if he was competent and as pure as an angel from heaven."[44]

Following an October visit by Tyler citizens to Reynolds, Pease asked him to appoint Captain Steelhammer to the Tyler post, recognizing the difficulty of placing troops everywhere citizens wanted them, but arguing that the short distance between Tyler and Van Zandt counties where the rebels "committed a most inhuman murder and many other acts of violence" justified the move. Violence was "driving a large number of loyal families [away] ... it is highly important that the officer in command should be one who comprehends the ... situation ...."[45]

Prominent Loyalist and convention delegate George W. Smith of Jefferson was murdered there on October 4, when the convention was in session. He was one of the few Carpetbaggers in the convention; he had come to Texas with the Army, stayed in Jefferson as a Freedman's Bureau teacher, and become active in Republican politics. B. W. Gray wrote Pease on October 14 that he had been in town during the murders of Smith and others, and "knowing how difficult it is, for the very facts to go out ... through the press, I ... give you my version ...." He said he knew the feelings and fears of many in town toward Smith, and Smith knew what they felt, too. "I advised him just before leaving Austin, that he ought not to return to Jefferson." Pease sent a heated letter to Reynolds about Smith's murder by what he called a "disguised and armed mob in the presence of the military in the city of Jefferson."[46]

Numerous controversial matters other than lawlessness, violence, and military control came before the Governor between July and December 1868. For example, land issues, complicated by laws written before, during, and after the rebellion, had to be settled. General Land Office Commissioner Joseph Spence, wrote to Pease, "The only law now in force ... for sale of public Domain is found ... in the Act of February 1860, amendatory of the Act of February 11, 1858 .... The Attorney General's opinion [is] that the Acts providing for the sale of alternate Sections and for the issuance of Script was repealed by the Acts of 20 October and 10th November 1866 .... The office has been governed by this opinion." Acting Comptroller George C. Rives wrote Pease about a payroll question: Should an officer of the provisional government be paid for the interval between his being ordered removed and his successor qualified? Rives wrote Pease that he did not know if he had the authority to answer, but he thought the officer was legally entitled to the salary. Pease's opinion on a personal matter was solicited by Sarah C. Brown of Austin, who, noting an apparent controversy, stated that she would not sell lots in the city because the land would be worth more when the railroad came in. She understood that a petition was circulating to remove her husband (Leander Brown) as Mayor because she refused to sell. She asked, "Doesn't a person have a right to determine worth of property?"[47]

The Governor remained involved in negotiations concerning the building of railroads. James H. Bell wrote from Houston, "Col. Baker thinks that the Central Rail Road ought to begin work on the branch from Brenham to Austin immediately" if the plan was acceptable to "their friends in New York." Baker expected Pease to "regulate acceptance of the 7% bonds so as to relieve yourself from all questionable responsibility in the matter ... it would not avail the company anything if you make your acquittance of their now existing indebtedness to the School Fund conditional upon its face."[48]

Hostilities between Indians and white settlers continued to demand the Governor's attention. One example involved Comanche brutality; and another, Anglo unwillingness to do what some considered just for the Coushattas. On the frontier south of Llano, Comanches attacked women and children in the home of John S. and Matilda Jane Friend in February 1868 while men were away. Two children, Malinda Ann Caudle and Temple Friend, survived as captives. In July, the governor issued a letter of credit to Leonard S. Friend (relationship unstated) under an 1866 legislative act to provide funds for the release of children or others captured by Indians. Pease appointed Friend as an agent to get the children and to draw up to fifteen-hundred dollars if needed. In May 1869 the children had still not been returned home. Pease wrote C. S. Parker, Commissioner of Indian Affairs, asking that the children be sent to Fort Richardson in Jack County, and if no payment provision was made by the United States, it would be paid by the state. To further ensure the children's well-being, the Governor wrote to the Parker County judge, J. H. Hunsberger, detailing the situation and asking that he contact a presumed relative in Parker County about the girl.[49]

The unsettled matter of state-granted land for the peaceable Coushattas arose again in 1868. The tribe, which had been in East Texas for about half a century, thrived by hunting, fishing, gathering, and farming. However, they were repeatedly forced to move as whites claimed land they lived on, even after the Republic made a grant to them. In 1855 when Pease was governor, the Legislature granted the tribe 6,400 acres in Polk County, but the grant amounted only to a promise on paper. Their relatives, the Alabamas, had a grant in Polk County, and most Coushattas lived with them.[50]

Pease received a petition in October 1868 for granting one-hundred acres to the Coushattas. The signers affirmed that the land would give the "peaceable and quiet" tribe room for homes. East Texan Unionist H. C. Pedigo wrote the governor at the request of Pease's private secretary about the Coushattas, stating that the tribe had "scarcely 100 souls" and "no means of procuring homes." Pedigo believed that they would likely remain in a state of "wretched indigence unless relieved by the government . . . ." He argued that "these Indians have some claim, if not upon the justice, at least [upon] the generosity of the state. During the War of the revolution they gave no aid whatever to the Mexicans but rendered assistance to the Texans ... supplying food to the soldiers and extending hospitality and encouragement to them." Pedigo wrote that the one-hundred acres prayed for in the October petition were "wholly insufficient" and that 1,280 acres would allow them to preserve their ancient tribal organization and laws. He noted that in 1854 when the Alabamas were settled in Polk County, they "were in the same destitute condition—Now they are prosperous." Unfortunately, mutual grudges and bad blood of long standing among the tribes rendered it "impracticable" for the tribes to live together, Pedigo wrote. Once again, nothing came of this initiative.[51]

Old acquaintances continued to write, usually to ask for favors. A letter from Edwin Waller, a signer of the Texas Declaration of Independence who worked with Pease in the early days of the Republic, began, "My dear old friend" and described a painful personal situation, "more than I can well bear, and remembering ... you in days of yore when we were friends and hoping that our Political differences [likely from the Civil War] will not have severed the friendly ties which bound us, I now appeal to you for aid." Waller's son, Hiram, had been Pease's "true friend ... and to prove it he still bears the mark of a Bowie Knife which was received when he and John A. Wharton got into that difficulty with Westall about you." What prompted Waller's letter was his son's murder of a man named Andrew. Waller assured Pease that the killing was accidental. "All that I have to ask you is to grant him a fair trial before twelve honest men ... ." He felt that the "misfortune ... [comes] upon me while in my old age [he was then sixty-seven] [and that] makes [it] the more painful for I am now very feeble and not able to assist him as I wish." He sent "kind wishes for your welfare and family."[52]

Amidst all the Governor's pressing problems, he remembered a tradition rooted deep in his New England heritage. He issued a proclamation for Thanksgiving Day in Texas on Thursday, November 26, 1868.[53]

Pease's correspondence with his beloved daughters sustained him. He wrote Julie on July 3, 1868, in response to her comments about Connecticut scenery, hoping she would remember her school days in Hartford "with pleasure .... I resided five years [there] and look back upon them as among the most pleasant years of my early life." He then made a passing reference but a valuable autobiographical comment on why he went to Texas: "I am not sure that my life would not have been more profitably spent if I had remained there, but I had a strong desire to try a new country." He mentioned a gift of two peaches that he would have given his girls if they have been present, but it would have been no sacrifice, since "You know I enjoy my tobacco greatly more than the nicest fruits." On July 6 he wrote Carrie, noting that school was closed and a long holiday lay ahead, but that unlike Texas girls who read nothing but novels once school is out "and think they have learned enough," he wanted his daughters "to think the time wasted, when they are not doing or learning something useful to themselves or others." He wanted them to have pleasure as well, and to that end they would be glad that Austin had music from "the band at the Capitol grounds every evening and sometimes there are as many as 5 or 6 hundred present, the music is fashionable and is said to be very fine, but I do not enjoy it as well as old fashioned times." He was eager to hear his girls play and sing and urged Carrie to buy sheet music to bring home.[54]

Carrie was at an age to enjoy travel, her "Papa" observed to her on September 7, and he asked her to describe what she was seeing. "You will find at Grandmas my letters written home on my first journey to the West. It may interest you to look over and see what changes have taken place in the Western country since that time." Pease wrote on October 3 to Carrie that he was becoming impatient for his family to come home to "dear Wood Lawn." He noted that he was proud of his daughters' ever-improving composition skills and handwriting, but he also admitted wistfully that they had left three years earlier as children but would come home as young ladies.[55]

The Governor's letters to Lucadia made his convictions even clearer than what he wrote to the commanders or his daughters. On September 12 he stated, "I cant give it up [office] while the Provisional [Government] lasts, but I shall not be a candidate for it under the new government, which I hope will be organized early in the spring." Days later he wrote "My Dear Wife," assuring her that Union men in Travis County were in no danger because enough troops kept the rebels in subjugation and will while Head Quarters remained there, "which will be as long as I remain in office." He then told her,

I cannot without disgrace give up my office while [this] government lasts, but God knows that I would gladly be rid of it, and nothing would induce me to take it again. No one at the north can conceive of the true conditions of affairs, there is not a week that passes that I do not hear of the wanton murder of ten or fifteen poor freedmen, and yet I am powerless to apply any remedy – If the people of the north knew the real conditions of affairs, they would not rest until mounted troops enough were sent here to garrison every county in the state, and make the people of each county where there are murders ... pay all the expense of keeping the troops. Nothing will save us but Grants election .... I know the democrats say that all the accounts of lawlessness ... here are told for political effect, but not half the truth has been told on the subject.[56]

In the daily business of civil government during Reconstruction, citizens might easily have forgotten that its very existence could not be taken for granted. Pease was well aware of that when he wrote to Canby in January 1869 about appropriations for state operating expenses, a subject that was not covered by Reconstruction laws. The Governor explained that previously the Legislature made appropriations biannually; hence, he had the Comptroller for Public Accounts made an estimate for 1869 and 1870. It was up to the General to order continuation of the civil government, "if in his judgment it is proper that it shall be continued." It was more than a polite deferential phrase; it was the truth.[57]

The still-miserable status of Freedmen and Pease's efforts to do what he could for them continued to occupy his mind in early 1869. Robert Stanfield of Hempstead wrote in January, "Governor, I have witnessed so much barbarity and cruelty from the whites to the Blacks, that I thought I would write you ... if it was known here that I had wrote it, my life would be the forfit." He believed that he spoke for the masses of the Freedmen of the vicinity, who "earnestly request of your honor that you send some one here to investigate the matter and make a proper report to the right authority so that we freed people can enjoy the freedom that was intended for us and ask nothing more. We have some friends among the whites but they are afrade to say a word." Even if the author was assisted by a literate friend in writing his letter, his statement that Freedmen wanted nothing more than the freedom intended for them was a profound observation that may have touched the Governor deeply.[58]

Pease did what he could. His concern for education for indigent black children was evident when he wrote Canby about an 1866 law providing for educating indigent white children. He had supposed it was unenforced since it was not compulsory, but Comal and Williamson counties were collecting taxes under it, and "it is clearly a violation of the spirit if not the letter of the civil rights law of the United States .... I submit that ... the law be suspended, and that it be so modified that the tax be collected from all persons ... and that it be expanded for the education of all indigent children without regard to color."[59]

A related subject of including black children in public education came to Canby's attention when Pease wrote about a question from San Antonio. City officials there realized that an 1866 law gave local police courts the power to form a school board vested with the power to divide the county into school districts, and the board would hence have the authority to disburse the portion of interest of the state school fund belonging to the county. Pease advised them not to proceed, because the law excluded black children, and San Antonio authorities concurred. Pease thought it best for the whole fund to remain in the Treasury.[60]

The Governor was also concerned about an 1866 apprentice law that harmed black children. He wrote Canby that the subject had come to his attention because Red River County was apprenticing colored children with no relatives. The law "ought never to be allowed." It made no educational provisions, and "many abuses have been practiced under it ... "White children never seemed to be apprenticed. The law "will doubtless be revised ... when we have a Legislature, but in the meantime it would seem proper that some good order should be issued that will correct any wrong ... ." Pease wrote a suggested order, with legal terms, for Canby.[61]

Lawless and violent conditions continued statewide, especially during the first part of the year. For example, an urgent request came to Pease in January from J. A. Wright, Anderson County Tax Assessor and Collector, asking for help "as matters grow more dark dayly, and it is impossible to arrest these outlaws ... without the aid of cavalry." Wright wondered if "Rebellion" was ever to be brought to a close. If not, he wrote, "let Gov. Pease, and all the members of Convention abandon their rights, and leave the county, for none of us are safe at our homes at night." Canby took notice. That letter and one from A. T. Monroe, a Crockett Convention delegate, motivated him to raise the number of troops, but he made no mention of cavalry.[62]

C. T. Garland updated the governor on conditions in Jefferson and the region in May: "There is, as yet, very little liberty of Speech in Northern Texas. No man would now dare to stump ... as a Radical. If the election occurs in July, no Republican votes of consequence will be cast ... on account of the absolute intolerance which prevails." Unionists were still cut off from society, he wrote, and their children were nearly excluded from schools.[63]

Violence continued in other regions as well. Judge A. B. Norton had to close his district court in Ellis County, and Pease endorsed the judge's recommendation that he and other members of the bar be attached to Palo

Pinto or Parker County. Days later, Norton asked for cavalry to stay with him as he tried cases in the district.[64] Injustice in Fort Bend County was brought to Canby's attention when Pease sent him clippings about an assault on Captain W. C. Rock in Richmond. The tax assessor-collector was charged with encouraging the assault, and the sheriff was charged with permitting it. Pease told Canby that he was "satisfied" that civil authorities could not give Rock redress.[65]

Another example of the consequences of crime came from Brownsville in Cameron County, where "exposure as a frontier county" on the Rio Grande created chronic problems for Mexican citizens, according to County Judge Jeremiah Galvan. His letter to an Army officer, forwarded to Pease, said about local citizens,

> They are subjected to more lawlessness and violence at the hands of strangers than any other American community. The constant disorders prevailing in Mexico ... account for this. ... Our jail is constantly full of criminals ... strangers to our ... language and laws ... .[66]

Letters reporting violence in counties had decreased greatly by September, but Pease received one from Judge Norton giving "a most deplorable account" of conditions in Ellis, Hill, Johnson, Tarrant, and Dallas counties. Pease recommended to Reynolds that since civil officers were not doing their duty, an "efficient" commissioned officer should investigate and if need be, perpetrators should be arrested and tried by a military commission.[67]

The personal cost of war and the violent era was very high, even for those who did not lose their lives or limbs in combat. "This miserable rebellion has broke me entirely up," T. B. Dooley lamented to the governor from Newport in Walker County:

> When the war broke out I had to go out in the confederate armey to save my neck .... when I got a good opportunity ... I went to the north and joined the U S. armey I was in the U S infantry three years .... I have got an onerable discharge. [My wife] made her braggs that she

intended to spite me for going [to the] Yankey armey .... I have bin trying to git divorced from her but it is all in vane. I am without friends or money ... I have got a passel of rebels to deal with they have made their brags that they intended to cost me $300 [or] they would cut my throat .... If you can do anything for me let me [k]now. I want to show these rebels that they cant have full say so if they was a bout one hundred of them hung we would be better off. I must come to a close by remaining your friend until Death.[68]

Because there were no social services except for families, friends, and churches for assisting people in distress, many needs went unmet, as Dooley's probably did. The only state institutions that provided care were the ones Pease had fostered in the 1850s while in office.[69]

The interim Governor still had traditional responsibilities, albeit with the commander's involvement. Criminal appeals of sentences were one category. For example, Pease sent Canby a copy of a notification to the sheriff of Smith County stating, "I have this day granted Jack Richardson a commutation of his punishment from hanging to imprisonment and hard labor for life in the State Penitentiary ... this is a command not to hang him ... but to take him to Huntsville." A Goliad lawyer wrote to explain the visit of Mrs. William Sansford, who was in Austin to see Pease on behalf of her husband. Pease had not issued an opinion, pending evidence, but "this lady's anxiety had grown almost to despair ... she couldn't wait any longer ... to know if her husband would be pardoned."[70]

The cost of operating the State Penitentiary was a major burden. It was leased in October 1868 to James A. McKee, but Pease wrote Canby on January 18, 1869, that McKee was abandoning his lease since he could not buy cotton machinery to keep all inmates at work. The institution has always been a heavy expense except during the rebellion when cotton was bought at normal prices and goods sold at very high prices. He projected operating costs of $90,000 to $100,000. He notified Canby on January 20 that he had no authority to accept McKee's resignation or any appropriation to pay debts; it was up to Canby to cover the emergency. A. T. Monroe, a Convention delegate, was appointed as financial agent for the Penitentiary, and Pease sent instructions to take inventory, execute a $100,000 bond, and pay all accounts. He asked Monroe for suggestions based on his experience about new business and management improvement. In February Canby received Monroe's request of $89,966 for three months with $61,725 for cotton and wool production and $2,200 for leather shoemaking. It was a large request, but Pease wrote Canby that he saw no other way to operate the Penitentiary. The structure then had 237 cells and 386 convicts, and cells were designed for only one man. Pease recommended expansion.[71]

Railroad issues continued to come before the Governor. The Buffalo Bayou, Brazos, and Colorado Rail Road Company ran into controversy over rates, as Pease explained to Acting Controller Rives. It was chartered by the Legislature during its third term, when regulations and rates were established. No changes had been made by the time Pease assured Rives that no other law had any bearing on the subject. Two days after Pease's message to Rives, the Governor sent to Canby a Colorado County citizens' memorial concerning the $6.00 rate for passage from Columbus to Harrisburg charged by that railroad, a charge that was "clearly in excess of what the law allows."[72]

As Governor of a state Pease had known from its beginning, he had a unique Texas history item to consider. The Secretary of State sent him a message that he forwarded to Reynolds about the condition of "what is called the Alamo Monument which stands in the Portico of the Capitol …. It has been greatly injured and is still … for want of a railing for its protection." Pease wanted an appropriation as suggested for repairs and to put a "substantial" iron railing around it. The paperwork from Philips did not survive in Pease's papers, nor did Reynolds' response.[73]

Political matters in 1869 continued as usual for months. For example, Republican leader C. B. Sabin, a longtime friend of Pease's, wrote him a pair of letters expressing warm personal comments but disgust with Texas politics. He began, "What is the matter that you do not write? I have scarcely heard from you since I have been [in Washington City] and I hope I have in no way offended." He had wanted to "edify" Pease about Union affairs and to write more often, because "I know full well that you needed the kind words of a friend perhaps more than I do." Referring to some conflicting quarrels and jealousies among friends, he assured Pease, "you are always so calm and well balanced that I naturally turned to you for sympathy … ." Later, Sabin wrote another letter that provided insight into Pease's character: "I received your kind letter … . I wish it had fallen my lot as it has yours to have been born with more self-reliance as well as sense and discretion." He was debating whether to open a law office in Washington or again in Houston, but "I must say I am sickened out with Texas politics … . It looks to me as though it would take a year or more to complete reconstruction."[74]

The last letter reporting violence in Pease's files as governor came in September after Judge Hardin Hart was wounded in an assassination attempt in North Texas. Pease wrote Reynolds, recommending that G. A. Everts be appointed as a special judge while Hart recovered.[75]

As violence decreased, economic improvement began to occupy the attention of more Texans, as evidenced by a letter from George W. Diamond in June. He wanted Pease to consider the "great benefits" of a railroad connection, and asked on behalf of Rusk County citizens if they could tax themselves to help build a line from Earpville in Upshur County to Henderson. He assured the Governor, "The people seen to have maturely considered the cost, and superior advantages" of a railroad connection, and wanted Pease to take the action and give them his cooperation.[76]

By the late spring, lessening violence gave way to heated political controversy at the state and local level. State Comptroller Morgan C. Hamilton, a longtime political adversary of the Governor, created "annoyance" by his "caprice and whims," as Pease wrote to Reynolds, when Hamilton refused to pay the salary of his private secretary, Henry B. Kinney, who had been appointed May 3. The comptroller claimed that the account for payment was not approved by the Governor, but as Pease wrote to Reynolds, "there is no law of this state that makes my approval of this account of any validity what-ever," and although Kinney was called a private secretary, his salary was paid by the state and so he was a state officer. Pease concluded his argument by saying, "I have been so much annoyed heretofore … by the Comptroller … that I do not feel disposed to submit to them any longer." It was a minor issue compared to other looming developments.[77]

Against the background of the state's ongoing issues and with the need to create a document that would permit Texas to return to the Union, the

Constitutional Convention went into its second session on December 7, 1868, for two more months. For most of that time they continued to debate matters other than a constitution. For instance, in early January Bastrop County delegates drew up a statement about activities of a vigilance committee organized there in late 1868 that threatened the lives of those who reported on them. Pease sent the document to Canby, noting that civil authorities, "if they had the nerve to do it, could only act upon information under oath, which few persons [will do since] their lives could be taken."[78]

Freedmen's rights to land, a subject of serious concern to the Governor, came before the Convention as a proposal in January to give them the same rights as whites. Pease wrote to Canby about it, pointing out that in 1866 a law passed that declared white persons could settle up to 160 acres in the vacant public domain not previously claimed. After the war, some Freedmen made settlements and improvements under this act, but there were county surveyors who refused to recognize them; in other cases, whites claimed the same land after blacks had, and the whites received valid certificates. Pease noted that it had always been state policy and practice to give land to actual settlers. He expected the Convention to pass the measure. He told Canby,

> "This act ... so far as it excluded colored men from its privileges, was certainly in violation of the spirit, if not the letter, of the Civil Rights Bill, and the freedmen ought not to be excluded .... But there is no authority here that has the power to protect them [but] the Commanding General.
>
> In my opinion, justice requires that this law shall be declared to apply to colored persons, as well as to white persons, and that in all cases where persons of color have ... taken steps to make settlements ... they shall have the same preference [as] whites. Such an order ... would be a great encouragement to those freedmen who are industrious and frugal.[79]

The complex weave of convention issues and conflicting political opinions continued from the summer over the topics of *ab initio*, division of the state, and railroads. The San Antonio *Express* had suggested that Pease's opposition to *ab initio* and dividing the state, as well as his support of a railroad ordinance, were related by his self-interest. It is possible that the value of his Austin area real estate would increase once the city was connected to the coast, but it is more likely that he thought the building of a H. & T. C. connection through Austin toward Dallas and the Red River would be of economic value to the state.[80]

San Antonio leaders disagreed with Pease and favored *ab initio* and state division, perhaps because they did not anticipate railroad connections in the immediate future, and they were worried that an H. & T. C. line through Austin would dominate the Central Texas economy. Convention radicals opposed Pease's agreement with the H. & T. C., and it was suggested that Pease had received part of the $250,000 that the railroad supposedly spent to get the ordinance passed. Reynolds, who had openly endorsed the radical wing of the Republican Party, later denied that he had acquiesced in the Pease agreement with the railroad, and ruled it null and void. Pease did not own stock in the railroad at the time, but he bought some later.[81]

Once the delegates focused on creating a new constitution, voting rights questions kept Republicans divided. Although the Governor had thought months before that limits on voting rights might be necessary, convention moderates argued a half-year later that most men should have the franchise, excepting only those who were excluded from office holding by the Fourteenth Amendment. The moderates had lost the support of the Union League and to succeed they needed support from more of those who had been Confederates. At the end, the proposed constitution had no significant disfranchisement provisions, but in reaching that decision delegates became more divided than ever. The convention could not achieve anything more and disbanded in disorder in February 1869. Oddly, it was up to Genl. Canby to collect convention records, consult members, and create a constitution.[82]

In mid-May, Pease wrote a lengthy letter to Reynolds, who had returned to Texas from Washington in March 1869 as the Fifth Military District commander. The letter outlined the proposed constitution and encouraged an early vote on it. Viewing the work of the delegates in a highly positive but not entirely realistic manner, Pease first noted that after "careful consideration of the condition of the state," delegates directed an election on the first Monday in July. However, Congress had passed a law requiring that an election must be by presidential order. Pease's opinion was that the election could be held as fairly in July as it could be later, and since "[t]he occupation of our people is mainly in agriculture … ," July was the best time to vote, because cotton required less work in that month than later. He also pointed out "a very perceptible improvement in the administration of criminal laws since the fourth of March last and a greater interest shown by our citizens in preservation of the public peace … ."

As for submission of the document whole or in part, Pease thought "it appears to be the desire of a considerable majority of the registered voters that it shall be submitted as a whole …" but others wanted a separate vote on who would have the franchise. He detailed sections and articles pertaining to the subject. Those who object do so "because they do not disfranchise those who participated in the rebellion; and as a general rule, those who desire a separate vote upon those provisions are those who object to, and intend to vote against the whole constitution, because they think it is too liberal to those who participated in the rebellion." He told Reynolds, "the effect of a separate submission on these sections, and a rejection of them, will be to leave nothing in the Constitution in regard to what persons shall exercise the right of suffrage, and the whole subject will be left open to be regulated by legislation." Such legislation could be prejudiced and capricious, he believed. Therefore, Pease recommended that the constitution should be submitted as it stood.

He also noted that the convention had passed 127 ordinances and declarations that were separately enrolled and signed. "The Constitution makes no mention of them, and they form no part of that instrument. They have never been published by authority, and the Convention made no provisions for taking a vote of the people on them." Furthermore, the measures had not been recognized by the military government, "and it is a mooted question, what effects, if any, is to be given to them by the future State Government." In Pease's view, many "are very objectionable and ought never to have been passed by such a body, elected as it was for a specific purpose and with limited powers." He recommended to Reynolds that the items be submitted to Congress with the constitution, with the recommendation that none have effect unless they were subsequently re-enacted by the state legislature.[83]

During the months following the constitutional convention the question of Pease's political future arose. Shortly before adjournment, moderate Republicans had asked A. J. Hamilton to run for governor. He began campaigning by asking Democrats and independents to stop arguing and unite. He had helped persuade the convention to pass a liberal suffrage clause. Pease may not have agreed entirely with his old friend's generous attitude toward the rebels, but he endorsed Hamilton's candidacy. Because the radical Republicans were running E. J. Davis for governor, some newspapers began supporting Pease as a compromise candidate. Newspaper publisher Flake thought that Pease should run for governor and Davis for lieutenant governor, but he also thought that somehow Pease should become the United States Senator after the election.[84]

Pease, perhaps having had more than enough of the governor's office, refused to run. He wrote J. C. Tracy of the Houston *Union* that he did not want to be considered and expressed his confidence in Hamilton. Tracy was sure that the only person who could bring the wings of the Republican Party together was Pease. The Governor held firm, hoping that the July election date would stick. Perhaps he entertained hopes that he would go to Washington as a senator-elect.[85]

Pease did not get the election date that he wanted, as Congress permitted Grant to set the day. Pease then tried to get the president to set a July election and pointed out that adherence to criminal law and preservation of public peace had been noticeable. Pease also asked his friend George Paschal, who was in Washington, to speak with Grant, but none of these efforts worked. The President set the election for November 30–December 3, 1869.[86]

Republican in-fighting continued. The radicals held a convention in June with mostly Black delegates who nominated Davis for governor and approved of the proposed constitution with its suffrage clause. Pease unsuccessfully tried to influence that convention. The end result was that national

Republican leaders assumed that the Texans had gained a consensus and that Davis was the nominee.[87]

These developments sent Pease to Washington in haste to explain Texas politics to the President, but Grant was no help and furthermore, he endorsed Davis. That summer, Federal posts were filled with radicals. Reynolds endorsed the radical ticket in an open, published letter that criticized Pease for failing to work for the Davis faction. Reynolds claimed that a win by Hamilton would defeat Republicanism in Texas and would leave the state "in the hands of the very men who, during the entire period of the rebellion, exerted every nerve to destroy the Union, and who have uniformly opposed the reconstruction laws." This vastly untruthful assertion may have been based on the loyalty of Reynolds to Grant.[88]

Pease responded to the Reynolds letter by resigning. He wrote on September 30, 1869, beginning with a statement concerning a published letter Reynolds had written to Grant in which Reynolds expressed opinions about Republican factions in Texas. Pease did not consider Reynolds's views "warranted by the course that has been pursued by those parties during the progress of reconstruction." The Governor noted that Reynolds had endorsed Davis and his followers, who "made the most strenuous and factious efforts" to prevent adoption of a constitution and to convince Congress to delay reconstruction of Texas. Reynolds's letter "also condemns Gen. Hamilton and his Supporters, among whom are not less than eight-tenths of the educated Republicans of the State, through whose influence a Constitution was adopted ... that secures to every citizen a perfect equality of civil and political rights."

Pease pointed out that since Reynolds wrote his letter, the Grant administration had removed many of the Republicans in Texas who were Hamilton supporters and replaced them with supporters of Davis. Pease also stated that "the influence and patronage" of the Military Commander in Texas and of the Grant administration was "being used in behalf of those Republicans who have exerted themselves to delay and defeat the reconstruction of the State ...." Such patronage was in opposition to the moderate Republicans, "who have, on good faith, used their influence to carry out its reconstruction strictly in accordance with the laws, and who have succeeded in that object, so far as the measure has been allowed to progress." He continued:

> It is well known that I was appointed to the position I occupy without being consulted. In accepting it, I was influenced solely by a desire to aid in carrying out the policy of Congress, which I consider to be the formation of a constitution giving equal and civil and political rights to all our citizens, and the election of officers who would administer it in good faith to secure that object. I have believed for some time past that the only mode of doing this, was by ratifying the new constitution, and electing a ticket headed by Gen. Hamilton.

He ended his letter and his twenty-six months in office with this statement:

> Under existing circumstances, I am unwilling to become, in any way responsible for the course being pursued by the Military Commander and the administration at Washington. I therefore respectfully resign the office of Governor of Texas.[89]

In reality, it must have been impossible for Pease to have had any respect left for Reynolds or Grant. From the time the Governor took a job he had not wanted, he had acted in good faith, following the law for the greater good of Texas. He had written to his daughter Carrie in March 1868 that he expected Reconstruction would last until the fall and he would have to remain as governor "unless he had the luck to be removed." Actually, he likely would have been removed had he not resigned. Marshall Pease attempted to take a moderate and balanced approach to the issues of Reconstruction. Unfortunately, most Texans of that era were not moderate or balanced in their views of critical issues.

Chapter 10

Life after Reconstruction, 1869–1905

"He went [as] his heart prompted him, and time shows he was not wrong."

Rev. Benjamin A. Rogers

E. M. Pease could have left politics in disgust once he resigned as provisional governor during Reconstruction in 1869, but his lifelong sense of duty and hope for the future of Texas kept him in public life. As he was about to leave office, a group of Houston Democrats made a plea for Conservatives, Democrats, and "National Republicans" to come together to save Texas from radicalism. The idea appealed to Pease, and he wrote that he would make speeches for A. J. Hamilton, who was running for governor. Pease promised to visit Comal, Bexar, Guadalupe, Gonzales, and Lavaca counties, advocating "a speedy removal of all political disabilities" after Texas rejoined the Union.[1] He was concerned that radical Republicans might take control of the Federal customs office in Galveston, where large sums were collected.[2] Fearing that the Grant administration was unaware of political dynamics in Texas, Pease, Hamilton, and others petitioned Senate Republicans in Washington to defer action on appointments until they had better information.[3] Amidst the turmoil, the radical E. J. Davis narrowly defeated the moderate Hamilton in the December 1869 gubernatorial race. Pease telegraphed Grant, stating that the election was invalid because no voting had occurred in Milam and Navarro counties, and he also joined a petition for a Federal investigation of votes elsewhere that were illegally counted for Davis. The Dallas *Herald* reported that Pease "ask(ed) that it not be accepted as a decision of the people .... [and said that] many thousands of fraudulent votes have been cast, and ... in numerous incidences neither the law nor the orders of the commanding general have been complied with."[4] These efforts produced no results. Davis backers, both Freedmen and whites, feared that Congress would not accept election results if a Democrat won. Although Reconstruction was almost over, General Reynolds still held control, and he declined to call a new election after being accused by Hamilton supporters of supporting Davis.[5] Therefore, with radicals controlling Texas, Grant signed legislation on March 30, 1870, allowing Texas representatives and senators to be seated in Congress. Pease could not prevail. More than a decade later he explained that he took office with the hope of saving Texas from the "chaos and disorder in which the rebellion had left her." As he remembered it,

> I used my best efforts to have the laws faithfully executed. I succeeded in some instances and would have done so in more if I had been properly sustained by the people and the military authorities. ... Notwithstanding the disorder and violence that prevailed, the material interests of the country prospered and our population increased very rapidly.[6]

Pease was unwilling to run again for governor, but he developed a more moderate position after the period when he had felt vindictive toward ex-Confederates. He abandoned radicalism, and once Texas returned to the Union in 1870, he worked to create a more moderate political movement, a position more in line with his character and temperament. To cultivate a moderate strategy, he met with A. J. Hamilton, J. W. Flanagan (elected to the United States Senate earlier in the year), and Democrats including James W. Throckmorton, Ben H. Epperson, and John Hancock. They developed opposition to measures passed by the radical Twelfth Legislature that included creation of a state militia and state police force and giving Governor Davis the power to declare martial law in any county. Pease was among thirty-one men who signed a petition to Congress that began, "We ... without regard to party or race, being thoroughly convinced that our civil liberties are in great danger, if they have not been actually overthrown by certain laws recently enacted by the Legislature ... [petition] Congress to save the good people from the grievous oppression of said laws." Nothing came of the petition in Washington, but it may have influenced the defeat of some radicals in the next round of elections in Texas.[7]

Pease stood opposed to Davis administration policies in spite of the political cost. As he wrote to Moses Austin Bryan, "The Democrats are hostile to me because I am a Republican, and those calling themselves Republicans, who are connected with the state government, are hostile to me because I speak plainly about their corruption and incompetency, consequently, I am without influence."[8] He gained a new ally when his former foe, Morgan C. Hamilton, left the Davis ranks and wrote Pease that he did not think Republicans could win the next election.[9] Hamilton emphasized corruption as an issue, but Davis also had a taxation problem. State and local taxes collected when Pease was governor had been about one million dollars, but by mid-1871, higher state salaries and education expenses, as well as an expanded government, resulted in the need for about six million dollars in tax money.[10] Pease knew that Texans would not tolerate such a large tax increase, and he led a group who called on voters statewide to hold county conventions to elect representatives to a state tax-payers' convention in Austin in September. He was chosen as one of Travis County's delegates.[11] The convention began on September 22 "in open air" on the corner of Congress Avenue and Pecan Street with "about 1000" present.[12] Pease was elected its president.[13] Ezekiel W. Cullen of Dallas, who nominated him, noted, "He is a Republican but an honest, straightforward man ... in Texas from the first and devoted to her interests."[14] Pease calculated that $800,000 was enough for government expenses. A committee was appointed to write a message to the people and confer with Davis, but the convention did not turn out as Pease had envisioned. He, Hamilton, and other moderate Republicans wanted to use it to convince voters to leave the radicals and support the moderates in the upcoming 1871 congressional election. They knew, however, they would need the support of Democrats. To that end, Pease supported John Hancock in a race against a Davis supporter, Edward Degener. Hancock won. Carrie Pease declared, "Papa voted for [Hancock] and is I suppose a Democrat, although he does not relish having Mama and I call him that."[15]

In 1872, growing dissatisfaction in the North, based on opposition to Grant and the radical movement in Republican ranks, resulted in the rise of the Liberal Republican Party. This movement appealed to moderates among the Texas Republicans, and John Hancock, writing from the United States House, encouraged Pease to go to the new party's Cincinnati convention: "It might be in your power to accomplish great good ... ."[16] At the meeting, which nominated Horace Greeley for president, Pease was elected chairman of the Texas delegation.[17] Thomas H. Stribling of San Antonio wrote Pease excitedly that the convention would "name the next president." Referring to the 1840 campaign of William Henry Harrison, he declared, "We are going to have a *Tippecanoe and Tyler too* campaign if I read the signs right."[18] Pease thought that the Greeley ticket would "bring a better condition of affairs" to Texas and the South.[19] During the campaign, the Harris County Democratic Party invited Pease to address a gathering that was planned as the largest one ever held in Texas. The invitation explained that, "Your many friends in this Section are desirous of meeting and *hearing* you .... Your great renown as a speaker will assist to carry the election ...."[20] Greeley's slate carried Texas, but Grant won the election. Conservative Democrats in Texas won most of the congressional and legislative races. Pease had tried hard to create a moderate political movement, but he could not. For the time being, he ceased his efforts, writing, "The Democrats are mostly rebels ... [and] those who have controlled what is called the Republican party ... have so little honesty and have [so] mismanaged our affairs, that no honest man can act with them."[21]

Pease soon devoted more time to his law practice, which he had resumed after the Civil War. Lucadia had written in 1870, "I suppose you will be better contented to have an office in town and practice your profession [although] I hoped you would take some rest now, having worked so hard all your life. I believe the Marshall blood which we inherit requires constant employment ... ."[22] For a year between 1870 and 1871, Pease had a law partner, E. B. Turner, but returned to solo practice once Turner was appointed a district judge. Pease's office was on Congress Avenue and Bois de Arc Street (later West Seventh Street).[23] In addition to practicing law, Pease turned to a new venture—banking. He had provided numerous private loans to people before banks were legal in Texas, and he must have been eager to be involved at last in a national bank. He wanted fellow Unionist George Brackenridge, owner of the San Antonio National Bank, to provide half the funds for a bank in Austin in 1872, but the deal fell through.[24] After the financial panic of 1873, Brackenridge become half owner and president of the First National Bank of Austin; Pease was vice president and senior officer in residence. The bank opened in the spring of 1874 in a large three-story building at a prominent location on the northwest corner of Congress Avenue and Pecan (later West 6th) Street.[25] Pease ran the bank successfully, based on his sound judgment of human behavior and business sense, and it also succeeded because the economy began to recover from the Panic of 1873.

Pease eagerly engaged in civic improvements that the Civil War had prevented for years. He was president of a gas company. With gas lights on Congress Avenue and "omnibuses" running, he wrote to Julie that the city would finally make Austin "like a northern city."[26] In 1877, he was president of the Travis Road and Bridge Company, which built a stone-pillared and wooden toll bridge across the Colorado River at Congress Avenue.[27] The Peases' Austin was becoming a modern city.

By 1874, thirty-eight years after the Texas Revolution, many of its participants had left Texas or died, and so the number of those who were present in 1836 was declining. Waves of new residents knew nothing of Texas history. Pease, who had come in 1835, must have wanted to re-establish himself proudly as an "Old Texian." When he was sixty-two in 1874, he participated in the founding of a state historical society. This group, led by Oran M. Roberts, then Chief Justice of the Texas Supreme Court, included Pease at an early-April organizational meeting, along with John H. Reagan, Guy M. Bryan, John S. "Rip" Ford, Homer S. Thrall, James B. Shaw (serving as Secretary), and others. Thrall reported to an April meeting that he was writing a history of Texas, and later he would review for the public his history "from the discovery of Texas to the Treaty of Onis." Because of inadequate funding and the ongoing political activities of its leaders, the organization failed.[28] Pease later helped to finance a comprehensive Texas history by Frank Johnson, who had participated in the Revolution.[29] Pease had also helped to found the Texas Veteran Association in 1873. Members were survivors of military action from 1835 to 1845; the main purpose of the group was to help members to acquire benefits of a pension that had been established by the Legislature in 1870. Pease himself was a beneficiary of that act: Until then, he could not, as a member of a volunteer company commanded by R. M. Coleman of Bastrop, receive land for his participation in the Revolutionary Army at Gonzales or at the Siege of Bexar. Letters of confirmation that Pease was at the Battle of Gonzales and the Siege of Bexar were written by Charles Mason of Gonzales County and by John W. Bunton of Hays County.[30] Pease served as an executive committee member of the Veteran Association from its founding until his death in 1883 and was its chairman for a time. Through this group, he resumed his close ties with Guy and Moses Austin Bryan, a friendship severed by the Civil War. Certificates of membership signed by Guy Bryan as president were issued posthumously to "Mr. E. M. Pease" and to "Mrs. E. M. Pease" in 1899.[31]

Just as he made personal peace with former secessionists, Pease reconciled politically with E. J. Davis and the Republican regulars by 1874. Although Davis had lost the governor's office to Democrat Richard Coke, Republicans still controlled Federal patronage in the state. Both Davis and Pease were concerned about the corrupt behavior of the customs collector in Galveston and urged his replacement. Grant agreed and wanted Pease to take the job. One of Pease's friends, W. W. Mills, wrote to him from Washington that Col. Benjamin H. Bristow, Secretary of the Treasury, was asked "to appoint you collector at Galveston and the nomination was made immediately and will be signed by the President." This was "done in full knowledge of your support of Mr. Greeley and with an honest purpose to improve the character of Federal officers in Texas." Mills called the appointment "tardy justice, but you know that exact justice is never possible in politics."[32] Pease knew that there was no higher level of Federal patronage in Texas, but he was uninterested in the position and wrote Secretary of the Treasury B. H. Austin that "it is one not suited to my habits of life ... and would require a removal of my residence to Galveston which would not be agreeable to my family."[33] Little could he say in a public document how much he valued being at home.

Between 1870 and 1875, Carrie, born in 1851, and Julie in 1853, continued their education and reached adulthood. No sooner had Lucadia and the girls gone north in mid-summer 1870 than Marshall wrote from Woodlawn, "I am very lonely here by myself, but get along very well with the servants. Emily was here .... [she] and her girls ask for you every day, and they send love."[34] Other household help was not as reliable as Emily, and a number of hired people came and went. The running of a very large house and farm was all but impossible without them. Lucadia's letters revealed her constant concern about Marshall's health: for example in the early 1870s, she was about to telegraph Marshall when she had not heard from him.[35] By mid-August, she resolved to never again leave him for so long, and she sent greetings to Emily and her children.[36] The girls' education was Lucadia's primary focus. To consider schools they went to Boston (at ages nineteen and seventeen), and Lucadia confessed, "They are both so near sighted, and so self willed, [sic] that they keep me ... troubled about them all the time." Soon, Julie was talking of going to Vassar. Lucadia stated she had "left the matter up to them."[37] Realizing that the family would be separated with Julie in Poughkeepsie, New York, and Carrie elsewhere with other plans, Lucadia knew that she must "sacrifice my feelings for their improvement." Carrie was thinking about voice and piano lessons because "she could not enter school, except in very low classes, which at her age she does not wish to do."[38] Lucadia reported good news in the fall: she went with Julie to Vassar, and she was "surprised and delighted that she passed the [entrance] examination" without any recent study. Lucadia left her there, where "she will have greater opportunities for improvement ... than at any school of which I have any knowledge. I shall miss her greatly, but as she wished to go to school, I think it was right ...." She "gave Mr. Vassar an order on Mr. Swanson for three hundred dollars ... ."[39] Julie took a year of remedial classes before beginning regular college-level work. The girls' lack of a sound education in Texas could not be made up by sporadic schooling in Connecticut, and no education during the Civil War cost them greatly. It surely pained their father, who had advocated public education for decades. His letters to his daughters in the 1870s show the affectionate and wise father that he was. He also wrote Carrie in October 1870 of his concern for his own mother's health at her advanced age, and he added another concern: "after the immense rain and flood that we have had ... all our creeks are running much higher than ever before since the settlement of the country. Many houses were swept away, a great amount of property destroyed, and many lives lost." High water in Shoal Creek would not have reached Woodlawn, but a flood would have wiped out property south of it, toward town. On a brighter note, he described improvements at Woodlawn: blinds were added in Carrie's room to make it cooler, and a new bath room, store room, and "Earth Closet" were being built on the first floor.[40] As October ended, the yellow fever quarantine was lifted in Galveston, and Texans were going home. Lucadia could have returned with Gail Borden and his wife, but she and Carrie did not, because she was hurriedly finishing Julie's winter wardrobe. She wrote Marshall, "You, nor no gentlemen I know, [realize] the bother and labor it is, to get a lady's wardrobe in wearing order, and I am most solicitous about Julie's having warm clothing." She asked if the railroad had been completed thirty miles beyond Brenham, because "it will be a great relief to have even that little taken from the carriage ride, or stage ride ... ."[41] From Vassar, Julie complained to her father about essay writing. He replied, "It amuses me ... that you cannot write a composition, when you write such excellent letters, what are letters but compositions?" He instructed her to write a composition at least once a week.[42]

Lucadia was in New York City during November with Susan Ward, the Pease's houseguest during the war. She commented to Marshall, "If you were here I should ask you, to go with me to hear Rip Van Winkle played, for womans rights woman as I am, I do not like going to theaters or many places of amusement without a gentleman."[43] On the way home, Lucadia and Carrie stopped in Washington, where Carrie noted cryptically, "Most of the interesting things have been taken to the Smithsonian Institute, but Washington ['s] coat and pants were hung up … ."[44] Lucadia must have recalled the day she had handled some of Washington's possessions on her way to Eltham Plantation. Thinking about clothes she had sewn for Julie to wear in cold New York, she suggested that she "had best get some canton flannel and make you two pairs of plain warm drawers. I shall feel so much more easy about your health, if you wear warmer drawers."[45] Back home in Austin, Lucadia noted a new ritual of writing to Julie on Sunday evening. That morning, Mr. Rogers preached "one of his long eloquent sermons … ." She also reported that an Austin woman,

> thinks girls have no occasion to study Latin or Greek, as she knows nothing of either, while I claimed that girls ought to be taught the sciences and the languages the same as boys—if their have health sufficient. Your Papa and myself miss you exceedingly but if you wish to remain at the college another year … I shall not be so selfish as to deny you such an opportunity for improvement. If you do not remain you will probably ever after regret it.[46]

Lucadia's thoughts remained focused on her girls in 1871. In mid-January, Carrie was at home, being "good company" and helping with "domestic matters," but saying she still might go to Vassar. Lucadia was pleased by Julie's improving "epistolary style," but "I would like it better if you could have written compositions or essays this year instead of [taking] double latin, [sic] tho' I suppose the Pres [sic] and Faculty of Vassar know better than I do, your most urgent needs." Meanwhile, among the household "servants," young Mary Eliza and Cloe were daily "attending the Wood Lawn seminary, for freed Colored females taught by Mrs. L. C. Pease." Lucadia noted that Vassar trustee Colonel Morgan L. Smith of New York, formerly of Brazoria County, visited Woodlawn and talked about the superiority of the college. He was "delighted" that Julie was there, and he wanted her to remain and graduate.[47] By April, Eliza, the daughter of the Pease's cook, Martha, had joined Lucadia's "seminary," and Marshall wrote that Chloe was "the best scholar."[48]

Marshall went to Hallettsville in March 1871 "to attend to an old suit which he has had there years before you were born," Lucadia explained to Julie. "He hopes this will be the last case in court which he will have to attend out of town … ."[49] The next month, Lucadia reported that he had been unwell for weeks, although he went to his office when she and Carrie thought he should not. He had no appetite and had "lost flesh."[50] A few days later he and Lucadia were at St. David's, where Lucadia noted "excitement": The Methodist minister had written to the Episcopal Bishop of Texas about a benefit for St. David's that had been given by the theater in town, "which was sinful in the eyes of the Methodists." Local newspapers "brought [the Rev. B. A.] Rogers out victorious," and he took his whole family to the Theatre to show I suppose his independence of Methodists opinion … ."[51] The Peases were his longtime supporters. Lucadia wrote little about politics, but events in May captured her attention:

> There was quite an excitement in the [Twelfth] Legislature here last week, which resulted in the turning out [of] the Speaker of the House, Mr. [Ira H.] Evans, for his opposition in giving subsidies to R. Road Companies … . There is great extravagance, and waste in the Legislature, so many members are carpetbaggers, and have no property in the State, that they don't seem to care how much they tax those who have.[52]

The summer in Austin was as hot and dry as usual. Lucadia commented that she and Carrie had not been to church for weeks because of "the great heat and what is worse the dust. There is now so much building in town and hauling rock, that the road past Mr. Raymond's is extremely uncomfortable." Hired household help abandoned Woodlawn for the city, and Lucadia made the droll observation, "I had begun to teach my family to live without eating, having dropped two of the three warm meals and was about the drop the other when our new woman came, and undid all by going back to the old way, [but] now is leaving, and I have it all to do over again."[53] It was so hot in August that Lucadia wrote Julie that although she was dressed only in stockings, slippers, and a chemise, the thought of sewing winter clothes made her even warmer, "but of our weather at present the less said about it the better." Lucadia was then probably living on fresh produce, dairy products, eggs, bread, and cornbread because she had no teeth, and she must have appreciated Marshall's arrival, "quite elated" with his melons. He also brought a box from Juliet that contained Lucadia's false teeth, which had been broken and were sent to the North, but broke again on the return trip. When Lucadia had her teeth removed years before in Connecticut, she made no mention then or later about what was used for replacements. Progress was being made in other ways, however. She wrote, "Our bath room &c is the greatest luxury [sic] imaginary."[54] This room only contained a tub. Lucadia noted as August ended that Carrie had accepted an invitation from George Graham to "go with him to night by moonlight to Barton Springs, with a party." This large, natural swimming pool with its cool water was already "quite a resort" with a house that sold ice cream.[55]

Free public schools, created under a legislative act passed by the Republican-controlled legislature in April 1871, opened on September 4, and "I should judge there were hundreds at the colored school, some men and women," Lucadia noted. Once Democrats regained full control of the state in 1876, they replaced the first "school system" with one that relied almost completely on local initiative. Accordingly, the Austin Graded School, the city's first public elementary school, opened in 1876 on a block west of downtown, set aside in 1839 for educational purposes. The Austin Public Free School System, a department of the City of Austin, began in 1881. Other progress in town was planned: a passenger depot for the anticipated railroad. Lucadia was delighted: "You know we consider the journey [to] Gton [Galveston, by coach] equal to half a trip, even if we were going the world round."[56] At home, Carrie was doing housework and "much sewing on the machine." However, "she is always underrating herself, and needs ... self esteem .... She is so much society for me, I dont [sic] know how I could live without her."[57] Lucadia responded to Julie's report of her "troublesome" hair length, suggesting, "Why not have it cut off and wear it short. I think it is much more becoming to you, and infinitely less care, which should be your great consideration .... If I were young again, I would have my hair cut short ... and wear it so all my life."[58]

During the October election for congressional members, Lucadia reported that it was "an exciting time among the men in town, Gov. Davis using every means in his power, fair and foul, particularly the latter, to elect his candidates .... Last week the Davisites had speech making, torch light processions, bands of music, hurrahing and shouting, and made the nights hideous with their demonstrations ...." Meanwhile, Lucadia's pupils, Mary Eliza and Cloe, wanted Julie to come home and were learning to spell so they could write to her.[59] Lucadia, thinking about Carrie's going to Vassar in the next school year, asked, "What do you think I can do when you are both away from me? I think I shall try to get a situation as chamber maid or scullion at Vassar ...." Perhaps she thought of leaving cooking to Aunt Martha, who had just surprised the family with fried chicken for breakfast, which, for being "duly praised," resulted in more for dinner.[60] The arrival of a "large photograph" of Julie excited the household; Cloe kissed it, and Emily proclaimed that Julie had become "fair."[61] Only weeks after contemplating Carrie's attending Vassar, Lucadia changed her mind: "I fear her eyes are not strong enough to allow her to study much. They become weak and painful ... in any constant employment." However, Lucadia noted that Carrie's penmanship had improved with practice and effort, and she sewed often and well; both tasks that required good eyesight.[62] In November the family attended the funeral of Lieutenant Governor Donald Campbell, a former state senator. The Masonic services were at the Capitol, "where a great display was made," Lucadia observed.[63] Shortly thereafter, a friend reported on the "great ball' for the new Speaker of the Senate to fill Campbell's place. It followed so soon after the funeral, it was called "the Campbell wake."[64]

Life at home was pleasant. Aunt Martha made excellent "wafles" [sic] although Lucadia remained fearful that her prized cook would take a job in the city. The day of Lucadia's letter, Aunt Martha had ridden to church with the Peases, "arrayed in a new red plaid dress, and almost rivalled, our beautiful Texas red birds [cardinals], in the brilliancy of her attire." Lucadia also reported that Mrs. Duval, wife of Judge Thomas H. Duval, "seemed surprised" that Julie remained for a second year at college. Lucadia wrote, piqued, "Many at this day have not outlived the old idea, that girls only need school education, enough to teach them to spell, read, and write ... by the time they are fourteen, when they are fitted to be leaders in society."[65] As the year came to an end, she described Thanksgiving: her table was decorated with evergreens, "miseletoe [sic]," red berries, and red roses, and Emily was "at the helm to see that everything was done to a turn .…." Lucadia was happy with the observation that had always meant so much to her.[66]

Two significant acts regarding the Pease homestead tract and a third development regarding their land occurred in the 1870s. In 1872, Pease made gifts of land to his former slaves, Emily Pease Woods and Sam Barber. These transactions were "in consideration of faithful service and for one dollar." The land was at the back of the property, west of the house, where Pease was growing grain.[67] The second significant gift of Pease land was to the City of Austin for a public park. Lucadia hesitated to sign the deed, because "I have so little confidence in the City authorities and their taste and judgment in beautifying" the land.[68] The next month, however, "E. M. Pease and his wife, L. C. Pease," deeded twenty-three acres within city limits on May 22, 1875, for a public park. Located on the western edge of Shoal Creek, this area was part of Pease's first purchase of land in Austin in 1855. Below the deed record, a plat showed the south end of the park, surrounded on the south and southwest by thirty-two lots framed by streets named for Texas Revolutionary heroes. Streets were to begin to the northwest with Houston Street (closest to the front yard at Woodlawn) and progress southeast with Rusk, Wharton, Lamar, Burleson, Archer, Baylor, and Ruiz. Cross streets were Jones, Zavala, Navarro, and the continuation of College Avenue, which became West 12th Street. This area was not developed as drawn, but it showed Pease's plan to honor Texas history, including the three native Mexican citizens who signed the Texas Declaration of Independence.[69] Lucadia observed that the plan "looks well on paper, and as the houses are airy [imaginary] ones, we can build them as tastefully and fine as we please."[70] The Austin City Council issued a resolution three months later to "Hon. E. M. Pease and Lady" accepting the acreage and extending thanks.[71] Eventually, in 1914, when the family formed the Enfield Realty and Homebuilding Company to begin developing their property as a residential neighborhood, the first section, Enfield A, showed the entrance to Pease Park at the north end of the 1500 block of Parkway Street, noted as Baylor Street on the 1875 deed.

After the park land was donated, the City did little but erect fences on it until the turn of the century. It was one of the earliest public parks established in Texas, and another example of the Peases' forward thinking about the public good. The Peases knew well that the land should never be developed with private lots, since they had seen Shoal Creek in serious floods over the years, and a park made the best use of the area. It would also preserve the natural beauty that Lucadia and Julie loved.

The third significant development involving their land occurred in 1876, once the family learned where the International and Great Northern Rail Road would run through their property. Lucadia wrote with relief that the tracks would be behind their house and would not have to be crossed to go into town.[72] The tracks were nearer the house than they liked—only about a thousand feet—and passed through their grain fields. The tracks remain in use, surrounded by Loop 1 in present-day Austin.

The years 1874 and 1875 were significant ones for the family: Carrie married, and Julie graduated from Vassar. Carrie had been courted by George Graham for several years. He was a son of Dr. Beriah and Lilly Graham, friends of the Peases. Julie responded to Carrie's engagement news by writing, "Dear little sister, if you love him and are happy, I am happy with you. Besides, I like George right well, and believe with him that he will get the dearest and best little woman the world contains."[73] George, who was born in Austin on April 27, 1847, was not known to be well-educated, and he had no profession. He was not one of the Austin business men whom Lucadia had envisioned earlier as a suitor, but he asked Marshall and Lucadia together for Carrie's hand in marriage. Greatly concerned about her daughter's future, she wrote to Julie,

> George took the opportunity to speak to us of his wish to marry Carrie, said he loved her, and would do all in his power to make her happy, etc. Your Papa replied … he wished her to consult her own happiness and if by marrying him it was secured, he was willing, etc. I remained silent, not approving of her choice, being ambitious to have her marry a man who had intellect enough to make their companionship improving to her. Then too he seems to be of a sickly

constitution ... However, if she really is attached to him and sees beauty, ease and grace of manner and intelligence ... she may be happy with him. How do you like your future brother in law?[74]

Julie responded,

> I agree with you perfectly in thinking that she is worthy of the best man in the land, and smartest .... But how in common sense is she ever to find one of this brilliant sort [?] You know what the young men of Austin are, and has she not selected as good a one as ... there is ... [?] She does not ... and I suppose never will know any one out of Texas, and if a swarm of such very charming and perfect men should emigrate to Texas, what chance would she have of seeing them, living way out in the country as we are. George's] chief attraction is the fact of his loving her dearly and truely [sic].[75]

Carrie and George married at Woodlawn on January 4, 1875, in a ceremony conducted by Edward B. Wright, Pastor of First Presbyterian Church."[76] Julie came home for the wedding, which was "very quiet" with "only about thirty being present ...." On their honeymoon the couple went with Julie as far as St. Louis, and Julie wrote, "we had a very good time there."[77] When they returned to Woodlawn, George began working on the farm. His help was needed, and having a trustworthy family member on the property was valuable.

Preparations began in early 1875 for the Peases' and Carrie's trip to Vassar for Julie's graduation. Julie declared, "You must look your best; Vassar is a critical place." She pointed out that she did not care about herself, "but other people make remarks." She insisted, "Papa should have a *new* and *fashionable* suit, especially if he sit[s] upon the platform .... Above all things, [he must have] a stylish hat." A cashmere dress would be "most suitable" for her mother.[78] As for honors at graduation, she warned Carrie, "if you or any of the family have a lingering hope that I will be among the favored few, please dispel that illusion Immediately."[79] She emphasized to her parents, "there is not the slightest chance of my having [an honor].

I have not worked for one, and in such a class as ours one must work with might and main." She knew that honors were more political than academic, and she did not respect the system.[80] Julie's firm position appeared to have contrasted with Lucadia's on the importance of an education. Lucadia had written,

> feeling my own deficiencies in education, and believing that women in the future are destined to fill situations which will require all the knowledge which the best of teaching can impart to them, I try to comfort myself by knowing we are giving you the best college ... the country affords, and that you are improving all its advantages .... Some day perhaps you will be a lecturer or orator.[81]

Julie's Bachelor of Arts in music and the arts reflected her true interests: she did not earn it for the purpose of teaching, as most young women did if they had the rare opportunity to attend college. She stated repeatedly that she wanted to return to Woodlawn, which she did, and her parents were delighted. She was secure in the knowledge that their wealth ensured that she did not need to earn a living or to marry. All three must have recognized that Julie's college experience was valuable, without regard to class rank or honors.

Before Julie returned home, her Papa's letters documented the illness of their longtime, treasured "servant," Emily Pease Woods. He wrote in April 1874 that he and "Mama" had "returned home [by] the rear of our lot and visited Emily, whose place looks comfortable." They (Emily, probably her husband, La Grande—also known as Grant—Woods, and possibly Emily's grown daughters and other family) "have about three acres cleared and planted in corn. They have also a small garden which Emily is very proud of. She is very thin and looks to be in miserable health."[82] Later he wrote, "poor Emily ... I fear she will not long be spared to us. Her new home is very comfortable, far better than her old residence for a sick person. Some of us will visit her every day to do what we can to relieve her suffering."[83] The next month, he wrote, "I rode over to see Emily this morning. She ... looks very feeble ... [but] is without pain."[84] He wrote days later that there was no hope for Emily's recovery; she was "sleeping very quietly" and he would not allow her to be awakened.[85] She died "very quietly" on August 11, 1874, and was buried the next day in the Colored Section of the City Cemetery.[86] Her white marble tombstone, which appears newer than the era in which she died, states that she was "aged 45 years." The engraved date on it, July 27, 1875, is incorrect. Emily had been in Marshall Pease's service as a slave and Freedwoman since December 1846, when he bought her and her mother in Brazoria. Hers is a case in which a former slave was cared for by her former master and his family, a family whose letters document that they loved her and whom she loved, and she died in her own home, on land that her former owner deeded to her in 1872.[87]

At mid-decade, Pease remained uninvolved in Republican Party leadership. When the chairmanship of the party's executive committee was vacant in April 1875, George Paschal, among other Pease friends, wanted him to run for the office, but Pease refused.[88] In 1876, he was willing to speak at an Austin rally for Rutherford B. Hayes, the Republican presidential candidate. E. J. Davis, who also addressed the rally, called Pease "a good and honest governor" who "came to the front in support of the Republican Party, which alone promised something to the country it had saved at the expense of blood and treasure." These comments did not motivate Pease to campaign more, and soon after the gathering in Austin, he and his family went to the Centennial Exposition in Philadelphia.[89] The following year, Pease worked on furthering public education in Austin. He was on a committee of school directors for the Austin Graded School, a public elementary school that served grades one through four, when the group met with representatives of the Peabody Fund in Tennessee. The fund provided grants to school districts in the South after the Civil War.[90] Pease returned to leadership of the Republican Party in Texas after Hayes was elected president and spoke to the state executive committee in 1877. He advocated doing "whatever would advance the cause of the party and its moral standard in the South," and stated that party reform was "absolutely necessary."[91] He followed with a letter to Hayes, stating that he had "no love or sympathy with the Democracy, that is, the Democrats of the South who deliberately brought upon us all our … sufferings since 1861." Nevertheless, he thought that a reconciliation policy was essential to "give peace and prosperity to the country ... ." Pease believed that "time and experience under the new order of things" were "slowly and silently doing their work in reconciling the hostile feeling between the races" in the South. He thought that with the conservative principles Hayes had advocated in his inaugural address, the trend could continue.[92] Hayes then considered Pease for the position of postmaster general, and wrote to Guy Bryan, asking what he thought of Pease's qualifications. Bryan replied, "Gov. Pease is the most deserving of notice among the Republicans in this state, being first in character, capacity and identification with the true interests of the country ... . He is able, honest and faithful, possessing thorough business habits and untiring industry, and with large experience in public office."[93]

Hayes offered Pease the position of collector of customs at Galveston (at an unknown date), and Pease wrote Treasury Secretary John Sherman in July 1878, "I do not now desire it. Nevertheless I have on reflection, concluded that I will accept the position if it is tendered to me ... . I prefer however that the appointment shall not be made until the term of Genl. [Benjamin G.] Shields expires in December next ... ."[94] Sherman's note, dated Sept. 2, 1878, included at the end of the letter a confirmation that the appointment would take effect upon the expiration of Shields's term. Hayes issued a certificate of nomination to Pease on January 22, 1879, stating his "special trust and confidence in the Integrity, Diligence, and Discretion of Elisha M. Pease."[95] At age sixty-seven, Marshall had finally been required to use his first name on an official document. The next step was a bond. Pease's business partners, Brackenridge and Harris, plus two other men put up $30,000 in bond money. "This I call as good a Bond as was ever given for that amount," Pease noted.[96] Lucadia commented to her sister that she wanted her husband to take the job because he was "in no active business at home" but "It is such a trial to M—and myself to go from home, that my conscience upbraids me for approving of his accepting the [sit]uation as he was disposed to decline it ... ."[97] Why she thought he was not working is unclear, because he was practicing law and managing a bank.

Sherman signed a document on February 12, 1879, stating that Pease had been appointed as Collector of Customs at Galveston.[98] The new collector was overqualified for the bureaucratic job, considering his extensive legal and administrative experience, but he knew the importance of having Federal income gathered at the Galveston port. He had to learn complex Federal regulations and the details of marine business, but he seemed to master those subjects without difficulty. Accounting, another topic that Pease handled well, involved no small numbers. For instance, duties on exports to foreign countries for cotton alone in 1875 totaled $663,850 and duties collected on all imports totaled $308,214 in 1880.[99] Pease was well-familiar with one of the biggest problems of the position: too many men wanted jobs during his entire term of office. Many seekers based their cases on their political leanings. Others were former clients or friends, including the Rev. B. A. Rogers of Austin. Few jobs were open, because the thirty-four positions were mostly filled, and Pease was unwilling to make changes without good reasons.[100]

His most difficult personnel problem was created by a predecessor who dismissed Norris Wright Cuney as a deputy inspector, apparently for racist reasons. Cuney, a native Texan born into slavery, was the mulatto son of a Texas planter. He went to Pennsylvania for an education in 1859 and after the war entered Republican politics in Texas. He never held elected office, but he was a leader locally in the Galveston community and statewide in the Republican Party.[101] His dismissal from the Custom House upset African American Republicans statewide and attracted attention in Washington. Pease received a letter from Texas Congressman Tom P. Ochiltree to Treasury Secretary John Sherman, stating with certainty that Cuney would accept the position of Inspector of Customs.[102] When Pease did not reappoint him right away, African Americans in Galveston complained.[103] In October, Pease wrote Sherman, making a case for an "increased Inspection force" because of the greater volume of business in the current fiscal year. Pease suggested that Cuney be appointed as Special Inspector, although the reason was that an employee was leaving, not because an additional position was justified. He wrote, "Mr. Cuney is an intelligent and well informed Colored man, perfectly competent to perform the duty, and formerly an Inspector in this District for several years." Sherman apparently did not accept the suggestion.[104] Pease admitted that he knew that "Negroes" in Galveston County had "frequently sent complaints to the Department that their race had not been sufficiently recognized in the nominations in this District."

He denied, however, having discriminated against African American applicants "when they were possessed of the proper qualifications."[105] Pease did rehire Cuney later. The latter's name is found among the signatories of letter that came to Pease in December, 1880, from twelve Customs House inspectors. The paper accompanied a carved wooden cane given to Pease just before he left office, "as a slight token of our esteem for you." It is a rare, remaining material example of appreciation for Pease; most evidence of gratitude for him at any time in his life is in writing.[106]

Because he held a political appointment, Pease was obligated to take part in the 1880 presidential campaign. He was a Galveston County delegate at the Republican state convention in Austin in March. The convention refused to elect Pease as its president after he was nominated by E. J. Davis, because Pease supported presidential hopeful John Sherman. Pease addressed the convention on Sherman's behalf, but the majority favored former President Grant.[107] Once James A. Garfield was nominated for president by the Republicans, Pease campaigned for him, but it was more than party loyalty: the Democratic candidate was General Winfield Scott Hancock, who had caused Pease such problems while he was governor during Reconstruction. At a Republican rally in Galveston, Pease spoke about the controversy, and that summer he went to Connecticut to speak on the same subject when asked to do so by the national Republican executive committee.[108] The Austin newspaper announced under its headline, "Ex-Governor Pease in the Light of Facts and History," that in the North, Pease was "telling how there had been no peace in the South for a Union man for these twenty years." The story pointed out that Pease's 1855 address to the Texas Legislature had made it clear that the Republicans were wrong and the Democrats were right. The story failed to account for the social and political changes since 1855.[109] By the time Pease returned to Texas later in the fall, he had finally had enough of politics and his position at the Customs House. He wrote Secretary Sherman that he was resigning effective January 1, 1881, "because my family desire to return to our old home at Austin and I am not willing to reside away from them." He stated that he was not leaving due to "any dissatisfaction with the ... office or with the Department." He also stated that his duties and responsibilities had increased seven-fold during his time in office because of the recovery of the national economy following the depression of the 1870s.[110]

While he was in Galveston, Pease wrote often to his family. A few weeks after he began work there, and even while Lucadia and Julie were with him, he wrote to Carrie, "Galveston can never be as pleasant to me as our old home, with you and George and the children and I shall never be entirely satisfied until I [am] back there again."[111] By early 1979 Carrie had given birth to three children: Marshall Pease Graham on October 15, 1875; George Thomas Graham on April 27, 1877; and Walter Pease Graham on November 5, 1878.[112] "Grandpa Pease" wrote loving notes to his grandsons that reflected his understanding of child development. He wrote to Carrie about his first grandchild when he was not yet two years old, "Tell [Marshall that Grandpa] has no little boys to play with … ."[113] He wanted young Marshall to learn the letters on his blocks, and to "be obedient to all the directions of his Papa and Mama." He sent kisses to the child, and to his younger brother. "Grandpa" wrote his namesake that he wanted to see his new "waggon," which "must be a big one to hold you and your Brother Walter. You must go slow with it, so as not to turn it over and hurt him."[114] He also wrote Carrie of his pleasure in recognizing Veteran Association members at their annual meeting, although he had not seen them in forty or more years.[115] He also wrote an affectionate letter to Lucadia's sister, Juliet, on the death of their mother, recalling, "She always treated me as a son and I feel her loss as much as I did when my own Mother died. Her life was a long and useful one … ."[116] At Woodlawn, George Graham must have been pleased to have been given "entire control of all the land and full authority to act … " in his father-in-law's absence.[117]

Pease's tasks in Galveston may have been dull to him, but one day, after he inspected a light house near Ashbel Smith's "comfortable" home in Galveston, he spent a "forenoon" with the doctor, his longtime friend, who gave him fruit and "some nice wine of his … made from mustang grapes."[118] As he approached retirement from his Customs position, Pease grew ever more impatient with his separation from Lucadia: he wrote her in October 1879, "We have too little of life left to waste it without each others [*sic*] society and companionship."[119]

When Pease returned home, he resumed his duties at the First National Bank and practicing law. He was not active in the Republican Party, but in the summer of 1881, the faint possibility of his being named to the United States Senate arose when Davis recommended to Republicans and Greenbacks in the Democrat-led Legislature that they vote for Pease. However, they supported James W. Throckmorton's attempt to unseat the incumbent, Samuel Bell Maxey.[120] Inevitably, Pease's history as a Democrat-turned-Republican gave him trouble with Democrats in control of state government. One unfortunate example involved The University of Texas, an institution Pease had dreamed of and worked to create since he was governor in the 1850s. In 1881, Governor O. M. Roberts responded to a request from Austin Democratic Senator A. W. Terrell, who nominated Pease for the university's first board of regents. Terrell learned that the majority of the senators opposed Pease because of his Unionist Republican views, and they requested that Roberts withdraw his nomination. Terrell reported to Pease, "The old man [Roberts] was furious ... at first refused to do it." He wrote to Pease, "This shows the feeling that I knew existed as strong as during the war although my friends have often assured me that I was mistaken."[121] Earlier, however, Pease had become a trustee of Austin's Tillotson Normal and Collegiate Institute. The filing of the school charter early in 1877 by the American Missionary Association of the Congregational Church, to educate "the colored people, and especially the training of competent teachers," made Austin a pioneering location for such education west of the Mississippi. The school was named for a minister from Connecticut, Rev. George Tillotson, who was a trustee along with Pease. Eight acres were purchased in east Austin by James Raymond and a Mr. Whitis for the school.[122] Later, Pease was named as a resource to designate an Austin agency that could provide builder's insurance for the new Tillotson building.[123] Lucadia wrote in 1881 that the school was in "successful operation" with "about ninety scholars ... some studying Latin." She observed an algebra class, "and found the negro's [sic] ahead of me in that."[124]

By the time Pease returned from his Customs House job in Galveston, Carrie and George had another child, Richard Niles (called Niles), born March 7, 1881. His birth was followed by Carrie Margaret, born September 7, 1882, the fifth child born to Carrie in only seven years. When Niles was born in a small house that George owned on Rio Grande Street, Carrie was so weakened by the birth that Lucadia and Julie went almost daily to help her, sometimes accompanied by Marshall.[125] George and Carrie's house had been built by George's father near his own home on Rio Grande Street. Lucadia wrote, "It has quite frustrated our plans, as we wished them to live on our side of [Shoal] creek … ." George and Carrie did stay with the Peases until early 1881, which was fortunate for everyone, because Lucadia and Julie were the caregivers of all the children and often Carrie and George's housekeepers.[126]

In August 1880, Carrie, accompanied by her mother and sister, went to New England to seek care for unnamed medical problems. Julie wrote, "Dr. Webster thinks she can help Carrie, but cannot say how long it may take. There is considerable the matter."[127] Medical issues must have been inevitable, with so many closely spaced births and with nonexistent obstetrical care. Carrie was also under the constant strain of having a child who was unwell. Walter, who had a lingering illness with intermittent fever, weight loss, and declining strength for months, died on September 24, 1881.[128] That day Marshall wrote to Carrie,

> We received with great sorrow your telegram of the 24th. It was not entirely unexpected after your dispatch of the previous Saturday, still we hoped and prayed that the result would be different. Nothing that I can say will lessen your grief over the loss of such a loving and loveable child as dear Walter was. Time alone can soothe the great affliction that has come over your household and enable you to think calmly of your present trials. We much fear that your own health will give way with the incessant care and watchfulness that the situation of your family has demanded from you for the last four months. You have the consolation of knowing that you have done everything in your power for the dear child who has gone to join his brother in another and a better world. And now you rest. With love from all here to all your family, and kisses … .[129]

This loving letter was followed by one to Julie, who was in Europe:

> We know how distressed you will be at the sad news ... of our darling
> Walter, who lived long enough to entwine himself around all our hearts.
> His memory will also be cherished ... [he] was such a blessing. Poor
> Carrie has a load to bear under which we hope she will not break down.
> We will be with her in a few days, but it will not be in our power to
> [lessen] her affliction that only comes with time.[130]

The grief of losing a child, the care of other young children, and the
physical strain of a fifth closely-spaced pregnancy took its terrible toll.
Marshall wrote to one of his sisters on November 9, 1882,

> Our darling Carrie died this morning at 7 a.m. You know that she had
> been in ill health for several months .... She gave birth to a Daughter on
> Tuesday [two days before] which left her too feeble to rally. The little
> girl is apparently healthy and quite large. We are all too overwhelmed
> to write more .... Will you be kind enough to communicate the sad
> news to Mr. Moore and Juliet by letter as we will not feel like writing
> for some time.[131]

Lucadia's brother-in-law C. R. Moor wrote, "You need not be told that
dear Carrie was one of the best of daughters, sisters, wives, mothers—patient,
loving, uncomplaining ... ."[132] An article about her noted that her deep faith
enabled her to say hours before her passing, "I am not afraid of death."
She was described as a kind friend, an unselfish daughter, a true-hearted wife,
and a self-sacrificing mother.[133]

Lucadia, thanked her "brother" (-in-law) in February 1883 for his
"kindest words of sympathy and consolation," but "it is a sorrow which must
abide with me as long as I live. Nothing has so helped me to bear the loss ...
as the love of ... the darling children she left to our care ... ."[134] Later she
wrote Juliet that young Marshall was sometimes riding horseback to the
bank, where George had become a clerk. Lucadia claimed "dear, loving,
sweet-tempered, sensitive, little Niles" as her own baby who cheered their

"sad household." Julie cared for "the dear little baby, whom [she] seldom leaves ...." Lucadia had "nothing to do about the housework," which made Julie's work arduous, "but with her energy of character and will to do, [she] cheerfully attends to everything."[135] Lucadia admitted in the spring, "Our dear Carrie's death nearly broke my heart."[136] That summer Lucadia reported that George's health had not been good while he had worked at the bank, and "he is never well when confined .... He has decided to go to a ranch at Brownwood, some four days journey from here by horseback ...." He had "dear little baby Sister" baptized in the Presbyterian Church and named her Carrie Margaret, "as her Mother told him just before her death ... [and] to call her Carrie.[137] Lucadia wrote her sister in July, "my years tell upon me and molehills seem like mountains." She had recently had her seventieth birthday. Niles was clinging to her, not letting her out of his sight, and the "poor little loving motherless boy ... whose father to whom he was most devoted" had left him. She wrote that it was a "great trial to George to go so far from his children, but his health is better when camping, and he likes his employment."[138]

That summer, Lucadia, Marshall, and Julie planned to go to Sulphur Springs in Lampasas, where "the change will do us all good." The springs feeding Sulphur Creek, known for their recreational and medicinal value, were only a day away by train. "Then should the children be sick, we could return home at once ...." She noted that Marshall had recently been in a horse and buggy accident, but he only suffered bruises and was thought to be healthy.[139] The trip had no apparent risk. The family went in mid-August, when "the weather was most oppressively warm, but we had ice all the time." Marshall rarely felt the summer heat as much as others did. With no warning, he suffered an attack (or series of attacks) of "congestive apoplexy," now generally thought to be strokes. Lucadia described what happened:

The twelve days of his sickness seem to me like a frightful dream ....
Through his sickness which at times was extremely painful, he was
unconscious of suffering, always saying he was better, and such
patience and sweetness and thoughtfulness for others comfort seems
more than human. Although his brain was affected from the first he

had his reason most of the [time] always knew all near him. Tho when the fever was the highest he was delirious. Even then doing everything we wished.

Lucadia also explained, "He was taken with congestive apoplexy of the brain, and Dr. [Thomas Dudley] Wooten now says, that considering his age, he thinks no human skill, after his first attack could have saved his life." She added, "he would not admit that he was much sick, calling it a bilious attack, which he sometimes had, but Julie and myself persuaded him to consent to our calling a Dr living there ...." They soon sent for Dr. Wooten in Austin, who "pronounced him in a critical condition." A Mr. McCall, who was an "excellent nurse," and Dr. [Robert J.] Brackenridge came from Austin. George Graham arrived. Of course, Marshall wanted to go home, but he could not be moved. He had "frequent paroxisms [*sic*] of prostration, when he seemed to suffer greatly, and his pulse would almost cease to beat, [but] when they had passed, he said he was in no pain, and at no time was conscious of suffering." The kindness that he had shown to others for years was repaid right away. A young man from Galveston came to nurse him. "He had been in the Custom House and said my dear husband was the best and dearest friend he had in the world. He was one of the most experienced and best of nurses, and scarcely left him .... His devotion to him and grief ... were like those of a son." Marshall Pease died in Lampasas on August 26, 1883. Lucadia's nephew, Harry Ladd of Austin, stayed with them "in our desolate home, and George was there until he had to return to his ranch. Julie, "though nearly heartbroken, attends to the children and everything for the comfort of all." Lucadia had begun her letter, "In my agony I am trying to write you. I know ... how deeply you feel for me now that the life of my life has gone from me forever ... The night he ceased to breathe, I thought I should die ... and I thought we would not long be separated. But I may live many many many long years to bear this sorrow." She knew that she needed to live in order to be present for her grandchildren, even though "the one whose constant thought was to make me happy I can never look upon again ...." She felt, "in death he was so beautiful, so calm so peaceful, it seemed a pleasant sleep. Oh I could not bear to have him taken from my sight." Lucadia questioned how she could live without him, but "I shall have to learn to be resigned, though all my feelings are so rebellious." She concluded her letter, "From the most perfect health and strength to be so suddenly taken away, but such a life fitted him at any moment for the great change." In her last comment, she acknowledged their faith in the change from life on earth to eternal life in the Kingdom of Heaven.[140]

Although it had been almost twenty years since the official close of the Civil War, and many Texans still did not appreciate Pease, he also had many friends. Some of them were with the Gulf, Colorado, and Santa Fe Railroad that had reached Lampasas in the preceding year. As a courtesy they sent a train at no charge to take the Governor's body, the family, and those with them back to Austin on the morning after his death.[141] The Pease's neighbor on adjoining property to the south of Woodlawn, former Confederate Brigadier General Nathan George Shelley, organized a group from the Austin Bar Association to meet the train and to make further arrangements.[142] Governor John Ireland ordered the flag over the Capitol lowered to half-staff, and state offices were closed. He offered the use of the House of Representatives so that the late governor's body could lie in state there, but Lucadia had his body brought to their cherished home for people to pay their respects. The day before the funeral, the Austin *Daily Statesman*, a Democratic paper, printed a formal tribute:

> As a member of society he was exemplary in every respect, and as a friend he was devoted and treasured; in the bosom of his family he was [a] beloved and honored husband and father, while at his hospi-table mansion were dispensed [many kindnesses] to so many devoted friends. THE STATESMAN, in chronicling the record of his many public services, cannot but extol him for his many private virtues. Memory of him will live in the hearts of many. [His family is named.] To them, in their great bereavement, THE STATESMAN extends the most heartfelt sympathy.[143]

The Austin *Daily Dispatch*, a Republican newspaper, published a lengthy article filled with praise and grief. It noted, "His public and private life was without a blot …. As a public officer and as a private citizen, he was the soul of honor. His integrity has never been questioned." In politics, he was "firm" in his conservative views "but never offensive," and he "commanded the esteem and respect of his fellow citizens of all parties." The *Dispatch* reported "a deep gloom" in the city, and the "solemn drapery of sorrow" hung at the First National Bank. As the Governor's body lay in a silver-trimmed casket in the parlor at Woodlawn, "hosts" of people came to pay their respects for two days. The paper reported, "Even in death the calm and benign look his face wore only reflected, let us hope, the bliss he enjoys in the higher spheres to which he has been called." For mourners, emotions ran high: "A solemn silence hung over everything, broken at times by muffled sobs." The widow stood by the casket, "bowed down with her affliction … the very personification of loving sorrow … and melted into unfeigned pity the hearts of all who saw her." In town, the Austin Bar Association issued formal tributes and resolutions, expressed intent to attend the funeral together, and planned to present their resolutions to the courts, including the Texas Supreme Court.

The *Dispatch* reported that taking the remains of "him who was so dearly loved … from a home and family he had made so happy, was the occasion of renewed weeping. The scene was affecting in the extreme." Coaches joined the procession all along its route. The funeral service was conducted on August 29 at St. David's Episcopal Church, where the Peases were members. "Every seat was occupied, and every available foot of standing room was crowded." The former rector, The Reverend Doctor Benjamin A. Rogers, delivered the eulogy. He noted the custom of the Episcopal Church to use the same rites for everyone, but it had become customary to gather from the lives of the "great ones" what may benefit survivors, and speak about those qualities. He and Pease had been friends for thirty years, and Rogers recalled Pease's "many public virtues … generous patriotic deeds … and private qualities for which those who knew him most intimately loved and revered him." He reviewed biographical facts of Pease's life, and remarked on the modest governor's "rare wisdom and worth" in both his public and private life. He "returned to public service again and again," in "almost continuous service" to Texas. Confronted with the political crisis that led to the Civil War, Pease "went …

on the side his heart prompted him, and time shows he was not wrong."[144] Finally, in lasting peace, after struggling for Texas since 1835, the governor's body was buried in the family plot in the city cemetery, only blocks from the Capitol and the Governor's Mansion, in the state that was a part of Mexico when he had "identified" with it shortly after his arrival nearly forty-eight years earlier.[145] He died three weeks before the University of Texas, which he had promoted for decades, held its first class on September 15, 1883.

Lucadia, widowed after almost thirty-three years of marriage to a man she loved with her whole heart, continued to pour out her grief in her letters, but slowly the family's life and events around her began to fill her pages. She stayed at Woodlawn, along with Julie and the grandchildren, who occupied her time. She wrote in early 1884 that the children's "severe colds ... make us very watchful and anxious ... you well know when one has been so terribly bereft, how the heart clings to those who remain to be loved and cared for .... "[146] Both she and Julie had work to do that they had never done before: Lucadia was executrix of her husband's will, but Julie did much of the extensive work it necessitated. Lucadia's energy had declined sharply after Carrie died, and even more so after her husband's death. The will was no small matter, requiring far more work than Marshall must have realized it would. He wrote his final will in April 1883, listing real estate holdings in twenty-five Texas counties. Some of the land was in his name, and some in both his and Lucadia's names. In Austin, the first property he bought and the Woodlawn acreage he bought from James B. Shaw totaled more than 425 acres.[147] Julie shouldered the majority of the work to administer the will, and served as property manager. Young Marshall Graham did some management work, including travel, and had an office in downtown Austin. He sent messages to his grandmother and aunt, asking their opinion of matters and reporting his work.[148]

"[A]t my age I cannot expect to remain long," Lucadia observed in March 1884. "Half of our family are now in the grave yard."[149] She was cheered by a visit from Carrie P. Richardson, Marshall's sister who had made an extended visit in Brazoria when Lucadia and Marshall were newlyweds. Like her brother, she had "a most retentive memory of persons she knew so long ago .... "[150] A trip to Poquonock was debated the next month, but Lucadia confessed to Juliet that she was "so old and broken" that such a trip seemed "insurmountable." Additionally, she had a question about the children: Carrie had asked George to let the Peases care for them, but she wondered whether he would consent to their being taken so far away, for so long, and Lucadia did not know what to do about the matter.[151] The family stayed home—in the heat. In July Lucadia "claim[ed] great credit for the effort ... to write you, as the temperature in the hall indicates at this hour, twelve noon, ninety-nine." She was enjoying summer fruit and vegetables, but she only weighed one hundred and fifteen pounds, "a low weight for me."[152] That fall, Julie enthusiastically took on home improvements that her father had planned, but which Lucadia had "no thought of attempting to do." The house was being painted, "which it has needed it for years."[153] Whether Lucadia was referring only to the wood trim that may have originally been painted white or whether she was thinking about the unpainted, sand-colored brick is unclear. This date was probably when the house was painted dark red. It was said, but there seems to be no proof, that the trim (including the columns) were painted forest green. Garish as those colors seem, especially on such a large house, they were in keeping with Victorian taste.[154]

A fire in the house caused great alarm in October 1884. Julie lit a fire in a new wood stove in the North Chamber, an upstairs bedroom, and then she went down to the parlor, where visitors were. Someone upstairs cried "Fire!" The North Chamber "seemed one blaze of fire, but it was only the mantlepiece, casing around it, nic nacs [sic] on it, and pictures on the wall. The smoke nearly suffocated us til the windows were opened. Everyone screamed water, and ran for it." A gentleman visitor ran to the kitchen and brought back a bucket of water; Julie brought water from the tank in the upstairs bathroom. Lucadia thought that nothing could save the house because everything in the room was combustible, but "plenty of water, and tearing away the woodwork soon put the fire out." In concluding news, Lucadia noted, "Uncle Sam [Barber] is now staying with us, most of the time. He calls this home, and Aunt Easter is here often, to have her stores replenished." Elderly Uncle Sam was the Freedman who was Marshall's slave as early as the 1840s and who drove the Peases to Austin in 1855. Aunt Easter was an elderly Freedwoman.[155]

The procession for the laying of the cornerstone at the new Capitol was a historic event witnessed by Lucadia, Julie, and the grandchildren on March 2, 1885. "There were crowds of people in the city and a fine procession, and we ... [hoped] all except the [baby] would remember the occasion," she wrote. The stone "is of Texas granite with an inscription of Texas 1836 and 1885, handsomely carved—There were addresses delivered, but we only saw the procession and came home. I will enclose ... a picture of the proposed building." The building was many times larger than the limestone edifice that was new when she and Marshall arrived in Austin in 1853.[156] Countless associations caused her to think about him. When she wrote to her sister on San Jacinto Day, she noted the anniversary and explained that she declined to go on a picnic, preferring to stay at home, alone. "Marshall always looked forward with so much interest to meeting the Veterans, and in talking over the scenes they had witnessed together, and while all days are sad ones, since he has been taken from me, still the return of anniversaries in which he took a part—are so fresh in my mind, it unfits me to see any company on such occasions."[157] In late 1885, finding household help remained a major problem. Lucadia and Julie cooked for themselves and enjoyed bakery bread, but the care of the large house and the children was more than they could do. Worse, in November 1885, "atrocious" murders in town caused Lucadia and Julie to feel "very timid and nervous." They hired one man to sleep upstairs and two in the former slave quarters, and "Julie has a loaded pistol under her pillow ... ."[158] Lucadia reported on a happier note that the children were "wild with excitement" when it snowed, and full of "hilarious joy ...." During Christmas, Lucadia was amused by the children's impatient waiting for Santa Claus, hanging their stockings early.[159] "Precocious" Niles prayed that he would not die, "but stay here to take care of Grandma, who is getting old." In the same letter, Lucadia reported that she attended services for Ashbel Smith, whose remains were buried in the State Cemetery. The funeral in the Capitol was attended by as many as two thousand people, James Raymond told her.[160] The first commencement of the University of Texas took place in June. Lucadia and Julie were present for one of its "many" exercises. All Lucadia noted was "the one girl, the first of her sex, who graduated [had] a great deal of attention ... bestowed on her ... and

[s]he also had a beautiful gold medal ... ."[161] Later that summer, Lucadia acknowledged the death of Sam Harris, her husband's longtime secretary and friend since their days in Brazoria: "Few can leave a better record of unselfish benevolence .... His time and means were given for the benefit of ... the children of his brother & sisters [who] have been educated and established in business by him ... ."[162]

The following year, Lucadia, stronger than she had been in years, remarked that she had borne heat and fatigue better than any of the others on a trip, thanks to her "strong constitution and habits of labor and exertion."[163] Still, she was grieving. In Janesville, Wisconsin, with Marshall's brother's family, she kept thinking about how he would have enjoyed them, but he was gone forever.[164] She felt equally miserable on return to Woodlawn, not only for Marshall's loss but also from the anniversary of Carrie's death, and even from the result of a two-year drought that had killed many of their plants and animals. Taking care of others continued anyway, with Christmas preparations for Aunt Easter and Uncle Sam and his wife, and Julie carried on the family's charity work for a widow with six children and others in extreme poverty.[165]

Lucadia and Julie opened Woodlawn to numerous visitors for the May 14, 1888, celebration of the completion of the Capitol. Lucadia expected Woodlawn to be filled to "its utmost capacity," but since "this event is one not likely to be repeated, in the lives of any now on this earth, we feel willing to take a great deal of trouble, in order to do our part."[166] That summer Woodlawn's apricot and other fruit trees begun producing again, and flowers were abundant, even a white moon vine that flowered on the upper gallery at night.[167] Property management required constant attention and created annoying issues. Lucadia had to write the county clerk that she did not understand an increased city tax rate. Furthermore, she had paid taxes, which should have maintained her street, delivered the mail, and provided street lighting, but "no city lights have ever shown upon [the] darkness" of her property.[168]

In the 1890s two notable people crossed Lucadia's path, both of whom became famous in art and literary circles over time. One was Elisabet Ney, a German sculptor who was well-known in European art and political circles when she and her husband moved to Texas in 1872. They bought "Liendo," the vast Groce plantation in Waller County, unaware that it could not support them without a large labor force. "Miss Ney," as she called herself, met Governor Oran Roberts, and in 1879 she spoke with a committee to consider his suggestion for statues in the new capitol building. The group liked her ideas, but the subject faltered over their desire for granite sculpture. With the support of Roberts, she won the contract for sculpting white marble statues of Stephen F. Austin and Sam Houston that were to be placed in the Texas exhibition at the Chicago Columbian Exposition in 1893. Only the Houston statue made it to Chicago, but it was widely acclaimed, and Ney's circle of friends and supporters grew. People slowly began to accept her unusual clothing (including work pants), short hair, and refusal to admit that she was married. She built a castle-like, blocky limestone studio and home, "Formosa," in Hyde Park, north of downtown Austin, and she went in search of patrons. Wearing a white Grecian tunic, she called on Lucadia Pease, who was impressed with the intelligence and energy of such an unconventional woman and made her a loan.[169] Lucadia wrote to Juliet, "We have a new acquaintance ... who came last night and staid [sic] with us. She wished to fund an Art Academy, and read to us a very interesting lecture she will deliver in the Capitol next Monday night."[170] Later Lucadia observed,

> I wish you could see our constant visitor Elisabet Ney the Sculptrice [sic]. She is very eccentric but so very intelligent that we all [find] her odd ways ... interesting. Her great idea is to establish an Art Academy here, and has offered her service for a years instruction In sculpture ... I think there is little prospect of her succeeding here, her ideas are on too grand a scale for Texas as it is at present.[171]

Bride Neill Taylor, a close friend of Julie's, said in a speech that because of the hospitality of Woodlawn, many other people learned of Ney's art: "Without the Pease home and influence Miss Ney would have had to fade away back into the bitter, heart-breaking solitude of Waller County. When she was hopeless, irritated, desperate, she went to spend a day or two at the Pease home. The atmosphere of the place was hope, comfort, and inspiration to her." Taylor added, "Mrs. Pease loaned her money ... in the first years here, and the fact that their personal approval and great social influence were behind her, added to the ... financial help without which she would ... have had to take her poverty back to Liendo."[172] Elisabet, who called the Niles children "beloved Brownies," sent them and Julie a note one afternoon announcing, "I just learned ... that in Hyde Park an *Electric tower festival* with *grand fireworks* shall take place to night [*sic*]." She asked, "Would not our children of Wood Lawn find *much*, and my dearest friend *some* enjoyment in witnessing it?" It would be seen from Lake Ney on her property, "at a quiet distance."[173] She was referring to the night that Austin's Moonlight Towers were turned on, May 6, 1895. The nearby tower was in Hyde Park at Speedway and West 41st Street.[174] During the years of their close friendship, the sculptor did not use any of the Peases as subjects except for the late Carrie Pease Graham; the family commissioned a bust, based on her photographs.[175]

During the 1890s, Lucadia also received three letters from an Austin man she did not know, but who asked her for a loan. The first two letters were written on note paper of her late husband's First National Bank—a fact that must have seemed odd to her. The first, on December 16, 1893, requested $600.00 and offered real estate as security. The writer stated, "I rather apprehend a change in affairs that may compel me to look out for other occupation .... I am sure my prospects are good." He admitted to being an employee of the First National Bank: "I wish to disclaim any using of what knowledge of your business affairs my situation may give me, but I make the application on a business basis." Lucadia must have quickly dismissed the poor judgment and audacity of the writer, but he wrote her again, days later, dropping the request to $500.00, based on real estate appraisals of "Mr. Ladd" (her nephew, Henry) and another man. He still did not state the purpose of the loan. Had Lucadia spoken with bank authorities about the conduct of their employee? She received a third letter on plain paper, dated January 8, 1894, asking for $300.00 "on my printing office which is worth at least $1000." He stated the terms of repaying the loan, and added, "I have been to San Antonio and have received considerable encouragement in the way of advertising and subscriptions. I want [to] use the money to extend my circulation by sending out several thousand ... sample copies ... ." He did not state his business, but he explained that the bank would not make the loan because of a law against granting loans with real estate or personal property as security. Again, Lucadia may not have replied, and her extant financial records show no loan was made. Undeterred, the writer sent a more forthcoming letter to Julie on January 19, 1894. He asked for $600.00 and explained that he wanted to begin a "weekly publication devoted to news and modern topics with special literary and original matter, something altogether different from anything in the State at present." It was to be illustrated. The letter was more gracious than those sent to Lucadia, but its author foolishly concluded that he would appreciate a written reply, "as I am always so busy that I never have an opportunity of conferring with you on the subject personally." Julie must have been as unimpressed as her mother was with such a poorly written request, and her financial records show no loan was made to the upstart. The writer of these letters signed himself "W. S. Porter"—William Sydney Porter. He later became known around the word as O. Henry, the creator of the modern short story. Porter was able to begin his publication, *The Rolling Stone*, later in 1894, the same year he resigned as a teller at First National Bank after being accused of embezzlement there. This odd set of circumstances has the irony of an O. Henry story, including the fact that Will Porter's words on his own behalf were not as well-written as those that won him fame.[176]

On the cusp of the twentieth century, Lucadia wrote that she liked to reminisce, but she embraced the present. She rode in that new invention, the automobile, in 1900, and wrote that she "enjoyed it greatly."[177] She commented briefly on the "terrible catastrophe" of the 1900 Galveston hurricane.[178] Lucadia returned to her Unitarian church roots when she was in the north, and wrote about a minister's preaching. She also reported that she had become "quite fat, and weigh 150 pounds, more than I ever weighed before."[179] She was surely delighted when the West Austin Ward School, formerly the Austin Graded School, was renamed for her late husband in 1902. Pease Elementary school, facing Rio Grande Street on the block designated for an academy in the original 1839 plan for the city, was one of the earliest public schools in Texas, but not the first. The 1869 Constitution required creation of free public schools, and in 1871 the Public School Law went into effect. Harrison County opened schools in October of that year.[180] The Austin Graded School opened October 2, 1876, with children grouped by age for grades one through four. Three public funds were combined to build it, but its two hundred-plus students were necessarily charged tuition from two to four dollars a month once the school fund was depleted every year, after about three months. Girls were taught on the first floor and boys, upstairs. In 1881, this school became part of the new Austin Public Free School system. When the city's ward schools were named for individuals in 1902, the first among them was named in honor of Pease. That meaningful choice would not have been lost on Lucadia, who must have remembered her husband's forty-year advocacy of public schools.[181] In 1903, before her ninetieth birthday, Lucadia attended an event that honored her and her late husband—a celebration at Pease Park on San Jacinto Day, twenty-eight years after she and Marshall had deeded the land to the City. Julie wrote, "They are improving 'Pease Park' a little and are to give a Fireman's picnic there. A road is being opened into it, on the town side of the creek, and it will be a very pretty drive."[182] The event, which was the opening ceremony for the park, included a speech by Alexander Penn Wooldridge that acknowledged the Peases' gift years before. Improvements included a stand for dancing and speakers. Lucadia wrote to her sister that it was "very gratifying that after so many years, that the city has begun to improve the Park which is naturally so capable of being made pleasant." She explained that the City "had made a small appropriation … used to make some drives and put up a small [structure] … ."[183]

In mid-summer Lucadia wrote to twenty-two year-old Niles, "There are so many things I wish to say to you so much advice to give you, but young people think they know more than the old, and they do in Science and many improvements of the age, but common sense and experience go with the old … ."[184] In mid-September, she mourned the death of her sister Juliet, but, as she wrote Niles, "she was ready at any time to go … ." Knowing flowers, she asked him to place a wreath on her grave made of bachelor buttons, because they would not wither.[185]

Twenty years after Marshall's death, his widow and daughter continued his legacy of protecting Texas history by joining the Texas State Historical Association. Their 1902 and 1903 membership cards were signed by Dr. Eugene C. Barker.[186]

With Juliet's passing, Lucadia's correspondence that documented the Peases' lives nearly came to an end, except for letters to her grandchildren. Her last extant letter was to Niles, dated September 15, 1903.[187] Only two brief newspaper articles and no letters document her decline and death. Under the sub-heading of "One of Austin's oldest and most beloved citizens dies at an advanced age … ." one newspaper story revealed that

> Something over a year ago, Mrs. Pease, who up to that time, though far advanced in life, had enjoyed unusual good health and physical preservation, had the misfortune to fall and break her hip, thereby dooming her to the role of an invalid. Notwithstanding this fact, however, she retained her natural cheerfulness and light-heartedness up to the very last … surrounded by those who knew and loved her in life.[188]

At the age of ninety-one, she departed this life on January 23, 1905, at 4:30 p.m. Services were to be held at her "suburban" home.[189] Her remains were placed next to Marshall's in their large family plot. At the time of her death, two of her daughters and three of her grandsons were also buried there.[190] Years later, Niles Graham installed a tall, pink granite obelisk in the center of the plot, carved with the names, dates, and locations of the births and deaths of the family.

Reflection on the lives of Marshall and Lucadia Pease leads to an admiration of their remarkable intelligence, patience, and kindness to those around them. Their love for each other was deep and unfailing. Their only serious character flaw, from a twenty-first century perspective, was their ownership of other human beings. However, as has been shown, Lucadia never said she owned anyone and after the war, wrote that she did not feel that she did; on the other hand, she referred to "Marshall's slaves" on more than one occasion. To twenty-first century observers, his views on race and slavery (prior to his changed opinion during Reconstruction) reflected the common prejudice of the age in which he lived. Other than this, Marshall's inability or unwillingness to write to his parents when he was young and far away from them was painful for both of them, and he was not known to apologize about the matter. As time went on, he became a good correspondent with his wife and daughters.

Thirty-six years separated the time between the day E. M. Pease left his post as Governor during the troubled era of Reconstruction and the day when Lucadia passed away in Austin with automobiles on the streets and Woodlawn no longer in the country. After Reconstruction, the former Governor had resumed his law practice, became co-owner of a bank, and contributed to civic improvements; he served the Federal government out of a sense of duty, not desire. He was still working late in his life and died suddenly. Marshall's and Lucadia's love of one another remained profound over time, and Lucadia was bereft without him. Her grief was magnified by the death, only months earlier, of their eldest daughter. Eventually Lucadia was able to embrace life again, becoming active and once more providing the hospitality that Woodlawn was known for. It must have been hard for her to be confined to bed with a broken hip after such an active life, but the report that she remained cheerful is a mark of her character. Although Marshall and Lucadia Pease died twenty-two years apart, they both left this life much as they lived it, with characteristic loving kindness.

Epilogue

Marshall was "identified with Texas," and Lucadia was "determined to like it."

lisha Marshall Pease claimed Texas as his home only months after arriving in January of 1835. At age twenty-three, he knew that the best way to "establish an independence"—that is, financial security—was to become a lawyer, and, amid such uncertain times, he must have known intuitively that he had the capacity to help create the future of Texas. Marshall, as he was known to his family, had to leave home and school at age fourteen and became a clerk. When he was twenty-one, he traveled from New England to the West, learned about Texas, and found an opportunity to read law in Mina (Bastrop). There, in October of 1835, he volunteered to fight in the first battle of the Revolution at Gonzales, and he served with the Texan Army at the Siege of Bexar. Afterward, his career in public service began as a clerk at the Convention of 1836, and the first draft of the Republic's Constitution is in his handwriting. Although he was the clerk of the committee, some of the organization and wording of the document may have been his own, accomplished under extreme pressure and uncertainty.

After the Revolution, young Pease joined John A. Wharton's law practice in Brazoria, where he passed the bar exam. His highly successful career, based on legal knowledge, ability to win cases, and wise judgment, enabled him to become a wealthy man and a public servant. He served in the first three state legislatures and later was a three-time governor. During the Second Legislature, as Chairman of the Judiciary Committee, he was responsible for much of the legislation that created the court system of the state. Following the adjournment of the Third Legislature, he left for Connecticut to claim his bride.

Lucadia Christiana Niles was called a "jewel" and an "angel" by Marshall's sisters, who knew her well. The couple were second cousins through the Marshall family with shared great-great grandparents. Marshall took his sisters' advice, and the couple became engaged in 1848. Lucadia was no ordinary woman. She was highly intelligent, had a good education, and like Marshall, she was mature, wrote well, and was willing to venture away from home. She also had the same sense of humor and the innate ability to love people. In 1838 she took a long trip, alone, to Virginia, ostensibly to be a tutor at a plantation; however, the real purpose of her months-long trip may have been to escape the amorous attention of another cousin. Amidst cultural differences and some homesickness, she remained curious, observant, and cheerful. Travel significantly enhanced her education. For example, having seen Jefferson's statue in the national Capitol, his words about equality echoed in her head when she witnessed slavery for the first time and tried to comprehend it. She also saw a lavish display of wealth in Virginia, and her distaste for such ostentation may have influenced her once she was wealthy herself. Lucadia and Marshall married when she was thirty-seven and he was thirty-eight. She tried to imagine near-tropical Texas and declared that she was "determined to like it," and she did. Both Marshall and Lucadia had the ability to accept change gracefully, a capacity that certainly made life easier for them.

E. M. Pease disliked "politiks" and vowed repeatedly to leave it, but yet he spent years of his life in public service. Being in the legislature had its difficulties, but he had the knowledge of the law and the interpersonal skills to create laws that shaped the state court system. Lucadia urged him to run for governor in 1853, convinced that he was the most qualified man in the state. Being governor was trying in the extreme at times, but he prevailed in the biggest issue of the time: resolving the debt of the Republic, and using the funds wisely for meeting human needs, especially in creating "asylums" for the blind, deaf, and mentally ill, and setting aside money for education. He led the campaign to construct the General Land Office building and Governor's Mansion. He believed in using public money wisely, a trait that he demonstrated over the years in many productive ways. To his great regret, public education could not be implemented in his time.

Pease, on becoming a wealthy nineteenth-century Southern gentleman, acquired slaves for his household and small farm. Like the leadership of the time, he called slavery "practical" because no other labor force was available. He expressed no moral objection to the practice, but Lucadia usually referred to the family's slaves as belonging to Marshall, not to her, and wrote after the Civil War that she did not regard any of them as ever being owned. He could not support the oncoming struggle over the institution and the lead up to the war. His attempt at moderation could not succeed, given the temperament of the times. He remained a Unionist on strong principle, but yet he retained his slaves. At high risk, he and his family stayed home in Austin during the war. Pease was appointed governor during the violence and disorder of Reconstruction, and he served out of a sense of duty, not desire. His experience proved valuable, although it was an all-but-impossible job. As Freedmen struggled for the vote, an education, and their very lives, Pease firmly supported their rights amidst many Texans who did not. Finally, after Reconstruction, Pease took one last political position at the Federal Customs House in Galveston, again out of duty.

Lucadia and Marshall often exchanged letters while Marshall was in Galveston; he wrote more and more urgently that he longed to be with her. Letters from the beginning of their marriage forward well document their lives and the times; it is clear that the personal cost of his career was high, and so were the months of separation when Lucadia took the children to Connecticut for school and to see their families. Their lives were truly committed to the loving and unfailing support of one another and to their family. When Lucadia declared herself "a women's rights woman," in the 1850s, he approved.

Marshall wrote that he wanted to be worthy of her love, and he was. When he died unexpectedly, she was bereft and thought she could not live long, but she survived more than twenty years. Their stately family home, Woodlawn, just west of Austin, had been a center of gracious hospitality, and Lucadia resumed that tradition after her husband's death. The Pease's middle daughter, Julie, who earned a degree from Vassar College, also lived at Woodlawn and reared there the three children of her late sister, Carrie Graham. The Peases enjoyed the pleasures of a high income, which they generously shared with those in need.

The outpouring of deep respect and great affection for the governor on his unexpected death at age seventy-one showed that he was revered on both sides of the divide that had split the state and nation so severely in the Civil War. He was valued for his judgment and honesty in holding fast to his convictions and for his unfailing kindness. When Lucadia died much later, she was remembered for her own humane qualities, loving-kindness being the greatest.

E. M. Pease observed near the end of his life that he had been "one of the people of Texas since the colonial days of Stephen F. Austin." This sweeping statement was also a typically modest, understated one: He participated in or led many of the events that brought about vast changes for almost half a century, from 1835 to 1883. Lucadia joined him in Texas in 1850 and lived to 1905, watching and participating in changes for fifty-five years. They left an extraordinary historical record that documents the development of Texas. Their record also provides examples in their own words of the ways that caring for others, guided by high principles of honesty, hard work, and careful thought, can be used for great good. May Texas, the place these remarkable people chose to call home, be blessed with many more such inspiring people in generations to come.

Endnotes

List of Abbreviations for Major Source Collections and Individuals in Endnotes

Pease Papers. The Pease, Niles, Graham Family Papers at the Austin History Center, Austin Public Library

Pease Records. Letters to and from E. M. Pease and other documents from his terms as Governor, Texas State Library and Archives Commission, Austin

EMP. Elisha Marshall Pease (E. M. or Marshall)

LCN. Lucadia Christiana Niles (birth name)

LCP. Lucadia Christiana Pease (married name)

CAP. Carrie Augusta Pease (birth name)

CPG. Carrie P. Graham (married name)

JMP. Julia (Julie) Maria Pease

LTP. Lorrain Thompson Pease

JN. Juliet Niles

JWH. John Woods Harris

Notes for Chapter 1

1. EMP partial autobiography on two handwritten, untitled, undated page fragments, Pease Papers. Evidence of the use of his name is in thousands of letters, both public and private, to and from him, as well as in business and legal documents in the Pease Papers and in letters and legal documents in the Pease Records.
2. The seven children were Maria Annunciade Caroline, who was born in 1810 and died in 1822; Elisha Marshall; Sarah, who died as an infant; Lorrain Thompson (named for his father), who was born in 1815; John James Rousseau, who was born in 1817; Sarah Maria, who was born in 1822; and Caroline Annunciade, who was born in 1826, Pease Papers.
3. *Annual Catalogue of the Course of Study, Westfield Academy, November 1826*, photocopy, Pease Papers; email of Jan Gryszkiewicz, Westfield Athenaeum, Westfield, MA to Elizabeth Whitlow, Mar. 1, 2016, on Academy archival material; no students named Pease were listed in the only extant catalogs of 1824, 1827, and 1828; Rev. Emerson Davis, Westfield Academy, Annual Catalogue 1826, p. 8, copy in Pease

Papers, original at Westfield Athenaeum. A reference to EMP's attendance for two terms is seen in *Biographical Encyclopedia of Texas* (New York, NY: Southern Pub. Co., 1880), 17.

4. Juliet was born in 1811, Lucadia Christiana in 1813, Maria Harriet in 1822, and Augusta Flora in 1825, Pease Papers.

5. LCP to EMP, Sept. 18, 1870, Pease Papers.

6. There is an extensive genealogy chart in an online link to the Pease Papers.

7. Letter from Teachers of Hartford Female Academy to Richard Niles (undated), LCN's history notes and report card, Pease Papers.

8. LCN's report card and tuition receipt, Pease Papers; Kathryn Kish Sklar, *Catharine Beecher: A Study in American Domesticity* (New Haven, CT: Yale University Press, 1973).

9. LCN to Sister, July 14, 1829 and Oct. 29, 1829, LCN to parents, Jun 21, 1832; tuition receipt and note from J. L. Hawks, undated, Pease Papers.

10. EMP partial autobiography; LCP to James D. Lynch, undated draft; EMP to CAP, Mar. 5, 1866, Pease Papers; Elisha Marshall Pease entry in James D. Lynch, *The Bench and Bar of Texas; Published by the Author* (St. Louis, MO: Nixon-Jones printing co., 1885), 221.

11. EMP to Gideon Welles, Feb. 20, 1833, and I. N. Pryor to Welles, Feb. 20, 1833, as quoted in Roger A. Griffin, "Connecticut Yankee in Texas: A Biography of Elisha Marshall Pease" (Ph. D. Dissertation, University of Texas, 1973), 11; EMP to LCN, Feb. 16, 1833, EMP to JMP, July 3, 1858, Pease Papers.

12. EMP to LTP, June 9, 13, 16, and 18, 1834 (quotation), E. M. Pease Transcripts of Letters and Documents in the Archives of the Grand Lodge of Texas, prepared by Dr. James D. Canter, Waco, Texas (hereinafter referred to as Pease Collection, Waco).

13. EMP to LTP, 1834, in the Grand Lodge Library Collection, Pease Papers.

14. EMP to LTP, 1834, in Grand Lodge Library Collection, Pease Papers.

15. EMP to LTP, July 2, 16, 1834, Pease Papers.

16. EMP to LTP, July 23, 1834 (first quotation); EMP to LTP, Aug. 2, 1834 (second quotation); EMP to LTP, Aug. 8, 1834 (third quotation); EMP to LTP, Aug. 13, 1834 (fourth quotation). Pease Papers.

17. Mary Austin Holley, *Texas: Observations—Historical, Geographical, and Descriptive—In a Series of Letters* (Baltimore, MD, 1836); EMP

handwritten account of arrival in Texas, undated photocopy in Pease Papers.

18. EMP partial autobiography, Pease Papers.

19. EMP partial autobiography. His observations about those he met are more extensive than noted here.

20. Ibid.

21. L. T. Pease, "Geographical and Historical View of Texas," in John M. Niles, *History of South America and Mexico; comprising Their Discovery, Geography, Politics, Commerce, and Revolutions, to which is annexed, A Geographical and Historical View of Texas, with a detailed Account of the Texian Revolution and War*, by Hon. L. T. Pease (2 vols., Hartford: H. Huntington, June 1837), I, 217–218; EMP to LTP, Nov. 27, 1835, Mar. 4, 1836, Pease Papers.

22. EMP partial autobiography, Pease Papers.

23. EMP to LTP, Feb. 15, 1841, Pease Papers.

24. EMP to Barrett, Sept. 15, 1835, Don Carlos Barrett Papers, Briscoe Center for American History, University of Texas at Austin.

25. EMP to LTP, Nov. 27, 1835; EMP account of the battle of Gonzales, undated manuscript, Pease Papers.

26. EMP to LTP, 1834, in Grand Lodge Library Collection, Pease Papers.

27. Proceedings of the General Council, in H. P. N. Gammel, comp., *The Laws of Texas, 1822–1897* (10 vols.; Austin,TX: Gammel Book Co. 1898–1902), I, 389; EMP to LTP, Nov. 27, 1835, Pease Papers (first quotation); EMP to Wyatt Hanks, Feb. 8, 1836, in Sam Houston Papers, Briscoe Center for American History, University of Texas at Austin (second quotation); Moses Austin Bryan to Beauregard Bryan, Sept. 25, 1889, Moses Austin Bryan Papers, Briscoe Center for American History, University of Texas at Austin.

28. "Proceedings of the General Council," in Gammel, comp., *Laws of Texas*, I, 796–797. The word "efficient," was in common use (EMP used it often) to refer to competency, but it has evolved to mean being productive without wasting time or effort; Pease to Wyatt Hanks, Feb. 8, 1836, photocopy in Houston papers (quotation); the document of the original land grant, in Spanish, is in the Pease Papers.

29. Proceedings of the General Council, in Gammel, comp., *Laws of Texas*, I, 807 (quotation); Proceedings of the Convention at Washington in Gammel, comp., *Laws of Texas*, I, 825–826. Washington-on-the-Brazos, as it became known during the Civil War, was known previously as Washington, and hence it is referred to by its proper name during the

Revolution. *Handbook of Texas Online*, Carole E. Christian, "Washington-on-the-Brazos, TX," accessed March 3, 2016, http://www.tshaonline.org/handbook/online/articles/hvw10.

30. EMP to LTP, Mar. 4, 1836, Pease Papers.

31. Proceedings of the General Council, in Gammel, comp., *Laws of Texas*, I, 813.

32. *The Diary of William Fairfax Gray, from Virginia to Texas, 1835–1837*, William P. Clements Center for Southwest Studies, Southern Methodist University, Dallas, TX, https://sites.smu.edu.swcenter/FairfaxGray/wg_cont.htm, 117–119. David Thomas was a delegate from Refugio and Chairman of the Committee for Organizing the Militia; Proceedings of the Constitutional Convention, in Gammel, comp., *Laws of Texas*, I, 894.

33. *Diary of William Fairfax Gray*, 124–125.

34. *Biographical Encyclopedia of Texas*, 17–18; Frank W. Johnson, *A History of Texas and Texans; Edited and brought to date by Eugene C. Barker with the assistance of Ernest William Winkler, To which are added historical, statistical and descriptive matter pertaining to the important local divisions of the State, and biographical accounts of the leaders and representative men of the state* (5 vols., Chicago, IL: American Historical Society, 1914) IV, 1610. Neither of these books cites the source(s) of their information, although Johnson and Pease knew each other. Johnson was an organizer of the Texas Veterans Association in which Pease was active.

35. Original draft, Constitution of the Republic of Texas, General Land Office, Austin.

36. EMP to LTP, March 29, 1836, Pease Papers.

37. EMP to Moses Austin Bryan, Mar. 30, 1836, Pease Papers.

38. Bryan to EMP, Jan. 22, 1877, M. A. Bryan Papers; EMP to L. T. Pease, March 29, 1836, EMP partial autobiography, EMP to L. T. Pease, May 26, 1836, Pease Papers.

39. EMP to LTP, March 4, March 9, and May 26, 1836, Pease Papers.

40. "Who is Governor Pease," Galveston *Civilian*, reprinted in Austin *Texas State Gazette*, Aug. 4, 1855; Pease to L. T. Pease, May 26, 1836, Pease Papers; William C. Binkley, ed., *Official correspondence of the Texan revolution, 1835–1836* (2 vols., New York, London, D. Appleton-Century, 1926), I, 507–508, II, 1090; *Biographical Encyclopedia of Texas*, 18.

41. EMP to LTP, September 10, 1836, Pease Papers.

42. Texas. Legislature. Senate, *Journals of the Senate of the Republic of Texas, First Session* (Columbia, IN: C. and T.H. Borden, 1836), 4; *Journals of the House of Representatives of the Republic of Texas, First Session* (Houston, TX: Office of the *Telegraph*, 1838) 5, 29; *Biographical Encyclopedia of Texas*, 18; Griffin, "Connecticut Yankee," 27–28. Lucadia Pease to James D. Lynch, n.d., Pease Papers; *Biographical Encyclopedia of Texas*, 18.

43. EMP to LTP, Jan. 8, 1837, Feb. 5, 1837, Pease Papers.

Notes for Chapter 2

1. EMP to LTP, Jan. n.d., 1837, Pease Papers.

2. John M. Niles, *History of South America and Mexico; Comprising Their Discovery, Geography, Politics, Commerce, and Revolutions, to which is annexed, A Geographical and Historical View of Texas, with a detailed Account of the Texian Revolution and War*, by Hon. L. T. Pease (2 vols., Hartford, IN: H. Huntington, June 1837). Niles, a United States Senator from Connecticut, had been a newspaper publisher and had written several books, including *A Gazetteer of the States of Connecticut and Rhode-Island* with maps of each state in 1819 and a biography of Oliver Hazzard Perry in 1821. *A View of South America and Mexico* ... was first published in 1825. The 1837 and 1838 versions with the Texas material also contained "A Map of Mexico and the Republic of Texas." The cartographer was unnamed; the engraver was T. Twitchel. The placement of rivers and towns are fairly accurate, but of course the boundaries were uncertain, except for the one with Louisiana. The Mexican federation is better outlined, but some internal state boundaries were unknown. The map, which is approximately eighteen inches square and on thin paper, was glued in to the book at the beginning of the Texas section, and folded in. It was hand-water colored in pastel green, pink, and yellow.

3. EMP to LTP, Feb. 5, 1837, Pease Papers. President Andrew Jackson's annual message, Dec. 22, 1836, had questioned whether Texas could survive and called its recognition "impolitic."

4. Francis R. Lubbock, *Six Decades in Texas: Or, Memoirs of Francis Richard Lubbock, Governor of Texas in War Time, 1861–1863: A Personal Experience in Business, War, and Politics*, ed. C. W. Raines (Austin, TX: Ben C. Jones & Co., 1900), 68–69; Gammel, comp., *Laws of Texas*, I, 1301–1303; Pease's bond, June 20, 1837, in Bonds and

Oaths of County and Republic Officers, 1837–1844, Records of the Secretary of State, TSLAC.

5. EMP to LTP, Aug. 4, 1837, EMP to John J. R. Pease, Aug. 4, 1837, Pease Papers.

6. EMP to Houston, Dec. 9, 1837, Houston Papers; *Handbook of Texas Online*, "Wharton, John Austin," accessed June 13, 2016, http://www.tshaonline.org/handbook/online/articles/fwh03.

7. District Court Minutes, Book A, p. 72, Records of the District Clerk, Apr. 10, 1838, Brazoria County Courthouse (originally in Brazoria); record book removed to Brazoria County Historical Museum, Angleton, Texas.

8. Hans W. Baade, "Law and Lawyers in Pre-Independence Texas," *Centennial History of the Texas Bar* (Burnet, TX: Eakin Press, 1981), 241–242.

9. *Handbook of Texas Online*, Joseph W. McKnight, "Law," accessed June 27, 2016, http://www.tshaonline.org/handbook/online/articles/jzlph.

10. Baron de Bastrop to Colonists: Proclamation, Aug. 4, 1823, as quoted in Gregg Cantrell, *Stephen F. Austin: Empresario of Texas* (New Haven, CT: Yale University Press, 1999), 134, 144; Michael Ariens, *Lone Star Law: A Legal History of Texas* (Lubbock: Texas Tech University Press, 2011), 7–9.

11. *Handbook of Texas Online*, Margaret Swett Henson, "Chambers, Thomas Jefferson," accessed July 01, 2016, http://www.tshaonline.org/handbook/online/articles/fch08.; Badde, "Law and Lawyers," 246; Rusk to Edward Harden, Sept. 16, 1845, quoted in William Ransom Hogan, *The Texas Republic: A Social and Economic History* (Norman: University of Oklahoma Press, 1946), 247.

12. Andrew Forest Muir, ed., *Texas in 1837* (Austin: University of Texas Press, 1968), 157, 160, 162.

13. *Diary of William Fairfax Gray*, 218–219.

14. Joseph W. McKnight, "Tracings of Texas Legal History: Breaking Ties and Borrowing Traditions," *Centennial History of the Texas Bar* (Burnet, TX: Eakin Press, 1981), 256; *Handbook of Texas Online*, Joseph W. McKnight, "Law," accessed June 27, 2016, http://www.tshaonline.org/handbook/online/articles/jzlph.

15. *Handbook of Texas Online*, "Wharton, John Austin," accessed June 26, 2016, http://www.tshaonline.org/handbook/online/articles/fwh03.

EMP to "Dear Sir" but unidentified, Dec. 10, 1838, Harris as Executor—see note to Messrs. Wharton, Harris, and Pease, 1838, regarding estate of John Sharp, Pease Papers.

16. *Handbook of Texas Online*, Amelia W. Williams, "Harris, John Woods," accessed June 28, 2016. http://www.tshaonline.org/handbook/online/articles/fha86.

17. EMP to LTP, July 10, 1838, Pease Papers.

18. "Elisha Marshall Pease," in Lynch, *Bench and Bar of Texas*, 221–250. The division of responsibilities was mentioned in an early biographical sketch of Pease, but extant records do not prove the point.

19. "Elisha Marshall Pease," in Lynch, *Bench and Bar of Texas*, 224; Hogan, *Texas Republic*, 252, 254.

20. Mark W. Lambert, "You can learn a lot about a man by the company he keeps: The legal practice of Texas Governor Elisha Marshall Pease (1812–1883)," presentation to Society of Southwest Archivists Annual Meeting, Houston, Texas, May 23, 2008.

21. Ibid.; John W. Harris to EMP, Apr. 5, 1846, Pease Papers.

22. Waller agreement, June 25, 1839; notice of legal agents, *Brazos Courier*, Sept. 3, 1839; Lewis C. Manson notes for collection, Jan. 1, 1840, Pease Papers.

23. Joseph Henry Polley Papers, Briscoe Center for American History, University of Texas at Austin; *Brazos Courier*, Dec. 3, 1839.

24. *Brazos Courier*, Oct. 6, 1840; Statement of fees charged to Isaac C. Hoskiss, undated, EMP Notes on Chambers Petitions of March 18, 1850 and April 4, 1850; Deposition of John P. Borden, Jan/ 20, 1840, EMP administrator of estate of James F. Perry; Deed of Partition, Sept. 1846, Pease Papers; Hogan, *Texas Republic*, 258; *Handbook of Texas Online*, Margaret Swett Henson, "Chambers, Thomas Jefferson," accessed June 11, 2016, http://www.tshaonline.org/handbook/online/articles/fch08.

25. Grayson's Bond, Jan. 1, 1846; William McNair to Harris and Pease, Nov. 11, 1848, Pease Papers.

26. M. W. Chapin to EMP, July 16, 1846. Receipt for payment of taxes, May 1, 1866, Pease Papers.

27. Receipts filed in 1840 legal papers, Pease Papers.

28. Receipts, legal services for John Sharp filed in 1840, Pease Papers.

29. New York and Republic of Texas forms for debt collection, Pease Papers.

30. Election Register, 1836–1842, 463, Records of the Secretary of State, TSLAC; Muster Roll, Captain John P. Gill's company of mounted volunteers, Mar. 20, 1842, Texas Militia Rolls, TSLAC; Yoakum, Henderson L. History of Texas From Its First Settlement in 1685 to Its Annexation to The United States in 1846 (2 vols., New York, NY: J.H. Colton & Co., 1856), II, 348–349; EMP to Sarah Marshall Pease, July 20, 1841, Pease Papers.

31. JWH to EMP, Feb. 14, 1846 (first through third quotation), JWH to EMP, Feb. 22, 1846, (fourth through sixth quotation), Pease Papers.

32. EMP to Sarah Marshall Pease, July 20, 1841, Pease Papers (first quotation); Lynch, Bench and Bar of Texas, 367–381 (second through fifth quotations.)

33. Johnson, History of Texas and Texans, IV, 1610 (first quotation); John W. Harris to EMP, Feb. 19, 1846, Pease Papers (second quotation).

34. JWH to EMP, Mar. 30, 1846 (first quotation), March 31, 1846 (second quotation), and April 5, 1846, (third quotation), Pease Papers.

35. Handbook of Texas Online, C. T. New, "Annexation," accessed July 20, 2016, http://www.tshaonline.org/handbook/online/articles/mga02.

36. LTP to EMP, Dec. 17, 1845, Pease Papers.

37. Election Returns, February 4, 1846, Records of the Secretary of State, TSLAC.

38. F. H. Merriman to EMP, Feb. 8, 1846; Robert Mills to EMP, Feb. 4, 1846, Pease Papers.

39. The House chamber was so crowded that a proposed resolution included the phrase, "no member be allowed to sit cross-legged, or put his legs upon his table so as to obstruct a passage between the tables." The proposal failed. Journals of the House of Representatives of the First Legislature of the State of Texas (Clarksville, TX: Standard Office, 1838), 442. Hereinafter the House of Representatives journals will be cited as HJ with the appropriate legislative session and page numbers.

40. HJ 1, 66.

41. HJ 1, 3–5, 9–12, 13–20; Journals of the Senate of the First Legislature of the State of Texas (Clarksville, TX: Standard Office, 1848), 12–17. Hereinafter the Senate journals will be cited as SJ with the appropriate legislative session and page numbers.

42. HJ 1, 22. The Judiciary Committee chairman was Peter W. Gray, son of the late William Fairfax Gray, whom Pease had known. The chairman, although only twenty-six, had legal experience and intelligence that served the committee well. See Handbook of Texas Online, Thomas W.

Cutrer, "Gray, Peter W," accessed July 24, 2016, https//www.tshaonline.org/handbook/onlinr/styivlrd/fgr25.

43. *HJ 1*, 31.
44. Gammel, comp., *Laws of Texas*, II, 1309.
45. *HJ 1*, 209.
46. *HJ 1*, 309–312.
47. Gammel, comp., *Laws of Texas*, II, 1438.
48. Ibid., 1452.
49. *HJ 1*, 135; Gammel, comp., *Laws of Texas*, II, 1600–1601.
50. Gammel, comp., *Laws of Texas*, II, 1461–1463.
51. *HJ 1*, 327.
52. *HJ 1*, 370.
53. *HJ 1*, 356.
54. *HJ 1*, 541.
55. *HJ 1*, 581.
56. Gammel, comp., *Laws of Texas*, II, 1600–1601.
57. *HJ 1*, 492.
58. Gammel, comp., *Laws of Texas*, II, 1315.
59. Ibid., 1475.
60. *HJ 1*, 324.
61. *HJ 1*, 334; Gammel, comp., *Laws of Texas*, II, 1429–1430.
62. *HJ 1*, 499; Gammel, comp., *Laws of Texas*, II, 1459–1460, 1462–1463.
63. Gammel, comp., *Laws of Texas*, II, 1625–1626.
64. *HJ 1*, 408; Gammel, comp., *Laws of Texas*, II, 1639–1644.
65. *HJ 1*, 94–95, 565; Gammel, comp., *Laws of Texas*, II, 1653–1664.
66. *HJ 1*, 247.
67. Gammel, comp., *Laws of Texas*, II, 1391.
68. *HJ 1*, 509, 556.
69. *HJ 1*, 572, Gammel, comp., *Laws of Texas*, II, 1597.
70. *HJ 1*, 443, Gammel, comp., *Laws of Texas*, II, 1551–1555.
71. *HJ 1*, 575–576.
72. *HJ 1*, 73.
73. *HJ 1*, 329; Gammel, comp., *Laws of Texas*, II, 1359.
74. *HJ 1*, 124.
75. *HJ 1*, 366.
76. *HJ 1*, 588.
77. Gammel, comp., *Laws of Texas*, II, 1626.
78. *HJ 1*, 615.
79. *HJ 1*. 560.

80. *HJ 1*, 564.
81. *HJ 1*, 702.
82. *HJ 1*, 733.
83. The House chamber was referred to as the "Hall." *HJ 2*, 15.
84. *HJ 2*, 78.
85. *HJ 2*, 13, 424.
86. *HJ 2*, 13.
87. *HJ 2*, 13, 14.
88. *HJ 2*, 21.
89. *HJ 2*, 22.
90. *HJ 2*, 28.
91. *HJ 2*, 15.
92. *HJ 2*, 71, 75.
93. *HJ 2*, 167–168.
94. Gammel, comp., *Laws of Texas*, III, 20–21.
95. Ibid., 208–209.
96. *HJ 2*, 404–406.
97. *HJ 2*, 480.
98. Gammel, comp., *Laws of Texas*, III, 151–153.
99. Ibid., 196–205.
100. Ibid., 284–285.
101. See David C. Humphrey, *Peg Leg: The Improbable Life of a Texas Hero Thomas William Ward* (Denton: Texas State Historical Association, 2009), 126–142, for an explanation of land law issues, Ward's role, and legislative action. See also *HJ 2*, 645–658, 693, 732–734, 842–852, and 861–863.
102. Gammel, comp., *Laws of Texas*, III 79–84, 29–30, 190.
103. Ibid., 291.
104. *HJ 2*, 232.
105. *HJ 2*, 93, 95.
106. *HJ 2*, 532.
107. Gammel, comp., *Laws of Texas*, III, 13.
108. Ibid., 163–181.
109. *HJ 2*, 557.
110. Gammel, comp., *Laws of Texas*, III, 113–120.
111. Ibid., 235–283.
112. *HJ 2*, 1002.
113. Gammel, comp., *Laws of Texas*, III, 286–297.
114. *HJ 2*, 260–261.

115. *HJ 2*, 108; Gammel, comp., *Laws of Texas*, III, 106–112.
116. *HJ 2*, 617, 683–684; Gammel, comp., *Laws of Texas*, III, 45–48.
117. Gammel, comp., *Laws of Texas*, III, 33–45.
118. *HJ 2*, 637.
119. *HJ 2*, 960; Gammel, comp., *Laws of Texas*, III, 72–75.
120. Gammel, comp., *Laws of Texas*, III, 215.
121. *HJ 2*, 627.
122. Gammel, comp., *Laws of Texas*, III, 137–138, 139.
123. *HJ 2*, 377–378.
124. *HJ 2*, 107.
125. *HJ 2*, 144.
126. *HJ 2*, 109.
127. Gammel, comp., *Laws of Texas*, III, 77–79.
128. *HJ 2*, 890; Gammel, comp., *Laws of Texas*, III, 311–316.
129. *HJ 2*, 1091–1092.
130. Gammel, comp., *Laws of Texas*, III, 210–232.
131. *SJ 3*, 205.
132. *SJ 3*, 3.
133. *SJ 3*, 7.
134. *SJ 3*, 9–10.
135. SJ 3, 98–99.
136. SJ 3, 98–99, 106.
137. *SJ 3*, 108–109.
138. *SJ 3*, 128; Gammel, comp., *Laws of Texas*, III, 627.
139. Gammel, comp., *Laws of Texas*, III, 640.
140. Ibid., 449.
141. *SJ 3*, 459.
142. *SJ 3*, 453.
143. Gammel, comp., *Laws of Texas*, III, 471.
144. LCN to EMP, May 10, 1850, Pease Papers.
145. Guy M. Bryan to EMP, July 3, 1850, Pease Papers.
146. Guy M. Bryan to EMP, Aug., 1850, n.d., Pease Papers.
147. Guy M. Bryan to EMP, July 3, 1850, Pease Papers.
148. EMP to LCP, Apr. 21, 1851, Pease Papers.
149. EMP to LCP, June n.d., 1851; LCP to "Mother," July 1, 1851; LCP to Maria N. Moore, August 4, 1851, Pease Papers.
150. JN to Maria N. Moore, Jan. 26, 1853, Pease Papers.
151. EMP to C. R. Moore, Mar. 17, 1853 (birth of Julie Maria, sometimes written "Julia Maria"), Pease Papers.

Notes for Chapter 3

1. Clarissa Clark to unaddressed recipient (LCN), Jan. 3, 1838, Pease Papers.

2. Thomas' last name is unknown, and no Cousin Thomas is mentioned elsewhere.

3. How Lucadia and her family knew or knew of the Bassetts is unknown. Descriptions of Lucadia's journey from Connecticut to Virginia are taken from LCN to Col. Richard Niles, Oct. 4, 1838, Pease Papers.

4. Lucadia may well have visited New York City, but there is no description of the route she took from Connecticut to Philadelphia.

5. The bronze statue, created by Pierre-Jean David d'Angers, shows Jefferson holding a quill pen in one hand, the quill pointed to his readable words in the other. The statue, placed in the Rotunda in 1834, was later relocated, but Lucadia made no mention of where she saw it, accessed Aug. 13, 2018, Notes from the Architect of the Capitol at https://www.aoc.gov/art/other-statues/ thomas-jefferson-statue.

6. Lucadia's niece, Christine Ladd-Franklin, born in 1847 to Eliphalet and Augusta Niles Ladd, was a Vassar College graduate and noted mathematician, logician, and psychologist who was quoted in a *Buffalo Express* article in April, 1918 on Niles family intelligence: "The first specific influence that led me toward serious intellectual pursuit was my mother's character and family circle. ... She was one of four sisters, all of whom were brilliant women." They would "return in the summers to our family home ... and there led a delightful intellectual life together", accessed June 30, 2016, Quoted in the Vassar College online alumni encyclopedia: vcencyclopedia.vassar.edu/alumni/Christine-ladd-franklin.html.

7. Malcom H. Harris, *Old New Kent County, Some Account of the Planters, Plantations, and Places in New Kent County*, vol. 1 (Malcolm Hart Harris: West Point, VA, 1977), 48. The Bassetts were among early arrivals in colonial Virginia. Title to the land that became Eltham Plantation was granted in 1669 to William Bassett, whose father of the same name had come from England. Land Patent Book, No. 6, 248, p. 50; descent from William Bassett, p. 42. Eltham became "one of the great plantations in Virginia for the whole of the Colonial Period," Harris stated. He wrote that the first brick home burned, according to an "account in the *Fredericksburg News*, 20 May 1875," and the bricks from the kitchen were sold much later to nearby Colonial Williamsburg

for its restoration. *New Kent, 50*, first quotation, 52; second quotation, 52; sale of bricks, 52.

8. The account of Lucadia's experiences while visiting Eltham in late 1838-early 1839 is taken from three very lengthy letters found in the Pease Papers: "Lucadia" (LCN) to "My dear Julie" (Juliet Niles), Nov. 3, 1838; "L" (LCN) to "My dear cousin Maria" (Maria Phelps), Dec. 15, 1838; and "My Dear Father," LCN to Richard Niles, January 11, 1839.

9. They may have been grandchildren of Bassett's brother or other relatives.

10. The Niles family's denominational choice is not stated directly in the Pease Papers, but Lucadia was married by a Universalist minister, and she made references much later in life to her appreciation of hearing Universalist sermons. The denomination had a number of churches in New England.

11. "Lu" (LCN) to "My dear Augusta" (Augusta Niles), Mar. 4, 1839, Pease Papers.

12. (LCN) to "My dear Mother" (Christiana G. Niles, but addressed to Richard Niles), May 11, 1839, Ibid.

13. "L" (LCN) "My dear Sister" (Juliet Niles), June 8, 1839, Ibid.

14. Lucadia was referring to Dr. Corbin Braxton, grandson of Carter Braxton, a signer of the Declaration of Independence, who built Chericoke in 1767. The house that Lucadia saw had been rebuilt by Dr. Braxton in the Federal style in 1828. Chericoke is in a National Historic District in King William County, and is on the National Register of Historic Places, property number 89994195, as well as the Virginia Landmarks Register. See https://www.dhr.virginia.gov/historic-registers, and https://en.wikipedia.org/wiki/List-of-plantations-in-Virginia.

15. "Lucadia" (LCN) to "Sisters," Jan. 25, 1843, "Lucadia" (LCN) to "Sisters," Jan. 25, 1843, Pease Papers.

16. Lucadia" (LCN) to unaddressed recipients, Mar.16, 1843, Ibid.

17. Lucadia" (LCP) to "Sisters" (letter addressed to J. (Juliet), M. H. (Maria), and A. F. [Augusta] Niles, Mar. 19, 1843, Ibid.

18. "Lu" (LCN) to unaddressed recipients, but letter is addressed to Richard Niles, Dec. 2, 1844, Ibid.

19. "Lu" (LCN) to Sisters, Dec. 3, 1844, Ibid.

20. "Lu" (LCN) to "My dear Sisters," (addressed to Maria H. Niles), Dec. 5, 1844, Ibid.

21. M. J. Welles to unnamed salutation (LCN), Dec. [no day] 1844, Ibid.

22. Lucadia" (LCN) to "My dear Sisters," Mar. 9, 1845, Ibid.
23. M. J. Welles to "My dear Ladies" (LCP and Caroline Pease), Feb. 4, 1845, Ibid.
24. Henry B. Andrews to "Dear Friend" (EMP), Jan. 16, 1846, Ibid.
25. Henry B. Andrews to "Dear Friend" (EMP), Jan. 26, 1846, Ibid.
26. E. M. Pease to "My Dear Brother" (John C. Robinson), Jan. 4, 1846, Ibid.
27. "Caroline" (Caroline Pease) to "My Dear Brother" (EMP), Jan. 25, 1846, Ibid.
28. Sarah M. Pease to "My Dear Son" (EMP), May 8, 1846, Ibid.
29. "Sister Maria" (Maria P. Robinson) to "Dear Brother" (EMP), June 2, 1846, Ibid.
30. Birth and death dates recorded by LCN in her own handwriting, sewn in to the family Bible, where the New Testament begins. Augusta Flora Niles Ladd, Collected Publications, Bible Collection Box 1, p. 1 of LCN's notes, Ibid.
31. "Sister Maria" (Maria P. Robinson) to "My Dear Brother" (EMP), Oct. 5, 1846, J. Booth to "My Dear Miss Niles" (LCN), July 8, 1847, Ibid.
32. "Lu" (LCN) to "My dear Sisters," Oct. 6–7, 1947, Ibid.
33. "Lu" (LCN) to "My dear Mother and Sisters," Oct. 14, 1847, Ibid.
34. "Lu" (LCN) to unaddressed recipients, Augusta Niles is named in first line, Oct. 28, 1847, Ibid.
35. "Jno. C. R." (J. C. Robinson) to "Brother" (EMP), Mar. 6, 1848, Ibid.
36. John J. R. Pease to "My Dear Brother" (EMP), May 28, 1848, Ibid.
37. EMP to CAP, Sept. 8, 1874, naming some of those buried in the Poquonock cemetery and their relationship to Carrie; LCP to EMP, quotation, Pease Papers.
38. "L. C. Niles" (LCN) to "Dear Cousin Marshall" (EMP), Nov. 9, 1848, Ibid.
39. "L. C. Niles" (LCN) to "Cousin Marshall" (EMP), Jan. 2, 1849, Ibid.
40. "L. C. Niles" (LCN) to "My Dear Marshall" (EMP), Mar. 2, 1849, Ibid.
41. "L. C. Niles" (LCN) to "My Dear Marshall" (EMP), Sept. 21, 1849, Ibid.
42. "Caroline" (Caroline Pease) to "My dear Brother" (EMP), Jan. 20, 1850, Ibid.
43. "L. C. Niles" (LCN) to "My Dear Marshall" (EMP), Mar. 29, 1850, Ibid.
44. Maria P. Robinson to EMP, Apr. 13, 1850, Ibid.

45. Guy M. Bryan to "Friend Pease" (EMP), July 10, 1850, Ibid.

46. Births, Deaths, Marriages 1704–1846, Windsor, Connecticut, Office of Town Clerk, v. 28, p 192. The location of the marriage was stated in LCP's hand-written notes on family history sewn into family Bible, Augusta Flora Niles Ladd, Collected Publications, Bible Collection, B 1, p 1 of notes, PGN Papers.

47. "Aunt Naomi" (Naomi Griswold) to "Niece" (LCP), Sept. 10 (1850), Pease Papers.

48. "Lucadia" (LCP) to "My Dear Augusta" (Augusta P. Niles), Sept. 23, 1850, Ibid.

49. "Lu" (LCP) to "Dear Sister Augusta" (Augusta N. Ladd), Oct. 18, 1850, Ibid.

50. "Lu" (LCP) to "My Dear Augusta" (Augusta N. Ladd), Nov. 5, 1850, Ibid.

51. "Lu" (LCP) to unnamed recipients, Nov. 16, 1850, Ibid.

52. "Marshall" (EMP) to "My Dear Wife" (LCP), Nov. 19, 1850, Ibid.

53. "Lucadia" (LCP) to "My Dear Mother and Sisters" (Christiana G. Niles and unnamed sisters) Dec. 3, 1850, Ibid.

54. "L" (LCP) to "My dear Sisters Maria and Augusta" (Maria Niles and Augusta N. Ladd) Dec. 22, 1850, Ibid.

55. "Lu" (LCP) to "My Dear Sisters," Jan. 18, 1851, Ibid.

56. "Lu" (LCP) to unnamed recipient, but named "My Dear Maria" (Maria P. Robinson) in first line, Feb. 12, 1851, Ibid.

57. No signature (LCP) to unaddressed recipient but named Augusta Niles in the first line, Mar. 2, 1851, Ibid.

58. (Unsigned) LCP to "My dear Augusta" (Augusta N. Ladd), Mar. 18, 1851, Ibid.

59. "Lu" (LCP) to "My Dear Maria," (Maria Niles) Mar. 30, 1851, Ibid.

60. "Lu" (LCP) to unaddressed recipient, but infers Juliet Niles, Apr. 15, 1851, Ibid.

61. "Marshall" (EMP) to "My Dear Lucadia" (LCP), Apr 21, 1851, Ibid.

62. "Lu" (LCP) to "My dear Augusta" (Augusta N. Ladd), May 26, 1851, Ibid. It was, after all, the nineteenth century, and it was not proper to discuss pregnancy, at least not in writing. It is also possible that other correspondence on the topic was not saved, since it was so personal.

63. E. M. Pease to "My Dear Lucadia" (LCP), June (no day) 1851, Ibid.

64. Marshall" (EMP) to "My Dear Lucadia" (LCP), June 14, 1851, Ibid.

65. Lu" (LCP) to "My Dear Mother" (Christiana G. Niles) Jul. 1, 1851, Ibid.

66. "Lucadia" (LCP) to "My dear Sister Maria" (Maria N. Moor), Aug. 4, 1851, Ibid.
67. "Lucadia" (LCP) to "My dear Sister Maria" (Maria N. Moor), Aug. 4, 1851, Ibid.
68. "Lucadia" (LCP) to "My dear Juliet" (Juliet Niles), Sept. 2, 1851, Ibid.
69. "Lucadia" (LCP) to "My dear Augusta" (Augusta N. Ladd), Sept. 18, 1851, Ibid.
70. No signature (LCP) to "My dear Augusta" (Augusta N. Ladd), Sept. 30, 1851, Ibid.
71. Short hair must have been a comparative description, since women did not wear their hair short for many more years.
72. "Lu" (LCP) to "Dear Juliet" (Juliet Niles), Oct. 21, 1851, Pease Papers.
73. "Lu" (LCP) to "My Dear Sister Maria" (Maria N. Moor), Oct. 28, 1851, Ibid.
74. Edward H. Cushing was later publisher of the *Houston Telegraph*.
75. "Lu" (LCP) to "My dear Marshall" (EMP), Nov. 12, 1851, Pease Papers.
76. "Marshall" (EMP) to "My Dear Wife" (LCP), Nov. 13, 1851, Ibid.
77. "L. C. N. P" (LCP) to "My Dear Sister Augusta" (Augusta N. Ladd), Mar. 1, 1852, Ibid.
78. "L. C. N. P." (LCP) to "My Dear Sister Juliet" (Juliet Niles), Mar. 18, 1852, Ibid.
79. "Marshall" (EMP) to "My Dear Wife" (LCP), Apr. 12, 1852, Ibid.
80. "Marshall" (EMP) to "My Dear Wife" (LCP), May 12, 1852, "Marshall" (EMP) to "My Dear Wife" (LCP), July [no day] 1852, Ibid. His height is not of record, but it was never mentioned in Pease Papers that he was either tall or short.
81. "Marshall" (EMP) to "My Dear Wife" (LCP), Aug. 2, 1852, Ibid.
82. "Juliet" (Juliet Niles) to "Dear Sister Maria" (Maria P. Moor), Oct. 29, 1952, Ibid.
83. "Juliet" (Juliet Niles) to "Dear Sister" (Augusta N. Ladd), Nov. 10, 1852, Ibid.
84. "Juliet" (Juliet Niles) to "My Dear Maria" (Maria P. Moor), Nov. 24, 1852, Ibid.
85. Lu" (LCP) to "My dear Sister" (Augusta N. Ladd, by content), Dec. 29, 1852, Ibid.
86. "Juliet" (Juliet Niles) to "Dear Sister" (Augusta N. Ladd, by content), Jan. 5, 1853, Ibid.
87. "Marshall" (EMP) to "My Dear Wife" (LCP) Jan. 10, 1853, Ibid.
88. "Marshall" (EMP) to "My Dear Wife" (LCP), Jan. 13, 1853, Ibid.

89. "Marshall" (EMP) to "My Dear Wife" (LCP), Jan. 17, 1853, Ibid.

90. "Juliet" (Juliet Niles) to "Dear Maria" (Maria N. Moore), Jan. 26, 1853, Ibid.

91. "Juliet" (Juliet Niles) to "Dear Maria" (Maria N. Moor) Mar. 11, 1853, Ibid.

92. "Marshall" E. M. Pease to "Dear Mother" (Christiana G. Niles), Mar. 17, 1853, Ibid.

93. "Juliet" (Juliet Niles) to "Dear Augusta" (Augusta N. Ladd), Mar. 23, 1853, Ibid.

94. "Lu" (LCP) to "My Dear Marshall" (EMP), Apr. 20, 1853, Ibid.

95. "Marshall" (EMP) to "My Dear Wife" (LCP), Apr. 24, 1853, Ibid.

96. "Marshall (EMP) to "My Dear Wife" (LCP), May 8, 1853. Ibid.

97. "Marshall" (EMP) to "My Dear Wife" (LCP), May 12, 1853, Ibid.

98. "Marshall" (EMP) to "My Dear Wife" (LCP), Jun. 18, 1853, Ibid.

99. "Marshall" (EMP) to "My Dear Wife" (LCP), July 2, 1853, Ibid.

100. "Lucadia" (LCP) to "My dear Marshall" (EMP), July 14, 1853, Ibid.

101. "Lucadia" (LCP) to "My Dear Marshall" (EMP), July 29, 1853, addendum to letter written July 28, 1853, Ibid.

102. "Marshall" (EMP) to "My Dear Wife" (LCP), July 28, 1853, Ibid.

103. "Marshall" (EMP) to "My Dear Wife" (LCP), Aug. 1, 1853, Ibid.

104. "Marshall" (EMP) to "My Dear Wife" (LCP), Aug. 15, 1853, Ibid.

105. "Marshall" (EMP) to "My Dear Wife" (LCP), Aug. 25, 1853, Ibid.

106. "Lucadia" (LCP) to "My dear Marshall" (EMP), Aug. 20, 1853, Ibid.

107. "Lucadia" (LCP) to "My dear Marshall" (EMP), Aug. 26, 1853, Ibid.

108. "Marshall" (EMP) to "My Dear Wife" (LCP), Aug. 26, 1853, Ibid.

109. "Marshall" (EMP) to "My Dear Wife," (LCP), Aug. 27, 1853, continued Aug. 28 and Aug. 29; quotes, Aug. 29, 1853, Ibid.

110. LCP to EMP, Sept. 2, 1853, Ibid.

111. LCP to EMP, Sept. 16, 1853, Ibid.

112. Mike Kingston, Sam Attlesey, and Mary G. Crawford, *The Texas Almanac's Political History of Texas* (Austin, TX: Eakin Press, 1992), 57.

113. EMP to LCP, Sept. 11, 1853 in a continuation of his Sept. 10, 1853, Pease Papers.

114. LCP to EMP, Sept. 26, 1853, and LCP to EMP, Sept.2, 1853 (regarding Elizabeth Marshall), Ibid.

115. EMP to LCP, Oct. 19, 1853, EMP to LCP, Nov. 2, 1853; receipt for passage of "Mrs. L. C. Pease" and children, Ibid.

116. EMP to LCP, Oct. 10, 1853, Ibid.

117. "Marshall" (EMP) to "My Dear Wife" (LCP), Nov. 2, 1853, Ibid.
118. "L. C. Pease" (LCP) to "Mother and Sisters" (Christiana G. Niles and unnamed sisters) Nov. 13, 1853, Ibid.

Notes for Chapter 4

1. LCP to Maria N. Moor Dec. 19, 1853, LCP to Augusta N. Ladd, Dec. 28, 1853, Pease Papers.
2. Susan Ward rented one of her rooms when her husband was United States Consul to Panama. Kenneth Hafertepe, *Abner Cook, Master Builder on the Texas Frontier* (Austin: Texas State Historical Association, 1992), 40; LCP to Maria N. Moor, Dec. 19, 1853, LCP to Sister, Jan. 13, 1854, LCP to Augusta N. Ladd, Dec. 28, 1853 (first quotation), LCP to Augusta N. Ladd, Jan. 13, 1854 (second quotation); Report of Guy M. Bryan, *SJ* 6, 38, on the capitol building.
3. Bell resigned November 23, 1853, to become a member of the United States House of Representatives and was succeeded by J. W. Henderson, who served as governor until Pease was sworn in.
4. Governor E. M. Pease, December 21, 1853–December 15, 1857, *Executive Record Book*, Pease Records.
5. Gubernatorial address of E. M. Pease, December 21, 1853, *SJ 5*, Part II, 3–4.
6. LCP to Augusta N. Ladd, Dec. 28, 1853, Pease Papers.
7. LCP to Sister, Jan. 13, 1854 (first and second quotation), LCP to Augusta N. Ladd, Dec. 28, 1853 (third quotation), LCP to Maria N. Moor, Dec. 19, 1853, EMP in attachment to letter of LCP to Juliet Niles, Jan. 21, 1854, Ibid.
8. Comptroller's Report, *SJ 5*, Part II, 8–9.
9. For payment to Texas by the United States, see: Aldon Socrates Lang, *Financial History of the Public Lands in Texas* (Waco, TX: Baylor University Bulletin 35, no. 1, July 1932) 42–45; and Thomas Lloyd Miller: *The Public Lands of Texas: 1519–1970* (Norman: University of Oklahoma Press, 1972), 61.
10. Governor's Message to the Gentlemen of the Senate and of the House of Representatives, *SJ 5*, Part II, 13, 15.
11. Ibid., 15–16; Edward Minor Gallaudet began teaching at the asylum in 1856 and later he led in creating the school that became Gallaudet University, accessed Sept. 3, 2017, https://www.britannica.com/biography/Edward_Minor_Gallaudet.

12. Governor's Message to the Gentlemen of the Senate and of the House of Representatives, *SJ 5*, Part II, 16–17.
13. Ibid., 17–18.
14. Ibid., 19–20.
15. Ibid., 20–21.
16. Ibid., 21–22.
17. Ibid., 22.
18. Ibid., 23.
19. Ibid., 23–24.
20. Ibid., 24.
21. Ibid., 24–25.
22. Gammel, comp., *Laws of Texas*, III, 1461–1465.
23. Governor's Message to the Gentlemen of the Senate and of the House of Representatives, *SJ 5*, Part II, 15.
24. Ibid., 15–16.
25. Governor's Message to the Gentlemen of the Senate and House of Representatives, *HJ 6*, Nov. 9, 1855, 34–35.
26. Gammel, comp., *Laws of Texas*, IV, 118–121; J. B. Shaw to EMP, August 24, 1855, Pease Papers.
27. Governor's Message to the Gentlemen of the Senate and of the House of Representatives, *SJ 5*, Part II, 17–19.
28. Gammel, comp., *Laws of Texas*, III, 1455–1459.
29. EMP to Gentlemen of the Senate and House, Jan.9, 1854, *SJ 5*, Part II, 86–88.
30. Gammel, comp., *Laws of Texas*, III, 1495–1498.
31. EMP to Jefferson Davis, Mar 13, 1854, Pease Papers.
32. Gammel, comp., *Laws of Texas* III, 1460, 1491.
33. LCP to JN, July 29, 1854, Pease Papers.
34. Edmund J. Davis to EMP, Mar 24, 1854, Pease Records. The word "Lipan" in the Pease Records was never fully designated to mean Lipan Apaches.
35. EMP to Edmund Davis, Mar. 24, 1854; EMP to Jefferson Davis, Mar. 24, 1854, Pease Papers.
36. EMP to R. S. Neighbors, Mar. 24, 1854. Robert S. Neighbors to EMP, Apr. 10, 1854, Pease Records.
37. EMP to Neighbors, April 20, 1854; Neighbors to EMP, May 2, 1854, Ibid.
38. EMP to Neighbors, May 8, 1854, Ibid.
39. "Public Meeting" document signed by J. A. Wilcox, John James, et al., in John D. McLeod, J. M. Carolan, et. al. to EMP, May 24, 1854, Ibid.

40. EMP to Smith, Aug. 8 (quotation) and Aug. 18; (Proclamation) Aug. 18, 1854, Ibid.

41. Smith to EMP, Oct. 25, 1855, EMP to–Oct. 29, 1855; "Circular" from EMP to Captains Giles S. Boggess, William Fitzhugh, John G. Waller, Charles E. Travis, and William Henry, Nov. 2, 1854, Ibid.

42. EMP to Smith, Nov. 4, 1854, Ibid.

43. EMP to Smith, June 20, 1855; C. R Wulfing et al., to EMP, Jun. 25, 1855, Ibid.

44. EMP to Smith, Jun 20, 1855, Ibid.

45. EMP to James H. Callahan, July 5, 1855, Callahan to EMP, Aug. 10, 1855, Ibid.; *Handbook of Texas Online*, Russell Woodall, "Callahan, James Hughes," accessed March 09, 2017.

46. EMP to C. Evans, et al., Sept. 5, 1855, EMP to Smith, Sept. 5, 1855, Pease Records.

47. EMP to Callahan, Oct. 10, 1855, Pease Records. For more information on the Callahan expedition, see Ronnie C. Tyler, "The Callahan Expedition of 1855: Indians or Negroes?" *Southwestern Historical Quarterly*, 4 (April 1967): 574–585. Tyler provides circumstantial evidence, but no conclusive proof, that Callahan may have intended to capture runaway slaves in Mexico. For a very different view, see Curtis Chubb, "Revisiting the Purpose of the 1855 Callahan Expedition, A Research Note," *Southwestern Historical Quarterly*, CXXI (April 2018), 416–429. Certainly, Callahan did not return to Texas with any slaves. The official archival records of Pease's terms as governor do not contain a document to him from Callahan that describes the expedition, but such a communication was extant, as evidenced by Pease's October 10 response to Callahan. The Pease Records do not include mention by anyone else about the expedition.

48. EMP to Smith, Oct. 13, 1855, Pease Records.

49. EMP to John D. Pitts, Dec. 18, 1855, Ibid.

50. EMP to Jefferson Davis, Sept. 23, 1854, Ibid.

51. Gammel, comp., *Laws of Texas*, III, 1543–1544.

52. Governor's Message to the Gentlemen of the Senate and of the House of Representatives, *SJ* 5, Part II, 17–19.

53. Gammel, comp., *Laws of Texas*, III, 1520.

54. Ibid., 1525.

55. Ibid., 1524.

56. Ibid., 1450, 1550–1552.

57. Ibid., III, 1542.

58. Governor's Message to the Gentlemen of the Senate and of the House of Representatives, *SJ 5*, Part II, 24; Gammel, comp., *Laws of Texas*, III, 1523.

59. EMP to Gentlemen of the Senate and House, Jan. 31, 1854, *HJ 5*, 340–342; Gammel, comp., *Laws of Texas*, IV, 128.

60. EMP to Gentlemen of the Senate and House, Jan. 20, 1854, *SJ 5*, Part II, 146 –147; Gammel, comp., *Laws of Texas*, III, 1474 –1476.

61. *Handbook of Texas Online*, George C. Werner, "Atlantic and Pacific Railroad," accessed July 26, 2017, http://www.tshaonline.orgt/handbook/online/articles/equ11 ; *Handbook of Texas Online*, George C. Werner, "Mississippi and Pacific Railroad," accessed July 26, 2017, http://tshttp://www.tshaonline.orgt/handbook/online/articles/equ5; S. S. McKay, "Texas and the Southern Pacific Railroad, 1845–1860" *Southwestern Historical Quarterly*, 35 (July 1931), 1–27.

62. Thomas J. Rusk to EMP, Apr. 19, 1854, Pease Papers; "Pacific Railroad," *American Railroad Journal: Steam Navigation, Commerce, Mining, and Manufacturies* (New York, NY: J. R. Schultze and Co.), Nov. 12, 1853, 728.

63. Certificate of Deposit, July 1, 1854, Award of Certificate for building Mississippi and Pacific Railroad, Aug. 4, 1854, Pease Records.

64. R. J. Walker and T. Butler King to EMP, Sept. 12, 1854, Pease Records.

65. B. F. Benton to EMP, Sept. 8, 1854, J. Pinckney Henderson to EMP, Sept. 11, 1854, Guy M. Bryan to EMP, Sept. 25, 1854, Pease Papers.

66. R. J. Walker and T. Butler King to James H. Raymond, Oct. 6, 1854, Pease Records.

67. EMP to James H. Raymond, Oct. 30, 1854, Nov. 2, 1854, Nov. 4, 1854, Pease Records.

68. EMP to James H. Raymond, Nov. 8, 1854, Pease Records.

69. Memucan Hunt to EMP, Nov. 18, 1854, Pease Papers.

70. Proclamation by the Governor of the State of Texas, Dec. 1, 1854, Pease Records; Guy M. Bryan to EMP, Dec. 26, 1854, Pease Papers.

71. M. B. Menard, W. Richardson, et al., to EMP, *Texas State Gazette*, Feb. 19, 1855, EMP to M. B. Menard, W. Richardson, et al., *Texas State Gazette*, Apr. 28, 1855.

72. Lorenzo Sherwood, a native New Yorker who moved to Galveston, served in the Legislature, and promoted the idea of state-owned railroads, was the probable source of Pease's plan. *Handbook of Texas Online*, Diana J. Kleiner, "Sherwood, Lorenzo," accessed August 18, 2017,

http://www.tshaonline.org/handbook/online/articles/fsh58; EMP to Menard et al., April 3, 1855, Pease Records.

73. Howard Wilcox [by] W. A. Wilcox, Apr. 24, 1854; EMP to President of the United States, May 8, 1854, Pease Records.

74. R. H. Anderson to T. J. Wood, Apr. 23, 1854, Thomas Harrison to EMP, Apr. 26, 1854, EMP to William Harvey, Apr. 28, 1854, Pease Records.

75. Pryor Lea to EMP, Feb. 4, 1854, EMP to Adrian Woll, Mar. 10, 1854, Adrian Woll to EMP, May 2, 1854, in both Spanish and English, Pease Records.

76. Gammel, comp., *Laws of Texas*, III, 1539–1540; Hafertepe, *Abner Cook*, 100–101. During the early days of the Governor's Mansion, it was referred to by various names such as the "governor's house" or "executive mansion."

77. Hafertepe, *Abner Cook*, 101–105.

78. Ibid., 69–70, 72, 93–102

79. LCP to JN and Augusta N. Ladd, Feb. 27, 1854, LCP to JN and Augusta N. Ladd, April 15, 1854, LNP to JN, addendum to letter of Oct. 6, 1854, LCP to EMP, Feb. [7]. 1855 (quotation), Pease Papers; description of house in Hafertepe, *Abner Cook*, 40–42.

80. LCP to EMP, Feb. 16, 1855, EMP to LCP, Jan. 28, 1855, Pease Papers.

81. LNP to EMP, Jan. 30, 1855, Ibid.

82. EMP to LCP, May 26, 1855, Ibid.

83. LCP to JN, Jan. 13, 1854. Feb. 9, 1854, Ibid.

84. LCP to JN and Augusta N. Ladd, Feb.27, 1854, Ibid.

85. LCP to JN, May 31, 1854, Ibid. Sam Harris was a brother of John W. Harris, Pease's law partner.

86. LCP to JN, Jul. 29, 1854, EMP to LCP, May 17, 1854, EMP to LCP, Feb. 20, 1855, EMP to LCP, May 28, 1855, Ibid.

87. Edward Goodman to EMP, Feb. 15, 1854, J. H. Fowler and A. G. Melton to EMP, Feb. 11, 1854, Richard Coke to EMP, Dec. 28, 1854, Pease Records.

Notes for Chapter 5

1. LCP to Augusta N. Ladd, July 27, 1855, Pease Papers.

2. J. Pinckney Henderson to EMP, June 23, 1856, Pease Papers.

3. Samuel A. Maverick, addressing a public meeting to nominate candidates for governor and lieutenant governor after Bexar County had not

sent representatives to the state Democratic convention; reported in *The Standard* (Clarksville), June 23. 1855.

4. Kingston, Attlesey, and Crawford, *Texas Almanac's Political History of Texas*, 57.

5. A. P. Thompson to EMP, Aug. 14, 1855, Pease Records.

6. LCP to JN, Aug. 23, 1855, Pease Papers.

7. LCP to JN, Nov. 14, 1855, Pease Papers. The reference to the Governor as a possible foreigner was a Know-Nothing attempt to cast doubt on his American citizenship.

8. LCP to Augusta N. Ladd, Dec. 14, 1855, Pease Papers. Ashbel Smith was then a member of the House of Representatives and a frequent visitor in the Pease home. They knew him well; he was born in Hartford in 1805 and came to Texas in 1837. Lucadia observed to Juliet Niles on Nov. 14, 1855, that it was said of him, he "will not marry unless he finds an heiress."

9. LCP to Augusta N. Ladd, Dec. 14, 1855, Pease Papers.

10. LCP to Maria N. Moore, Jan. 14, 1856, Pease Papers.

11. The Sixth Legislature met from November 5, 1855, through February 6, 1856, and resumed in an "Adjourned Session" from July 7 to September 1. The Adjourned Session would function as a called session; officers and committee assignments were continuous. Much of the major legislation of the Sixth Legislature would be passed at the Adjourned Session.

12. LCP to Augusta N. Ladd, Nov. 14, 1855, Pease Papers.

13. EMP Biennial Message, Nov. 6, 1855, *SJ 6*, 8.

14. Ibid., 8–11.

15. Gammel, comp., *Laws of Texas*, IV, 227–229.

16. Biennial Message of EMP to the Sixth Legislature, *SJ 6*, 11–12. The poll tax had nothing to do with voting. It was a head tax; that is, a tax on individuals, for the purpose of increasing revenue. The poll tax in 1855 was based on an amended law of February 11, 1850. Gammel, comp., *Laws of Texas*, III, 621.

17. EMP Biennial Message, Nov. 6, 1855, *SJ 6*, 12–13.

18. Ibid., 13–16.

19. Ibid., 16–17.

20. Ibid., 17–18.

21. Ibid., 18–19.

22. Ibid., 20–23.

23. Ibid., 23–29.

24. Ibid., 29–31.

25. Ibid., 31; Gammel, comp., Laws of Texas, IV, 247–249.

26. EMP Biennial Message, Nov. 6, 1855, *SJ 6*, 36–38; Gammel, comp., *Laws of Texas*, IV, 186–187, 195–196. (Callahan's expedition is discussed in more detail and fully documented in Chapter 4.)

27. EMP Biennial Message, Nov. 6, 1855, *SJ 6*, 39; Gammel, comp., *Laws of Texas, IV*, 258–259.

28. EMP Biennial Message, Nov. 6, 1855, *SJ 6*, 39–40; Gammel, comp., *Laws of Texas, IV*, 249.

29. EMP Biennial Message, Nov. 6, 1855, *SJ 6*, 42–43; Gammel, comp., *Laws of Texas, IV*, 231–232, 236.

30. EMP Biennial Message, Nov. 6, 1855, *SJ 6*, 43.

31. EMP Message to Members of the Senate and the House, July 7, 1856, *SJ 6*, Adjourned Session, 6–7.

32. Ibid., SJ 6, 7.

33. The printed journals of the Sixth Legislature omitted the passage of the law concerning the codes; hence, the topic is not in Gammel's *Laws of Texas*. However, the original signed bill is in the bill files of the State Archives (see microfilm rolls 1579 and 1580) and is also available on the TSLAC Texas Digital Archives. The codes were bound and printed by the Galveston *News* Office, 1857. The appropriation bill of the Adjourned Session is in Gammel, comp., *Laws of Texas*, IV, 517. The Texas Legislative Reference Library has posted the "Codes of 1856" or the "Old Codes" at www.lrl.state.tx.us/collections/oldcodes.cfm.

34. EMP Message to Members of the Sixth Legislature, Adjourned Session, *SJ 6*, 8.

35. Ibid., 7–8.

36. Ibid., Gammel, comp., *Laws of Texas*, IV, 461–463.

37. Gammel, comp., *Laws of Texas*, IV, 525–526, 529, 449–455, 475–476, 503.

38. Ibid., 85, 457–458, 478–479, 489–492, 494, 502–503.

39. EMP to Gentlemen of the Senate and House, *SJ 6*, 14–18, quotation p. 15.

40. *HJ 6*, 316.

41. EMP to LCP, Aug. 6, 1856, Pease Papers.

42. Gammel, comp., *Laws of Texas*, IV, gives the date as Aug. 16, 1856, 622–624.

43. EMP Message to the Senate, July 8, 1856, *SJ 6*, 11–12.

44. Gammel, comp., *Laws of Texas*, IV, 427–431, 388–391.

45. Ibid., 466–467, 499–500.

46. Ibid., III, 239.

47. LCP to JN, Jan. 17, 1856, Pease Papers.

48. EMP to A. H. Cook, Feb. 27, 1856, Pease Records.

49. LCP to Sister, April 7, 1856, Pease Papers.

50. EMP to LCN, June 9, June 10, June 11, 1856, Pease Papers.

51. EMP to LCP, June 14, June 18, 1856, Pease Papers.

52. EMP to LCP, Jun. 16–17, 1856, Pease Papers. "Macauly" was apparently the English historian Sir Thomas Babington Macaulay, who promoted progressive ideas. Pease later bought copies of Macaulay's books for the State Library.

53. EMP to LCP, Aug. 24, 1856, LCP to EMP, July 2, 1856, Pease Papers.

54. EMP to LCP, July 26, 1856, Pease Papers.

55. EMP to LCP, June 12, 1856, and quotation, continuation on June 14, Pease Papers. The peas must have been black-eyed peas since it was summer, and the pork was ham that Lucadia cured.

56. EMP to LCP, June 18, 1856, Aug. 14, 1856, July 21, 1856 (continued July 23), Aug. 3, 1856, Pease Papers.

57. EMP to LCP, June 21, 1856, June 24, 1856, Pease Papers.

58. EMP to LCP, July 1–2, 1856, Pease Papers.

59. EMP to LCP, July 9, 1856, Pease Papers.

60. EMP to LCP, Sept. 10, 1856, LCP to EMP, Oct 8, 1856, LCP to EMP, June 15, 1856, LCP to EMP, July 2, 1856, EMP to LCP, July 21, 1856, Pease Papers.

61. H. H. Haynie to EMP, July 10, 1856, EMP to H.H. Haynie, July 1856, Pease Records; *HJ 6*, 30–31, 49–50.

62. EMP to LCP, July 15, 1856, LCP to EMP, July 16, 1856, Pease Papers.

63. EMP to LCP, July 23, 1856, July 26, 1856, Aug. 3, 1856, Pease Papers.

64. EMP to LCP, Aug. 3–5, 1856, Pease Papers.

65. EMP to LCP, Aug. 10–13, 1856, Pease Papers.

66. EMP to LCP, Aug. 24, 1856, Pease Papers.

67. EMP to LCP, Aug. 24–27, 1856, Pease Papers.

68. EMP to Gentlemen of the Senate, *SJ 6 Adj.*, 153–154; Gammel, comp., *Laws of Texas*, IV, 595.

69. EMP to Gentlemen of the Senate and House, *SJ 6 Adj.*, 153–154; Gammel, comp., *Laws of Texas*, IV, 444.

70. James Guthrie to James B. Shaw, Oct. 1, 1856, Pease Records.

71. O. T. Branch to EMP, Oct. 20, 1856, Pease Records.

72. W. M. Fowler to EMP, Oct. 27, 1856, S.A. Maverick to EMP, Nov. 19, 1856, Pease Records. A well was subsequently dug.

73. Jno. Twohig to EMP, Nov. 29, 1856, Pease Records.

74. Committee on Claims and Accounts to House Speaker, *HJ 6*. 254–260. Likewise, Mrs. Margaret McCormick, on whose cow pasture the Battle of San Jacinto had been fought, was not paid for the loss of her beeves that had been slaughtered to feed the Texas Army and the Mexican prisoners.

Notes for Chapter 6

1. H. H. Edwards to EMP, Dec. 21, 1856, Pease Records. The Nacogdoches Archives had been transferred to the Secretary of State in Austin in 1850, although wooden state buildings were unsafe.

2. John R. Baylor to EMP, Dec. 10, 1856, Pease Records. Baylor was dismissed the following year over this matter and feuding with his supervisor, Robert Neighbors. See *Handbook of Texas Online*, Jerry Thompson, "Baylor, John Robert," accessed July 04, 2017, http://www.tshaonline.org/handbook/online/articles/fbaat.

3. D. E. Twiggs to L. Thomas, June 16, 1857, and note on the back of the letter, Pease Records.

4. John A. Wilcox to EMP, Apr. 17, 1857, May 1, 1857, May 22, 1857, Aug. 4, 1857, Pease Records.

5. Antonio Flores et al., July 27, 1857, Pease Records. This episode and its subsequent events became known as the "Cart War," but Governor Pease's Records and the legislative journals show that no name was attached to the episode at the time.

6. EMP to D. E. Twiggs, Aug. 13, 1857, D. E. Twiggs to EMP, Aug. 20, 1857, Pease Records.

7. D. E. Twiggs to EMP, Aug. 29, 1857, EMP to D. E. Twiggs, Sept. 26, 1857, Pease Records.

8. J. A. Wilcox to EMP, Sept. 17, 1857, Nicandor Valdez et al. to EMP, Sept. 17, 1857, Pease Records.

9. D. E. Twiggs to EMP, Sept. 19, 1857, Pease Records.

10. EMP to Twiggs, Oct. 2, 1857, J. M. McNutt to EMP, Oct. 7, 1857, Pease Records.

11. J. M. McNutt to EMP, Oct. 14, 1857, Pease Records. Subsistence and forage rations for the troops that Pease called into service were named in a letter to him by Alexander H. Roads on Oct. 13, 1857.

He was to supply all rations but hay at San Antonio and on the road to Port Lavaca. Troops were to receive beef, salted pork or bacon, flour, beans, coffee, sugar, candles, soap, and salt, plus corn for the horses.

12. Jno. Withers to EMP, Oct. 14, 1857, Pease Records.

13. G. H. Nelson to EMP, Oct 14, 1857, Jno. Withers, Army Special Orders, Oct. 20, 1857, Pease Records.

14. Manuel Robles Pezuela to Lewis Cass, Oct. 14, 1857, Oct. 19, 1857, Pease Records.

15. Lewis Cass to EMP, Oct. 24, 1857, Pease Records.

16. G.H. Nelson to EMP, Nov. 8, 1857, Pease Records.

17. E. A. Stevens to G. H. Nelson, Nov. 24, 1857, G. H. Nelson to EMP, Nov. 28, 1857, Pease Records.

18. G. H. Nelson to EMP, Dec. 17, 1857, EMP to G. H. Nelson, Dec. 19, 1857, Pease Records.

19. EMP to Gentlemen of the Senate and House, *SJ* 7, 37, 82–83.

20. EMP to Lewis Cass, Dec. 10, 1857, Pease Records.

21. William Fields to EMP, Feb. 5, 1857, Apr. 9, 1857, Jun. 20, 1857, Sept. 16, 1857, Oct. 15, 1857, Oct. 17, 1857, Pease Records.

22. Robert Cruzbar to EMP, June 10, 1857, Pease Records.

23. James L. Smither to EMP, Jun. 30, 1857, J. H. Littlefield to EMP, Jul. 4, 1857, Pease Records.

24. EMP to Gentlemen of the Senate and House, Nov. 4, 1857, *SJ* 7, 13–23.

25. William Crain to EMP, Feb. 18, 1857, Pease Records. It is unknown whether the governor answered or whether this letter referred to James Long, who was killed in 1822 and whose widow Jane Long received a league and labor of land in present-day Waller County.

26. B. E. Tarver to EMP, June 22, 1857, Pease Records.

27. Minutes of the Board of School Commissioners, Mar. 21, 1857, Pease Records. The governor's secretary was termed a "Private Secretary" but that meant that the secretary worked only for the governor in his official role.

28. M. F. Locke et al. to EMP, Nov. 1, 1857, E. Adeane Barlow to EMP, Jul. 6, 1857, Pease Records.

29. EMP to Gentlemen of the Senate and House, Nov. 25, 1857, *SJ* 7, 121.

30. Message of the Governor of the State of Texas to the Seventh Legislature, Nov. 4, 1857, *SJ* 7, 13–14.

31. Ibid., 14–15.

32. Ibid., 15–19.
33. Ibid., 19–20.
34. Ibid., 20–22.
35. Ibid., 22–23.
36. *Handbook of Texas Online*, George C. Werner, "Mississippi and Pacific Railroad," accessed July 24, 2017, http://www.tshaonline. org/handbook/online/articles/eqm05.
37. *SJ 7*, 25–26.
38. Texas north of the Red River was the area from the river north to 36 degrees 30 min between the 100th and 103rd Meridians.
39. *SJ 7*, 28–31.
40. P. Bremond to EMP, Apr. 30, 1857, Aug. 11, 1857, Pease Records.
41. *SJ 7*, 31.
42. *SJ 7*, 32.
43. *SJ 7*, 32–33.
44. *SJ 7*, 33–35.
45. EMP to Senate & House, Dec. 3, 1857, Pease Records.
46. *SJ 7*, 36–37.
47. Ibid., 37–38.
48. Ibid., 38.
49. Ibid., 38–39.
50. EMP to Gentlemen of the Senate and House of Representatives, *HJ 7*, 243.
51. *SJ 7*, 36; Gammel, comp., *Laws of Texas*, IV, 515. The basement library room was shown in the floor plan of the Capitol in 1883.
52. E. H. Cushing to EMP, May 28, 1857, S. S. Nichols to EMP, June 15, 1857, July 18, 1857, Aug. 3, 1857, S. S. Nichols to EMP, Oct. 9, 1857, Pease Records.
53. Wiley and Halstead to EMP, Sept. 5, 1857, Pease Records.
54. S. S. Nichols to [Governor], Dec. 11, 1857; EMP Certification and Statement. Dec. 24, 1857, Pease Records.
55. Thanksgiving Proclamations by the Governor of Texas, 1854, 1855, 1856, Pease Records; LCP to Augusta N. Ladd, Dec. 14, 1855, Pease Papers.
56. Proclamation by the Governor of Texas, Nov. 1, 1856, Pease Records; LCP to Sister, Nov. 29, 1857, Pease Papers.
57. EMP Valedictory Address to the Seventh Legislature, Dec. 21, 1857, *HJ 7*, Appendix, 4–5.
58. Ibid., 5–6.

Notes for Chapter 7

1. Bryan to EMP, May 30, 1857, Pease Papers.
2. EMP to Bryan, June 17, 1857, Bryan Papers.
3. EMP to Bryan, June 17, 1857, Bryan Papers.
4. EMP to Bryan, June 17, 1857, Bryan Papers.
5. Sam Houston, speech at Tremont Temple, Boston, Massachusetts, Feb. 22, 1855, in Amelia W. Williams and Eugene C. Barker, eds., *The Writings of Sam Houston, 1813–1863* (6 vols., Austin: University of Texas Press, 1938–1843), VI, 172, 176.
6. Bryan to EMP, Sept. 12, 1857, Pease Papers; EMP to Bryan, Sept. 23, 1857, Bryan papers.
7. EMP Message to the Gentlemen of the Senate and House of Representatives, Nov. 4, 1857, *SJ 7*, 12–39.
8. EMP, Second Inaugural Address to Gentlemen of the Senate and House of Representatives and fellow-citizens, *SJ 6*, Dec. 21, 1855, 250.
9. *Southern Intelligencer* (Austin), Apr. 29, 1857.
10. EMP to LCP, Mar. 14, 1858, re return to practice, Harris to EMP, Jan. 30, 1858, re meeting with "Mr. Mills" and schedule, Pease Papers.
11. S. M. Swenson to EMP, Jun. 19, 1858, EMP to LCP, Oct. 7, 1858, Pease Papers.
12. F. Flake to EMP, May 23, 1859, Pease Papers. The word "Democracy" was used as a collective term for "Democrats." Harris to EMP, Feb. 1 and Mar. 15, 1859, Pease to Flake, undated draft filed w/ Flake to Pease, May 23, 1859, Pease Papers.
13. EMP to Flake, May 23, 1859, Pease Papers.
14. Thomas H. Stribling to EMP, June 18, 1857, July 8, 1857, Pease Papers.
15. EMP to Hamilton Stuart, Editor, *Civilian* (Galveston), July 5, 1859, printed in the July 5 section of the paper published July 9, 1859.
16. *Civilian and Gazette Weekly* (Galveston) July 12, 1859.
17. Huntsville *Item* (n.d.) reprinted in *State Gazette* (Austin), June 25, 1859.
18. "Letter of E. M. Pease," *State Gazette* (Austin), July 23, 1857.
19. For a summary of Unionism, see *Handbook of Texas Online*, Walter L. Buenger, "Unionism," accessed Dec. 28, 2017, http://www.tshaonline.org/handbook/online/articles/mzu01. For additional information, see Walter L. Buenger, *Secession and the Union in Texas* (Austin: University of Texas Press, 1984).

20. *Southern Intelligencer*, (Austin) Sept. 5, 1860; Frank H. Smyrl, "Unionism in Texas, 1856–1861," *Southwestern Historical Quarterly*, 68 (October 1964), 178–179.

21. *Southern Intelligencer* (Austin), Sept. 5, 1860 on Pease's role in Unionist politics.

22. *Alamo Express* (San Antonio), Sept. 24, 1860; Smyrl, "Unionism in Texas," 172–195.

23. LCP to JN, Dec. 4, 1860, Pease Papers.

24. LCP to Sister, Feb. 11, 1860, Feb. 22, 1860, Pease Papers.

25. LCP to Sister, Feb. 11, 1861, LCP to Sisters, Mar. 19, 1861, Pease Papers.

26. EMP Tax Records: Travis County, Texas, Tax Records, 1860, Abstract 287, microfilm, Austin History Center. Pease's taxable Travis County property in 1860 would have been valued at more than $700,000 in 2020.

27. *Texas State Gazette* (Austin), Sept. 21, 1861; A. W. Terrell, "The City of Austin from 1839–1865," *Quarterly of the Texas State Historical Association*, 14, (Oct. 1910): 120.

28. *Texas State Gazette*, June 15, 1861; Marshall *Texas Republican*, Oct. 12, 1861.

29. LCP to "Sister," Aug. 30, 1865, Pease Papers. Hancock, who had been expelled from the Legislature for refusal to take the Confederate oath, practiced law during the first part of the war, having told his clients that he would not practice in Confederate courts. Daniel W Hancock, "The Political and Congressional Career of John Hancock, 1865–1885," (M. A. Thesis, University of North Texas, 1996); Handbook of Texas Online; Anne W. Hooker, "John Hancock" accessed Jan. 10, 2018, http://www.tshaonline.org/handbook/online/articles.

30. LCP to Maria N. Moor, Aug. 30, 1865, Pease Papers.

31. Niles Graham mentioned the incident, based on his grandmother's story. R. Niles Graham to Harriet Graham, Apr. 30, 1931, Pass in Pease Papers.

32. "Interrogatories and Writ of Garnishment," issued to EMP, Jan. 24, 1862; court documents, Dec. 21, 1861, Feb. 5, 1862, May 28, 1863, Jan. 12, 1864, filed as case 1457, "Confederate States v. E. M. Pease," Confederate District Court Records, Western District of Texas, held in Federal Records Center, Fort Worth, Texas. For explanation of the sequestration acts of the United States and of the Confederacy and the work of the Western District Court, see: T. R. Havins, "Administration

of the Sequestration Act in the Confederate District Court for the Western District of Texas, 1862–1865," *Southwestern Historical Quarterly*, 43 (Jan. 1940) 300–301, 307, 321. Original documents of Lorrain T. Pease's land grants are First Class Headright, 19 Feb 1892, Bexar-000685; Bounty grant, 12 Feb 1849; Bexar 000577; and Donation Grant, 14 Jan 1852, Bexar 000901, all in Texas Land Grant Records, Archives and Records Program, Texas General Land Office, Austin, Texas.

33. LCP to "Sister," Aug. 30, 1865, EMP Journal of Accounts, beginning December, 1856, Pease Papers. (The 2019 value of $47,000 in 1860 was more than $1,420,000.)

34. James Hammond Trumbull, ed., *History of Hartford County, Connecticut, 1633–1884* (2 vols. Boston: 1886), II, 159. Whether he, Lucadia, or someone else wrote the account is unknown.

35. Joseph Moreland to E. M. Pease, Dec. 25, 1855, vol. K, 114, Travis County Deed Record Book, Travis County Courthouse, Austin, Texas. The boundaries are unclear in the original deed.

36. LCP to Maria N. Moor, Jan. 14, 1856; LCP to JN, Jan. 17, 1856 (quotation) Pease Papers. Mechanics were generally free men in construction and other trades.

37. LCP to Augusta N. Ladd, Feb. 3, 1856, Receipt to EMP from Abner Cook, Feb. 3, 1857, in Household Accounts folder, 1855, Pease Journal of Accounts, Pease Papers.

38. LCP to Sister, Feb. 10, 1857, LCP to Augusta N. Ladd, Apr. 3, 1858 (first quotation), LCP to Maria N. Moor, May, 1858 (second quotation), EMP to Wife, May 9, 1858 (third quotation), Pease Papers.

39. Samuel Harris to EMP, Dec. 12, 1858, James B. Shaw to EMP, Mar. 22, 1859, LCP to Husband, Apr. 12, 1859 (first quotation) and Apr. 20, 1859 (second quotation), Pease Papers.

40. James B. Shaw to EMP, Mar. 22, 1859, August 10, 1859 promissory note; January 1860 payment information in EMP Incoming Correspondence, Pease Papers.

41. Hafertepe, *Abner Cook*, 88–92; "Woodlawn Historic Structures Report," Section 104 of "Woodlawn: 6 Niles Road, Austin, Texas, Technical Package" (a large, un-paginated, loose-leaf notebook), Austin, Texas: General Land Office, n.d. When Woodlawn was in state control because it was bequeathed to the University of Texas, this report was assembled to inform potential buyers of the historical value and physical condition of the property.

42. LCP to Sister, Oct. 31, 1859 (first quotation), LCP to Christiana Niles, July 26, 1859 (second and third quotation), LCP to Sister, Nov. 7, 1859 (fourth quotation), LCP to Sister, Nov. 9, 1860 (fifth quotation), JMP to RNG, 1903 (sixth through ninth quotations), LCP to Sister, Oct. 31, 1859, LCP to Sister, Feb. 17, 1860 (tenth quotation), Pease Papers.

43. United States Eighth Census (1860), Travis County, Texas, Schedule 3 (Productions of Agriculture), Record Group 29 (National Archives, Washington, D.C.); E. M. Pease agreement with F. S. Schieffer, Nov. 1, 1865, HB File, Niles Road 6 (Woodlawn), AHC. The 2019 value of $12,000 in 1860 was more than $363,000.

44. LCP to "Sister," Aug. 30, 1865, Pease Papers.

45. EMP to CP, Feb. 24, 1866, Pease Papers; Deed, E. M. Pease to International and Great Northern Railroad, Oct. 10, 1876, v. 27, p. 82, Travis County Clerk's Office, Travis County Courthouse Annex, Austin, TX.

46. Farming and gardening references: LCP to Sister, Mar. 19, 1863, EMP to Carrie Pease, Feb. 24, 1866 (first quotation), vegetables and watermelons, JMP to Mamma, Oct. 20, 1873, orchard with fig and peach trees, LCP to Sister, Oct. 31, 1859, JMP to Carrie Pease, May 1872, William Watson Rosedale Nurseries receipt, Brenham, TX, Feb. 21, 1891, for peach and plum trees; smokehouse, JMP to Mamma, May 22, 1879, Gidion [artist] "Old Pease Barn" line drawing, Royal Order of Jesters program, Oct. 21, 1933, Pease Papers; Reuben T. Ford, "A Topographical Map of the City of Austin Including the City Outlots also known as the Government Tract," (Austin: De Cordoba and Withers, January 1872), AHC map L-0004-1872.

47. Hafertepe, *Abner Cook*, xvii; *Polk's Morrison & Fourmy Austin City Directory* 1916 (Houston: Morrison & Fourmy Directory Company, Inc., 1916), 22; *Geology of the Austin Quadrangle*, United States Geological Survey, 1902, AHC map P-0036, shows landform prior to significant human alterations and notes the underlying limestone varieties in the area, including the Pease estate.

48. LCP to JN, Feb. 22, 1861, Pease Papers.

49. LCP to JN, Apr. 5, 1861, Pease Papers.

50. LCP to JN, Apr. 20, 1861, Pease Papers.

51. LCP to Mrs. Richard Niles, Jul. 26, 1859, Pease Papers.

52. LCP to Sister, Feb. 17, 1860, LCP to EMP, Mar. 28, 1860, Pease Papers.

53. LCP to Sister, May 31, 1860, Pease Papers.

54. LCP to Sister, Aug. 30, 1865, Pease Papers.

55. LCP to Maria N. Robinson, Aug. 30, 1865 (first quotation), LCP to Sister, Mar. 19, 1863, LCP to Sisters, Feb. 20, 1857 (second quotation), LCP to Mother, July 26, 1859 (third quotation), Pease Papers.

56. LCP to Sister, Jan. 1861 (quotation); LCP to Husband, Jan. 18, 1866, LCP to Sister, Sept. 18, 1865, Pease Papers. For a biography of Ward that includes documentation of his marital relationship, see David C. Humphrey, *Peg Leg: the Improbable Life of a Texas Hero, Thomas William Ward, 1807–1872* (Denton: Texas State Historical Association 2009).

57. C. E. Townsend to EMP, May 9, 1861, Pease Papers.

58. EMP to Carrie Pease, Aug. 10, 1863, Pease Papers.

59. LCP to Sister, Jun. 14, 1865, (first quotation); LCP to Sister, Aug. 30, 1865 (second quotation), Pease Papers.

60. Although the Peases kept detailed records of all sorts, no list of the Pease slaves at any one time or any comprehensive list of their purchase and sale dates has survived in the Pease Papers.

61. EMP to LCP, Nov. 19, 1850, LCP to Maria N. Moor and Augusta N. Ladd, Dec. 22, 1850, LCP to Sisters, Jan. 21, 1851, LCP to Augusta N. Ladd, Mar. 2, 1851, Pease Papers.

62. JN to Augusta N. Ladd, Nov. 10, 1852; JN to Sister, Jan. 5, 1853, Pease Papers.

63. EMP to LCP, Jan. 10, 1853; JN to Sister, Jan. 5, 1853, Pease Papers.

64. EMP to LCP, Jun. 18, 1856, Pease Papers.

65. LCP to EMP, Jul. 2, LCP to EMP, Aug. 7, 1856, Pease Papers.

66. For an understanding of slavery in Texas, see Randolph B. Campbell, *An Empire for Slavery: The Peculiar Institution in Texas, 1821–1865* (Baton Rouge, Louisiana State University Press, 1989).

67. LCP to Maria N. Robinson, Feb. 12, 1851 (first quotation), LCP to Augusta Ladd, Mar. 18, 1851 (second quotation); Pease Papers.

68. LCP to JN, Apr. 15, 1851, Pease Papers.

69. LCP to JN, July 29, 1854, Pease Papers. Juliet declared a number of times that she had no plans to marry.

70. LCP to EMP, June 5, 1854 (first quotation); EMP to LCP, July 9, 1856 (second quotation); EMP to LCP, July 15, 1856; EMP to LCP, Aug. 3, 1856, Pease Papers.

71. EMP to Maria Moor, Dec. 31, 1856 (first quotation); EMP to LCP, June 12, 13, 1856 (second quotation), Pease Papers.

72. LCP to Sister, May 31, 1854, Pease Papers.

73. LCP to Maria N. Moor, Dec. 31, 1857 (quotations); LCP to JN, Jan. 4, 1858, Pease Papers.

74. LCP to Maria N. Moor, Feb. 12, 1851, LCP to Augusta N. Ladd, March 18, 1851, JN to Maria N. Moor, Jan. 26, 1853, JN to Augusta N. Ladd, Jan. 5, 1853, LCP to Sister, May 31, 1854, Pease Papers.

75. EMP to LCP, Jul. 23, 1856, LCP to JN and Augusta Ladd, April 11, 1855, Pease Papers.

76. EMP to LCP, Jun. 13, 1856, LCP to EMP, Oct. 7, 1853, Pease Papers.

77. EMP to LCP, Nov. 2, 1853 (first quotation); LCP to Augusta N. Ladd, May 5, 1855 (second quotation), LCP to EMP, Sep. 19, 1860 (third quotation), Pease Papers.

78. LCP to Maria Moor, Mar. 30, 1851, Pease Papers.

79. JN to Sister, Jan. 5, 1853, Pease Papers.

80. EMP to LCP, Aug. 26, Sept. 14, 1853, Pease Papers.

81. EMP to LCP, Oct. 2, 1853, EMP to LCP, Oct.17, 1853, Pease Papers.

82. LCP to Maria N. Robinson, Feb. 12, 1851 on Sam waiting table, EMP to LCP, Sept. 29, 1853, on Little Sam's illness. Pease Papers.

83. LCP to EMP, Oct. 7, 1853, LCP to EMP, July 14, 1853, Aug. 26, 1853, Sept. 16, 1853, Pease Papers.

84. LCP to Maria N. Moor, Mar. 30, 1851, Pease Papers.

85. EMP to LCP, June 9, 1856, EMP to LCP, July 9, 1856, EMP to LCP, Aug. 24, 1856, EMP to LCP, Jan. 10, 1857, LCP to Augusta N. Ladd, June 15, 1857, Pease Papers.

86. LCP to EMP, June 5, 1854, EMP to LCP, June 18, 1856, Pease Papers.

87. LCP to Sister, July 20, 1857, [Bill of Sale?]Edward McDonnell and Rachel McDonnell, April 18, 1857, Pease Papers.

88. Clinton Terry to E. M. Pease, Dec. 10, 1853, LCP to Maria N. Robinson, Dec. 19, 1853, LCP to JN, continued from Jan. 21, 1854, Pease Papers.

89. LCP to EMP, June 5, 1854, EMP to LCP, May 25, 1856, June 21, 1856, Nov. 6, 1856; LCP to Augusta N. Ladd, Apr. 10, 1857, LCP to Sister, July 20, 1857, Pease Papers.

90. LCP to Augusta N. Ladd, May 5, 1855, Contract with J. M. Prewitt, May 5, 1856, Pease Papers.

91. JN to Uncle Jared, Mar. 9, 1853, Pease Papers.

92. Sam Harris to EMP, May 20, 1860, Pease Papers.

Notes for Chapter 8

1. L. W. Groce to EMP, May 27, 1865, Pease Papers. The *Galveston News* also endorsed the idea in June.

2. E. H. Cushing to EMP, June 12, 1865, Pease Papers.

3. "Juneteenth" is discussed in Campbell, *Empire for Slavery*, 246–251. LNP to Maria N. Moor, Aug. 30, 1865, Pease Papers.

4. For a survey of Reconstruction in Texas, see Carl H. Moneyhon, *Texas after the Civil War: The Struggle of Reconstruction* (College Station: Texas A&M University Press, 2004).

5. EMP to Carrie Pease, Mar. 2, 1865, Pease Papers.

6. Ben H. Proctor, *Not Without Honor: The Life of John H. Reagan* (Austin: The University of Texas Press, 1962), 172–174.

7. "Speech Delivered by Hon. E. M. Pease at Turner Hall, Galveston, TX, July 1, 1880," Pamphlet in Pease Papers.

8. See Griffin, "Connecticut Yankee," 189, 207 (Fn. 15).

9. E. M. Pease and Swante Palm, "Personal Papers: Political documents: Reports of committee appointed by Gov. A. J. Hamilton to investigate state treasury," Swante Palm Papers, Briscoe Center for American History, University of Texas, Austin. Report hereinafter cited as Pease and Palm Report. This is a draft copy in EMP's hand, but with few changes shown. The original, which does not survive in state records, was probably transcribed from this, as was true with many EMP documents; reference to creation of second board, 22.

10. Pease and Palm Report, 2.

11. Ibid., 3–8.

12. Ibid., 10, 13. Cotton cards were rectangular wooden paddles with fine wire teeth that were used in place of cotton gins in small scale production. When cotton was pulled by hand through a pair of cards, seeds were separated from fiber many times faster than by hand-picking the seeds. These cards were manufactured in the North.

13. Ibid., 13, 15–16, quotation, 21.

14. Ibid., 22, 25.

15. Ibid., 37–53.

16. Alfred H. Kelly and Winfred A. Harbison, *The American Constitution: Its Origins and Development* (New York, Norton, 1963) quotation from court ruling, 480–481; William W. Pierson, Jr., "Texas versus White," *Southwestern Historical Quarterly*, 18 (April 1915), 341–367; "Texas versus White, II, 19 (July 1916), 1–36; Carl H. Moneyhon, *Republicanism in Reconstruction Texas* (Austin: University of Texas Press, 1980), 100; Handbook of Texas Online, "Texas v. White," accessed March 21, 2018.

17. LCP to JN, Mar. 31, June 14, Aug. 30, and Sept. 18, 1865, Pease Papers.

18. Custer and his wife, Elizabeth, had pleasant parties with Austinites during their stay, and he was thought to be courtly. Rumors circulated that Custer commandeered Woodlawn for a residence, but the house was locked while the Peases were in the North, and Elizabeth Custer's book described the Blind Asylum. Where Custer's soldiers were buried near the creek is unknown. Julie recalled years later that after a flood, she saw unearthed caskets, which were reinterred elsewhere. EMP to JMP, Mar. 8, 1866, Sept 12, 1868, LCP to EMP, Oct. 11, 1868, R. Niles Graham to Harriet Graham, Apr. 30, 1931, Pease Papers; Elizabeth Bacon Custer, *Tenting on the Plains, or General Custer in Kansas and Texas* (New York, NY: Harper & Brothers, 1895). Will Erwin, Senior Historian of the State Cemetery in Austin, confirmed that if these troops were reinterred there, their remains were moved again, possibly to Fort Sam Houston, the nearest Federal cemetery, probably in 1883. Will Erwin to Elizabeth Whitlow by telephone, Mar. 23, 2018.

19. EMP to Carrie Pease, Jan. 20, Feb. 8, Mar. 2, 5, 16, 1866, Pease Papers.

20. Randolph B. Campbell, *Grass–Roots Reconstruction in Texas, 1865–1880*, (Baton Rouge, Louisiana State University Press, 1997), 10–11.

21. EMP to CP, April 9, 1866, Pease Papers.

22. EMP Campaign Circular in Austin *Southern Intelligencer*, May 1, 1866.

23. Cushing to EMP, Mar. 24, 1866; Crockett *Sentinel*, n.d., quoted in Dallas *Herald*, May 5, 1866.

24. *Huntsville Item*, reprinted in *Austin Southern Intelligencer*, Apr. 20, 1866.

25. EMP to JMP, May 8, 1866, EMP to CP, May 18, 1866, Pease Papers; Executive Record Book No. 281, 224–227, Pease Records.

26. Gideon Welles, *Diary of Gideon Welles: Secretary of the Navy under Lincoln and Johnson* (Boston: Houghton Mifflin Co., 1911), ii, 568–569.

27. EMP to CP, Mar. 2, 30, 1866, Pease Papers.

28. Griffin, "Connecticut Yankee," 45.

29. Campbell, *Grass-Roots Reconstruction*, 11–12.

30. Welles, *Diary*, Dec. 13, 1866, 641–642.

31. Campbell, *Grass-Roots Reconstruction*, 12–13.

32. Griffin, "Connecticut Yankee," 56: Pease to unnamed recipient, Apr. 6, 1867, reprinted in Austin *Southern Intelligencer*, Apr. 25, 1867.

33. Maria Robinson to EMP, Apr. 14, 1867; LCP to EMP, June 18, 1867; EMP to CP, Aug. 3, 1867, Pease Papers.

34. Welles, *Diary*, June 12, 1867, 105–106.
35. Paul Casdorph, *A History of the Republican Party of Texas, 1865–1965* (Austin, TX: Pemberton Press, 1965), 4; EMP to CP, July 11, 1867, Pease Papers; Austin *Texas State Gazette*, July 13, 1867.
36. Griffin, "Connecticut Yankee," 65.
37. EMP to Griffin, July 22, 1867, Pease Papers.
38. Griffin, "Connecticut Yankee," 68.
39. Welles, *Diary*, July 30, 1867, 146–147.
40. EMP to Griffin, July 22, 1867, Pease Papers. Caldwell was named a Supreme Court Associate Justice on October 18.
41. EMP to CAP, Aug. 3, 1867, Pease Papers.
42. J. M. Burroughs to EMP, Sept. 3, 1867, Pease Papers (first four quotations); C. B. Sabin to EMP, Sept. 9, 1867, (fifth quotation) Pease Records, E. H. Cushing to EMP, no month, 2, 1867, Pease Papers (sixth quotation), Jasper Starr to EMP, Oct. 21, 1867, Pease Records (seventh quotation).
43. EMP to Griffin, written on back of a letter to A. H. Latimer to Griffin, Aug. 12, 1867, Pease Records, TSLAC.
44. C. B. Sabin to EMP, Aug. 7, 1867 (first quotation), Palm and others to EMP, Aug. 16, 1867. The appointment date is noted on the back side of the letter (second quotation), Pease Records.
45. Sheridan to Griffin, U.S. Military Telegraph, Galveston, Aug. 28, 1867, handwritten copy to Pease, Pease Records.
46. Printed circular from Head Quarters, District of Texas, Galveston, Sept 10, 1867, Pease Records.
47. Edmund J. Davis to "major" [Thaddeus McRae, Private Secretary], Sept. 25, 1867, Pease Records.
48. H. A. Swartout to EMP, Sept. 15, 1867, Pease Records, (first quotation); EMP to LCP, Sept. 28, 1867, Pease Papers (second, third, and fourth quotations).
49. EMP to Brig. Genl. James Oakes, Sept., 16, 1867, Pease Records.
50. W. B. Caraway to unnamed person, Sept. 30, 1867 (first quotation); Charles A. Russell to EMP, Oct. 2, 1867 (second quotation); Alex Anderson to EMP, Dec. 25, 1867 (third quotation); Pease Records.
51. James P. Newcomb to EMP, 1867, Unnamed correspondent in Bowie County to EMP, 1867, Pease Records.
52. J. B. McCormick, Tax Assessor and Collector, Denton County to M. C. Hamilton, Comptroller, Dec. 4, 1867, forwarded to EMP from Hamilton, Pease Records.

53. W. K. Baylor to Griffin, Aug. 31, 1867; EMP to Griffin, Sept. 16, 1867, Pease Records.

54. Griffin to EMP, Sept. 11, 1867, Pease Records.

55. W. B. Pace to EMP, Aug. 18 (first quotation), Aug. 26 (second quotation); EMP to James Oakes, Aug. 30, 1867 (third quotation), Pease Records.

56. Henry Cheatham to EMP, Aug. 17, 1867; General Orders No. 37, Pease Records.

57. B. F. Buckley and others to EMP, Aug. 20, 1867, Aug., 1867, Pease Records.

58. Colbert Caldwell to EMP, Aug 20, 1867, Pease Records.

59. Colbert Caldwell to EMP, Sept. 3, 1867, Pease Papers.

60. M. H. Goddin to EMP, Nov. 30, 1867, Pease Records.

61. Genl. James Oakes to EMP, Oct. 2, 1867, Pease Records.

62. Livingston Lindsay to EMP, Sept. 30, 1867 (first quotation), Oct. 2, 1967 (second quotation); Lindsay to EMP, Oct. 9, 1867 (third and fourth quotation), Pease Records.

63. R. W. Kennon to EMP, Oct. 15, 1867 (first and second quotation); S. E. Edwards, Brenham, June 20, 1868 (third quotation), Pease Records.

64. R. W. Kennon to EMP, Oct. 15, 1867, S. W. Perkins to EMP, Oct.,1867, E. P. Hunt to EMP, Oct., 1867, Pease Records.

65. Joseph Spence to EMP, Sept. 4, 1867 (first quotation); M. C. Hamilton to EMP, Nov. 11, 1867, EMP to Joseph Reynolds, Nov. 14, 1867 second to fourth quotation, Pease Records.

66. Matthew Symington to EMP, Oct. 10, 1867, Pease Records.

67. A.J. Hamilton to EMP, Oct. 28, 1867; EMP to M. C. Hamilton, Dec. 3, 1867, Pease Records.

68. Sophie Wilson to EMP, Dec. 20, 1867, Pease Records.

69. EMP to LCP, Oct. 29, 1867; S. M. Swenson to EMP, Dec. 12, 1867, Pease Papers.

70. S. M. Swenson to EMP, Dec. 16, 1867, Pease Papers.

71. William Stone to Lieutenant N. S. McCafferty, Dec. 14, 1867, G. H. Noonan to William Stone, Dec. 16, 1867 (first and second quotations), Brevet Lieutenant Colonel W. G. Mitchell to EMP, Dec. 1867 (third and fourth quotations), Pease Records.

72. EMP to LCP, Oct. 19, 1867 (first quotation), Oct. 29, 1867 (second quotation), Pease Papers.

Notes for Chapter 9

1. EMP to Brevet Lieutenant Colonel W. G. Mitchell, Jan. 17, 1868, Pease Papers. Two printed copies and his hand-written draft of the letter are in the folder.

2. Winfield S. Hancock to EMP, Mar. 9, 1868, Pease Papers.

3. Pease's reflections on Buchanan are in, "Speech Delivered by Hon. E. M. Pease at Turner Hall, Galveston, Texas, July 12, 1880," p. 10, Pamphlet in Pease Papers.

4. The Eighth Census of 1860 showed that 8,784 slaves, the largest number of blacks in any county in the state, lived in Harrison County where Marshall is the county seat. They made up 59 percent of the population. Randolph B. Campbell, *A Southern Community in Crisis: Harrison County, Texas, 1850–1860* (Austin: Texas State Historical Association Press, 1983), 20–21.

5. C. C. Caldwell to Major Longley (meant for Governor Pease), January 2, 1868, Pease Records.

6. Donald Campbell and B. W. Gray to EMP, May 1, 1868, Pease Records, Campbell to Pease, May 6, 1868, Pease Records.

7. C. T. Garland to EMP, May 11, 1868, Pease Records.

8. William Phillips to EMP, Feb. 10, 1868, Pease Records.

9. J. N. Williams to EMP, Feb. 19, 1868, Mar. 20, 1868, Apr. 8, 1868, Pease Records.

10. J. F. Johnson to EMP, Apr. 10, 1868, Pease Records.

11. B. W. Musgrove to EMP, May 15, 1868, Pease Records.

12. EMP handwritten note, n. d., Pease Records; Jacob Weber to A. M. Bryant, May 31, 1868, Pease Records.

13. John L. Lovejoy to EMP, Jun. 10, 1868, Pease Records.

14. Robert McMann to EMP, June, 1868, Pease Records.

15. Jeremiah Hamilton to EMP, Mar. 25, 1868, Pease Records, G. Schutze to EMP, Mar. 28, 1868, and Apr. 4, 1868, Pease Records.

16. Edmund J. Davis to EMP, Mar. 8, 1868, Pease Records.

17. Jeremiah Galvan to EMP, Feb. 6, 1868; P. D. Alexander, Mar. 30, 1868 (first quotation), T. S. Anderson to EMP, May, 1868 (second quotation); J. M. Kammheimer to EMP, Mar. 24, 1868 (third quotation); J. J. Reynolds to EMP, Apr. 8, 1868; Pease Records.

18. EMP to J. J. Reynolds, Jun. 19, 1868, Letterpress Vol. 1, 8–14, Pease Records.

19. EMP to J.J. Reynolds, Jun 23, 1868, Letterpress Vol. 1, 17–18, Ibid.

20. Isaac Y. Williams to EMP, Mar. 16, 1858, Hamilton to EMP, Apr. 14, 1868, F. P. James and N. A. Handsey [?] to EMP, Jun. 14, 1868, Pease Records.

21. William S. Rawson, Harrisburg, PA. to EMP, Feb. 25, 1868, A. G. Moore to EMP, Mar. 27, 1868, John W. Harris to EMP, May 6, 1868, Pease Records.

22. EMP to CAP, Jan. 10, 1868, EMP to My Dear Daughters, Jan. 18, 1868, EMP to My Dear Daughters, Feb. 14, 1868, EMP to JMP, Mar. 14, 1868, EMP to CAP, Mar. 21, 1868, Pease Papers.

23. EMP to "My Dear Daughters," May 7, 1868 (first to fifth quotation); EMP to CAP, June 7, 1868 (sixth) quotation; EMP to JMP, June 14, 1868; EMP to CAP, June 24, 1868 (seventh quotation), Pease Papers.

24. Moneyhon, *Texas after the Civil War*, 87; LNP to Juliet Niles, Feb. 11, 1868, Pease Papers.

25. C. T. Garland to EMP, May 11, 1868, D. M. McAdoo to EMP, June 13, 1868, Pease Records.

26. EMP to Reynolds, July 28, 1868, Letterpress 1, Pease Records; Austin *Weekly Republican*, June 24, 1868.

27. Moneyhon, *Texas after the Civil War*, 89.

28. *Journal of the Reconstruction Convention which Met at Austin, Texas, June 1, A. D., 1868, 1ˢᵗ session* (Austin, 1870), 3, 14–15; *Austin Tri-Weekly Texas State Gazette*, Mar. 26, 1869; *Dallas Herald*, June 6, 13, 1868.

29. *Journal of the Reconstruction Convention*, 1ˢᵗ Session, 15–16.

30. Moneyhon, *Texas after the War*, 96.

31. Ernest W. Winkler, ed., *Platforms of Political Parties in Texas* (Austin: Bulletin of the University of *Texas*, 1916, No. 53),112–114; *Proceedings of the Republican State Convention*, Assembled at Austin, August 12, 1868 (Austin, 1868), 5–6.

32. Campbell, *Grass-Roots Reconstruction in Texas*, 16–17.

33. Ramsdell, *Reconstruction in Texas*, 228–229; *Journal of the Reconstruction Convention 1868*, 1ˢᵗ session, 907, 939; Copy of ordinance in Gammel, comp., *Laws of Texas*, VI, 58–59; C. E. Morse to W. R. Baker, Sept. 3, 1868, in *Houston Tri-Weekly Union*, Nov. 3, 1869; EMP to Reynolds, Oct. 5, 1868, Reynolds to EMP, Oct. 30, 1868, EMP to Reynolds, Dec. 3, 1869, Copy of agreement between EMP and H. & T. C., Nov. 30, 1868, Pease Records.

34. Moneyhon, *Texas after the War*, 96–97.

35. C. T. Garland to EMP, Aug. 1868, Pease Records.

36. D. Campbell to EMP, Aug. 25, 1868, K. R. S. identified as "Knights of the Rising Sun" in Campbell to EMP, Sept. __, 1868, D. Campbell to EMP, Aug. 25, 1868, Pease Records.

37. D. Campbell to Colbert Caldwell, Sept. 3, 1868, Campbell to EMP, Sept. 1868, N. V. Board to EMP, Oct. 12, 1868, Pease Records.

38. A. B. Norton to EMP, Oct. 20, 1868, Nov. 3, 1868, Nov. 25, 1868, Pease Records. General E.R.S. Canby replaced Reynolds as commander of the Fifth Military District from November 1868 to March 1869.

39. E. P. Upton to EMP, Jul. 22, 1868, Pease Papers; E. P. Upton to EMP, Pease Records.

40. Edward R. S. Canby to EMP, Dec. 31, 1868, Pease Records.

41. EMP to Reynolds, July 1, 1868, Letterpress 1, 35–37, Pease Records.

42. EMP to Reynolds, July 16, 1868, Letterpress 1, 57–58, Pease Records.

43. EMP to Reynolds, July 28, 1868, Letterpress 1, 86–86, Pease Records.

44. EMP to Reynolds, Oct. 2, 1868, Letterpress 1, 201–203, Pease Records.

45. EMP to Reynolds, Oct. 22, 1868, Letterpress 1, 256–257, Pease Records.

46. Moneyhon, *Texas after the War*, 88, 96; B. W. Gray to EMP, Oct 14, 1868, Pease Papers; EMP to Reynolds, Oct. 30, 1868, Letterpress 1, 266–267, Pease Records; *Handbook of Texas Online*, Mark Odintz, "SMITH, GEORGE WASHINGTON," accessed May 21, 2020, http://www.tshaonline.org/handbook/online/articles/fsm21.

47. Joseph Spence to EMP, Dec. 21, 1968, George C. Rives to EMP, Dec. 1868, Sarah C. Brown to EMP, Oct. 1, 1868, Pease Records.

48. James H. Bell to EMP, November 23, 1868, Pease Records.

49. Letter of Credit to L. S. Friend, July 18, 1868, No. 180, James M. Day and Dorman Winfrey (eds.) *Texas Indian Papers 1860–1916* (4 vols., Austin: Texas Library and Historical Commission, 1961), IV, 266–267; EMP to Charles E. Mix, Sept. 1, 1868, Letterpress 2, 137–138, EMP to C. S. Parker, May 17, 1869, Letterpress 2, 278–279, EMP to J. H. Hunsberger, May 17, 1869, Letterpress 2, 280–281, Pease Records; Johnie Lee Reeves, "LEGION VALLEY MASSACRE," *Handbook of Texas Online*, accessed November 6, 2015 (http://www.tshaonline.org/handbook/online/articles/btlkt).

50. *Handbook of Texas Online*, Howard N. Martin, "ALABAMA-COUSHATTA INDIANS," accessed May 21, 2020, http://www.tshaonline.org/handbook/online/articles/bma19.

51. H. C. Pedigo to EMP, Dec. 8, 1868, Pease Records.

52. Edwin Waller to EMP, Aug. 21, 1868, Pease Records. See Charles D. Spurlin, "WALLER, EDWIN," *Handbook of Texas Online*, accessed December 8, 2015 (http://www.tshaonline.org/handbook/online/articles/fwa38).

53. Thanksgiving Proclamation by EMP, November 1868, Pease Records.

54. EMP to JMP, July 3, 1868 (first to third quotation), EMP to CAP, July 6, 1868 (fourth and fifth quotation), Pease Papers.

55. EMP to CAP, Sept. 7, 1868 (first quotation); EMP to CAP, Oct. 3, 1868 (second quotation), Pease Papers.

56. EMP to LCP, Sept. 12, 1868, EMP to LCP, Sept. 18, 1868, Pease Papers.

57. EMP to Edward R. S. Canby, Jan. 13, 1869, Letterpress 2, 68–70, Pease Records.

58. Robert Stanfield to EMP, Jan. 11, 1869, Pease Records.

59. EMP to Canby, Feb. 19, 1869, Letterpress 2, 147–148, Pease Records.

60. EMP to Canby, Feb. 24, 1869, Letterpress 2, 153–154, Pease Records.

61. EMP to Canby, Mar. 4, 1869, Letterpress 2, 162–164, Pease Records.

62. J. A. Wright to EMP, Jan. 13, 1869, Edward R. S. Canby to Pease, Jan. 16, 1869, Pease Records.

63. C. T. Garland to EMP, May 21, 1869, Pease Records.

64. EMP to Canby, Mar. 19, 1869, Letterpress 2, 175; Mar. 23, 1869, Letterpress 2, 188; Mar. 29, 1869, Letterpress 2, 197, Pease Records.

65. EMP to Canby, Jan. 18, 1869, Letterpress 2, 75–76, Pease Records.

66. Jeremiah Galvan to Louis V. Caziare, Feb. 6, 1869, Edward R. S. Canby to EMP, Mar. 13, 1869, Pease Records.

67. EMP to Reynolds, Sept. 5, 1869, Pease Records.

68. T. B. Dooley to EMP, Apr. 26, 1869, Pease Records.

69. Proclamation of E. M. Pease, Apr. 19, 1869, Pease Records.

70. EMP to Canby, Apr. 6, 1869 (first quotation), E. R. Lane to EMP, Apr. 8, 1869 (second quotation), Pease Records.

71. EMP to Canby, Jan. 18, 1869, Letterpress 2, 77–79, EMP to Canby, Jan. 20, 1869, Letter Press 2, 89–90, EMP to George C. Rives, Jan. 22, 1869, Letterpress, 91–92, EMP to Thaddeus C. Bell, Jan. 23, 1869, Letterpress 2, 96–97, EMP to A. D. Monroe, Jan. 26, 1969, Letterpress 2, 99, EMP to Canby, Feb. 13, 1869, 138–139, EMP to Canby, Letterpress 2, 157–158, Pease Records.

72. EMP to George C. Rives, Jan. 16, 1869, Letterpress 2, 71, EMP to Canby, Jan. 18, 1869, Letterpress 2, 83, Pease Records.

73. EMP to Reynolds, May 11, 1869, Letterpress 2, 259, Pease Records.

74. C. B. Sabin to EMP, Jan. 28, 1869 (first to fourth quotations), C. B. Sabin to EMP, May, 1869 (fifth to sixth quotation), Pease Records.

75. EMP to Reynolds, Sept. 9, 1869, Letterpress 2, 327–328, Pease Records.

76. George W. Diamond to EMP, Jun. 5, 1869, Pease Records.

77. EMP to Reynolds, May 31, 1869, Letterpress 2, 288–292, Pease Records.

78. EMP to Edward R. S. Canby, Jan. 5, 1869, Letterpress 2, 51–53, Pease Records.

79. EMP to Canby, Jan. 19, 1969, Letterpress 2, 85–86, Pease Records.

80. San Antonio *Daily Express*, July 22, 23, 26, 1868, EMP to LCP, Sept. 13, 1868, EMP to JMP, Dec. 31, 1871, Pease Papers; Charles S. Potts, *Railroad Transportation in Texas* (Austin, 1909), 39–40.

81. Austin *Daily Republican*, Feb. 21, 23, and Apr. 8, 1869; Houston *Tri-Weekly Union*, Dec. 4, 1869; S. M. Swenson to EMP, Nov. 26, Nov. 28, 1869, Pease Papers.

82. Campbell, *Grass-Roots Reconstruction*, 16–17.

83. EMP to Reynolds, May 17, 1869, Letterpress 2, 267–277, Pease Records.

84. Austin *Daily Republican*, Apr. 23, 1869; Pease to the Austin *Republican*, n.d., Austin *Weekly Republican*, Oct. 13, 1869; Austin *Tri-Weekly Texas State Gazette*, Apr. 2, 23, 1869; Houston *Tri-Weekly Union*, Oct. 7, 13, 1869.

85. J. C. Tracy to EMP, April 18, 1869, EMP to CAP, Nov. 15, 1867, Mar. 21, 1868, S. M. Swenson to EMP, May 27, 1868, C. B. Sabin to EMP, Feb. 22, 1869, Pease Papers.

86. Pease to Reynolds, May 17, 1869, Letterpress 2, 367–276, Pease Records; Thaddeus McRae to Pease, Jun. 5, 1869, Pease Papers.

87. Campbell, *Grass-Roots Reconstruction in Texas*, 18–19; Austin *Daily Republican*, July 30, 1869.

88. Reynolds to Grant, Sept. 4, 1869, in Austin *Weekly Republican*, Oct. 13, 1869; Pease, MS Diary, June 30, July 19, 1869, Pease Papers; Austin *Daily Republican*, July 30, 1869.

89. EMP to Reynolds, Sept. 30, 1868, Letterpress 2, 334–336, Pease Records.

Notes for Chapter 10

1. EMP to J. D. Giddings "and others," Sept. [n.d.] 1869, Pease Papers.

2. Customs duties were the principal source of revenue for the Federal government during the nineteenth century.

3. EMP, et al., "To the Republican Senators of the United States," Nov. 29, 1869, Houston *Tri-Weekly Union*, Dec. 29, 1869.

4. Dallas *Herald*, Jan. 15, 1870.

5. Moneyhon, *Texas after the Civil War*, 117.

6. E. M. Pease, "Speech Delivered by Hon. E. M. Pease at Turner Hall, Galveston, TX, July 1, 1880," Pamphlet in Pease Papers.

7. "Petition of the People of Texas to Congress, to Guarantee to the People a Republican form of Government," 1870, Daily Republican Office, booklet, Pease Papers.

8. EMP to Moses Austin Bryan, Feb. 20, 1871, Bryan Papers.

9. Hamilton to EMP, May 20–21, 1871, Pease Papers.

10. Edmund Thornton Miller, *A Financial History of Texas*. (Austin: University of Texas, 1917) 160–167.

11. Austin *Tri-Weekly Democratic Statesman*, Aug. 22, 1871.

12. Austin *Democratic Statesman*, Sept. 26, 1871.

13. O. M. Roberts in Dudley G. Wooten, *Comprehensive History of Texas* (2 vols., Dallas, TX: William G. Scarff, 1898), II, 193; *Handbook of Texas Online*, Carl H. Moneyhon, "TAX-PAYERS' CONVENTION," accessed August 02, 2020, http://www.tshaonline.org/handbook/online/articles/vft01.

14. Austin *Tri-Weekly Democratic Statesman*, Sept. 23, 1871.

15. CAP to JMP, n. d. (original penciled as Nov. 1871), Pease Papers.

16. John Hancock to EMP, Mar. 28, 1872, Pease Papers.

17. For EMP's role, see Dallas *Herald*, May 11, 1872; State representatives listed on letterhead from Head-Quarters National Committee Liberal Republicans and endorsing Greeley, Pease Papers.

18. Thos. H. Stribling to "Gov." [EMP], Apr. 14, 1872, Pease Papers.

19. EMP to JMP, May 2, 1872, Pease Papers.

20. Thos. B. Horrand to EMP, Pease Papers.

21. EMP to JMP, Feb. 1, 1874, Pease Papers.

22. LCP to EMP, Sept 18, 1870, Pease Papers.

23. EMP to JMP, Sept. 12, 1871, Pease Papers.; "Pease & Turner, Attorneys at Law, Austin, Texas," calling card, n.d., Austin Files: Biography, E. M. Pease, AHC.

24. G. W. Brackenridge to EMP, Jun. 8, 1872, Pease Papers.

25. EMP to JMP, Apr. 12, 1874, Pease Papers; Photograph of bank, Austin Files, AHC.

26. CAP to JMP, n. d. [1871 penciled in an archival note], EMP to JMP, Jan. 25, 1874, Pease Papers.

27. Austin *Weekly Democratic Statesman,* Mar. 22, 1877; Austin *Daily Democratic Statesman,* Mar. 15, 1877.

28. For a history of efforts to form a state historical association that preceded the Texas State Historical Association, see Richard B. McCaslin, *At the Heart of Texas: One Hundred Years of the Texas State Historical Association* (Austin: TSHA, 2007), 1–19. Lists of attendees at the organizational meeting and comments of Thrall are found in the Austin *Daily Democratic Statesman,* Apr. 9, 23, 1874.

29. Frank Johnson to EMP, July 8, 1879. Oct. 19, 1879; Thomas J. Devine, statement of pledges to pay for Johnson's history, to be paid to EMP, April 1879 (EMP's notation on the back states October 1879), Pease Papers.

30. E. M. Pease, Republic Claims files, Archives Division, Austin, Texas State Library.

31. Certificates of membership in Texas Veteran Association, Pease Papers.

32. W. W. Mills to EMP, Oct. 11, 1874, Pease Papers.

33. EMP to B. H. Austin, Oct. 24, 1874, Pease Papers.

34. EMP to JMP or CAP, July 11, 1870, Pease Papers.

35. LCP to EMP, July 24, 1870, Pease Papers.

36. LCP to EMP, Aug. 14, 1870, Pease Papers.

37. LCP (unsigned) to EMP, July 31, 1870, Pease Papers.

38. LCP (unsigned) to EMP, Aug. 28, 1870, Pease Papers.

39. LCP to EMP, Sept. 25, 1870, Pease Papers.

40. EMP to CAP, Oct. 27, 1870, Pease Papers.

41. LCP to EMP, Oct. 30–Nov. 6, 1870, Pease Papers.

42. EMP to JMP, Nov. 20, 1870, Pease Papers.

43. LCP to EMP, Nov. 29, 1870, Pease Papers.

44. CAP to JMP, Dec. 10, 1870, Pease Papers.

45. LCP to JMP, Dec. 10, 1870. This letter is a continuation of Carrie's letter to Julie, same date. Pease Papers.

46. LCP to JMP, n.d. 1870, Pease Papers.

47. LCP to JMP, Jan. 15, 1871, Pease Papers.

48. EMP to JMP, Apr.16, 1871, Pease Papers.

49. LCP to JMP, Mar. 5, 1871, Pease Papers.

50. LCP to JMP, Apr. 16, 1871, Pease Papers.

51. LCP to JMP, Apr. 22, 1871, Pease Papers.

52. LCP to JMP, May 14, 1871, Pease Papers.

53. LCP to JMP, July 30, 1871, Pease Papers.

54. LCP to JMP, Aug. 8, 1871, Pease Papers.

55. LCP to JMP, Aug. 29, 1871, Pease Papers.

56. LCP to JMP, Sept. 4, 1871, Pease Papers.

57. LCP to JMP, Sept. 10, 1871, Pease Papers.

58. LCP to JMP, Sept. 17, 1871, Pease Papers.

59. LCP to JMP, Oct. 4, 1871, Pease Papers.

60. LCP to JMP, Oct. 15, 1871, Pease Papers.

61. LCP to JMP, Oct 24, 1871, Pease Papers.

62. LCP to JMP, Oct. 27, 1871, Pease Papers.

63. LCP to JMP, Nov. 12, 1871, Pease Papers.

64. LCP to JMP, Nov. [no day] 1871, Pease Papers.

65. LCP to JMP, Nov. 19, 1871, Pease Papers.

66. LCP to JMP, Dec. 3, 1871, Pease Papers.

67. E.M. Pease granted land to Emily and La Grande (Grant) Woods, and to Samuel Barber on July 9, 1872. Travis County Deed Records, County Clerk's Office, Travis County Courthouse, Austin.

68. LCP to JMP, Apr. 4, 1875, Pease Papers.

69. Deed of E. M. and L.C. Pease to City of Austin, May 22, 1875; Travis County Deed Records, Vol. 20, 323–325, County Clerk's Office, Travis County Courthouse, Austin.

70. LCP to JMP, Summer, 1875, Pease Papers.

71. City of Austin Resolution, Aug. 25, 1875, copy in E. M. Pease Biographical Folder in Austin Files, AHC.

72. E. M. Pease, Deed to the International and Great Northern Rail Road, Oct. 13, 1876, and Feb. 7, 1879; LPC's comments to JN, Oct. 22, 1876, Pease Papers.

73. JMP to CAP, Jan. 10, 1874, Pease Papers.

74. LCP to JMP, Feb. 8, 1874, Pease Papers.

75. JMP to LCP, Feb. 22, 1874, Pease Papers.

76. Certificate of Marriage and Marriage Announcement, Pease Papers.

77. JMP to LCP, Jan. 13, 1875, Pease Papers.

78. JMP to Carrie P. Graham [CPG], Mar. 25, 1875, Pease Papers.

79. JMP to CPG, Mar. 22, 1874, Pease Papers.

80. JMP to EMP and LCP, Mar. 22, 1875, Pease Papers.

81. LCP to JMP, Jan. 31, 1874, Pease Papers.

82. EMP postscript on LCP to JMP, May 10, 1874, Pease Papers. This note indicates that since her property was in the rear of their lot, west of the Pease home, in or near their grain fields.

83. EMP to JMP, Jun. 7, 1874, Pease Papers.

84. EMP to JMP, Jul. 26, 1874, Pease Papers.

85. EMP to LCP, Aug. 9, 1874. Pease Papers.

86. EMP to LCP, Aug. 16, 1874, Pease Papers.

87. The originally designated "Colored Section" of the original city cemetery was first seen by the author in the spring of 2015. Robert E. Tieman,
Oakwood Cemetery Austin Texas, Register of Gravestones (n.p. 2006).
The body of Emily Pease Woods was buried beside that of Sananah
Pease, who died in 1866. The body of Chloe Pease, who died in 1891,
was placed next to Emily's. They were buried in an unmarked plot in
Section 4, once designated as "Colored Grounds" with a wrought iron
marker for the section that was removed sometime after the spring of
2015 when the author first saw it.

88. G. Paschal to EMP, May 10, 1875, Pease Papers.

89. Austin *Daily Democratic Statesman, Jun. 25, 1876*; LCP to CPG and
JMP, Jul. 23, 1876, Pease Papers.

90. Austin *Weekly Democratic Statesman*, Feb. 8, 1877.

91. Austin *Daily Democratic Statesman*, Feb. 22, 1877.

92. EMP to Hayes, Mar. 9, 1877, Pease Papers.

93. Guy Bryan to Hayes, June 24, 1877, in Ernest W. Winkler, ed.,
"The Bryan-Hayes Correspondence," *Southwestern Historical Quarterly*,
XXVII (Jan. 1924): 242; Bryan to EMP, June 24, 1877, Pease Papers.

94. EMP to John Sherman, July 30, 1878, Applications for Appointments
as Custom Service Officers, 1833–1910, Records of the Treasury
Department, Record Group 56, National Archives and Records Administration (NARA), College Park, Maryland.

95. Certificate of nomination, January 22, 1879 (oversize document),
Pease Papers.

96. EMP to LCP, Feb. 5, 1879, Pease Papers.

97. LCP to JN, Feb. 14, 1879, Pease Papers.

98. Appointment document, Feb. 12, 1879, Pease Papers.

99. Statistical notes for the Galveston Custom House, Ibid.

100. Examples of applications to Pease from Robert Mills, Feb. 2, 1879,
John Hancock, Feb. 13, 1879, and B. A. Rogers, Feb. 14, 1879, "List
of Employees of the U. S. Customs Service, District of Galveston,
January, 1879, Pease Papers.

101. Paul Douglas Casdorph, "Norris Wright Cuney and Texas Republican
Politics, 1883–1896," *Southwestern Historical Quarterly*, 68 (Apr. 1965):
455–464.

102. Tom P. Ochiltree to John Sherman, June 30, 1879, Pease Papers.

103. William R. Evans, petition of Galveston County Republican Executive Committee to Sherman, Aug. 23, 1879, Pease Papers.

104. EMP to Sherman, Oct. 25, 1879, Pease Papers.

105. EMP's undated draft of letter attached to E. M. Moore to EMP, Dec. 18, 1879, Pease Papers; *Handbook of Texas Online*, Merline Pitre, "CUNEY, NORRIS WRIGHT," accessed July 16, 2019; http://www.tshaonline.org/handbook/online/articles/fcu20. Douglas Hales. *A Southern Family in White and Black: The Cuneys of Texas* (College Station: Texas A&M University Press, 2003), 81.

106. Day and Night Inspectors note to EMP accompanying cane, Pease Papers. [The cane, inscribed "with Christmas compliments," is in the Governor's Mansion collection.]

107. Proceedings of the Republican State Convention ... 1880 (Austin, 1880), 4; Austin *Daily Democratic Statesman*, Mar. 26, 1880; flyer promoting John Sherman for President in 1880 and advocating creation of "Sherman Clubs", Pease Papers.

108. Julius Schutze to EMP, Jul. 13, 1880, R. N. Lane to EMP, Jul. 30, 1880, Pease Papers.

109. Austin *Weekly Democratic Statesman*, Sept. 16, 1880.

110. EMP to Sherman, Nov. 19, 1880, E. M. Pease file, Collectors of Customs Applications, Galveston, Texas, RG 56, NARA, College Park, MD.

111. EMP to CPG, Mar. 3, 1879, Pease Papers.

112. Marshall's birth recorded in EMP to JMP, Oct. 16, 1875, Pease Papers.

113. EMP to CPG, Aug. 18, 1878, Pease Papers.

114. EMP to "Grandson Marshall," Aug. 12, 1879, Pease Papers.

115. EMP to CPG, Apr. 22, 1879, Pease Papers.

116. EMP to JN, May 8, 1879, Pease Papers.

117. EMP to George Graham, July 10, 1879, Pease Papers.

118. EMP to LCP, Aug. 11, 1879, Pease Papers

119. EMP to LCP, Oct. 22, 1879, Pease Papers.

120. Dallas *Daily Herald*, Jan. 28, 1881; Alwyn Barr, *Reconstruction to Reform, Texas Politics 1876–1906* (Austin: University of Texas Press, 1971), 60–61.

121. Terrell to EMP (draft) Apr. 1, 1881, filed with Terrell to Pease, Pease Papers.

122. Austin *Weekly Democratic Statesman*, Feb. 15, 1877, mentions existence of a charter, but not its date.

123. B. D. Pike to E. B. Wright, Jan. 29, 1880, Pease Papers. No records of trustee's meetings are extant in the Pease Papers or in records at Huston-Tillotson University. The school merged with Samuel Huston

College in 1952; it later became Huston-Tillotson College, and finally Huston-Tillotson University.

124. LCP to JN, May 28, 1881, Pease Papers.

125. EMP to JMP, Jul. 8, 1881, Pease Papers.

126. LCP to JN, Sept. 27, 1875, Dec. 1, 1880, Pease Papers.

127. JMP to EMP, Aug. 1, 1880, Pease Papers.

128. EMP to JMP, June 30, 1881, July 8, 1881, Pease Papers.

129. EMP to CPG, Sept. 24, 1881, Pease Papers.

130. EMP to JMP, Oct. 9, 1881, Pease Papers.

131. "Your affectionate Brother" (EMP) to "My Dear Sister" (unnamed), Nov. 9, 1882, Pease Papers.

132. C. R. Moor to EMP, Nov. 15, 1882, Pease Papers.

133. "In Memoriam," newspaper clipping, n.d., n.p., Austin Files, Biography, Beriah Graham and family, AHC.

134. LCP to "My dear Brother" (unnamed), Feb. 1883, Pease Papers.

135. LCP to JN, Feb. 10, 1883, Pease Papers.

136. LCP to JN, April 3, 1883, Pease Papers.

137. LCP to "My dear Sister," Jun. 19, 1883, Pease Papers.

138. LCP to JN, Jul. 18, 1883, Pease Papers.

139. LCP to JN, Jul. 28, 1883, Ibid.; *Handbook of Texas Online*, "SULPHUR CREEK (LAMPASAS COUNTY)," accessed Mar. 8, 2019, http://www:tshaonline.org/handbook/online/articles/rbshq.

140. LCP to JN, no date, 1883, Pease Letters.

141. "Special to the (Austin) Statesman," Lampasas, Aug. 27 (1883), Austin Files: Biography, Elisha Marshall Pease, AHC.

142. "Action of the Austin Bar," n.d., n.p., Austin Files, Biography, Elisha Marshall Pease, AHC.

143. Austin *Daily Statesman*, Aug. 28, 1883.

144. "The Illustrious Dead: Ex Gov. E. M. Pease Passes Away ... ." Austin *Daily Dispatch*, published after burial of EMP on Aug. 29, 1883, Pease Papers.

145. The Pease plot is in Section 4, Lot 102.

146. LCP to JN, Jan. 21, 1884, Pease Papers.

147. E. M. Pease: Last Will and Testament. Office of the Travis County Clerk, Travis County Courthouse, Austin. Pease stated that the homestead land was 425 acres, plus the acreage in blocks 7, 8, and 9 in his 1855 purchase, which was not totaled.

148. Marshall Graham died suddenly at the age of thirty from an unstated cause at Woodlawn in December 1905, leaving Julie to resume total

responsibility for the family's business affairs. *Austin Statesman* funeral notice, Pease Papers.

149. LCP to JN, Mar. 6, 1884, Pease Papers.

150. LCP to JN, Apr. 1, 1884, Pease Papers.

151. LCP to JN, May 28, 1884. Pease Papers.

152. LCP to JN, July 22, 1884, Pease Papers.

153. LCP to JN, Nov. 1, 1884, Pease Papers.

154. Black-and-white photographs taken by the United States Historic American Building Survey (HABS) in 1937 make the house appear so dark it has almost no features except for white trim added once Niles and Anita G. Graham took possession of the house after Julie's death in 1918. HABS photos of exterior and interior of Woodlawn, Homer H. Lansbury, photographer: www.loc.gov/pictures/resource/ hhh.tx0267photos.1562923pd?co=hh; copies of pictures in _____ 6 Niles Road file, AHC; dark red paint on a brick in a wall, shown to the author, 2018.

155. LCP to JN, Nov. 1, 1884, Pease Papers.

156. LCP to JN, Mar. 24, 1885, Pease Papers.

157. LCP to JN, Apr. 21, 1885, Pease Papers.

158. LCP to JN, Nov. (no day) 1885, Pease Papers.

159. LCP (no signature) to JN, Jan. 14, 1886, Pease Papers.

160. LCP to JN, Jan. 31, 1886, Pease Papers.

161. LCP to JN, Jun. 28, 1886, Pease Papers.

162. LCP to JN, Sept 12, 1886, Pease Papers.

163. LCP to JN, Jul. 22, 1887, Pease Papers.

164. LCP to JN, Oct. 31, 1887, Pease Papers.

165. LCP to JN, Nov. 20, 1887, Pease Papers.

166. LCP to JN, Mar. 6, 1888, Pease Papers.

167. LCP to JN, Jun. 9, 1888, Pease Papers.

168. LCP to Frank Brown, Jul. 12, 1889, Pease Papers.

169. Henry B. Diedmann, "Elisabet Ney, Sculptor," *Southwestern Historical Quarterly*, LXV (Oct. 1961): 177.

170. LCP to JN, Dec. 12, 1893, Pease Papers.

171. LCP to JN, Jul. 23, 1894, Pease Papers.

172. Mrs. Thomas F. (Bride Neill) Taylor, "Julia Pease: A talk delivered before the Texas Fine Arts Association," n. d. (following JMP's death in January 1918) typescript, Austin Files, Biography Julia Pease, AHC.

173. Elisabet Ney to JMP, "1 o'clock" (May 6, 1895), Pease Papers.

174. The original thirty-one towers in the center of the city were powered by electricity generated at the Austin dam on the Colorado River. These 150-foot towers atop fifteen-foot iron pedestals held six lamps that cast a bluish-white light. Technology changed with time, but the lights continue to cast "moonlight." Surviving towers were designated landmarks by the State Historic Preservation Board in 1976.
175. The bust is on display at the Elisabet Ney Museum in Austin.
176. W. S. Porter to LCP, Dec. 16, 1893, Dec. 27, 1892, and Jan. 8, 1895, W. S. Porter to Julia [sic] Pease, Jan. 17, 1894, B 83, Pease Papers; *Handbook of Texas Online*, Connie Patterson, "PORTER, WILLIAM SYDNEY," accessed March 29, 2019, *http://www.tshaonline.org/handbook/online/articles/fpo20*. In 1895, Porter terminated his publication and moved to Houston. When he was put on trial in Austin, he refused to admit or deny charges against him and was sent to a Federal penitentiary.
177. LCP to RNG, Mar. 17, 1900, Pease Papers.
178. LCP to JP, Sept 14, 1900, Pease Papers.
179. LCP to RNG, Dec. 10, 1900, Pease Papers.
180. Randolph B. Campbell, *A Southern Community in Crisis: Harrison County, Texas, 1850–1880* (Austin: TSHA Press, 2016 ed.), 319–323.
181. "The Austin Graded School—Its Operation and Other Items ...." Austin *Weekly Statesman*, Oct. 12, 1876; Mildred Jackson, "History of Pease School," a class paper written for Education 584.3 [presumably at the University of Texas], Jun. 3, 1925; opening date and tuition charges, Austin *Daily Democratic Statesman*, Sept. 8, 1878; for more detailed information, Austin Files, Public Schools——Elementary, Pease before 1970, AHC, APL; Michael Miller, conversation with the author, Aug. 17, 2019, on the Austin Public Free School System having been a City department until it was separated with its own tax base and school board in 1955 as the Austin Independent School District.
182. JMP to Margaret (Carrie Margaret Graham), Apr. 19, 1903, Pease Papers.
183. LCP to JN, Apr. 22, 1903, Pease Papers.
184. LCP to RNG, Jul. 5, 1903, Pease Papers.
185. LCP to RNG, Sept. 15, 1903, Pease Papers.
186. Membership cards, Pease Papers.
187. LCP to RNG, Sept. 15, 1903, Pease Papers.
188. Newspaper clipping in Pease Papers.

189. Austin *Statesman*, Jan. 30, 1905.
190. Marshall Pease Graham, Carrie and George Graham's firstborn, worked in the Pease real estate business at the turn of the century, writing his grandmother and aunt about their property around the state. He asked Julie, for instance, about a one dollar an acre offer from a Mr. Raymond on thirteen thousand acres in Hutchinson County, Jan. 9, 1903, Pease Papers. Marshall died at the age of thirty, at Woodlawn, on Saturday, December 9, 1905, and his funeral was to be held there on December 11, according to an Austin *Statesman* notice on December 10. Neither the notice nor letters in the Pease Papers explain circumstances.

Bibliography

Primary Sources

Archival sources

Archives of the Grand Lodge of Texas, Waco, Texas.

 E. M. Pease Transcripts of Letters and Documents.

Austin History Center, Austin Public Library

 Austin Files, Biography.

 Pease, Graham and Niles Family Papers.

 Travis County, Texas, Tax Records, 1860, microfilm.

 Reuben T. Ford, "A Topographical Map of the City of Austin Including the City Outlots also known as the Government Tract," (Austin, TX: De Cordoba and Withers, January 1872), AHC map L-0004-1872.

 Geology of the Austin Quadrangle, United States Geological Survey, 1902, AHC map P-0036.

Brazoria County Historical Museum, Angleton, Texas.

 District Court Minutes, Book A, Records of the Brazoria County District Clerk.

Briscoe Center for American History, University of Texas at Austin

 Barrett, Don Carlos. Papers.

 Bryan, Moses A. Papers.

 Houston, Sam. Papers.

 Palm, Swante. Papers.

 Polley, Joseph Henry. Papers

Federal Records Center, Fort Worth, Texas.

 Confederate District Court Records, Western District of Texas.

National Archives, Washington, D.C.

 United States Eighth Census (1860), Travis County, Texas, Schedule 3 (Productions of Agriculture), Record Group 29.

 Applications for Appointments as Custom Service Officers, 1833–1910, Records of the Treasury Department, Record Group 56.

Texas General Land Office, Austin, Texas.

 Original draft, Constitution of the Republic of Texas.

 Texas Land Grant Records: Lorrain T. Pease land grants; First Class Headright, 19 Feb 1892, Bexar-000685; Bounty grant, 12 Feb 1849; Bexar 000577; and Donation Grant, 14 Jan 1852, Bexar 000901.

"Woodlawn Historic Structures Report," Section 104 of "Woodlawn: 6 Niles Road, Austin, Texas, Technical Package."
Texas State Library and Archives, Austin
E. M. Pease, Governor's Records.
Bonds and Oaths of County and Republic Officers, 1837–1844, Records of the Secretary of State.
Election Register, 1836–1842, Records of the Secretary of State.
Election Returns, 1845, Records of the Secretary of State.
Texas Militia Rolls.
Republic Claims files.
Travis County Clerk's Office, Courthouse, Austin, Texas.
Travis County Deed Records.
Probate Papers.

Newspapers

Austin *Daily Democratic Statesman*, 1877.
Austin *Daily Republican*, 1869.
Austin *Democratic Statesman*, 1871.
Austin *Southern Intelligencer*, 1856–1860.
Austin *Texas State Gazette*, 1855–1865.
Austin *Tri-Weekly Democratic Statesman*, 1871.
Austin *Tri-Weekly Texas State Gazette*, 1869.
Austin *Weekly Democratic Statesman*, 1877.
Austin *Weekly Republican*, 1869.
Brazoria *Brazos Courier*, 1839–1840.
Dallas *Herald*, 1868–1870.
Galveston *Civilian and Gazette Weekly*, 1859–1860.
Tri-Weekly Houston Union, 1869.
Marshall *Texas Republican*, Oct. 12, 1861.
San Antonio *Alamo Express*, Sept. 24, 1860.
San Antonio *Daily Express*, 1868.

Published Documents

Gammel, H. P. N., comp. *The Laws of Texas, 1822–1897*. 10 volumes. Austin, TX: Gammel Book Co., 1898–1902.
Journals of the House of Representatives of the State of Texas [1st–12th Legislatures]. Austin, 1846–1871.

Journal of the Reconstruction Convention which Met at Austin, Texas, June 1, A. D., 1868, 1ˢᵗ session. Austin, 1870.

Journals of the Senate of the State of Texas [1ˢᵗ–12ᵗʰ Legislatures]. Austin, 1846–1871.

Proceedings of the Republican State Convention, Assembled at Austin, August 12, 1868, Austin, 1868.

Winkler, Ernest W. ed., *Platforms of Political Parties in Texas.* Austin: Bulletin of the University of *Texas,* 1916, No. 53.

Published Correspondence, Memoirs, Diaries, Travelers' Accounts, and Contemporary Books

Biographical Encyclopedia of Texas. New York, Southern Pub. Co., 1880.

Binkley, William C., ed. *Official Correspondence of the Texan Revolution, 1835–1836.* 2 vols. New York, London: D. Appleton-Century, 1926.

Custer, Elizabeth Bacon. *Tenting on the Plains, or General Custer in Kansas and Texas.* New York, NY: Harper & Brothers, 1895.

Day, James M., and Dorman Winfrey, eds. *Texas Indian Papers 1860–1916.* 4 vols. Austin: Texas Library and Historical Commission, 1961.

Gray, William Fairfax, *The Diary of William Fairfax Gray, from Virginia to Texas, 1835–1837.* Dallas, TX: William P. Clements Center for Southwest Studies, Southern Methodist University, 1997.

Holley, Mary Austin. *Texas: Observations—Historical, Geographical, and Descriptive—In a Series of Letters.* Baltimore, 1836.

Houston, Sam. *The Writings of Sam Houston, 1813–1863.* Edited by Amelia W. Williams and Eugene C. Barker, 6 vols. Austin: University of Texas Press, 1938–1943.

Johnson, Frank W. *A history of Texas and Texans; Edited and brought to date by Eugene C. Barker with the assistance of Ernest William Winkler, To which are added historical, statistical and descriptive matter pertaining to the important local divisions of the State, and biographical accounts of the leaders and representative men of the state.* Chicago, IL: American Historical Society, 1914.

Lubbock, Francis R. *Six Decades in Texas: Or, Memoirs of Francis Richard Lubbock, Governor of Texas in War Time, 1861–1863: A Personal Experience in Business, War, and Politics.* Edited by C. W. Raines. Austin, TX: Ben C. Jones & Co., 1900.

Muir, Andrew Forest, ed. [Anonymous] *Texas in 1837.* Austin: University of Texas Press, 1968.

Niles, John M. *History of South America and Mexico; Comprising Their Discovery, Geography, Politics, Commerce, and Revolutions, to which Is Annexed, A Geographical and Historical View of Texas, with a Detailed Account of the Texian Revolution and War, by Hon. L. T. Pease.* 2 vols. Hartford, IN: H. Huntington, 1837.

Polk's Morrison & Fourmy Austin City Directory 1916. Houston, TX: Morrison & Fourmy Directory Company, Inc., 1916.

Trumbull, James Hammond. ed., *History of Hartford County, Connecticut, 1633–1884.* 2 vols. Boston, MA: Edward L. Osgood, 1886.

Welles, Gideon. *Diary of Gideon Welles: Secretary of the Navy under Lincoln and Johnson.* 3 vols. Boston, MA: Houghton Mifflin Co., 1911.

Winkler, Ernest W. ed. "The Bryan-Hayes Correspondence." *Southwestern Historical Quarterly* 27 (Jan. 1924).

Wooten, Dudley G. *Comprehensive History of Texas.* 2 vols., Dallas, TX: William G. Scarff, 1898.

Yoakum, Henderson L. History of Texas from Its First Settlement in 1685 to Its Annexation to the United States in 1846. 2 vols., New York, NY: J.H. Colton & Co., 1856.

Secondary Sources

Books

Ariens, Michael. *Lone Star Law: A Legal History of Texas.* Lubbock: Texas Tech University Press, 2011.

Barr, Alwyn. *Reconstruction to Reform, Texas Politics 1876–1906.* Austin: University of Texas Press, 1971.

Buenger, Walter L. *Secession and the Union in Texas.* Austin: University of Texas Press, 1984.

Campbell, Randolph B, *An Empire for Slavery: The Peculiar Institution in Texas, 1821–1865.* Baton Rouge, Louisiana State University Press, 1989.

Campbell, Randolph B. *Grass-Roots Reconstruction in Texas, 1865–1880.* Baton Rouge: Louisiana State University Press, 1997.

Campbell, Randolph B. *A Southern Community in Crisis: Harrison County, Texas, 1850–1860.* Austin, Texas State Historical Association Press, 1983.

Cantrell, Gregg. *Stephen F. Austin: Empresario of Texas.* New Haven, CT: Yale University Press, 1999.

Casdorph, Paul D. *A History of the Republican Party of Texas, 1865–1965.* Austin, TX: Pemberton Press, 1965.

Hafertepe, Kenneth. *Abner Cook, Master Builder on the Texas Frontier*. Austin: Texas State Historical Association Press, 1992.

Hales, Douglas. *A Southern Family in White and Black: The Cuneys of Texas*. College Station: Texas A&M University Press, 2003.

Harris, Malcom H. *Old New Kent County, Some Account of the Planters, Plantations, and Places in New Kent County*. West Point, VA: Malcolm Hart Harris, 1977.

Hogan, William Ransom. *The Texas Republic: A Social and Economic History*. Norman: University of Oklahoma Press, 1946.

Humphrey, David C. *Peg Leg: The Improbable Life of a Texas Hero Thomas William Ward*. Denton: Texas State Historical Association Press, 2009.

Kelly, Alfred H., and Winfred A. Harbison. *The American Constitution: Its Origins and Development*. New York, NY: Norton, 1963.

Kingston, Mike, Sam Attlesey, and Mary G. Crawford. *The Texas Almanac's Political History of Texas*. Austin, TX: Eakin Press, 1992.

Lang, Aldon Socrates. *Financial History of the Public Lands in Texas*. Waco, TX: Baylor University Bulletin 35, no. 1, July 1932.

Lynch, James D. *The Bench and Bar of Texas; Published by the Author*. St. Louis, MO: Nixon-Jones printing co., 1885.

McCaslin, Richard B. *At the Heart of Texas: One Hundred Years of the Texas State Historical Association*. Austin: Texas State Historical Association Press, 2007.

Miller, Edmund Thornton. *A Financial History of Texas*. Austin: University of Texas, 1916.

Miller, Thomas Lloyd Miller. *The Public Lands of Texas: 1519–1970*. Norman: University of Oklahoma Press, 1972.

Moneyhon, Carl H. *Texas after the Civil War: The Struggle of Reconstruction*. College Station: Texas A&M University Press, 2004.

Moneyhon, Carl H. *Republicanism in Reconstruction Texas*. Austin: University of Texas Press, 1980.

Potts, Charles S. *Railroad Transportation in Texas*. Austin, 1909.

Proctor, Ben H. *Not Without Honor: The Life of John H. Reagan*. Austin: University of Texas Press, 1962.

Ramsdell, Charles William. *Reconstruction in Texas*. Austin: University of Texas Press, 1970.

Sklar, Kathryn Kish. *Catharine Beecher: A Study in American Domesticity*. New Haven, CT: Yale University Press, 1973.

Tieman, Robert E. *Oakwood Cemetery Austin Texas, Register of Gravestones*. Austin: *n.p.*, 2006.

Articles, Dissertations, and Unpublished Papers

Baade, Hans W. "Law and Lawyers in Pre-Independence Texas." *Centennial History of the Texas Bar*. Burnet, TX: Eakin Press, 1981.

Chubb, Curtis. "Revisiting the Purpose of the 1855 Callahan Expedition, A Research Note." *Southwestern Historical Quarterly* 121 (April 2018), 416–429.

Casdorph, Paul D. "Norris Wright Cuney and Texas Republican Politics, 1883–1896." *Southwestern Historical Quarterly* 68 (April 1965), 455–464.

Dielman, Henry B. "Elisabet Ney, Sculptor." *Southwestern Historical Quarterly* 65 (Oct. 1961), 157–183.

Griffin, Roger A. "Connecticut Yankee in Texas: A Biography of Elisha Marshall Pease." Ph.D. dissertation, University of Texas, 1973.

Hancock, Daniel W. "The Political and Congressional Career of John Hancock, 1865–1885." M.A. thesis, University of North Texas, 1996.

Havins, T. R. "Administration of the Sequestration Act in the Confederate District Court for the Western District of Texas, 1862–1865." *Southwestern Historical Quarterly* 43 (Jan. 1940), 295–322.

Lambert, Mark W. "You can learn a lot about a man by the company he keeps: The legal practice of Texas Governor Elisha Marshall Pease (1812–1883)," presentation to Society of Southwest Archivists Annual Meeting, Houston, Texas, 2008.

McKay, S.S. "Texas and the Southern Pacific Railroad, 1845–1860." *Southwestern Historical Quarterly* 35 (July 1931), 1–27.

McKnight, Joseph W. "Tracings of Texas Legal History: Breaking Ties and Borrowing Traditions." *Centennial History of the Texas Bar*. Burnet, TX: Eakin Press, 1981.

Pierson, William W. Jr., "Texas versus White." *Southwestern Historical Quarterly* 18 (April 1915), 341–67; and "Texas versus White, II." 19 (July 1916), 1–36.

Smyrl, Frank H. "Unionism in Texas, 1856–1861." *Southwestern Historical Quarterly* 68 (October 1964), 172–195.

Terrell, A.W. "The City of Austin from 1839–1865." *Quarterly of the Texas State Historical Association* 14 (Oct. 1910), 113–128.

Tyler, Ronnie C. "The Callahan Expedition of 1855: Indians or Negroes?" *Southwestern Historical Quarterly* 70 (April 1967), 574–585.

Index

B

J

O

P

U

V

W